Springer Proceedings in Business and Economics

More information about this series at http://www.springer.com/series/11960

Nesrin Ozatac · Korhan K. Gökmenoglu
Editors

Emerging Trends in Banking and Finance

3rd International Conference on Banking and Finance Perspectives

 Springer

Editors
Nesrin Ozatac
Eastern Mediterranean University
Famagusta, Cyprus

Korhan K. Gökmenoglu
Department of Banking and Finance
Eastern Mediterranean University
Famagusta, Cyprus

ISSN 2198-7246   ISSN 2198-7254   (electronic)
Springer Proceedings in Business and Economics
ISBN 978-3-030-13194-4   ISBN 978-3-030-01784-2   (eBook)
https://doi.org/10.1007/978-3-030-01784-2

This Springer imprint is published by the registered company Springer Nature Switzerland AG
The registered company address is: Gewerbestrasse 11, 6330 Cham, Switzerland

Contents

The Determinants of Nonperforming Loans: The Case of Turkey

Korhan K. Gökmenoğlu, Emmanuela G. Kenfack,
and Barış Memduh Eren[✉]

Department of Banking and Finance, Eastern Mediterranean University,
Famagusta, North Cyprus, Turkey
{korhan.gokmenoglu, emmanuela.kenfack, baris.eren}@emu.
edu.tr

1 Introduction

Just as during previous financial crises, the 2007–2008 global financial crisis rose from the accumulation of poor-quality assets in a merry economic atmosphere (Shiller 2012). Because of the euphoric and unmonitored risk appetite of financial institutions, the mortgage market crash became inevitable, resulting in panic and fear and driving almost all financial markets across the globe into a crippled condition that led to multiple bank failures. Given the difficult situation at the time, government bailouts were granted to financial institutions considered "too big to fail" in an attempt to prevent another Great Depression (Grgurić 2011). The role assumed by banks during that period highlights the importance of sound monitoring in asset quality as a tool in guarding against potential crises. As a result, research into the impact of asset quality increased significantly (Barseghyan 2010; Espinoza and Prasad 2010; García-Marco and Robles-Fernández 2008; Khemraj and Pasha 2009; Masood and Stewart 2009; Messai and Jouini 2013; Podpiera and Weill 2008).

As defined by the BASEL II, a loan is considered as non-collectible when it is not repaid over a period of 90 days. The NPL has gained increased significance as an indicator of asset quality. Many researchers have suggested the accumulation of poor-quality loans acts as a key determinant of bank failure, which is one of the reasons for systemic risk (Demirguc-Kunt and Detragiache 1997; Laeven and Valencia 2008). Research investigating failing financial institutions found a persistent increase in NPLs preceding bank failures (Akyurek 2006; Berger and De Young 1997; Cucinelli 2015; Skarica 2014). For this reason, understanding the factors driving changes in NPLs will help regulators adopt better precautionary tools to prevent further bank failures and economic stagnation.

Turkey experienced two serious financial crises in 2000 and 2001 that caused significant deterioration in economic conditions, especially in the banking system. To overcome these problems and establish a sound economic system, an extensive reform program was put into place by Turkish government. As a part of the reform program, to restructure the Turkish banking system, a multistep procedure was applied. The main objective was to restructure public banks, settle banks taken over by the Saving Deposit Insurance Fund of Turkey, rehabilitate the private banking system, strengthen

N. Ozatac and K. K. Gökmenoglu (eds.), *Emerging Trends in Banking and Finance*, Springer Proceedings in Business and Economics,
https://doi.org/10.1007/978-3-030-01784-2_1

surveillance and supervision, and increase the level of efficiency and competition among banks (the Banking Regulation and Supervision Agency (BRSA) 2010). The strict supervision and regulatory framework implemented by the Central Bank of the Republic of Turkey was one aspect of the reforms (Özatay and Sak 2002). Structural reforms implemented in the Turkish banking sector following the crises stabilized the Turkish banking environment—the balance sheet structure of all banks significantly improved and the distortions made by public banks were reduced. Comprehensive institutional reforms, along with the sound monetary and fiscal policies, resulted in significant improvement amid better macroeconomic conditions (Akyurek 2006) and strengthened Turkey's banking system.

The global financial crisis of 2007–2008 caused crippling financial conditions all over the world. The adverse effects of the crisis on the Turkish economy were not as significant as they were in other developed and emerging economies, such as China, India, Russia, South Africa, and Brazil (Comert and Colak 2014), mostly because of the structural reforms implemented in the early 2000s. Although Turkey's much stronger banking system a result of the extensive institutional reforms and strong supervision over those of the previous decade helped the country partially absorb the global shock, Turkey was not totally immunized against the adverse global conditions. Global crises had significant adverse effects on the Turkish banking sector. The banking sector's volume of credit was significantly reduced by the last quarter of 2008 because of a slowdown in economic activities, a high unemployment rate, low credit demands, and an increase in the cost of external financing (Aysan et al. 2016). In 2009, the ratio of NPLs to total loans reached to its highest level since 2006 (BRSA 2009). These negative impacts from the Crises made NPLs an important indicator of the performance in studying the banking sector of Turkey.

The purpose of this study is to investigate the determinants of NPLs by considering two factors that are likely to explain changes in NPLs: macroeconomic and bank-specific factors. The first shows the domestic and international impacts of economic conditions on bank performance, and the latter is related to internal impacts in the banking sector. BIST 100, IPI, the cross-exchange rate between EUR/TL and USD/TL, and the changes in NPLs are used as proxies for the state of the economy. Bank-specific factors, ROA and ROE, are used to measure the impact of managerial efficiency. Rather than using a sample of banks, we use sectoral data from the entire banking sector for these variables. The structural reforms done in the Turkish banking sector at the beginning of the last decade encouraged the use of time series data covering the period of 2006–2015, with quarterly frequency. The time span under investigation is ideal because it covers the period before and after the global financial crisis. Our sample may be an important source of information to explain the determinants of NPLs. Our study will make use of time series econometrics tools such as the Johansen cointegration, the vector error correction model (VECM), and the Granger causality test in finding the long-run and causal relationship and also estimating the long-run coefficients of independent variables.

Section 2 is the literature review of the previous studies on the determinants of NPLs, Sect. 3 defines the data and methodology, Sect. 4 concentrates on the empirical results, and Sect. 5 is the conclusion.

2 Literature Review

In recent years, researchers have examined the determinants of NPLs, mostly in response to the growing desire to understand the factors that significantly account for financial sector vulnerability. The literature explains the factors that determine NPLs as arising from two sources. First, there are macroeconomic sources such as GDP growth and inflation (Fofack 2005; Klein 2013), unemployment (Makri et al. 2014), and real interest rates (Keeton and Morris 1987; Messai and Jouini 2013). Second, bank-specific factors such as managerial efficiency (Matthews 2013; Podpiera and Weill 2008) and bank size (Berger and De Young 1997; Louzis et al. 2012) are likely to influence the capacity of borrowers to repay their loans.

Studies investigating the relationship between macroeconomic variables and the quality of loans have attempted to relate the economic situation with the soundness of banks. When the economy expands, a minimal amount of bad loans are recorded because of sufficient available income to meet payment deadlines. As the economy booms, loans tend to be granted without proper evaluation of creditworthiness, whereas recessions are characterized by an increase in NPLs (Messai and Jouini 2013). Pioneering studies such as that of Keeton and Morris (1987) evaluated the loan losses of a sample of 2,470 commercial banks in the United States for the period of 1979–1985. The study suggested that the conditions of the local economy, along with the low performance of some industries, accounted for the variation in loan losses. According to Espinoza and Prasad (2010), the ratio of NPLs to total loans grows in proportion to a decreasing rate of economic growth and increasing risk aversion and interest rates. Louzis et al. (2012) examined the factors influencing NPLs in different loan categories (consumer loans, business loans, and mortgages) for the Greek banking system. They found that for all the categories, NPLs can be explained mainly by changes of the macroeconomic fundamentals, such as GDP, unemployment, interest rates, and public debt. Skarica (2014) studied the variations of NPL ratios in some European countries over the period of Q3:2007 to Q3:2010 with the use of aggregate country-level data, and their results revealed that high NPLs are mainly due to economic contraction. Chaibi and Ftiti (2015) found that policies encouraging higher economic growth and employment worked positively toward reducing NPLs in France and Germany. According to Dimitrios et al. (2016), output gap could be a significant variable in explaining variations in NPLs.

In addition to macroeconomic fundamentals, a number of studies suggest bank-specific factors such as profitability, capital size, and managerial efficiency affect NPLs. Among these factors, managerial efficiency has been intensely studied, proxied by variables such as ROE and ROA. According to the "bad management" hypothesis suggested by Berger and De Young (1997), banks operating with poor credit monitoring and lack of control over operating expenses experience decreased cost efficiency, which, in turn, increases banks' credit risks. Therefore, as one of the measurements of credit risks, inferior bank management leads to a rise in NPLs. Berge and DeYoung found that poor management and moral hazard were positively linked to variations in NPLs. These findings were also confirmed by the work of Godlewski (2014), who used ROA as a proxy for managerial efficiency. The results showed a negative relationship between the banks' managerial inefficiency and the level of NPL ratio to total loans. Podpiera and Weill (2008) used cost efficiency as a proxy for management quality to determine its causal link with NPLs. Granger causality tests showed a unidirectional causality running from managerial inefficiency to NPLs, with emphasis on the benefits of undertaking schemes to improve managerial performance. Louzis et al. (2012) found similar results in the case of Greece. Researchers found the role of management was a prominent source for mitigating credit risk. More recent findings, such as those of Vardar and Özgüler (2015) and Bardhan and Mukherjee (2016), confirmed previous research on the importance of managerial supervision in determining the evolution of NPLs.

The management performance of banks and NPLs can also be positively related. Rajan (1994) explained that borrowers' ability to repay their obligations is not easily observable, whereas earnings are immediately recognized by the markets. Bank managers who are aware of this can inflate their current earnings by altering their credit policies. For instance, lending new funds, changing the terms of loans, and weakening the conditions of covenants can all be used to hide the size of bad loans. As a result, past earnings might be positively related to future NPLs. García-Marco and Robles-Fernández (2008) used a panel data of 129 Spanish banks covering a period of 1993–2003 and found that higher ROEs led to more risk and a higher probability of defaults. Meanwhile, Boahene et al. (2012) examined six Ghanaian banks and concluded that a higher NPL was positively associated with ROE as a result of policy changes in their credit management as well as alterations in their lending interest rates, fees, and commissions.

Some studies investigated the impact of the combination of macro and bank-specific factors affecting the performance of loans. For instance, Messai and Jouini (2013) suggested that GDP growth and ROA have a negative effect on NPLs, whereas unemployment and the real interest rate influence NPLs positively. Using the United States as a case study, Sinkey and Greenawalt (2013) found a significant positive relationship between NPLs and both internal factors such as high interest rates and excessive lending and external factors such as deteriorating economic conditions. More recently, Dimitrios et al. (2016) investigated the determinants of NPLs in the Euro area and, similar to previous studies, found that both bank-specific and macroeconomic variables play significant roles explaining changes in NPLs (Tanasković and Jandrić 2015; Vogiazas and Nikolaidou 2011).

In the case of Turkey, several studies investigated the determinants of NPLs. Yücememiş and Sözer (2010) studied NPLs in the Turkish banking sector during periods of crisis and found that NPLs act as a leading indicator for the general state of the economy. They also argued that the 2001 banking sector reforms suppressed the potential growth of Turkish banks' NPLs during the 2007–2008 crisis as compared to the period of the 2001 financial crisis. Karahanoglu and Ercan 2015 used the VAR methodology and Granger causality test to study the relationship between NPLs, BIST 100, and the exchange rates of TL/USD and TL/EUR and IPI serving as proxies to analyze the general economic conditions over the period of 2005–2015. The results showed a positive relationship between the macroeconomic proxies and NPLs. According to Vardar and Özgüler (2015), a stable long-run relationship exists between NPLs and macroeconomic variables, whereas in the short run the nature of the relationship is limited and unidirectional. Islamoglu (2015) analyzed the relationship between NPLs and commercial loans, interest rates, and public debt stock/GDP ratios and concluded that NPLs are significantly affected by those factors. The work of Us (2017) suggested that the 2007–2008 crisis affected the dynamics of NPLs in the Turkish banking sector differently across various banks. According to his findings, the policy implications were uneven and varied among different banks.

3 Data, Model Specification and Methodology

In this paper, time series data covering the period of 2006–2015 with quarterly frequency[1] is used. BIST 100, IPI, EUR and USD are used as proxies for the state of the economy while ROA and ROE are used as proxies for the managerial efficiency. The data sources are as follows; the Turkish Statistical Institution (TUIK) for IPI, the Banking Supervisory Body (BRSA) for ROA and ROE, the Central Bank of Republic of Turkey (TCMB) for EUR, USD and NPL and Borsa Istanbul for the BIST 100.

This paper suggest that the ratio of NPLs to total loans of the Turkish banking sector can be determined by several macroeconomic factors which include BIST 100, IPI, EUR an USD and bank-specific factors; ROA and ROE of the banking industry. The functional relationship is illustrated as follows:

$$NPL = f\ (BIST,\ IPI,\ EUR,\ USD,\ ROA,\ ROE) \tag{1}$$

In order to avoid a potential multicollinearity problem that can be arisen from having correlated independent variables, two different models are constructed. All the variables are converted into logarithmic form and the functional relationship is expressed as:

$$\text{Model 1}: \ln NPL_t = \beta_0 + \beta_1 \ln SUE_t + \beta_2 \ln EUR_t + \beta_3 \ln ROE_t + \mu_t \tag{2}$$

$$\text{Model 2}: \ln NPL_t = \beta_0 + \beta_1 \ln BIST_t + \beta_2 \ln USD_t + \beta_3 \ln ROA_t + \mu_t \tag{3}$$

where "ln" is used to denote the logarithmic form of the variables under investigation. β_0 is the coefficient of the constant term while β_1, β_2, and β_3, represent the partial coefficients of the independent variables for each specified model. Finally, the stochastic term is represented by u_t.

3.1 Methodology

Prior to any estimation, all variables must be tested for unit root. This study uses the Augmented Dickey-Fuller (ADF) (Dickey and Fuller 1981) and Philip-Perron

---

[1]A quadratic match-sum method was used to convert annual data into quarterly frequency. This method was equally used by Sbia et al. (2014) in their article "A contribution of foreign direct investment, clean energy, trade openness, carbon emissions and economic growth to energy demand in UAE" see in reference section.

6   K. K. Gökmenoğlu et al.

(PP) (Philip and Perron 1988) unit root tests. Following the finding that all series are I (1), the Johansen co-integration test was applied to determine whether the series converge to equilibrium in the long-run (Johansen and Juselius 1990). The VECM was used to estimate the long and short-run coefficients of the co-integrated independent variables. Lastly, the causal relationship between the investigated variables is determined by applying the Granger causality test (Engle and Granger 1987).

3.2 Unit Root Tests

This paper employs the ADF (Dickey and Fuller 1981) and PP (Philip and Perron 1988) unit root tests to verify the level of integration of the variables. The null hypothesis for both ADF and PP tests states that the series have unit root while the alternative hypothesis rejects this claim by suggesting stationarity. Given Eq. 4, the variables are said to have unit root when $\phi = 1$ and to be stationary when $\phi < 1$. The ADF was introduced as an advancement of the DF (Dickey-Fuller) test in order to overcome the problem of autocorrelated error terms. The regression for the ADF test is given as:

$$\Delta Y_t = \phi\, \gamma_{t-1} + \sum_{i=1}^{p} \alpha_i Y_{t-1} + \mu_i \tag{4}$$

The PP test only differs from the ADF unit root test on how it treats autocorrelation and heteroscedasticity in residual terms. PP allows for serial correlation whereas ADF approximates the ARMA structure of the residuals by including an autoregressive parameter in the test's regression.

3.3 Co-integration Test

Economic theory often suggests that nonstationary variables have a long-run equilibrium relationship. Johansen co-integration test (Johansen 1988) checks if there is convergence in the long-run for two or more series. The Johansen test suggests cointegration in the presence of at least one cointegrating vector. The tests' regression is given as;

$$Y_t = \mu_t + \Pi_1 Y_{t-1} + \cdots\cdots + \Pi_k Y_{t-k} + \mu_t + \text{e} \qquad (\text{for, } t=1,\ldots T) \tag{5}$$

where Π_t, Π_{-1}, ..., Π_{t-k} respectively represents level and lagged vectors of the n variables which are assumed to be I(1) in the model; $\Pi_1 \ldots \Pi_k$ are the coefficients of a (n × n) dimensioned matrix; μ_t is the intercept vector and e a vector of consisting of random errors. The trace statistic which is used to determine the number of cointegrating vectors among the variables and it is obtained by using the Eigen values (Johansen and Juselius 1990). The trace statistic (λ Trace) can be determined by the formula below:

$$\lambda \text{ trace } = -T \sum \ln(1 - \lambda_i), \ i = r+1,\ldots,n-1$$

The null and alternative hypotheses are given as

$$H_0 : V = 0 \qquad H_1 : V \geq 1$$
$$H_0 : V \leq 1 \qquad H_1 : V \geq 2$$
$$H_0 : V \leq 2 \qquad H_1 : V \geq 3$$

3.4 Vector Error Correction Model (VECM)

In presence of the long run equilibrium relationship which is determined by the co-integration test, the long and short-run coefficients of the independent variables are estimated using the VECM. The model is estimated by the equation below;

$$\Delta \ln\text{NPL} = \beta_0 + \sum_{(i-1)}^{n} \beta_1 \ln NPL_{(t-j)} + \beta_1 \Delta \ln SUE_{(t-j)} + \beta_2 \Delta \ln EUR_{(t-j)} + \beta_2 \Delta \ln ROE_{(t-j)} \beta_4 \varepsilon_{(t-1)} + \mu_t$$

$$(6)$$

$$\Delta \ln\text{NPL} = \alpha_0 + \sum_{(i-1)}^{n} \alpha_1 \ln NPL_{(t-j)} + \alpha_2 \Delta \ln BIST_{(t-j)} + \alpha_3 \Delta \ln USD_{(t-j)} + \alpha_4 \Delta \ln ROE_{(t-j)} \alpha_5 \varepsilon_{(t-1)} + \mu_t$$

$$(7)$$

Δ shows the change in the independent variables and $\varepsilon_{(t-1)}$. is the lagged error correction term. Where β_1 shows the speed by which the disequilibrium in short and long-run values is adjusted by a contribution of the independent variables.

3.5 Granger Causality Test

The next step after confirming an existing long-run relationship between variables is to determine the direction of this relationship using the Granger causality test (Granger 1988). According to this test, the lagged variables (Y_{t-1} and X_{t-1}) are regressed with the non-lagged variables. If the independent variable's coefficient is found to be statistically significant, that would imply that it occurs before the dependent variable and hence "Granger causes" it. The equations for this test are given below as;

$$Y_t = \sum_{i=1}^{m} \lambda_i Y_{t-1} + \sum_{j=1}^{m} \delta_j X_{t-j} + \mu_{1t} \qquad (8)$$

$$X_t = \sum_{i=1}^{n} \alpha_i Y_{t-1} + \sum_{j=1}^{n} \beta_j X_{t-j} + \mu_{2t} \qquad (9)$$

From the above equation, the relation between the Y and X are said to be bidirectional when δ and α are both significant, unidirectional when just one coefficient from both equation is significant and finally independent when both coefficients are not significant.

4 Empirical Results

4.1 Unit Root Test

The ADF and PP unit root tests results show that the series are non-stationary at level for all variables but they become stationary after obtaining their first difference. This implies that the variables are I(1). As a result, OLS (Ordinary Least Square) methodology will give biased results for beta estimations hence; VECM will be more suitable if a long-run relationship exists among variables. The summary of the unit root tests can be seen in Table 1.

4.2 Co-integration Test

The Johansen test performed on the series identifies the presence of 2 co-integrating equation(s) for the first model and 4 co-integrating equation(s) for the second model at 5% level of significance. This indicates an equilibrium relationship for both models in the long-run. Tables 2 and 3 illustrate the Johansen cointegration test results.

4.3 Vector Error Correction Model Results

The Johansen cointegration results showed the existence of a long-run relationship between NPL and the independent variables. Next, the long and the short-run coefficients of the independent variables are estimated using the VECM. Prior to this, the optimal lag was determined using Akaike and Schwarz information criterions. For this study a lag period of 1 was chosen in accordance with the Schwarz criterion, since it gave consistent results for both models as seen from the Tables 4 and 5.

From the lag length results, the optimal lag period of one-quarter was selected to perform the VECM in order to obtain the long and short-run coefficients. The results obtained are as follows;

Substituting the results obtained from the tables, the long-run estimates for the cointegrating equations are given in Table 6 and 7 for both models as follows:

$$Model\ 1: LNNPL = \beta_0 + 1.28560 \ln EUR + 2.95932 \ln ROE + 5.48067 \ln IPI + \varepsilon_t \tag{10}$$

$$Model\ 2: LNNPL = \beta_0 + 2.09093 \ln BIST + 3.26683 \ln USD + 4.69321 \ln ROA + \varepsilon_t \tag{11}$$

From the results above, the first model suggests that lnNPL converge to its long-run equilibrium level at a 12% speed of adjustment every quarter by the contribution of the independent variables IPI, ROE, and EUR. Meanwhile, the second model suggests a 10% speed of adjustment in NPLs by the contribution of BIST, USD, and ROA to converge to its long equilibrium. The results obtained from both models are suggesting that short-run changes in the independent variables do not have any significant impact on the level NPL. The long-run the stochastic equations can be interpreted as follows;

Table 1. ADF, PP unit root test results

Statistics	lnNPL	lag	lnBIST	lag	lnEUR	lag	lnUSD	lag	lnIPI	Lag	lnROE	lag	LnROA	lag
Level														
τT (ADF)	−2.99	2	−2.76	9	−2.55	4	−3.01	8	−3.19	2	−2.94	9	−2.80	9
$\tau\mu$ (ADF)	−2.11	1	0.15	9	−1.01	4	0.65	9	−0.82	1	1.24	9	0.76	9
τ (ADF)	−1.27	1	1.41	9	−1.10	3	−1.54	5	1.03	1	1.12	9	1.44	9
τT (PP)	−1.88	4	−2.65	1	−2.77	2	−2.22	1	−2.02	4	−2.34	2	−2.30	2
$\tau\mu$ (PP)	−1.75	4	−1.17	1	−2.03	2	−0.83	2	−0.93	4	−0.67	2	−0.17	2
τ (PP)	−0.94	4	0.64	1	−0.76	2	−1.59	3	1.72	4	−1.59	2	1.21	2
First difference														
τT (ADF)	−3.72**	3	−6.43*	7	−5.03*	3	−12.72*	7	−3.48***	7	−11.93*	7	−12.07*	7
$\tau\mu$ (ADF)	−3.77*	3	−5.43*	7	−5.11*	3	−9.58*	7	−3.21**	0	−7.12*	7	−5.28*	7
τ (ADF)	−3.82*	3	−4.41*	7	−2.76*	4	−2.76*	7	−3.04*	0	−4.56*	7	−3.62*	7
τT (PP)	−3.29***	3	−3.95**	1	−3.54**	2	−4.01**	1	−3.26***	3	−3.78**	2	−3.84**	2
$\tau\mu$ (PP)	−3.32**	3	−3.97*	1	−3.49**	2	−4.06*	2	−3.31**	3	−3.84*	2	−3.85*	2
τ (PP)	−3.36*	3	−3.98*	1	−3.60*	3	−3.95*	2	−3.10*	3	−3.69*	3	−3.68*	3

Note The variables in the table are in logarithmic form. τT shows the most realistic model with the trend and intercept; $\tau\mu$ shows the model with only intercept and no trend; τ represents the model with neither intercept nor trend. The numbers in the lag column represent the lag-length used in ADF test to remove autocorrelation in the error terms. When using PP test, numbers in the lag column represent Newey-West Bandwidth (as determined by Bartlett-Kernel). *, **, and *** denote rejection of the null hypothesis at the 1%, 5%, and 10% levels, respectively

Table 2. Johansen co-integration test result for model 1

Number of CEs	Eigenvalue	Trace statistic	Critical (5%)	Prob.
None[*]	0.9758	172.5198	47.8561	0.0000
At most 1[*]	0.6128	42.4126	29.7971	0.0011
At most 2	0.1928	9.2041	15.4947	0.3468
At most 3	0.0476	1.7073	3.8415	0.1913

Note Trace test indicates 2 co-integrating equation(s) at 5% significance, [*] denotes rejection of the null hypothesis at the 5% significant level

Table 3. Johansen co-integration test result for model 2

Number of CEs	Eigenvalue	Trace statistic	Critical (5%)	Prob.
None[*]	0.4500	59.9482	47.8561	0.0000
At most 1[*]	0.4281	37.2349	29.7971	0.0058
At most 2[*]	0.2427	16.0006	15.4947	0.0419
At most 3[*]	0.1333	5.4363	3.8415	0.0197

Note Trace test indicates 4 co-integrating equation(s) at 5% significance. [*] denotes rejection of the null hypothesis at the 5% significant level

Table 4. Results for the VAR lag order selection criteria (model 1)

Lag	AIC	SC
0	−7.5651	−7.3892
1	−17.6225	−16.7428[*]
2	−18.2759[*]	−16.6924
3	−17.9501	−15.6628
4	−17.7203	−14.7292

Note *Denotes lag order selected by the criterion

Table 5. Results for the VAR lag order selection criteria (model 2)

Lag	AIC	SC
0	−2.8675	−2.6916
1	−14.1814	−13.3016[*]
2	−14.7013	−13.1177
3	−14.53	−12.2426
4	−14.8266[*]	−11.8355

Model 1: On average when the Euro to TRY exchange rate appreciates by 1%, NPL will increase by 1.28560%. A 1% increase in the Turkish level of industrial production will cause NPLs to increase by 5.48067%. When the Turkish banking sector's average ROE increases by 1%, NPLs will rise by 2.95932%.

Table 6. VECM results (model 1)

Description	Variable	Coefficient	Standard error	t Statistic
Speed of adjustment	ΔlnNPL	-0.12096^*	0.03203	-3.7771
Short-run coefficients	ΔlnIPI(1)	1.77268	1.31093	1.35223
	ΔlnEUR(1)	-0.063275	0.21646	-0.29232
	ΔlnROE(1)	-0.099285	0.23388	-0.42452
Long-run coefficients	lnIPI(-1)	5.48067^*	1.47387	3.71856
	lnEUR(-1)	1.28560^*	0.55375	2.32163
	lnROE(-1)	2.95932^*	0.68816	4.30031

Note *Denotes that coefficients are significant at 1%

Table 7. VECM results (model 2)

Description	Variable	Coefficient	Standard error	t Statistic
Speed of adjustment	ΔlnNPL	-0.10164^*	0.02355	-4.31619
Short-run coefficients	ΔlnBIST(1)	-0.042561	0.15463	-0.27523
	ΔlnUSD(1)	-0.243322	0.36196	-0.67223
	ΔlnROA(1)	0.381426	0.24287	1.57052
Long-run coefficients	lnBIST(-1)	2.09093^*	0.55175	3.78962
	lnUSD(-1)	3.26683^*	0.65823	4.96307
	lnROA(-1)	4.69321^*	1.02167	4.59369

Model 2: An average increase in Istanbul's stock market index by 1% will cause the level of NPL to increase by 2.09093%. Also, a 1% increase in the banking sector's average ROA will cause NPL to increase by a percentage of 4.69321; and lastly, a 1% appreciation of dollar to TRY will cause NPLs to increase by 3.26683%.

4.4 Granger Causality

In order to determine the causal relationship between the variables, the Pairwise Granger causality tests were applied using the same lag length as in the VECM. The null hypothesis of this test indicates non-causality and the alternative hypothesis in the case of a rejection indicating causality between the dependent and independent variables. The test results are illustrated in Table 8.

Granger causality test results show that there is a bi-directional relationship between NPL and ROA. This indicates that when there is a change in ROA, the level of NPL changes as well. This causal relationship can be inferred that the managerial efficiency is an important determinant of bad loans in the Turkish banking sector. In addition, there are unidirectional causal relationships running from EUR, USD and ROE to NPL. Causality test results suggest a possible depreciation of Turkish Lira against foreign currencies might affect the default risk of loans. Moreover, the causal relationships from ROE and ROA to NPL support the significance of managements' impact on NPL for the case of Turkey.

Table 8. Granger causality results

Dependent variable	F-statistics (probability values)						
	lnNPL	lnBIST	lnEUR	lnUSD	lnIPI	lnROE	lnROA
lnNPL	–	0.958 (0.53)	0.628 (0.76)	1.206 (0.39)	1.206 (0.39)	1.977 (0.16)	4.326 (0.02)
lnBIST	0.805 (0.63)	–	0.424 (0.90)	9.221 (0.00)	0.868 (0.59)	11.442 (0.00)	2.150 (0.13)
lnEUR	2.744 (0.07)	4.237 (0.02)	–	2.068 (0.14)	2.374 (0.10)	2.329 (0.11)	25.215 (0.00)
lnUSD	3.594 (0.03)	13.006 (0.00)	2.198 (0.13)	–	2.303 (0.11)	3.809 (0.03)	9.189 (0.00)
lnIPI	1.368 (0.32)	1.240 (0.38)	0.507 (0.85)	0.280 (0.97)	–	1.372 (0.32)	4.121 (0.02)
lnROE	10.920 (0.00)	2.683 (0.08)	1.044 (0.48)	5.011 (0.01)	4.209 (0.02)	–	1.814 (0.19)
lnROA	6.468 (0.00)	2.496 (0.09)	5.202 (0.01)	16.017 (0.00)	2.589 (0.08)	0.923 (0.55)	–

5   Conclusion and Policy Implications

This research aimed to extend the existing literature on NPLs by empirically investigating the factors accounting for changes in NPLs for the Turkish banking sector. Given that Turkey is a developing country, banking sector activities assume a crucial role in the health of the overall economy because in developing countries, commercial banks dominate the market of financial intermediation. This study covered the period of 2006–2015 and used data with quarterly frequency in analyzing the effects of macroeconomic variables IPI, BIST 100, EUR, USD, and the sectoral variables of ROE and ROA of Turkish banks on NPLs. In this regard, the study found a long-run relationship between the variables of interest using Johansen's cointegration test.

In line with expectations, the macroeconomic findings suggest a positive relationship between foreign exchange rate appreciation and the level of NPLs in the Turkish banking sector. This positive relationship could be justified by the presence of an insufficient savings in the Turkish economy. This gap pushes most domestic firms to employ foreign currency borrowing as a means of finance, thus rendering them highly sensitive to changes in these currencies which may pose a problem in loan repayment (for similar findings, see Du and Schreger 2016; Karahanoglu and Ercan 2015). Also, given the fact that Turkey's financial markets are still fairly attached to traditional products and the use of derivative products to finance hedging activities is still under development, the increase of this burden on Turkish home companies may render them more liable to possible defaults on bank loans in the event of an appreciation in these currencies. The study's results have realistically demonstrated the relationship between currency change and NPLs. Other macroeconomic variables, such as LnBIST and LnIPI, were found to be positively related to NPLs as well. A plausible reason could be excessive lending by banks, which might be caused by high growth in production and financial markets. Because of excessive lending, the overall financial stability of the sector can deteriorate (Dell'Ariccia and Marquez 2006). Also, the bank-specific factors measured by ROA and ROE exhibited a significant positive relationship with NPLs. These findings can be supported by Rajan's (1994) argument that manipulating credit policy to boost current earnings could be positively linked with future increases in the level of NPLs, a relationship observed in similar studies (Boahene et al. 2012; García-Marco and Robles-Fernández 2008; Macit 2012).

Although the determinants of NPLs were explored in the literature for Turkey, ROA and ROE variables were mostly ignored in the empirical studies. This paper contributes to the existing literature by including these variables to examine the management related to bank-specific factors on NPLs. Despite the positive developments of macroeconomic indicators following the series of structural changes and reforms, managerial inefficiency in the Turkish banking sector still has an impact. Therefore, regulatory authorities must ensure that involved institutions participate within confined rules and regulated frameworks. Apart from this, an increase in the amount of NPLs combined with stock exchange and production growth can be a sign of economic overheating. Therefore, constructive responses to numerous factors at both macro and micro levels may prove vital for the success of Turkish economy.

References

Akyurek, C. (2006). The Turkish crisis of 2001: a classic? *Emerging Markets Finance and Trade, 42*(1), 5–32.

Aysan, A., Ozturk, H., Polat, A., & Saltoğlu, B. (2016). Macroeconomic drivers of loan quality in Turkey. *Emerging Markets Finance & Trade, 52*(1), 98–109.

Bardhan, S., & Mukherjee, V. (2016). Bank-specific determinants of nonperforming assets of Indian banks. *International Economics and Economic Policy, 13*(3), 483–498.

Barseghyan, L. (2010). Non-performing loans, prospective bailouts, and japan's slowdown. *Journal of Monetary Economics, 57*(7), 873–890.

Banking Regulation and Supervision Agency (BRSA). (2009). *Financial markets report.*

Banking Regulation and Supervision Agency (BRSA). (2010). From crisis to financial stability (Turkey experience). *Banking Regulation and Supervision Agency Working Paper.*

Banking Regulation and Supervision Agency (BRSA). (2017). *Financial data of the banking sector.* Retrieved from http://www.bddk.org.tr/WebSitesi/english/Reports/Financial_Data/ Financial_Data.aspx.

Berger, N., & De Young, R. (1997). Problem loans and cost efficiency in commercial banks. *Economic and Policy Analysis, 21*(6), 849–870.

Boahene, S. H., Dasah, J., & Agyei, S. K. (2012). Credit risk and profitability of selected banks in Ghana. *Research Journal of Finance and Accounting, 3*(7), 6–14.

Borsa Istanbul. (2017). *Index data.* Retrieved from http://www.borsaistanbul.com/en/data/data/ index-data.

Central Bank of the Republic of Turkey (TCMB). (2017). *Exchange rates.* Retrieved from http:// www.tcmb.gov.tr/wps/wcm/connect/TCMB+EN/TCMB+EN/Main+Menu/STATISTICS/ Exchange+Rates.

Chaibi, H., & Ftiti, Z. (2015). Credit risk determinants: evidence from a cross-country study. *Research in International Business and Finance, 33*, 1–16.

Comert, H., & Colak, S. (2014). The impacts of the global crisis on the Turkish economy and policy responses. *Economic Research Center Working Papers*, 14–17.

Cucinelli, D. (2015). The impact of non-performing loans on bank lending behavior: evidence from the Italian banking sector. *Eurasian Journal of Business and Economics*, 8(16), 59–71.

Dell'Ariccia, G., & Marquez, R. (2006). Lending booms and lending standards. *The Journal of Finance*, 61(5), 2511–2546.

Demirguc-Kunt, A., & Detragiache, E. (1997). The determinants of banking crises-evidence from developing and developed countries. *New York: World Bank Publications*.

Dickey, A., & Fuller, A. (1981). Likelihood ratio statistics for autoregressive time series with a unit root. *Econometrica: Journal of the Econometric Society*, 1057–1072.

Dimitrios, A., Helen, L., & Mike, T. (2016). Determinants of non-performing loans: evidence from euro-area countries. *Finance Research Letters, 18*, 116–119.

Du, W., & Schreger, J. (2016). Sovereign risk, currency risk, and corporate balance sheets. *Harvard Business School BGIE Unit Working Paper No. 17-024*.

Engle, F., & Granger, W. (1987). Co-integration and error correction: representation, estimation, and testing. *Econometrica: Journal of the Econometric Society*, 251–276.

Espinoza, R., & Prasad, A. (2010). Nonperforming loans in the GCC banking system and their macroeconomic effects. *IMF Working Paper No. 10/224*.

Fofack, H. (2005). Non-performing loans in sub-Saharan Africa: causal analysis and macroeconomic implications. *World Bank Policy Research Working Paper No. 3769*.

García-Marco, T., & Robles-Fernández, M. D. (2008). Risk-taking behavior and ownership in the banking industry: the Spanish evidence. *Journal of Economics and Business, 60*(4), 332–354.

Godlewski, C. J. (2014). The determinants of multiple bank loan renegotiations in Europe. *International Review of Financial Analysis, 34*, 275–286.

Granger, W. (1988). Some recent development in a concept of causality. *Journal of Econometrics, 39*(1), 199–211.

Grgurić, I. (2011). Too big to fail: the inside story of how Wall Street and Washington fought to save the financial system and themselves. *Financial Theory and Practice, 35*(1), 130–133.

Islamoglu, M. (2015). Predictive power of financial ratios with regard to the Turkish banking industry: an empirical study on the stock market index. *Asian Economic and Financial Review, 5*(2), 249–263.

Johansen, S. (1988). Statistical analysis of cointegration vectors. *Journal of economic dynamics and control, 12*(2–3), 231–254.

Johansen, S., & Juselius, K. (1990). Johansen maximum likelihood estimation and inference on cointegration-with applications to the demand for money. *Oxford Bulletin of Economics and statistics, 52*(2), 169–210.

Karahanoğlu, I., & Ercan, H. (2015). The effect of macroeconomic variables on non-performing loans in Turkey. *The Journal of International Social Research*, 8(39), 883–892.

Keeton, W., & Morris, C. (1987). Why do banks' loan losses differ? *Economic Review, 72*(5), 3–21.

Khemraj, T., & Pasha, S. (2009). The determinants of non-performing loans: an econometric case study of Guyana the Caribbean. *Centre for Banking and Finance Biannual Conference on Banking and Finance*. St. Augustine, Trinidad.

Klein, N. (2013). Non-performing loans in CESEE: determinants and impact on macroeconomic performance. *IMF Working Paper No. 13/72*.

Laeven, L., & Valencia, F. (2008). Systemic banking crises: a new database. *IMF Working Paper No. 08/224*.

Louzis, D., Vouldis, A., & Metaxas, V. (2012). Macroeconomic and bank-specific determinants of non-performing loans in Greece: a comparative study of mortgage, business, and consumer loan portfolios. *Journal of Banking and Finance, 36*(4), 1012–1027.

Macit, F. (2012). Bank specific and macroeconomic determinants of profitability: evidence from participation banks in Turkey. *Economics Bulletin, 32*(1), 586–595.

Makri, V., Tsagkanos, A., & Belles, A. (2014). Determinants of non-performing loans: the case of Eurozone. *Panoeconomicus, 61*(2), 193–206.

Masood, O., & Stewart, C. (2009). Determinants of non-performing loans and banking costs during the 1999–2001 Turkish banking crisis. *International Journal of Risk Assessment and Management, 11*(1–2), 20–38.

Matthews, K. (2013). Risk management and managerial efficiency in Chinese banks: a network DEA framework. *Omega (United Kingdom), 41*(2), 207–215.

Messai, A. S., & Jouini, F. (2013). Micro and macro determinants of non-performing loans. *International Journal of Economics and Financial Issues, 3*(4), 852, 860.

Özatay, F., & Sak, G. (2002, April). The 2000–2001 financial Crisis in Turkey. In *Brookings Trade Forum* (pp. 121–160).

Philip, P., & Perron, P. (1988). Testing unit root in time series. *Biometrica, 75*, 335–345.

Podpiera, J., & Weill, L. (2008). Bad luck or bad management? Emerging banking market experience. *Journal of Financial Stability, 4*(2), 135–148.

Rajan, R. G. (1994). Why bank credit policies fluctuate: a theory and some evidence. *The Quarterly Journal of Economics, 109*(2), 399–441.

Sbia, R., Shahbaz, M., & Hamdi, H. (2014). A contribution of foreign direct investment, clean energy, trade openness, carbon emissions and economic growth to energy demand in UAE. *Economic Modelling, 36, 191–197.*

Shiller, R. J. (2012). *The subprime solution: How today's global financial crisis happened, and what to do about it.* Princeton: Princeton University Press.

Sinkey, J., & Greenawalt, M. (2013). Loan-loss experience and risk-taking behavior at large commercial banks. *International Journal of Economics and Financial Issues, 5*(1), 43–59.

Skarica, B. (2014). Determinants of non-performing loans in central and Eastern European countries. *Financial Theory and Practice, 38*(1), 37–59.

Tanasković, S., & Jandrić, M. (2015). Macroeconomic and institutional determinants of non-performing loans. *Journal of Central Banking Theory and Practice, 4*(1), 47–62.

Turkish Statistical Institute (TUIK). (2017). *Industry statistics.* Retrieved from http://www.turkstat.gov.tr/UstMenu.do?metod=temelist.

Us, V. (2017). Dynamics of non-performing loans in the Turkish banking sector by an ownership breakdown: the impact of the global crisis. *Finance Research Letters, 20*, 109–117.

Vardar, G., & Özgüler, I. C. (2015). Short term and long term linkages among nonperforming loans, macroeconomic and bank-specific factors: an empirical analysis for Turkey/Takipteki krediler, makroekonomik ve banka özellikli faktörler arasındaki uzun ve kısa dönemli ilişkiler: Türkiye için ampirik bir analiz. *Ege Akademik Bakış, 15*(3), 313–325.

Vogiazas, S. D., & Nikolaidou, E. (2011). Investigating the determinants of nonperforming loans in the Romanian banking system: An empirical study with reference to the Greek crisis. *Economics Research International, 2011*, 1–13.

Yücememiş, B. T., & Sözer, İ. A. (2010). Türk bankacılık sektöründe takipteki krediler: Mukayeseli kriz performansı. *Avrupa Araştırmaları Dergisi, 18*(1–2), 89–119.

Determinants of External Debt: The Case of Malaysia

Korhan Gokmenoglu[(✉)] and Rabiatul Adawiyah Mohamed Rafik

Department of Banking and Finance, Eastern Mediterranean University,
Famagusta, North Cyprus, Turkey
korhan.gokmenoglu@emu.edu.tr, rabiah90@gmail.com

1 Introduction

External debt, which is mainly used for financing the gap between a country's national savings and required investment (Michael and Sulaiman 2012), has been considered an important source for countries to finance their economic growth and, ultimately, improve the standard of living for their citizenry. Obtaining external financial resources with a lower interest rate than the domestic rate is an important advantage for the borrower country. The acquisition of cheap additional resources is especially important for investments in urgent/time-sensitive projects and infrastructure (Ogunmuyiwa 2011), and they enable the country to spread risk across a longer period, which facilitates economic growth.

Developing countries have several common characteristics, such as lower productivity, insufficient human resources, and institutional problems, which plague the investment environment and hinder economic growth (Atique and Malik 2012; Bullow and Rogoff 1989; Rahman 2012), resulting in low per capita income. However, one of the most important problems for these countries is a lack of sufficient financial resources (Ezeabasili et al. 2011) that results from insufficient tax revenue, trade deficits, inadequate foreign exchange earnings (Imimole et al. 2014), and a shortage of domestic savings (Collignon 2012). Financial resources insufficiency hinders investment, leads to scarce capital stock, and creates a vicious cycle of poverty.[1] Given their lack of sufficient financial resources, developing countries have to resort to external sources to finance their savings-investment gap. Obtaining external financial resources enables a country to finance its investment, accumulate required capital stock for fast economic growth, and reduce poverty (Edo 2002; Schclarek 2004). In this respect, external debt, which channels resources from resource-abundant countries to resource-scarce developing countries, is an important way for the latter to finance economic growth, which will lead to globally efficient use of capital.

Nevertheless, it is widely believed that external debt contributes to economic growth, especially in developing countries, by providing additional resources; however, there are also concerns about it. First of all, external debt contributes to economic growth only if it is not deadweight debt (Oke and Boboye 2012; Udoka and Anyingang

---

[1] For the theoretical framework that justifies the need for external borrowing by developing countries, see McFadden et al. (1985).

© Springer Nature Switzerland AG 2018
N. Ozatac and K. K. Gökmenoglu (eds.), *Emerging Trends in Banking
and Finance*, Springer Proceedings in Business and Economics,
https://doi.org/10.1007/978-3-030-01784-2_2

2012), which means that it is utilized efficiently and effectively for productive investments. Second, the effect of external borrowing on economic growth also depends on the level of the debt. Above a certain threshold, external debt can become detrimental to economic fundamentals (Okosodo and Isedu 2011), investment (Awan et al. 2011; Cholifihani 2008), and economic activities (Sachs 1989), and it can hinder economic growth (Ajayi 1991; Amasoma 2013; Georgantopoulos et al. 2011; Hayati 2012; Morgan and Kawai 2013; Pattillo et al. 2004; Shakar and Aslam 2015; Stanescu 2013). Reinhart and Rogoff (2010) argued that countries with more than 90% external debt-to-GDP ratio experienced a weakening in their GDP growth rate. Excessive debt accumulation constitutes an obstacle to sustainable economic growth (Kumar and Woo 2010) and poverty reduction (Berensmann 2004; Maghyereh and Hashemite 2003).[2]

In addition to its detrimental effect on economic growth, excessive indebtedness also hinders the ability of a debtor nation to settle its future obligations comfortably, makes the country unable to meet its debt obligations (Were 2001), and plunges the country into a vicious circle of indebtedness, thus making its economy vulnerable to financial crises. In fact, a feedback effect exists between financial crises and the indebtedness of a country. On the one hand, a high debt level makes a country prone to be hit by a financial crisis; on the other hand, a financial crisis causes a significant increase in the debt level of a country. Therefore, sustainability of foreign debt financing became one of the most important topics for policy makers and economists after a series of developing countries were hit by "debt crises" during the 1970s and 1980s (Abrego and Ross 2001; Barro 1989; Barro and Lee 1994; Clements et al. 2003; Cline 1984; McFadden et al. 1985). Even before bad memories of these catastrophic events faded away, in 2007, mostly developed countries were hit by one of the biggest financial crises in history (Arestis and Sawyer 2009; Baldacci et al. 2010; Cheong et al. 2011; Dyson 2014). The 2007 crisis brought questions of sustainability of external debt and its effect on economic growth to the top of the economic agenda (Ali and Mustafa 2012).

Malaysia is a developing country that has achieved mixed success and faces challenges with the utilization of external debt. Malaysia achieved one of the most successful macroeconomic performances among all developing countries (Athukorala 2010) following the New Economic Policy (NEP), which was adopted in 1971 with the aim of transforming Malaysia into an industrialized country. Success was outstanding, and the country experienced an average growth rate of 11.1% between 1996 and 2005 (Carter and Harding 2010). However, the country also experienced two severe financial downturns during the last 2 decades. First, in 1997, the country was hit by a severe financial crisis, and Malaysia lost 50% of its GDP (Athukorala 2010). To avoid a systematic collapse of the financial system, part of the banking system was acquired by the government, and the recovery from the crisis was financed mainly with foreign debt. Pegging the ringgit to the U.S. dollar in September 1998 caused domestic debt to be replaced by external debt (Zakaria et al. 2010), and the external debt position of the country deteriorated even more. A decade later, in 2007, the global financial crisis hit the country and caused a 20% loss in capital markets, massive capital outflow, and a

---

[2]For counter arguments, see Panizza and Presbitero (2014).

decline in manufacturing exports, which forced the Malaysian government to rely heavily on external debt. Malaysia's external debate increased dramatically after these two financial crises (Fig. 1).

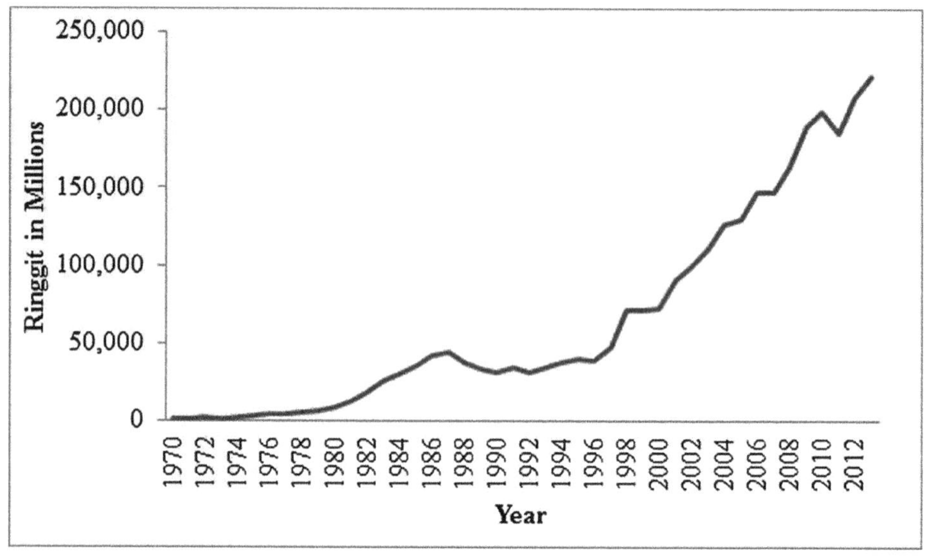

Fig. 1. Chart depicting Malaysia's external debt.

Even though Malaysia's external debt-to-GDP ratio is still lower than that of some developed countries, the rate of increase of the debt is alarming (The Malaysian Insider 2015). Malaysia had the highest federal deficits among Association of Southeast Asian Nations countries between 2000 and 2009 (Narayanan 2012). Also, the attitude of decision makers; for example, a debt ceiling that aims to avoid the overreliance on debt (Arnone et al. 2010) has been raised multiple times over the past decade (Investment Frontier 2013; Loganathan et al. 2010); is the other concern. A significant increase in Malaysia's debt over the past 2 decades and its sensitivity to external shocks have led to major concerns for the country regarding the sustainability of its external debt. If this trend continues, Malaysia could become the victim of the next external shock, which, in turn, would make the debt position of the country even worse.

Given these facts, determinants of Malaysia's external debt provide relevant information for making policy recommendations. In this research, we analyze the impact of four macroeconomic variables—namely, gross domestic product (GDP), exchange rate (EXR), recurrent expenditure (REXP), and capital expenditure (CEXP), on the external debt of Malaysia for the period of 1970–2013 by employing time series econometric methods. To investigate the long-run and causal relationship among these variables, we employed the Johansen cointegration test, vector error correction model, and Granger causality tests.

In the next chapter, we review the literature. In Sect. 3, we provide the data and methodology. We present the empirical analysis and findings in Sect. 4, and we conclude and offer recommendations in Sect. 5.

2 Literature Review

There is vast literature on debt studies, the majority of which focuses on the relationship between debt and macroeconomic fundamentals. Many of these studies elaborate this relationship on a theoretical basis, such as the debt overhang hypothesis (Krugman 1988); the Laffer curve (Arnone et al. 2010; Pattillo 2002); the dual gap model (Bacha 1990), the tax smoothing model (Barro 1979), the political economy model (Alesina and Tabellini 1990), and the theory of political budget cycles (Nordhaus 1975). Also, many empirical studies have looked at the effects of external debt on macroeconomic variables such as economic growth (Akram 2015; Babu 2014; Mankiw et al. 1990), interest rates (Elmendorf and Mankiw 1998; Rahman 2012), and economic well-being (Hallett and Oliva 2015).

Since the 1970s, mainly as the result of a series of financial crises, the determinants and sustainability of debt have become major concerns and have been studied intensely by the scholars. Nevertheless, studies present a number of interrelated factors as contributors of debt accumulation, and it is possible to divide this literature into two parts by taking into account the main approach of the researchers. The first group of researchers argued that global developments such as external/global shocks (Siddique 1996), capital flight (Tiruneh 2004), interest rate shocks (Hajivassiliou 1987), oil price shocks (Menbere 2004), and deterioration in terms of trade and the real effective exchange rate (Easterly 2002) were the main reason for countries' debt. It is widely accepted that external shocks have a negative effect on the indebtedness of countries. However, this approach might give the impression that debt problems are out of the governments' hands. Nevertheless, such an approach could be useful to warn countries that some external factors might cause debt unsustainability and put the policy makers of sovereign nations in a passive position. Conversely, the second group of researchers claimed that some internal factors, such as poor policy making and economic mismanagement (Easterly 2002), unrealistic macroeconomic policy (Burnside and Dollar 2004), excessive government spending (Edo 2002), variability in export revenue and government expenditure (Ajayi and Khan 2000), primary budget deficits (Bilquees 2003), fiscal deficits (Folorunso and Falade 2013), and balance of payments (Kemal 2001) were the main determinants of indebtedness for countries. These factors are mainly under the control of governments, so this view acknowledges that the effectiveness of a country's economic and political policies has a direct influence on its amount of debt (Cumberworth and Milbourne 1996), and better policies can help to ensure the debt sustainability of a country.

Other than external shocks and government policies, many social and political factors are considered as determinants of debt and its sustainability, including trade liberalization (Sabahat and Butt 2008), initial income (Eaton and Gersovitz 1981), poverty and income instability (Tiruneh 2004), inequality and polarization (Woo 2003), institutional and sociopolitical factors (Colombo 2009), irresponsible and corrupt governments (Menbere 2004), the effects of different political systems (Haggard and Kaufman 1992), and unchecked rule in a resource-rich country (Sarr et al. 2011). Cumberworth and Milbourne (1996) indicated that external debt was closely linked to the economic model used by a country. Countries with similar unfavorable economic, social, cultural, and political policies had a higher likelihood of relying on external debt (Bonga et al. 2014). The supply of external debt is sometimes based on the needs of the recipient country, making it possible for developing countries to benefit from the financing of operations in another country (Zeaiter 2008).

Studies have investigated the effect of Malaysia's external debt on the macroeconomic fundamentals of the country. Daud et al. (2013) investigated the relationship between Malaysia's external debt and economic growth and found that external debt had a positive, significant effect on the growth rate. However, when they took into consideration the threshold effect, they found that the positive contribution of the debt existed up to an optimal level of debt, but above a certain threshold, external debt became detrimental to the economic growth rate. This result is an important motivation behind studies that investigate the determinants of external debt for Malaysia. Pyeman et al. (2014) studied the determinants of the external debt of Malaysia for the years 1972 through 2012. Their empirical findings showed that gross domestic product, exports, and foreign direct investment were important indicators affecting the external debt of the country. Loganathan et al. (2010) focused on the sustainability of the external debt of Malaysia for the years 1988 through 2008. Their findings showed that there was both a short- and long-run relationship between external debt and several macroeconomic fundamentals—namely, government revenue, balance of payments, and government reserves. The results indicated that Malaysian external debt would be sustainable eventually, based on adjustments in the macroeconomic variables. However, when this article was written, the effects of the 2007 crisis had not been felt completely; in 2008, Malaysia's debt position deteriorated significantly. Thus, the sustainability of Malaysia's external debt problem is more severe today than during the precrisis period.

3 Model and Data

In this research, we investigate determinants of external debt by employing four macroeconomic variables: the gross domestic product (GDP), exchange rate (EXR), recurrent expenditures (REXP), and capital expenditures (CEXP) for the period of 1970–2013 for Malaysia. The data were obtained from the World Bank, International Monetary Fund (IMF), and Malaysia's Ministry of Finance databases. The functional relationship among these variables is specified in Eqs. 1 and 2 represents the econometric model of our study:

$$ED = f(GDP, EXR, REXP, CEXP) \qquad (1)$$

$$ED_t = \beta_0 + \beta_1 GDP_t + \beta_2 EXR_t + \beta_3 REXP_t + \beta_4 CEXP_t + \varepsilon_t \qquad (2)$$

where

ED	External debt,
GDP	Gross domestic product,
EXR	Exchange rate,
REXP	Recurrent expenditure,
CEXP	Capital expenditure,
and β_1, β_2, β_3, β_4	are their coefficients, respectively.

In our study, variables are used in logarithmic form, and the estimated equation is given below:

$$\ln ED_t = \beta_0 + \beta_1 \ln GDP_t + \beta_2 \ln EXR_t + \beta_3 \ln REXP_t + \beta_4 \ln CEXP_t + \varepsilon_t \qquad (3)$$

The effect of GDP growth on the external debt—in other words, the expected sign of β_1—is ambiguous. From one perspective, an increase in the GDP may result in a decrease in external debt due to the existence of domestically generated financial resources and alternatives to debt such as export revenues and taxation (Benedict et al. 2014). According to this view, if a country has more income, it will require less external funding, which might reduce the need for borrowing. In contrast, higher GDP growth may increase utilization of external financing because GDP growth increases the ability of a country to borrow by providing collateral. Like a firm, a country can access debt for debt-financed projects that will bring profit and become a viable source of financial capacitation (Memon et al. 2014).

A higher exchange rate means a weaker local currency against the other currencies. We expect a highly significant, positive β_2 coefficient (Awan et al. 2011; Bader and Magableh 2009; Imimole et al. 2014), which implies a value loss in currency will increase external debt. This happens for two reasons. First, "a strong exchange rate indicates the stability and strength of an economy (Meesook 2001) and the participation in export-oriented production (Awan et al. 2015). In contrast, a weaker exchange rate is an indication of weaknesses in the domestic economy, which may lead to a need for external financing. Second, a value loss of the currency increases the amount of external debt, which is denominated in foreign currency. So we should expect an increase in the accumulation of external debt, especially following a depreciation of the domestic country.

Recurrent expenditures are a significant proportion of a country's budget and have a stable nature. This situation implies that it is hard to cut recurrent expenditures in the short run, and most of the revenues available to the government are directed toward financing recurrent expenditures (Ribiero et al. 2012). It is common, especially for developing countries, to borrow in order to finance recurrent expenditures So we expect a positive and significant β_3 coefficient. As part of the integral investment in infrastructure and other necessities, governments require significant capital. For many developing countries, budgetary constraints result in a reliance on external finance to cover these expenditures. Capital expenditures financed through external debt are the key in determining the level of investment in the provision of services and amenities to the citizens (Awan et al. 2015). As in recurrent expenditure, we expect a positive coefficient for capital expenditures.

4   Methodology and Empirical Findings

This section is a discussion of the findings from the empirical analysis. Using unit root tests, cointegration analysis, vector error correction estimations, and Granger causality tests, we investigated the relationship among the variables used in our models outlined in Sect. 3.

4.1   Descriptive Statistics

Descriptive statistics of the variables used in our model are given in Table 1.

As shown in Fig. 2, there was an upward trend in all of the variables except the exchange rate. This indicates the existence of a unit root problem in our data. Due to this, a formal unit root testing will be applied.

Table 1. Descriptive analysis

Statistic	LNED	LNCEXP	LNEXR	LNGDP	LNREXP
Mean	24.132	9.267	1.051	25.663	10.214
Median	24.372	9.303	0.995	25.684	10.313
Maximum	26.125	10.874	1.367	27.617	12.260
Minimum	20.900	6.586	0.777	23.295	7.679
Std. dev.	1.515	1.183	0.185	1.285	1.281
Skewness	−0.652	−0.506	0.396	−0.179	−0.242
Kurtosis	2.360	2.372	1.760	1.914	2.170
Observations	44	44	44	44	44

Note L denotes the natural logarithm

4.2   Unit Root and Stationary Test Results

Prior to any time series analysis, to avoid any spurious regression, first integration order of the data has to be investigated. For this purpose ADF (Dickey and Fuller 1981), PP (Phillips and Perron 1988) unit root and KPSS (Kwiatkowski et al. 1992) stationarity tests are applied.

ADF has three different specifications, the first one includes neither intercept nor trend (model 4a), second one includes an intercept (model 4b), and the third one contains both the trend and intercept (model 4c).

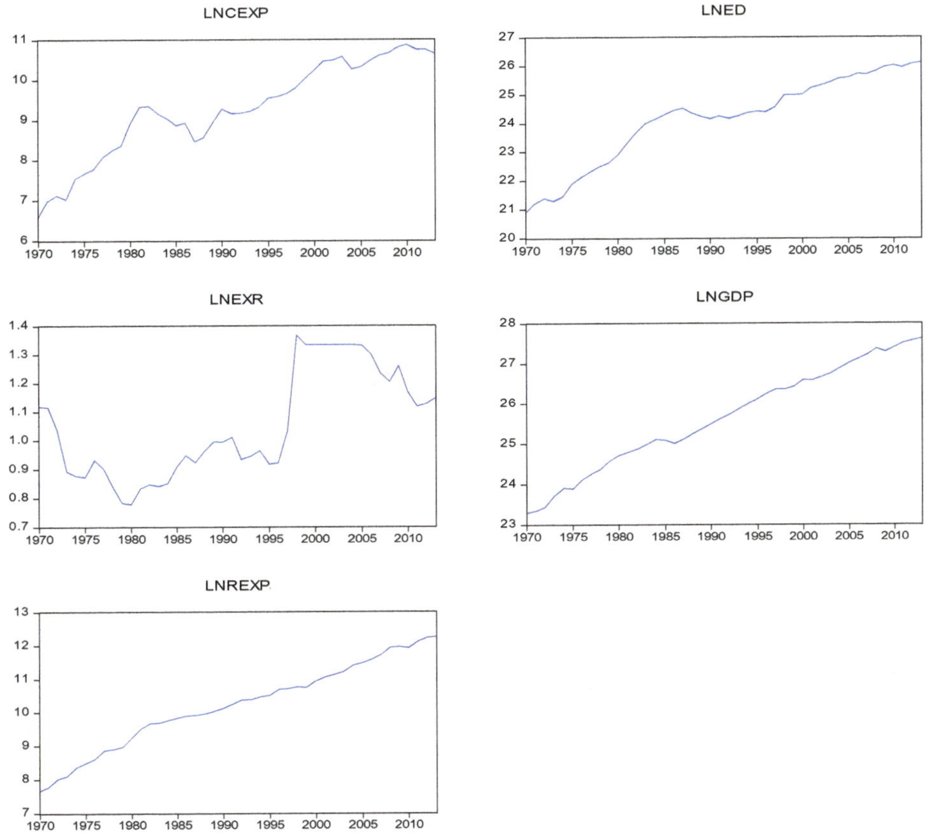

Fig. 2. Time series plot of the variables under natural logarithm

$$\Delta Y_t = \gamma\, Y_{t-1} + \alpha \sum \Delta Y_{t-1} + \varepsilon_t \tag{4a}$$

$$\Delta Y_t = \beta_1 + \gamma\, Y_{t-1} + \alpha \sum \Delta Y_{t-1} + \varepsilon_t \tag{4b}$$

$$\Delta Y_t = \beta_1 + \beta_2 t + \gamma\, Y_{t-1} + \alpha \sum \Delta Y_{t-1} + \varepsilon_t \tag{4c}$$

Both ADF and PP tests have the null hypothesis that a series contains a unit root against the alternative hypothesis of stationarity.

H_0: $\gamma = 0$ (Y_t has a unit root, or $_{Yy}$ *is* nonstationary)
H_1: $\gamma < 0$ (Y_t is stationary)

KPSS test differs from ADF and PP test in terms of its hypothesis. Null hypothesis of KPSS test states that series is stationary. Because of this difference, KPSS test can be applied as a confirmatory analysis.

The summary of the unit root test results can be seen in Table 2. We fail to reject the null hypothesis under ADF and PP, while we reject the null hypothesis under KPSS which means that the variables are integrated of order one, I(1).[3] Thus, the use of OLS regression analysis will lead to a spurious result (Choi 2015). Instead, a cointegration test is better suited for the data.

Table 2. ADF, PP unit root and KPSS stationary test results

	lnED	Lag	lnGDP	Lag	lnEXR	lag	lnREXP	lag	lnCEXP	Lag
Statistics (level)										
τT (ADF)	3.29^{***}	4	2.10	0	2.36	0	2.46	4	2.32	1
$\tau\mu$ (ADF)	1.77	1	1.78	0	1.18	0	2.02	0	1.75	1
τ (ADF)	2.29	1	8.92	0	0.14	0	7.91	0	2.68	0
τT (PP)	1.76	3	2.11	1	2.36	0	2.53	4	2.30	0
$\tau\mu$ (PP)	2.44	3	1.78	0	1.18	0	2.13	4	2.31	1
τ (PP)	3.51	4	8.52	3	0.17	1	6.98	3	2.32	2
τT (KPSS)	0.15^{**}	5	0.41^{***}	4	0.12^{***}	4	0.14^{***}	5	0.09	4
$\tau\mu$ (KPSS)	0.78^{*}	5	0.84^{*}	5	0.53^{**}	5	0.83^{*}	5	0.79^{*}	5
First diff										
τT (ADF)	4.31^{*}	0	6.45^{*}	0	5.01^{*}	0	2.44	3	5.21^{*}	0
$\tau\mu$ (ADF)	4.09^{*}	0	6.04^{*}	0	5.03^{*}	0	2.48	3	5.08^{*}	0
τ (ADF)	3.11^{*}	0	1.46	2	5.09^{*}	0	1.45	3	4.59^{*}	0
τT (PP)	4.36^{*}	1	6.48^{*}	2	4.94^{*}	5	6.18^{*}	2	5.18^{*}	3
$\tau\mu$ (PP)	4.06^{*}	2	6.03^{*}	3	4.95^{*}	5	5.84^{*}	0	5.08^{*}	2
τ (PP)	3.08^{*}	1	2.60^{**}	4	5.02^{*}	5	2.72^{*}	1	4.59^{*}	1
τT (KPSS)	0.09	3	0.04	0	0.12^{**}	2	0.14^{**}	3	0.08	0
$\tau\mu$ (KPSS)	0.32	4	0.29	2	0.15	2	0.35	1	0.27	1

Note lnED, lnGDP, lnEXR, lnREXP, lnCEXP represent logarithmic forms of external debt; gross domestic product; exchange rate; recurrent expenditure and capital expenditure respectively. τ_T represents the most general model with a drift and trend; τ_μ is the model with a drift and without trend; τ is the most restricted model without a drift and trend. Both in ADF and PP tests, unit root tests were performed from the most general to the least specific model by eliminating trend and intercept across the models. *, **, and *** denote rejection of the null hypothesis at the 1%, 5%, and 10% levels, respectively. Tests for unit roots have been carried out in E-views

4.3   Cointegration Results

After confirming that all variables are I(1), we proceeded to investigate the long-run relationship among variables. Johansen and Juselius (1990) cointegration test was used to investigate any possible long-run relationship among nonstationary variables. This

---

[3] To determine whether series are stationary or not we also investigate grapy of the data and ACF graphs. Both show that, compatible with formal unit root test results, all series are integrated order of 1.

test is based on the direct examination of cointegrating vector autoregressive (VAR) illustration.

$$Y_t = \alpha_1 Y_{t-1} + \alpha_2 Y_{t-2} + \cdots + \alpha_k Y_{t-k} + \varepsilon_t \tag{5}$$

Cointegration test is sensitive to lag length. So, prior to a cointegration test, first the optimal lag length should be determined. By using Akaike, Schwarz and Hannan-Quinn information criterions, the optimal lag selection turns out to be one as seen in Table 3.

Table 3. VAR lag order selection criteria results

Lag	AIC	SC	HQ
0	0.917782	1.126.755	0.993878
1	**−10.88721***	**−9.633381***	**−10.43064***
2	−1.057.379	−8.275.099	−9.736.735
3	−1.071.086	−7.367.308	−9.493.325

Note *Denotes lag order selected by the criterion

Table 4. Cointegration test results

Null hypothesis	Trace statistics	5% critical value	1% critical value
H_0: r = 0	69.570*	68.52	76.07
H_0: r $\leq$ 1	35.698	47.21	54.46
H_0: r $\leq$ 2	18.079	29.58	35.65

Note *Denotes rejection of the null hypothesis at 5% critical value level

The result of the Johansen cointegration test is given in Table 4. The null hypothesis of 'no cointegrationg vector' was rejected in favor of the alternative hypothesis of 'one cointegrating vector', which means that a long-run relationship exists among LNED and, LNCEXP, LNEXR, LNGDP, and LNREXP. The normalized cointegrating coefficients are stated in Table 5.

Table 5. Normalized cointegrating coefficients

lnED	lnEXR	lnGDP	lnREXP	lnCEXP
1.000000	−0.086271	0.782960	−0.861093	−0.979664
	(0.25133)	(0.31983)	(0.34866)	(0.13550)

Note Standard error in parentheses

Therefore, the long-run cointegrating vector can be written as;

$$LNED = 0.0862 \ln EXR - 0.7829 \ln GDP + 0.861 \ln REXP + 0.9796 \ln CEXP + \varepsilon_t$$

$$(6)$$

The presence of one cointegation vector between the variables makes it possible to estimate VECM and to capture the dynamic adjustment. To determine the significance of the normalized cointegrating coefficients and estimate error correction term we estimate VECM.

4.4   Vector Error Correction Model Results

Based on the Granger representation theorem, if there is cointegration (long-run equilibrium relationship) among nonstationary variables, there has to be an error correction representation (Engle and Granger 1987) as well. VECM provides the short-run and long-run relationships between foreign debt and the explanatory variables. If the coefficients are significant in the short-run only, then the impacts of explanatory variables are transitory. Relationship between Y_t and X_t with an error correction specification can be represented as follows:

$$\Delta Y_t = \beta_0 + \beta_1 \Delta X_t - \pi \hat{e}_{t-1} + \varepsilon_t \qquad (7)$$

where β_1 is the short-run coefficient. VECM estimation results are given in Table 6.

Table 6. VECM results

Result	Variable	Coefficient	SE	t Statistic
Speed of adjustment	ΔlnED	−0.258	0.089	−2.875
Short-run relationship	ΔlnEXR(−1)	0.581	0.350	1.605
	ΔlnGDP(−1)	0.225	0.287	0.722
	ΔlnREXP(−1)	0.065	0.251	−0.231
	ΔlnCEXP(−1)	0.261	0.117	−0.746
Long-run relationship	lnEXR(−1)	−0.086	0.251	−0.343
	lnGDP(−1)	0.783*	0.319	2.448
	lnREXP(−1)	−0.861*	0.349	−2.469
	lnCEXP(−1)	−0.979*	0.135	−7.230

Note *Indicates that the coefficient is significant

As seen in Table 6, error correction term is negative and statistically significant at $\alpha = 0.01$ with a coefficient of 0.258 which means ED of Malaysia convergences to its long-run equilibrium level by 26% speed of adjustment every year by the contribution of CEXP, EXR, GDP, and REXP. The long-run relationships can be interpreted as, if GDP increases by 1%, ED will decrease by 0.783%, a 1% increase in REXP leads to a 0.861% increase in ED, and a 1% increase in CEXP leads to a 0.979% increase in ED.

These results are compatible with our prior expectations. However, the coefficient of exchange rate is not significant.

4.5   Granger Causality Test Results

The Granger causality test is performed in order to investigate any possible causal relationship among the variables of the estimated model. The equations for the causality test are illustrated below;

$$Y_t = Y_{t-1} + X_{t-1} + u_{1t} \tag{8}$$

$$X_t = X_{t-1} + Y_{t-1} + u_{2t} \tag{9}$$

The null hypothesis of the test states that there is no causal relationship among the variables. The Granger causality test was applied under the VECM specification as discussed in Sysoev and Sysoeva (2015). Table 7 presents the results of the Pairwise Granger Causality Tests.

Table 7. Granger causality test results

Dependent variables	ΔlnED	ΔlnCEXP	ΔlnREXP	ΔlnEXR	ΔlnGDP	Inferences
ΔlnED	–	0.25879	1.71000	4.14970**	0.20572	ΔlnED $\geq$ ΔlnEXR
ΔlnCEXP	27.5466*	–	0.1197	3.90003***	0.15055	ΔlnCEXP $\geq$ ΔlnED, ΔlnCEXP $\geq$ ΔlnEXR
ΔlnREXP	4.76526**	0.79693	–	4.26148**	0.04004	ΔlnREXP $\geq$ ΔlnED, ΔlnREXP $\geq$ lnEXR,
ΔlnEXR	0.34701	1.05560	0.61151	–	0.21385	–
ΔlnGDP	4.53058**	6.11882**	10.2191*	5.50632**	–	ΔlnGDP $\geq$ ΔlnED, ΔlnGDP $\geq$ lnCEXP, ΔlnGDP $\geq$ lnREXP, ΔlnGDP $\geq$ ΔlnEXR

Note *, **, and *** denote rejection of the null hypothesis at the 1%, 5%, and 10% levels, respectively

The results given in Table 7 indicate that there are one-way causal relationships running from CEXP to ED and EXR, from ED to EXR, from REXP to ED, and from GDP to ED, CEXP, EXR and REXP. These findings imply that CEXP, REXP and GDP Granger causes of external debt. There is a unidirectional causality from external debt to EXR. This findings show us, higher indebtedness level will affect the level of exchange rate. No bidirectional causal relationship is observed among the variables.

5 Conclusion

In this study, we investigated determinants of Malaysia's external debt by employing four macroeconomic variables: GDP, exchange rates, recurrent expenditures, and capital expenditures. The cointegration test indicates that there is a cointegrating vector under the optimal lag selection of one. VECM test results show that there is no significant short-run relationship among the variables, but there is a long-run relationship that is compatible with the results of the cointegration test. The Granger causality test indicates that external debt precedes the exchange rate depreciation. Also, as we expected, current expenditure, capital expenditure, and GDP precede external debt in Malaysia.

Our results show that the Malaysian government can manage to reduce external debt by increasing GDP, hence the government relies on GDP for the repayment of external debt. Conversely, any increase in capital or recurrent expenditures will increase the external debt level. Thus, controlling recurrent expenditures is an effective way to control external debt. However, any reduction in capital expenditure will affect economic growth as well, which, in turn, could cause an increase in external debt. So the government's priority should be controlling recurrent expenditures. Also, government efforts to incentivize domestic saving will help to finance capital expenditure without relying heavily on external resources.

Also, there is a need for the government to put in place policies capable of ensuring quality deployment of external debt through budgeting rules, such as the Fiscal Responsibility Act. The government should build modern project management methods into budgeting systems to ensure a high capital budget implementation rate. Malaysian institutions such as the Public Procurement Bureau must be reformed and strengthened to create an enabling platform to allow the private sector to take the driver's seat in infrastructure development and investment through public-private partnership (PPP) models. To address the need for creative budgeting using PPP models, Malaysia needs to deemphasize the role of government in the markets, diversify the economy, and build strong institutions to bring forth faster development. Reform of the country's subsidy system, including removal of subsidies in certain industries to enhance competitiveness, will help both cost reduction and GDP growth, which will help reduce external debt. Subsidies must not create rent-seeking behaviors but incentivize production and efficiency. Ending petroleum product subsidies will encourage private investors to come into that sector, increasing the availability of products, ensuring citizen welfare, and saving much-needed foreign reserves. Finally, the surreptitious concealment of extra budgetary items and recurrent expenditures through creative accounting methods, outside of procedures approved by parliament, should be eradicated.

References

Abrego, L., & Ross, D. (2001). Debt relief under the HIPC initiative: Context and outlook for debt sustainability and resource flow. IMF Working Paper Series, Working Paper No. 144, IMF, Washington.

Ajayi, S. I., & Khan, M. S. (2000). *External debt and capital flight in Sub-Saharan Africa*. International Monetary Fund.

Ajayi, S. L. (1991). *Macroeconomic Approach to External Debt-The case of Nigeria* (No. RP_08).

Akram, N. (2015). Is public debt hindering economic growth of the Philippines? *International Journal of Social Economic, 42*(3), 202–221.

Alesina, A., & Tabellini, G. (1990). A positive theory of fiscal deficits and government debt. *The Review of Economic Studies, 57*(3), 403–414.

Ali, R., & Mustafa, U. (2012). External debt accumulation and its impact on economic growth in Pakistan. *The Pakistan Development Review, 51*(4), 79–96.

Amasoma D. (2013). Analysis of the relationship between fiscal deficits and external sector performance in Nigeria. *Journal of Economics and Sustainable Development, 4*(11), 80–87.

Arestis, P, & Sawyer, M. (2009). Path dependency and demand-supply interations in macroeconomics analysis. *Path Dependency and Macroeconomics,Basingstoke, Palgrave Macmillan,* 1–36.

Arnone, M., Bandiera, L., & Presbitero, A. F. (2010). *External debt sustainability: theory and empirical evidence.* Retrieved on September 16th 2016 from http://core.ac.uk/download/pdf/9311316.pdf.

Athukorala, P. (2010). *Malaysian Economy in Three Crises.* Working Paper No. 2010/12, Crawford School of Economics and Government, Arndt-Corden Department of Economics.

Atique, R., & Malik, K. (2012). Impact of domestic and external debt on the economic growth in Pakistan. *World Applied Sciences Journal, 20*(1), 120–129.

Awan, R. U., Anjum, A., & Rahim, S. (2015). An econometric analysis of determinants of external debt in Pakistan. *British Journal of Economics, Management and Trade, 5*(4), 1–10.

Awan, A., Asghar, N., & Rehman, H. U. (2011). The impact of exchange rate, fiscal deficit and terms of trade on external debt of Pakistan. *Australian Journal of Business and Management Research, 1*(3), 10.

Babu, J. O. (2014). External debt and economic growth in the East Africa community. *African Journal of Business Management, 8*(21), 1011–1018.

Bacha, E. L. (1990). A three-gap model of foreign transfers and the GDP growth rate in developing countries. *Journal of Development Economics, 32*(2), 279–296.

Bader, M and Magableh, I.K. (2009). An enquiry into the main determinants of public debt in Jordan: an econometric study. *Dirasat Administrative Sciences, 36*(1), 181–190.

Baldacci, E., Gupta, S. and Mulas-Granados, C. (2010). Restoring Debt Sustainability After Crises: Implications for the Fiscal Mix. IMF Working Paper No 232.

Barro, R. (1989). Economic Growth in a Cross-Section of Countries. NBER Working Paper Series, No. 3120, National Bureau of Economic Research, USA, September 1989.

Barro, R. J. (1979). On the determination of the public debt. *J. Polit. Econ. 87* (5), 940–971 (Part 1, October).

Barro, R., and Lee, J. (1994). "Sources of EconomicGrowth", Carnegie-Rochester Conference Series on Public Policy, 40(9), 1–36.

Benedict, I., Ehikioya, I. L., & Asin, O. M. (2014). Determinants and sustainability of external debt in a deregulated economy: A Cointegration analysis from Nigeria (1986–2010). *American International Journal of Contemporary Research, 4*(6), 201–214.

Berensmann, K. (2004). New ways of achieving debt sustainability beyond the enhanced HIPC initiative. *Intereconomics 39*(6), 321–330.

Bilquees, F. (2003). An analysis of budget deficits, debt accumulation, and debt instability. *The Pakistan Development Review, 42* (3), 177–195.

Bonga, W. G., Chirowa, F., Chiminya, J., & Strien, M. V. (2014). World de-dollarisation: economic implication of de-dollarisation in Zimbabwe (introduction of special coins). *Available at SSRN 2534972.*

Bullow, J., & Rogoff, K. (1989). Sovereign debt: is to forgive and forget? *The American Economic Review, 79*(1), 43–50.

Burnside, C., Dollar, D. (2004). Aid, policies, and growth: revisiting the evidence. World Bank Policy Research Working Paper 3251.

Carter, C., & Harding, A. (2010). *Special Economic Zones in Asian Market Economics.* Routledge.

Cheong K. W., Yong, E. M., Lye, K. H., Tan, K. E., & Tee, W. S. (2011). Debt, Budget Deficit and Economic Growth of Malaysia. Unpublished thesis, Universiti Tunku Abdul Rahman, Malaysia.

Choi, I. (2015). *Almost all About Unit Roots: Foundation, Developments and Applications.* UK: Cambridge University Press.

Cholifihani, M. (2008). A cointegration analysis of public debt service and GDP in Indonesia. *Journal of Management and Social Sciences, 4*(2), 68–81.

Clements, B., Bhattacharya, R., & Nguyen, T. Q. (2003). *External Debt, Public Investment,and Growth in Low-Income Countries.* IMF.

Cline, W. (1984) International Debt: Systemic Risk and Policy Response. Institute of International Economics: Washington, DC.

Collignon, S. (2012). *Europe's Debt Crisis, Coordination Failure and International Effects.* Working Paper No. 370.

Colombo, E. (2009). The Politics of External Debt in Developing Countries. Craigwell.

Cumberworth, M., & Milbourne, R. (1996). External debt and liabilities: Evidence from a Cross Section of Countries. *Economic Record, 72*(218), 201–213.

Daud, S. N. M., Ahmad, A. H., & Azman-Saini, W. N. W. (2013). Does external debt contribute to Malaysia economic growth? *Ekonomskaistraživanja – Economic Research 26*(2), 346–363.

Dickey, D. A., & Fuller, W. A. (1981). Likelihood ratio statistics for autoregressive time series with a unit root. *Econometrica: Journalof the Econometric Society, 49*(4), 1057–1072.

Dyson, K. (2014). *States, Debt, and Power: 'Saints and Sinners' in European History and Integration.* OUP Oxford.

Easterly, W. (2002). How did heavily indebted poor countries become heavily indebted? Reviewing two decades of debt relief. *World Development, 30*(10), 1677–1696.

Eaton, J. & Gersovitz, M. (1981). Debt with potential repudiation: theoretical and empirical analysis. *The Review of Economic Studies*, 289–309.

Edo, S. E. (2002). Financial management analysis of contributions of external and domestic factors to foreign debt accumulation in Nigeria and Morocco. *Journal of Financial Management & Analysis, 15*(2), 69.

Elmendorf, D. W., & Mankiw, N. G. (1998). *Government Debt.* Working Paper No. w 6470.

Engle, R., & Granger, C. (1987). Cointegration and error correction representation: estimation and testing. *Econometrica, 55*(2), 251–276.

Ezeabasili, V. N., Isu, H. O., & Mojekwu, J. N. (2011). Nigeria's external debt and economic growth: an error correction approach. *International Journal of Business and Management, 6*(5), 156.

Folorunso, B. A., and Falade, O. E. (2013). Relationship between fiscal deficit and public debt in Nigeria: an error correction approach. *Journal of Economics and Behavioral Studies, 5*(6):346–355.

Georgantopoulos A.G., et al. (2011). The interrelationship between military expenditure and external debt: patterns of causation in Northern Africa Countries. *Journal of Economics and Behavioral Studies, 3*(4), 264–273.

Haggard, S., & Kaufman, R. R. (1992). The politics of economic adjustment: International constraints, distributive conflicts, and the state. Princeton University Press.

Hajivassiliou, V. A. (1987). The external debt repayments problems of LDC's: an econometric model based on panel data. *Journal of Econometrics, 36*(1), 205–230.

Hallett, A.H., and Olivia, J.C.M. (2015). The importance of trade and capital imbalances in the European debt crisis. *Journal of Policy Modelling, 37*(2), 229–252.

Hayati, A. R. (2012). The relationship between budget deficit and economic growth from Malaysia's perspective. *International Proceedings of Economics Development and Research, 38*, 54–58.

Imimole, B., Imoughele, L. E., & Okhuese, M. A. (2014). Determinants and sustainability of external debt in a deregulated economy: a cointegration analysis from Nigeria (1986–2010). *American International Journal of Contemporary Research, 4*(6), 201–214.

Investment Frontier. (2013). *7 Countries with debt ceilings or limits. page. investment frontier. Oct 8. 2013.* Retrieved April 10, 2016, from Investment Frontier: http://www.investmentfrontier.com/2013/10/08/7-countries-with-debt-ceilings-or-limits.

Johansen, S., & Juselius, K. (1990). Maximum likelihood estimation and inferences on cointegration—with applications to the demand for money. *Oxford Bulletin of Economics and Statistics, 52*(2), 169–210.

Kemal, A.R (2001). Debt Accumulation and its implications for growth and poverty. *The Pakistan Development Review, 40*(4), 263–281.

Krugman, P. R. (1988). *Financing vs. Forgiving a Debt Overhang.* Working Paper No. 2486.

Kumar, M. S., Woo, J. (2010). Public Debt and Growth. IMF Working Papers, 10/174. International Monetary Fund.

Kwiatkowski, D., Phillips, P. C., Schmidt, P., & Shin, Y. (1992). Testing the null hypothesis of stationarity against the alternative of a unit root. *Journal of Econometrics, 54*(1), 159- 178.

Loganathan, N., Sukemi, M. N., & Sanusi, N. A. (2010). External debt and macroeconomics performance in Malaysia: sustainable or not? *Global Economy and Finance Journal, 3*(2), 122–132.

Maghyereh, A., and Hashemite, U. (2003). External debt and economic growth in Jordan: the threshold effect. *Economia Internazionale/International Economics, 56*(3), 337–355.

Mankiw, N. G., Romer, D., & Weil, D. N. (1990). *A contribution to the empirics of economic growth.* Working Paper No. w3541. National Bureau of Economic Research.

McFadden, D., Eckaus, R., Feder, G., Hajivassiliou, V., & O'Connell, S. (1985). 'Is there life after debt? An econometric analysis of the creditworthiness of developing countries', in: Smith, G. W. and Cuddington, J. T., 'International Debt and the Developing Countries', A World Bank Symposium, 1985, pp. 179–209.

Meesook, K. (2001). *Malaysia: From Crisis to Recovery* (Vol. 207). International Monetary Fund.

Memon, P. A., Rus, R. B., & Ghazali, Z. B. (2014). Firm and macroeconomic determinants of debt: Pakistan evidence. *Social and Behavioural Sciences, 172*(1), 200–207.

Menbere, W. T (2004). An empirical investigation into the determinants of external indebtedness. *Prague Economic Papers, 3*, 261–277.

Michael, O., & Sulaiman, L. A. (2012). External debt, economic growth and investment in Nigeria. *European Journal of Business and Management, 4*(11), 67–75.

Morgan, P. J., & Kawai, M. (2013). Long-term issues for fiscal sustainability in emerging Asia. *Public Policy Review, 9*(4), 751- 770.

Narayanan, S. (2012) Public Sector Resource Management. In: Malaysia's Development Challenges: Graduating from Middle (eds.) Hal Hill, ThamSiew Yean, Ragayah Haji Mat Zin, Rouledge, 131–154.

Nordhaus, W. D. (1975). The political business cycle. *The review of economic studies, 42*(2), 169–190.

Ogunmuyiwa, M. (2011). Does external debt promote economic growth in Nigeria? *Current Research Journal of Economic Theory, 3*(1), 29–35.

Oke, M. O., & Boboye, I. (2012). Effect of external debt on economic growth and development of Nigeria. *International Journal of Business and Social Science, 3*(12), 297–304.

Okosodo, L. A. & Isedu, M. O. (2011). The impact of external debt burden on the growth of agricultural and manufacturing sectors in the Nigerian economy (1980–2008). *Interdisciplinary Journal of Contemporary Research in Business, 3*(2), 1–15.

Panizza, U., & Presbitero, A. F. (2014). Public debt and economic growth: is there a causal effect. *Journal of Mcroeconomics 41,* 21–41.

Pattillo, C. (2002). *External debt and growth.* Retrieved on September 16th 2016 from http://www.imf.org/external/pubs/ft/fandd/2002/06/pattillo.html.

Pattillo, C., Poirson, H., & Ricci, L. (2004). *What are the Channels through which external Debt Affects Growth?* Retrieved on September 16th 2016 from https://www.imf.org/external/pubs/ft/wp/2004/wp0415.pdf.

Phillips, P., & Perron, P. (1988). Testing for a unit root in time series regression. *Biometrika, 75*(2), 335–346.

Pyeman, J., Noor, N. H. H. M., Mohamad, W. M. F. W., & Yahya, A. A. (2014). Factors Affecting External Debt in Malaysia: An Empirical Investigation. Proceedings of the 1st AAGBS International Conference on Business Management 2014.

Rahman, N. (2012). How federal government's debt affect the level of economic growth? *International Journal of Trade, Economics and Finance, 3*(4), 323–326.

Reinhart, C. M., & Rogoff, S. K. (2010). Growth in a time of debt. *American Economic Review, 100*(2), 573–578.

Ribiero, M. P., Villafuente, M., Baunsgaard, T., & Richmond, C. J. (2012). *Fiscal Frameworks for Resource Rich Developing Countries.* International Monetary Fund.

Sabahat, Z., & Butt, M. S. (2008). Impact of Trade Liberalization on External Debt Burden: Econometric Evidence from Pakistan. Munich Personal RePEc Archive (MPRA) Paper No. 9548.

Sachs, J. (1989). "The Debt Overhang of Developing Countries", in Calvo, G, R Findlay, P Kouri and J Macedo, eds., Debt, Stabilisation and Development: Essays in Memory of Carlos Diaz Alejandro, Oxford, Basic Blackwell, pp. 80–102.

Sarr, M., Bulte, E., Meissner, C. & Swanson, T. (2011). On the looting of nations. *Public Choice, 148*(3–4), 353–380.

Schclarek, A. (2004). *Debt and Economic Growth in Developing and Industrial Countries.* Working Paper 2005/34. Lund University Department of Economics.

Shakar, S. A., & Aslam. M. (2015). Foreign direct investment, human capital and economic growth in Malaysia. *Journal of Economic Cooperation and Development, 36*(1), 103–132.

Siddique, M. A. B. (1996). The external debt problem of Sub-Saharan Africa: 1971–1990. *The South African Journal of Economics, 64*(2), 100–124.

Stanescu, M. C. (2013). The effects of the economic crisis on the public debt of the member states of European Union. *Romanian Economic and Business Review, 8*(1), 7–18.

Sysoev, I. V., & Sysoeva, M. V. (2015). Detecting changes in coupling with granger causality method time series with fast transient processes. *Physica D, 309*(1), 9–19.

The Malaysian Insider, (2015). *Malaysia economy stable despite 50% debt to GDP ratio.* Retrieved on September 16th 2016 from http://www.themalaysianinsider.com/malaysia/article/malaysian-economy-stable-despite-50-debt-to-gdp-ratio-says-chua-bernama.

Tiruneh, M. W. (2004). An empirical investigation into the determinants of external indebtedness. University of Munich, Empirical Research Group, Munich and Institute of Slovak and World Economics Slovak Academy of Sciences, Bratislava, Slovakia.

Udoka, C.O., & Anyingang, R.A. (2012). The effect of interest rate fluctuation on the economic growth of Nigeria 1970–2010. *International Journal of Business and Social Science, 3*(20), 295–302.

Were, M. (2001). *The Impact of External Debt on Economic Growth in Kenya: An Empirical Assessment.* WIDER Discussion Paper No 116, United Nations University.

Woo, J. (2003). Economic, political, and institutional determinants of public deficits. *Journal of Public Economics, 87*(3), 387–426.

Zakaria, Z., Hussein, Z. H., Noordin, N. B., & Sawal, B. M. (2010). Financial Crisis of 1997/1998 in Malaysia: causes, impacts and recovery plans. *Voice of Academic, 5*(1), 1–18.

Zeaiter, H. F. (2008). *Determinants of Soverreign-Debt Default in Developing Countries.* The University of Wisconsin-Milwaukee.

Asset Allocation, Capital Structure, Theory of the Firm and Banking Performance: A Panel Analysis

Nader Alber[(⊠)]

Faculty of Commerce, Ain Shams University, Cairo, Egypt
naderalberfanous@yahoo.com

1 Introduction

Financial Banks should construct their financial structure according to the regulatory constraints. According to (Vittas 1992), financial regulation aims at 3 main objectives: stability, efficiency and fairness. Table 1 illustrates banks' financial structure for a sample of 15 countries at the end of 2013, as follows:

The constructing of banking financial structure should meet the requirements of regulatory constraints that include liquidity, capital adequacy.

<u>Regarding Liquidity</u>, risks are due to two reasons: the first is represented by liabilities side, where depositors withdraw of their deposits, and this requires sufficient liquidity to meet these requirements. And the second is due to assets side, where the bank should have sufficient liquidity to give required facilities to their borrowers (Saunders 1994, pp. 293–4).

<u>Regarding Capital Adequacy</u>, it has been related to risk, for the extent that make us see that the function of capital in banks is to absorb banking operations risks. As financial intermediaries, banks have, not only their risks, but also risks of other firms.

In the early seventies of the last century, many banks had been bankrupt, and many others had not acceptable levels of capital adequacy. For these reasons "Basle Committee" aimed to develop a unified standard for measuring bank capital adequacy. Basle accord began in 1975, and was modified in 1983 under supervision of International Settlement Bank. In Dec. 10, 1987, the Committee decided that capital adequacy ratio should be 7.25% as a minimum at the end of 1989, and 8% at the end of 1992. The Committee determined the components of the ratio, where its numerator includes core capital and supplementary capital, and its dominator includes 4 categories representing 4 levels of risk (Sinkey 2002, p. 271), where each level was weighted according to its level of risk, from 0 to 20%, to 50%, to 100% as risk level increases.

In 1993, the Committee suggested to add a third category to the capital. This category includes subordinated debt, which cover market risk only through issuing bonds at a rate exceeding the market rate. In Dec., 11, 1995, the central banks governors of the G10 accepted this agreement, and decided application before 1998. It seems that the first ratio issued in 1988 hasn't been sensitive to banking risks, even after modification of 1998. This leads "Basle II", which includes 3 major dimensions:

N. Ozatac and K. K. Gökmenoglu (eds.), *Emerging Trends in Banking and Finance*, Springer Proceedings in Business and Economics, https://doi.org/10.1007/978-3-030-01784-2_3

Table 1. Banks' financial structure for a sample of 15 countries at the end of 2015

Country	Liquid assets	Gov. investments	Non-gov. investments	Loans	Other assets	Deposits	Equity	Other liabilities
Algeria	0.0872	0.1359	0.5023	0.004	0.269	0.7396	0.070	0.1902
Egypt	0.1134	0.4051	0.3548	0.069	0.057	0.7932	0.114	0.0928
Iraq	0.3375	0.0631	0.1727	0.160	0.266	0.6172	0.099	0.2837
Jordan	0.1518	0.2335	0.4148	0.120	0.079	0.5719	0.143	0.2845
Kuwait	0.0532	0.0292	0.6045	0.197	0.115	0.7052	0.135	0.1589
Lebanon	0.3322	0.2285	0.2518	0.161	0.025	0.6715	0.086	0.2423
Libya	0.6685	0.0000	0.1853	0.040	0.105	0.8494	0.048	0.1011
Morocc	0.0248	0.0565	0.6510	0.024	0.243	0.4722	0.089	0.4380
Oman	0.0688	0.0254	0.6789	0.088	0.138	0.6972	0.188	0.1148
Qatar	0.0385	0.1989	0.5418	0.179	0.041	0.5560	0.121	0.0385
Saudi A.	0.1058	0.0946	0.5935	0.111	0.094	0.7405	0.119	0.1009
Sudan	0.1864	0.0980	0.4674	0.061	0.187	0.5696	0.169	0.2607
Tunisia	0.0487	0.0546	0.6794	0.030	0.186	0.5501	0.138	0.3117
UAE	0.1152	0.0723	0.4497	0.205	0.157	0.5818	0.138	0.2797
Yemen	0.1160	0.4442	0.1945	0.198	0.047	0.8019	0.078	0.1200

Source Arab Monetary Fund (2015) Economic Statistics Bulletin of Arab Countries

the first is the minimum requirements of capital, the second is the auditing control, and the third is market discipline (Saunders and Cornett 2003, 524; Pujal 2001, pp. 36–39).

Spina (2013) elaborates how Basel III presents substantial improvement upon previous versions by requiring an increase in the quantity and quality of capital. Although the nominal capital requirement continues to be 8% of risk-weighted assets, as in Basel I and II, the new rules specify that at least 75% of the total capital must be Tier 1 Capital, thus 25% in Tier 2 Capital (as opposed to 50/50 prescribed in previous versions). Furthermore, Tier 1 is divided into two categories, Common Equity Tier 1 (at least 4.5% of a bank's RWA), and Additional Tier 1 (generally preferred stock and additional paid-in capital that otherwise does not satisfy the criteria for Tier 1).

<u>Efficiency</u> measurement is an aspect of firm performance that is measured with respect to an objective; it can be measured with respect to maximization of output, maximization of profits, or minimization of costs. Scale economies, scope economies, and X-efficiency are different aspects of performance. Scale and scope economies refer to selecting the appropriate outputs, while X-efficiency refers to selecting the appropriate inputs. Typically, scale economies refer to how the firm's scale of operations (its size) is related to cost. Scope economies refer to how the firm's choice of multiple product lines is related to cost (Mester 2003, p. 2).

Data envelopment analysis (DEA) is a mathematic technique developed in operations research and management science and over the last 40 years, the field of its usage has been extensively updated. DEA is a non-parametric linear programming technique that measures the relative efficiency of a group of decision making units (DMUs) which receive multiple inputs to produce multiple outputs.

DEA, first proposed by Charnes et al. (1978) and applied by Sherman and Gold (1985) is based on earlier work initiated by Farrell (1957). DEA has become a popular technique in bank efficiency analysis since its first application by Berger and Humphrey (1997) provides an international survey of efficient frontier analysis of financial institution performance. Maletić et al. (2013, p. 845) addresses the basics of DEA methods: CCR (Charnes, Cooper and Rhodes), BCC (Banker, Charns and Cooper) and AP (Andersen and Petersen).

The most basic models of DEA are CCR, BCC, Additive and SBM. CCR and BCC models are radial and aim to minimize inputs while keeping outputs at least the given output levels (*input-oriented*) or attempt to maximize outputs without requiring more of any of the observed input values (*output-oriented*). The combination of both orientations in a single model is called additive model. Additive models treat the slacks (the input excesses and output shortfalls) directly in objective function, but it doesn't have the ability to measure the depth of inefficiency by a scalar similar to θ^* in CCR-type models (Shafiee et al. 2013, p. 2).

DEA models that project units on the efficient frontier by reducing resources are termed *input minimization* models, and those that augment outputs are termed *output maximization* models. A DEA benchmarking model is unambiguously specified once we determine its inputs and outputs, and specify the linear programming formulation that fits the envelopment surface and projects the inefficient units on the efficient frontier (Soteriou and Zenios 1997, p. 24).

The choice of inputs and outputs is perhaps the most important task in employing DEA to measure the relative efficiency of the DMUs. Two approaches are widely used to identify a bank's inputs and outputs, the production approach (e.g.; Sherman and Gold 1985), and the intermediation approach (e.g.; Yue 1992). Under the production approach, banks are treated as a firm to produce loans, deposits, and other assets by using labor and capital. However, banks are considered as financial intermediaries to transform deposits, purchase funds and labors into loans and other assets under the intermediation approach. More specifically, deposits are treated as an input under the production approach and an output under the intermediation approach.

<u>Regarding Financial Stability</u>, many global, regional and governmental bodies are established for its promotion. The Financial Stability Board (FSB) is established to address financial system susceptibilities and to drive the development and implementation of strong regulatory, supervisory, and other policies which enhance financial stability. Also, the Financial Stability Forum (FSF) has been set up by the G-7 in the wake of the Asian crisis in 1999, with an expanded membership (drawn mainly from the G-20).

In US, the legislation Restoring American Financial Stability Act of 2010 focuses on how to promote the financial stability. The UK Financial Services Authority (FSA) requires stricter capital rules than those proposed by the Basel Committee on Banking Supervision (BCBS). The European Central Bank (ECB) is in charge of monitoring and assessment of financial stability. Presently, the Committee of European Banking Supervisors (CEBS) provides regular bank sector analysis, performs assessments on banking risks, to be reported to the European Union political institutions.

Schinasi (2004) lists the key principles for defining financial stability as a generic concept, embodying the varied aspects of the financial system. The author addresses that financial stability relates not only to the absence of financial distress but also to the capability of the financial system to limit, contain, and deal with such situations. Schinasi (2006) addresses "stability" as the ability of financial system to resolve systemic risks. He argues that financial system is stable if the system is capable to perform three key functions: (1) allocation of resources from savers to investors; (2) assessment, pricing, and allocation of financial risks; (3) and absorption of financial and economic shocks.

Dobravolskas and Seiranov (2011) addresses two kinds of stability and two kinds of factors violating stability. The authors argue that financial stability characterizes smooth flow of funds between savers and investors, while monetary stability characterizes ability to preserve stable level of prices for goods and services and to keep acceptable levels of currency fluctuations. They divide factors violating stability of financial system into external and internal factors. The first group includes macroeconomic disproportions in production and consumption, saving and investment processes, and the second arises from imperfect nature of financial markets.

Swamy (2011) analyzes the determinants of banking sector soundness, as measured by banking stability index (BSI) in the context of an emerging economy banking sector. This study considers the core set of soundness indicators for the construction of the index for the Indian financial system during the period 1997–2009.

In brief, this study tries to answer these four main questions:

- How to build up an "optimal financial structure" in terms of the "theory of the banking firm" under constraints of liquidity and capital adequacy?
- How to construct an index of "optimality of bank financial structure"? By other words: How to use regulatory constraints as determinants of optimality?
- Does "optimality index of bank financial structure" affect the banking efficiency?
- Does "optimality index of bank financial structure" affect the financial stability?

The paper is arranged as follows: after this introduction, Sect. 2 reviews research literature. Section 3 is for the suggested model and Sect. 4 is for empirical work, presenting results, discussing how these results answer research questions with a robustness check. Section 5 summarizes the paper and provides remarks about conclusions.

2 Literature Review

This section tries to present some of previous work, which has been conducted in the fields of theory of the banking firm, financial stability and banking efficiency.

Regarding the "theory of the banking firm", portfolio theory aims at determining the "optimal mix of assets", where (Markowitz 1952) depends on 2 main criteria: risk and return. The theory explains how to calculate the optimal weights; that have the maximum level of return at the same level of risk, or the minimum level of risk at the same level of return. On the other hand, "optimal capital structure" is still a controversy issue, regarding the debate among theories explaining this optimality.

Most studies take in account the dependence relationships among items of the 2 sides of balance sheet, while few ones (e.g.; Klein 1971; Sealey 1985) argue that loans function is independent of deposit function. The Perceiving trend takes the 2 sides of balance sheet in account. (Pringle 1973) assumes that (Klein 1971) is concerning with a case study. So, its results could not be generalized. (Murphy 1972) insists on building a comprehensive theory of a banking firm, which should concerns with liquidity management, portfolio selection, and service pricing at the same time.

Broaddus (1972) is one of the famous studies determining the optimal weights of liquidity and loans, using linear programming, where the objective function is to maximize the average profitability of liquidity and loans, within constraints of liquidity, minimum level of loans, and balance sheet. (Cohen 1972) uses also linear programming techniques to determine the optimal weights of cash and quasi cash, investment in securities, loans, current deposits, certificates of deposits, and capital. The study objective function is to maximize net income within constraints of capital it risky assets ratio, maximum deposit lending ratio, and legal reserve ratio.

Fama (1980) assumes that there's no optimal capital structure for banks depending on MM theory. He considers 2 main constraints: Liquidity (reserve requirements), and deposit pricing. For Liquidity constraint, he sees that banks are performing the role of "Portfolio manager", and constructing a "personal portfolio" for each depositor. He considers "reserve requirements" as direct taxes on deposit returns. (Buser et al. 1981) does not agree with (Fama 1980). They determine the optimal ratio of debts to assets (D/A)* without existence of deposit insurance system, and with its existence, where they denote this ratio (D/A)**.

There're many other studies that analyze bank capital structure. Otsberg and Thomson (1996) determines the optimal capital structure of banks, within legal requirements of capital adequacy and market forces. Karna and Graddy (1982) shows —using data of BHCs from 1969 to 1976—that optimal capital structure which maximizes ROE is determined when liabilities to assets ratio = 18.4, Where ROE = 12.3%. Orgler and Taggart (1983) analyzes optimal bank capital structure within a special perspective, depending on *agency theory*, while (Hutchison 1995) concerns with deposit pricing, within liquidity constraints, depositors utility, and market competition.

Francis (1978) categorizes assets into 5 items: cash and quasi cash, governmental investment, mortgage loans, business loans, and consumption loans. Liabilities are categorized into 3 items: current deposits, saving deposits, and equity rights. Using data of 869 banks, during period from 1966 to 1971, optimal weights of above-mentioned items are determined. Francis uses *Lagrange Function* which maximizes ROE within definitional constraints, and legal reserve constraint.

Baltnesperger (1980) develops his famous model, by which bank assets are divided into two items: reserves (for providing liquidity) and revenue-assets (for providing profitability), and bank liabilities are divided, also, into 2 items: deposits and equity rights. The study aims to make the optimal division between the 2 items of the 2 sides of bank balance sheet. This optimality is determined using profitability function which includes revenues of loans and investments, paid interests, liquidity costs, capital adequacy costs, indirect costs, and opportunity cost of equity.

Sealy (1985) proposes optimal weights of deposits, loans, and liquidity. According to this model, deposits are a function of their interest rate, while loans are determined in light of market competitive circumstances. **Sealy**'s model aims to maximize profits before taxes.

Elyasiani et al. (1995) shows that functions of deposit supply and loans demand are dependent (one on the other), which doesn't agree with *separation theory* of **Sealy**'s model. It shows that costs related to deposits side and those related to loans side occur simultaneously, and it aims to maximize net present value of profits within constraints of balance sheet and legal reserve requirements. Using quarterly data of 150 BHCs from the first quarter of 1981 to the second quarter of 1981, the study determines the optimal weights of deposits, loans, and legal reserve balances.

Regarding "banking stability", Schaeck et al. (2007) investigates the implications of competitive bank behavior with 38 countries for the period 1980–2003. They find that competition reduces the likelihood of a crisis and increases time to observing crisis. Berger et al. (2009) supports the "competition-fragility" view using over 8235 banks in 23 developed countries for the years 1999–2005. Besides, Uhde and Heimeshoff (2009) analyzes over 2600 banks across the EU-25 during the period from 1997 to 2005 and their empirical results are consistent with the "concentration-fragility" view.

Amidu and Wolfe (2009) analyzes a panel dataset of 978 banks, during the period 2000–2007. Macro data is obtained from the World Development Indicator of the World Bank and International Financial Statistics database. They use H-statistic and the Lerner index as measures of the degree of competition in the banking sector, employ three stage least squares (3sls) estimation techniques, and investigate the significance of diversification in the competition-stability relationship. The core finding is that competition increases stability as diversification across and within both interest and non-interest income generating activities of banks increases.

Demirgüç-Kunt and Detragiache (2011) studies the effect of compliance with the Basel core principles for effective banking supervision on bank soundness. Using data for more than 3000 banks in 86 countries, the authors find that neither the overall index of compliance with the Basel core principles nor the individual components of the index are robustly associated with bank risk measured by Z-scores. This may cast doubt on the usefulness of the Basel core principles in ensuring bank soundness.

Dobravolskas and Seiranov (2011) investigates the reasons of financial instability, during the 2007–2008 crisis and studies the ways of rebuilding financial stability in the process of post-crisis regulatory reforms. Findings show that violation of stability is a result of deregulation processes in major financial markets since 1980s on the one hand, a result of inadequacy of national micro-prudential regulators on the other hand. The article studies how these targets are met in post-crisis regulatory reforms, in USA, the European Union and Lithuania.

De Nicolò et al. (2011) develops a dynamic model of a bank exposed to both credit and liquidity risk, and analyzes the impact of capital regulation, liquidity requirements and taxation on banks' optimal policies and metrics of efficiency of intermediation and social value. The authors argue that the inverted U-shaped relationship between bank lending, bank efficiency, social value and regulatory capital ratios indicates the existence of optimal levels of regulatory capital.

Results indicate that mild capital requirements increase bank lending, bank efficiency and social value relative to an unregulated bank. Also, findings show that liquidity requirements reduce bank lending, efficiency and social value significantly.

Buston (2012) shows the net impact of two opposing effects of active risk management at banks on their stability. This has been applied on US BHCs using a sample of an unbalanced panel containing 7253 observations and 2276 banks, from 2005 to 2010. Empirical evidence supports the effects of active risk management at banks on their stability and show that active risk management banks are less likely to fail during the crisis of 2007–2009.

Wagner (2004) finds that increasing liquidity in normal times doesn't affect stability, as measured by banks probability of default. By contrast, he argues that an increase in asset liquidity in times of crisis reduces stability. Wen and Yu (2013) elaborates the effects of bank stability on market concentration, financial deepening, bank income structure and international debt situation by using panel data for 18 emerging countries. Results supports that concentration affects financial stability in banking industry.

Schaeck and Cihak (2013) assemble a panel dataset from BankScope for European banks for the period 1995–2005. The sample covers Austria, Belgium, Denmark, France, Italy, Germany, Luxembourg, Netherlands, Switzerland, and the U.K, and consists of 17,965 bank-year observations for 3325 banks. Results indicate that competition robustly improves stability via the efficiency channel.

<u>Regarding "banking efficiency"</u>, Aly et al. (1990) uses CCR model to evaluate the technical, scale, and allocative efficiencies of 322 USA banks in 1986. The number of full-time staff, fixed asset, capital and loanable fund are chosen as inputs; while real estate loan, commercial and industrial loan, consumer loan, miscellaneous loan, and current deposit are chosen as outputs.

Andersen and Petersen (1993) proposes ranking model that shows how much the unit can "get worse" but still be efficient. Superefficient units are those with efficiency of over 100%, the most efficient is the one which is highest ranked, while the units with efficiency less than 100% are inefficient and therefore ranked lower.

Soteriou and Zenios (1997) has indicated that analyzing banks' efficiency should include branches, service quality, operations, and profitability, simultaneously. The authors develop a framework for combining strategic benchmarking with efficiency benchmarking of the services offered by bank branches. They use 3 DEA models: an operational efficiency model, a quality efficiency model and a profitability efficiency model. Empirical results indicate that superior insights can be obtained by analyzing operations, service quality, and profitability simultaneously than the information obtained from benchmarking studies of these 3 dimensions separately.

Berger and Humphrey (1997) documents 130 studies of financial institution efficiency, as applied on 21 countries, from multiple time periods, and from various types of institutions, including banks, credit unions, and insurance companies. Results suggest that progress has been made on efficiency measurement rather than that has been made in explaining the differences in performance (i.e., profitability or efficiency) across institutions. Athanassopoulos and Giokas (2000) examines 47 branches of the Commercial Bank of Greece and uses the DEA results to implement the proposed changes in the bank performance measurement system.

Milind (2003) carries out the banks efficiency analysis in India on the basis of two models. Model A inputs are: interest expenses, non-interest expenses, and outputs: net interest income, net non-interest income, and model B inputs are: deposits, employees, and outputs: net loans, non-interest income). Fries and Taci (2004) compares the performance of 289 banks in 15 post-communist countries, using an intermediate approach. The results show that foreign banks are more competitive and have better results in cost efficiency than domestic banks.

Carvallo and Kasman (2005) investigates the cost efficiency of a sample of 481 Latin American and Caribbean banks in 105 countries over the years from 1995 to 1999 using a stochastic frontier model (SFA). They use three inputs: loans, deposits, and other earning assets and three prices of factors of production: the price of labor, the price of purchased funds, and the price of physical capital. Results indicate that on average, very small and very large banks are significantly more inefficient than large banks.

Efficiency of Canadian banks has been investigated by Avkiran (2006) and Wu et al. (2006). Avkiran (2006) applies DEA using a sample of 24 Canadian foreign bank subsidiaries in year 2000. The outputs include loans, securities and non-interest income, while inputs include deposits, non-interest expenses and equity multiplier. Wu et al. (2006) integrates the DEA and neural networks (NNs) to examine the relative branch's efficiency of a big Canadian bank. The authors observe 142 banks in Canada, and monitor the number of employees and costs for input indicators; while for output they monitor deposits, income and bank loans.

Sakar (2006) in Turkey analyzes 11 banks and monitors input: branch numbers, employees per branch, assets, loans, deposits, and outputs: ROA, ROE, interest and non- interest assets. Hassan and Sanchez (2007) examines banking performance using DEA. The authors estimate and compare the efficiency and productivity of seven Latin American countries (Argentina, Brazil, Chile, Colombia, Ecuador, Mexico and Venezuela) during the period from 1996 to 2003. The study finds that most of the sources of inefficiencies are regulatory rather than technical. This means that bank managers do not choose the correct (optimal) input and output mix, because they are not forced to do so by government regulations or market conditions.

Moh'd Al-Jarrah (2007) uses DEA approach to investigate cost efficiency levels of banks operating in Jordan, Egypt, Saudi Arabia and Bahrain over 1992–2000. The estimated cost efficiency is further decomposed into technical and allocative efficiency at both variable and constant return to scale. Later on, the technical efficiency is further decomposed into pure technical and scale efficiency. Results show that cost efficiency scores range from 50 to 70% with some variations in scores depending on bank's size and geographical locations. Avkiran (2009) applied non-oriented network slacks-based measure in domestic commercial banks of United Arab Emirates (UAE), using non-oriented, non-radial SBM modeling.

Alber (2011) considers the effects of banking expansion on profit efficiency of the Saudi banks. This has been conducted using a sample of 6 commercial banks (out of 11), and covering the period from 1998 to 2007. Profit efficiency has been measured using the ratio of actual profitability to the best one, which a similar bank can realize. Tests indicated that we could accept hypotheses regarding the effects of "availability of phone banking", "number of ATMs" and "number of branches" on profit efficiency of

Saudi banks. Al-Farisi and Hendrawan (2012) examines the impact of capital structure on performance of conventional and Islamic banks, by using profit efficiency approach. They measure profit efficiency score for each bank in Indonesia during the period from 2002 to 2008 by using distribution free approach (DFA). Result indicate that banks' capital ratio have a negative effect on their profit efficiency.

Maletić et al. (2013) uses DEA technique in case of measuring operation efficiency of the banking sector in Serbia, which currently has 33 banks. Input and output indicators differ according to the used models A and B. According to Model A, inputs include interest expenses and non-interest expenses, while outputs include interest income and net non-interest income. According to Model B, inputs include deposits and employees, while outputs include loans and operating income.

Shafiee et al. (2013) evaluates the efficiency of an Iranian bank using dynamic SBM model in DEA during three consecutive terms considering net profit as a good link and loan losses as a bad link. Each branch in each term expends money on labor salaries and operating expense as inputs to produce loans as output. In each term some loans become non-performing, because of unable borrowers to make full or even partial payment.

Thayaparan and Pratheepan (2014) focuses on total factor productivity growth and its decomposition of commercial banks in Sri Lanka, as applied on two state banks and four private banks over the period 2009–2012. By using DEA, total factor productivity and its components are measured in terms of efficiency change, technical efficiency change, pure efficiency change and scale change. Interest income and loans are considered as outputs and deposits, total assets, number of staff and interest expenses are considered as inputs. Results indicate that, all six banks operate averagely at 87.2% of overall efficiency and that less performance is achieved due to the less progress in technical change than efficiency change. The overall results conclude that private banks are more efficient than state banks.

Comparing with previous work, the current study tries to:

- Propose an index of "optimality of bank financial structure" in terms of the "theory of the banking firm", while previous work tend to address the optimal financial structure without comparing with actual one.
- Investigate the effect of "optimality of bank financial structure" on both of banking efficiency and financial stability, while previous work tend to address them separately without this framework.

3   The Suggested Model

3.1   Variables Used

Before constructing the model, two kinds of variables are needed: the first represents items from bank balance sheet and the second represents items from income statement. These two categories are illustrated as follows (Tables 2 and 3):

Table 2. Items of bank balance sheet

Variable	Sign	Variable	Sign
Cash %	W1	Deposits %	W6
Cash in bank %	W11	Volatile deposits %	W61
Due from banks %	W12	Stable deposits %	W62
Due from CBE %*	W13	Equity	W7
Gov. investment %	W2	Capital %	W71
Loans %	W3	Reserves and R. earnings %	W72
Volatile loans %	W31	Complementary capital % (for capital adequacy)	W73
Stable loans %	W32	Other liabilities %	W8
Non-gov. investment %	W4	Other comp. capital %	W81
Other assets %	W5	Due to banks %*	W82
		Others %	W83

% refers to the item percentage compared with total assets

* It's assumed that W13 = W82, as it's a zero game at the long run

Table 3. Items of bank income statement

Variable	Sign	Calculation	Notes
Loans returns %	R1	R1 = W3 × C1	C1: loans interest rate
Other returns %	R2		
Deposit costs %	R3	R3 = W6 × C2	C2: deposit cost rate
Deposit interests %	R31	R31 = W × C21	C21: deposit interest rate
Deposit insurance cost %	R32	R32 = W6 × C22	C22: deposit insurance cost rate
Other expenses %	R4		
Interests of complementary capital %	R5	R5 = (W73 + W81) × C3	C3: interest rate for complementary capital
Taxes	R6	R6 = (R1 + R2 − R3 − R4 − R5) × t	t: tax rate

% refers to the item percentage compared with total assets

3.2 Objective Function

The model aims at maximizing Return on Equity (ROE), and it could be used to maximize other objective functions (i.e.; ROA, profitability of lending and net profitability of lending).

3.3 Constraints

The model aims at maximizing ROE within the following constraints:

3.3.1 Definitional Constraints

where

$$W1 + W2 + W3 + W4 + W5 = 1 \tag{1}$$

$$W6 + W7 + W8 = 1 \tag{2}$$

3.3.2 Legal Reserve Ratio Constraint

where

$$W12 \geq (W6 \times S) \tag{3}$$

where S: Legal Reserve Ratio.

3.3.3 Legal Liquidity Ratio Constraint

where

$$(W11^{*} + W13 + W2) \geq (W6 \times L) \tag{4}$$

where L: Legal Liquidity Ratio

3.3.4 Capital Adequacy Constraints

where

$$((W3 + W4 + W5) \times A) \times W7 \tag{5}$$

where A: Capital Adequacy Ratio

$$W2 + W3 + W4 \leq W6. \tag{6}$$

3.3.5 Maximum Lending Constraint

where

$$W3 \leq W6 \times M \tag{7}$$

where M: Maximum Lending Ratio.

3.4 Algorithm

The algorithm of the proposed model could be illustrated by the following steps:

3.4.1 Determining W5* and W8*

Where W5* is W5 that maximizes ROE, and W8* is W8 that maximizes ROE. So, the model have to maximize ROE: ROE = f (W5), and to maximize ROE: ROE = f (W8).

3.4.2   Determining W11*

where

$$W11^* = W31 + W61 \tag{8}$$

W31 could be estimated using regression where W3 is the dependent variable, and time is the independent one. By estimating confidence intervals, we can get W31, where confidence intervals are estimated by the following:

$$W3 \pm (t/2 \times \text{standard error}) \tag{9}$$

So,

$$W31 = (t/2 \times \text{standard error}) \tag{10}$$

And by the same way, we can estimate W61.

3.4.3   Determining W1*, W2*, W3*, W4*, W6* and W7*

Using *Lagrange Function* for objective function, considering constraints, leads to the following:

$$W12^* = W6^* S \tag{11}$$

$$W1^* = W11^* + W12^* + W13^* \tag{12}$$

$$W2^* = W6^* \times L - W11^* - W13^* \tag{13}$$

$$W3^* = W6^* \times M \tag{14}$$

$$W4^* = 1 - W1^* - W2^* - W3^* - W5^* \tag{15}$$

$$W6^* = ((1 - W8^*) - A)/(1 + (S + L) \times A) \tag{16}$$

$$W7^* = 1 - W6^* - W8^* \tag{17}$$

3.5   Optimality Index of Bank Financial Structure

After determining optimal weights of balance sheet items, as illustrated above, it's simple to calculate the Optimality Index of Bank Financial Structure, as follows:

3.5.1   Calculating Optimality of Assets (OA)

$$\mathbf{O1 = (|W1 - W1^*| + |W2 - W2^*| + |W3 - W3^*| + |W4 - W4^*| + |W5 - W5^*|)/2} \tag{18}$$

3.5.2 Calculating Optimality of Liabilities (OL)

$$\mathbf{O1} = (|\mathbf{W6} - \mathbf{W6}_*| + |\mathbf{W7} - \mathbf{W7}_*| + |\mathbf{W8} - \mathbf{W8}_*|)/2 \qquad (19)$$

3.5.3 Calculating Optimality Index (OI)

$$\mathbf{OI} = (\mathbf{OA} + \mathbf{OL})/2 \qquad (20)$$

4 Testing Hypotheses

Banking efficiency is measured by DEA technique according to Constant Returns to Scale (CRS) efficiency. So, Banking efficiency is measured as follows:

$$\mathbf{Banking\ Efficiency = CRS} \qquad (21)$$

Financial stability is measured by Z-score that indicates the number of standard deviations that a bank's profit must fall to drive it into insolvency.

$$\mathbf{Z} = (\mathbf{ROA} + \mathbf{E/A})/\sigma_{\mathbf{ROA}} \qquad (22)$$

where ROA is return on assets, E/A denotes the equity to asset ratio and σ ROA is the standard deviation of return on assets.

This paper tries to test the following 2 hypotheses:

(1) There's no significant effect of "optimality of bank financial structure" on "bank efficiency", where:

$$\mathbf{CRS = f(OI)} \qquad (23)$$

This means that alternative hypothesis Ha: $\beta \neq 0$ versus null hypothesis Hb: $\beta = 0$, where β is the regression coefficient of the above-shown function.

(2) There's no significant effect of "optimality of bank financial structure" on "bank financial stability", where:

$$\mathbf{Z = f(OI)} \qquad (24)$$

This means that alternative hypothesis Ha: $\beta \neq 0$ versus null hypothesis Hb: $\beta = 0$, where β is the regression coefficient of the above-shown function.

Table 4 illustrates descriptive statistics of optimality index (OI), banking efficiency (CRS) and financial stability (Z_SCORE) for a sample of 15 MENA countries and cover the period from 2004 to 2013:

Table 4. Descriptive statistics of optimality index, efficiency and financial stability

Variable	OI	CRS	Z_SCORE
Mean	0.926776	0.926776	24.65634
Median	0.976704	0.976704	21.33371
Maximum	1.000000	1.000000	64.46805
Minimum	0.389085	0.389085	−1.036303
Std. dev.	0.132625	0.132625	13.09133
Skewness	−2.824592	−2.824592	0.892286
Observations	150	150	150

Source Collected and processed by the researcher

Table 5. Testing the first hypothesis using OLS and GMM techniques

Variable	Coefficient	Std. error	t-Statistic	Prob.
Panel (1) Dependent Variable: CRS Technique: OLS				
C	0.714650	0.058777	12.15875	0.0000
OI	0.272825	0.074402	3.666910	0.0000
R-squared	0.083286			
F-statistic	13.44623			
Prob. (F-statistic)	0.000342			
Panel (2) Dependent Variable: CRS (−1) Technique: GMM				
C	0.229545	0.006301	36.43167	0.0000
OI	0.437684	0.035826	12.21695	0.0000
R-squared	0.084567			
J-statistic	13.44623			
Prob. (J-statistic)	0.381989			

To test the research hypotheses, a panel data regression has been conducted using OLS and GMM techniques. The Generalized Method of Moments (GMM method) uses lagged values of explained variables as instrumental variables to fix the problem of endogeneity. GMM is also malleable enough to include serial correlation and unobserved heterogeneity into the model.

Regarding the first hypothesis, Table 5 illustrates how optimality of bank financial structure" affect "bank efficiency", as follows:

Table 5 supports the significance of "optimality index" effect on "banking efficiency" with explanation power of 8.33% using OLS technique and of 8.46% using GMM technique.

Regarding the second hypothesis, Table 6 illustrates how optimality of bank financial structure" affect "financial stability", as follows:

Table 6 supports the significance of "optimality index" effect on "financial stability", with explanation power of 2.76% using OLS technique and of 15.49% using GMM technique.

Table 6. Testing the second hypothesis using OLS and GMM techniques

Variable	Coefficient	Std. error	t-Statistic	Prob.
Panel (1) Dependent Variable: Z_SCORE Technique: OLS				
C	12.60902	5.975510	2.110116	0.0365
OI	15.49462	7.564047	2.048456	0.0423
R-squared	0.027571			
F-statistic	4.196173			
Prob. (F-statistic)	0.042282			
Panel (2) Dependent Variable: Z_SCORE (−1) Technique: GMM				
C	0.522271	0.028688	18.20488	0.0000
OI	−15.54103	0.621259	−25.01536	0.0000
R-squared	0.154927			
J-statistic	14.65379			
Prob. (J-statistic)	0.329462			

5 Summary and Concluded Remarks

This paper attempts to propose a measure of "optimality of bank financial structure" in terms of the "theory of the banking firm" under constraints of liquidity, capital adequacy.

Results show that "optimality of bank financial structure" may affect each of "banking efficiency"; and "financial stability". This has been conducted using panel analysis according to OLS and GMM techniques, as applied on a sample of 15 MENA banking systems, over the period from 2004 to 2015.

References

Alber (2011) "The Effect of Banking Expansion on Profit Efficiency of Saudi Banks, **2nd International Conference on Business and Economic Research**, Malaysia: Langkawi, 14–16 March 2011.

Al-Farisi, A. & Hendrawan, R. (2012) "Effect of Capital Structure on Banks Performance: A Profit Efficiency Approach Islamic and Conventional Banks Case in Indonesia," **International Research Journal of Finance and Economics** 86, 6–19.

Aly, H., Grabowski, R., Pasurka, C. & Rangan, N. (1990) "Technical Scale and Allocative Efficiencies in US Banking: An Empirical Investigation," **Review of Economics and Statistics** 72 (2) 211–218. Retrieved from: http://dx.doi.org/10.2307/2109710.

Amidu, M. & Wolfe, S. (2009) "Bank Competition, Diversification and Financial Stability," **22nd Australasian Finance and Banking Conference 2009**. Available at SSRN: http://ssrn.com/abstract=1341863.

Andersen, P. & Petersen, N. (1993) "Procedure for Ranking Efficient Units in Data Envelopment Analysis," **Management Science** 39(10) 1261–1264.

Arab Monetary Fund (2015) **Economic Statistics Bulletin of Arab Countries.** Retrieved from: http://www.amf.org.ae/en/content/economic-statistics-bulletin-arab-countries.

Athanassopoulos, A. & Giokas, D. (2000) "The Use of Data Envelopment Analysis in Banking Institutions: Evidence from the Commercial Bank of Greece," **Interfaces** 30, 81–95. Retrieved from: http://dx.doi.org/10.1287/inte.30.2.81.11678.

Avkiran, N. (2006) "Using DEA in Benchmarking," **JASSA** 2 (2). Retrieved from: www.finsia. com/docs/default.../2_2006_dea_benchmarking.pdf?sfvrsn.

Avkiran, N. (2009) "Opening the Black Box of Efficiency Analysis: An Illustration with UAE Banks," **Omega** 37, 930–941. Retrieved from: http://dx.doi.org/10.1016/j.omega.2008.08. 001.

Baltensperger, E. (1980) "Alternative Approaches to the Theory of Banking Firm," **Journal of Monetary Economics** 6, 1–37.

Berger, A. & Humphrey, D. (1997) "Efficiency of Financial Institutions: International Survey and Directions for Future Research," **Journal of Operational Research** 98, 175–212.

Berger, A., Klapper, L. & Turk-Ariss, R. (2009) "Bank Competition and Financial Stability," **Journal of Financial Services Research** 35(2) 99–118.

Broaddus, A. (1972) "Linear Programming: A New Approach to Bank Portfolio Management," **Federal Reserve of Richmond**, Nov., 3:11.

Buser, S., Chen, A. & Kane, E. (1981) "Federal Deposit Insurance, Regulatory Policy, and Optimal Bank Capital," **Journal of Finance** 36, 51–60.

Buston, C. (2012) "Active Risk Management and Banking Stability," Available at: http://dx.doi. org/10.2139/ssrn.2049390.

Carvallo, O. & Kasman, A. (2005) "Cost Efficiency in the Latin American and Caribbean Banking Systems," **Journal of International Financial Markets Institution and Money** 15, 55–72.

Charnes, A., Cooper, V. & Rhodes, E. (1978) "Measuring the Efficiency of Decision Making Units," **European Journal of Operational Research** 2, 429–444. Retrieved from: http://dx. doi.org/10.1016/0377-2217(78)90138-8.

Cohen, K. (1972) "Dynamic Balance Sheet Management: A Management Science Approach," **Journal of Bank Research**, winter, 9–19.

De Nicolò, G., Gamba, A. & Lucchetta, M. (2011) "Capital Regulation, Liquidity Requirements and Taxation in a Dynamic Model of Banking," **Discussion Paper 2011–090**, Tilburg University, Center for Economic Research.

Demirgüç-Kunt, A. & Detragiache, A. (2011) "Basel Core Principles and Bank Soundness Does Compliance Matter?" **Journal of Financial Stability** 7 (4) 179–190.

Dobravolskas, A. & Seiranov, J. (2011) "Financial Stability as the Goal of Post-Crisis Regulatory Reforms," **Business Systems and Economics** 1 (1) 101–114.

Elyasiani, E., Kopecky, K. & Van Hoose, D. (1995) "Costs of Adjustment, Portfolio Separation, and the Dynamic Behavior of Bank Loans and Deposits," **Journal of Money, Credit and Banking** 27, 955–974.

Fama, E. (1980) "Banking in the Theory of Finance," **Journal of Monetary Economics** 6, 39–57.

Farrell, M. (1957) "The Measurement of Productive Efficiency," **Journal of the Royal Statistical Society**, Series A, General, 120 (Part 3) 253–281. Retrieved from: http://dx.doi. org/10.2307/2343100.

Francis, J. (1978) "Portfolio Analysis of Asset and Liability Management in Small—, Medium —, and Large—Sized Banks," **Journal of Monetary economics** 3, 112–134.

Fries, S., Taci, A. (2004) "Cost Efficiency of Banks in Transition: Evidence from 289 Banks in 15 Post-Communist Countries," **Journal of Banking and Finance** 29, 55–81.

Hassan, K. & Sanchez, B. (2007) "Efficiency Determinants and Dynamic Efficiency Changes in Latin American Banking Industries," Retrieved from: http://ssrn.com/abstract=1087045.

Hutchison, D. (1995) "Retail Bank Deposit Pricing: An Inter-temporal Asset Pricing Approach," **Journal of Money, Credit, and Banking** 27, 217- 231.

Karna, A. & Graddy, D. (1982) "Bank Holding Company Leverage and the Return of Stockholders Equity," **Journal of Bank Research** 13.

Klein, M. (1971) "A Theory of the Banking Firm," **Journal of Money, Credit, and Banking** May, 297–304.

Maletić, R., Kreća, M., & Maletić, P. (2013) "Application of DEA Methodology in Measuring Efficiency in The Banking Sector," **Economics of Agriculture** 60(4) 843–855.

Markowitz, H. (1952) "Portfolio Selection," **The Journal of Finance** 8, 77–91.

Mester, L., (2003) "Applying Efficiency Measurement Techniques to Central Banks," **FRB of Philadelphia Working Paper # 03-13**. Retrieved from: http://ssrn.com/abstract=572442 or http://dx.doi.org/10.2139/ssrn.572442.

Milind, S. (2003) "Efficiency of banks in a developing economy: the case of India," **European Journal of Operational Research** 148, 662–671.

Moh'd Al-Jarrah, I. (2007) "The use of DEA in Measuring Efficiency in Arabian Banking," **Banks and Bank Systems Journal** 2(4) 21–30.

Murphy, N. (1972) "Costs of Banking Activities: Interactions between Risk and Operating Costs: A Comment," **Journal of Money, Credit and Banking**, Aug., 614:615.

Orgler, Y. & Taggart, R. (1983) "Implications of Corporate Capital Structure for Banking Institutions," **Journal of Money, Credit and Banking** 15, 212–221.

Otsberg, W. & Thomson, J. (1996) "Optimal Financial Structure and Bank Capital Requirements: An Empirical Investigation," **Journal of Money, Credit and Banking** 29, 73–93.

Pringle, J. (1973) "A Theory of the Banking Firm," **Journal of Money, Credit and Banking** 5.

Pujal. A. (2001) "Un Nouveau Ratio de Solvabilité en 2004," **Banquemagazine** 622, 36–39.

Şakar, B. (2006) "A Study on Efficiency and Productivity of Turkish Banks in Istanbul Stock Exchange using Malmquist DEA," **Journal of American Academy of Business** 8 (2) 145–155.

Saunders, A. (1994) **Financial Institutions Management: A Modern Perspective**. Ill.: Irwin & Inc.

Saunders, A.& Cornett, M. (2003) **Financial Institutions Management: A Risk Management Approach**. 4th ed.; McGraw-Hill.

Schaeck, C. & Cihák, M. (2013) "Competition, Efficiency, and Stability in Banking", **Financial Management** (forthcoming).

Schaeck, K., Cihák, M. & Wolfe, S. (2007) "Are Competitive Banking Systems More Stable?," **Journal of Money, Credit and Banking** 41(4) 711–734.

Schinasi, G. (2006) **Safeguarding Financial Stability: Theory and Practice**. Washington, D. C.: International Monetary Fund.

Schinasi, G. (2004) "Defining Financial Stability," IMF Working Paper, **International Capital Markets Department, International Monetary Fund**, WP/04/187.

Sealy, C. (1985) "Portfolio Separation for Stockholders Owned Depository Financial Intermediaries," **Journal of Banking and Finance** 9 (4) 477–490.

Shafiee, M., Sangi, M., & Ghaderi, M. (2013) "Bank Performance Evaluation using Dynamic DEA: A Slacks-Based Measure Approach," **Journal of Data Envelopment Analysis and Decision Science**, 1–12.

Sherman, H., Gold, F. (1985) "Bank Branch Operating Efficiency: Evaluation with Data Envelopment Analysis," **Journal of Banking and Finance** 9, 297–316.

Sinkey, J. (2002) **Commercial Bank Financial Management**. 6th ed., N.Y.: Prentic Hall.

Soteriou, A. & Zenios, S. (1997) "Efficiency, Profitability and Quality of Banking Services," **Working Papers # 97–28**, Center for Financial Institutions, Wharton School, University of Pennsylvania.

Spina, J. (2013) "Banking Regulation and Basel III," Available at SSRN: http://ssrn.com/abstract=2248075.

Swamy, V. (2011) "Banking System Resilience and Financial Stability: An Evidence from Indian Banking," Available at: http://ssrn.com/abstract=2060744.

Thayaparan, A., & Pratheepan, T. (2014) "Evaluating Total Factor Productivity Growth of Commercial Banks in Sri Lanka: An Application of Malmquist Index," **Journal of Management Research** 6 (3) 58–68.

Uhde, A. & Heimeshoff, U. (2009) "Consolidation in Banking and Financial Stability in Europe: Empirical Evidence," **Journal of Banking & Finance** 33(7) 1299–1311.

Vittas, D. (1992) **Financial Regulation: Changing the Rules of the Game**. 1st. ed.; Washington: The World Bank.

Wagner, W. (2004) "The Liquidity of Bank Assets and Banking Stability," Available at http://ssrn.com/abstract=556128.

Wen, S. & Yu, J. (2013) "Banking Stability, Market Structure and Financial System in Emerging Countries," **Journal of Applied Finance & Banking** 3(3) 1–13.

Wu, D., Yang, Z. & Liang, L. (2006) "Using DEA-Neural Network Approach to Evaluate Branch Efficiency of a Large Canadian Bank," **Expert Systems with Applications** 31(1) 108–115.

Yue, P. (1992) "Data Envelopment Analysis and Commercial Bank Performance: A Primer with Applications to Missouri Banks," **Federal Reserve Bank of St. Louis Review** 74.

Does Research and Development Expenditure Impact High-Technology Export in Turkey: Evidence from ARDL Model

Elma Satrovic[1]([✉]) and Adnan Muslija[2]

[1] Çağ University, Tarsus, Turkey
elmasatrovic@cag.edu.tr
[2] University of Sarajevo, Visoko, Bosnia and Herzegovina
adnanmuslija@msn.com

1 Introduction

The relationship between research and development expenditure and high-technology export in Turkey has not been explored quite extensively in previous studies. Therefore, there is a need to present official statistics on these economic terms of interest in order to show great potential in terms of both, research and development expenditure and high-technology export.

In terms of research and development expenditure, special attention is given to the last observed years. Therefore, Turkish Statistical Institute indicates that research and development expenditure in Turkey went up by 18.8% in 2014 to reach TRY 17.6 billion (USD 6.1 billion) compared to 2013. Moreover, spending has surpassed 1% of the country's total GDP, with private-sector outlay accounting for almost half, at 49.8%. In terms of 2013, it is important to emphasize that the country has spent 0.95% of GDP on R&D efforts. R&D expenditure in Turkey is expected to account for 3% of the country's GDP by 2023. Since this paper analyses the relationship between research and development expenditure and high-technology export, it is important to emphasize that Turkey provides special investment incentives in the form of tax exemptions and cuts, as well as financial support, to improve vital industries' technological competitiveness and innovation capacity.

The Graph 1 summarizes official statistics on research and development expenditure in Turkey over the period 1995–2014. Until the year 2004, there was a slight increase in research and development expenditure. However, it is important to emphasize that after the year 2004, research and development expenditure has increased exponentially. Overall trend indicates the increase in research and development (R&D) expenditure in Turkey over the observed period.

On the other hand, high-technology export reports dynamic trends. Exponential increase is reported in the years until 2000. After that, there is a drop in the variable of interest until the year 2003. From the year 2003 on, there is an increase in high-technology export with drops that are not that serious like in the period 2000–2003. This can be summarized by Graph 2.

N. Ozatac and K. K. Gökmenoglu (eds.), *Emerging Trends in Banking and Finance*, Springer Proceedings in Business and Economics,
https://doi.org/10.1007/978-3-030-01784-2_4

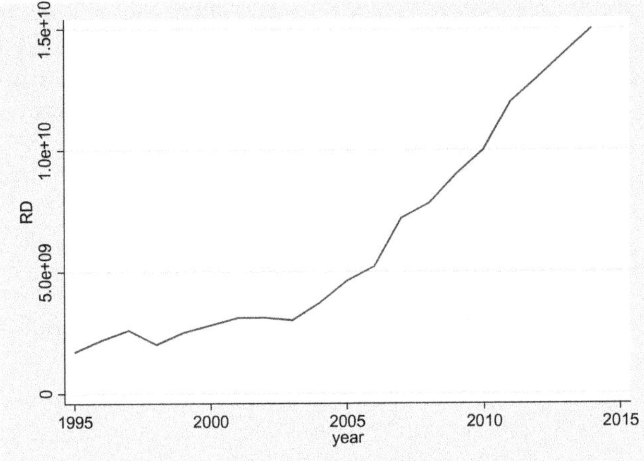

Source: Authors

Graph 1. Research and development (R&D) expenditure statistics in Turkey. *Source* Authors

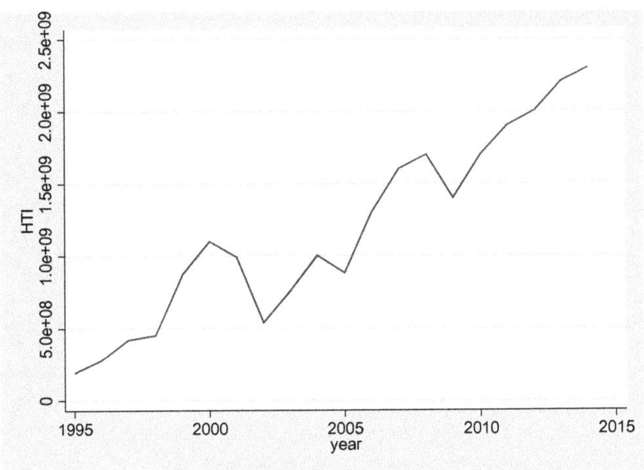

Source: Authors

Graph 2. High-tech export in Turkey. *Source* Authors

Frolov and Lebedev (2007) indicate that high-technology industry consists of: arms and ammunition production; production of engines and turbine other than aircraft; automobile and motorcycle engines; production of centrifuges, calendars, and vending machines, manufacturing of nuclear reactors and its components, manufacturing of helipad, aircraft, and other flying machines; manufacturing of spacecraft including boosters and manufacturing of automobile. Therefore, an improvement in research and development can significantly contribute to high-technology export taking into account that aforementioned industries heavily rely on research and development.

The paper proceeds as follows. Section 2 summarizes previous empirical studies on the relationship between the research and development expenditure and high-technology export. Data, variables and methodology are described in detail in Sect. 3. Empirical results are reported and interpreted in Sect. 4. Main conclusions are summarized at the end of this paper.

2 Literature Review

Previous studies indicate that one of the most effective ways for the countries to overcome recession is to increase export. In terms of export special attention is given to the high-technology export since it is considered to be the most dynamic (Sandu and Ciocanel 2014). Taking this into account, the determinants of high-technology export have been explored quite extensively in recent studies. The determinants are explored quite extensively since policy makers are looking for the most effective way to stimulate high-technology export.

Sandu and Ciocanel (2014) have also indicated that research and development intensity can influence high-technology export taking into account its positive impact on firm's capacities to produce high-technology products. It is also expected to improve national intellectual capital as well as the number of patent applications. In addition, research and development as well as innovation are strongly connected to the firm's capabilities to assimilate high-technology knowledge in order to increase the competitiveness of high-technology products. Taking this into account, this part of the paper summarizes the results of previous studies that analyze the relationship between the research and development expenditure and high-technology export.

Research and development (R&D) investment is considered to play a crucial role in developing high-tech industries in Han et al. (2017). The authors have investigated the impact of investments in domestic high-tech industries on relative R&D efficiency across China's high-tech sectors. For this purpose authors have used Data Envelopment Analysis (DEA). The obtained results indicate that there is no increase in overall R&D over the period 1998–2009 despite to the fact that the R&D expenditure has increased by 2188%. This research suggests that high-technology industry in China suffers from the inefficiency in technology commercialization process.

Girma et al. (2008) have investigated the relationship between research and development and export activity concerning the possibility of the reverse causality. Therefore, the research question states whether R&D stimulates export or occurs as the result of the increased export in the country. The obtained results indicate that previous exporting experience improves the innovative capability of Irish firms. However, a significant relationship is not reported in terms of British firms.

The relationship between high technology exports and GDP per capita levels is analyzed in Usatbas and Ersin (2016). The authors have used the case of Turkey and South Korea. They have observed the period ranging from 1989 to 2014. For the purpose of the research the authors have used ADF, PP unit root and KPSS stationarity tests as well as Zivot-Andrews single break and Lee-Strazicich two break unit root tests. Lastly, authors have tested for cointegration using Engle-Granger and Johansen tests by incorporating the break dates as exogenous dummy variables. The obtained results indicate differences between South Korea and Turkey. The results suggest that, in the future, Turkey should increase the investments in human capital and R&D directed to high tech exports in order to accelerate the economic growth.

Gani (2009) has observed countries with higher levels of technological achievement to explore the relationship between economic growth and high-technology export. The observed countries have been classified into three groups based on technological achievement index as: technological leaders, potential leaders and dynamic adopters. The obtained results indicate a significant positive impact of high-technology exports on growth of the technological leader countries. The impact for the other countries is not reported to be significant. The authors indicate that the main policy implication is that low-income countries with lower levels of technological achievement and growth may need to focus on new product development with high technological content so as to be competitive in the global trading environment as well as to enhance their growth and development.

Lo Turco and Maggion (2015) have been exploring whether or not innovation promotes the export probability of the firms. They have been reported that the joint adoption of both innovation strategies fosters Turkish firms' first time export entry in rich destination markets. Nevertheless, innovation improves firms' export probability. The authors have also indicated that product innovation matters in particular for exporting to developing economies, while process innovation reinforces the role of product innovation for exporting to richer markets.

Based on the results obtained in up-to-date studies, the positive relationship between the research and development expenditure and high-technology export is expected. Therefore, it is expected that high level of the research and development contributes to high-technology export in the case of Turkey.

3 Data and Methodology

3.1 Data

The data, used to estimate the causal relationship between the research and development expenditure and high-technology export in Turkey are collected over the period 1995–2014. Economic freedom is used as a control variable. The data on high-technology export are collected from the World Bank database while the data on the research and development expenditure are collected from OECD. The Heritage Foundation database is used as a source of the data on economic freedom.

The first challenging task for authors was to find the adequate proxy variable of the research and development. For the purpose of this analysis, research and development expenditure (*RD*) is taken as a proxy variable of research and development. OECD indicates that this variable includes gross domestic R&D expenditure by sector of performance (business enterprise, government, higher education, private non-profit, and total intramural) and by source of funds (business enterprise, government—

including public general university funds—higher education, private non-profit and funds from abroad—including funds from enterprises and other funds from abroad).

On the other hand, there is a need to find appropriate proxy variable of high-technology export.

Usman (2017) and Yoo (2008) indicate that appropriate proxy variable of high-technology exports is high-technology exports (current US\$—*HTE*). The World Bank defines high-technology exports as products with high R&D intensity, such as in aerospace, computers, pharmaceuticals, scientific instruments, and electrical machinery. This variable is considered appropriate in this study as well.

In terms of control variable, it is important to emphasize that Heckelman (2000), Dawson (2003) and Ozcan et al. (2017) indicate that the Index of Economic Freedom (*EFI*), is appropriate proxy variable of economic freedom. Therefore, this variable is accepted in this paper as well. The Heritage Foundation indicates that the economic freedom is "the fundamental right of every human to control his or her own labor and property". In economic societies where people enjoy economic freedom, they have an opportunity to freely work, produce, consume and make investments. The Heritage Foundation also indicates that economic freedom is expected to bring greater prosperity and its ideals are strongly associated with healthier societies, cleaner environments, greater per capita wealth, human development, democracy and poverty elimination.

Economic freedom measure is based on 12 qualitative and quantitative factors that are grouped into four pillars of economic freedom namely: 1. rule of law that includes: property rights, government integrity and judicial effectiveness, 2. government size that includes: governments spending, tax burden and fiscal health, 3. regulatory efficiency that includes: business freedom, labor freedom and monetary freedom as well as 4. open markets that include: trade freedom, investment freedom and financial freedom. Score ranges between 0 and 100. Higher-score is associated with better economic freedom.

3.2   Methodology

Methodology used in this paper can be summarized as follows. The analysis starts by calculating the most important measures of descriptive statistics. Moreover, the stationarity of variables will be explored using the appropriate tests. In addition, Johansen cointegration test will be used to examine the cointegrating relationship between the research and development expenditure and high-technology export. Granger causality test will be used to examine the causal relationship between economic terms of interest (Satrovic and Muslija 2017). Lastly, ARDL panel data approach will be applied to deal with possible estimation issues running from reverse causality. Engle and Granger (1987) two-step approach for testing the existence of a long-run relationship can be summarized as follows under the assumption $(y_t, x_t)'$ is a vector of $I(1)$ variables (Satrovic 2017): 1. Run an OLS regression for the model in levels and test whether the residuals are stationary and 2. Estimate an EC (error correct) model with the lagged residuals from the first step included as EC term (provided they are stationary).

4 Empirical Results

The empirical results section starts by presenting descriptive statistics. The highest value of HTE is reported for the year 2014 while the lowest is reported for the year 1995. When it comes to RD, the highest value is reported for the year 2014 while the lowest is reported for the year 1995. In terms of EFI, the highest value of 65 is obtained in the year 2014 while the lowest value of 51 is obtained in the year 2005. Since standard deviations imply high volatility for the observed period and in order to ease interpretation, natural logarithm of the selected variables is calculated. Therefore, the obtained coefficients will be interpreted as elasticities. Table 1 summarizes the obtained results.

Table 1. Descriptive statistics

Stats	THE	RD	EFI
Mean	1180000000	6230000000	59
SD	649000000	4440000000	4
Max	2300000000	15000000000	65
Min	190000000	1700000000	51
Skewness	0.167	0.763	−0.589
Kurtosis	1.873	2.118	2.288
Meas. unit.	USD	USD	%

Source Authors

Furthermore, information criterion procedures (Schwarz's Bayesian information criterion (SBIC), the Akaike's information criterion (AIC), and the Hannan and Quinn information criterion (HQIC)) are used to determine the number of lags needed. Table 2 summarizes the obtained results. The obtained results of all of the three criteria agree that the appropriate number of lags to be used in this research is 3 (Satrovic 2017).

Table 2. The number of lags needed

Lag	LL	LR	Df	P	FPE	AIC	HQIC	SBIC
0	−659.132				6.60E + 35	88.151	88.15	88.2454
1	−626.495	65.275	4	0	1.50E + 34	84.3326	84.3296	84.6158
2	−621.509	9.9717	4	0.041	1.30E + 34	84.2012	84.1962	84.6732
3	−615.145	12.728*	4	0.013	1.1e + 34*	83.886*	83.8789*	84.5468*
4	−611.52	7.2486	4	0.123	1.40E + 34	83.9361	83.927	84.7857
5	−607.292	8.4569	4	0.076	2.10E + 34	83.9056	83.8945	84.9441

Source Authors

* indicates lag order that is selected by the information criterion

In addition, Augmented Dickey-Fuller (ADF) test is used to investigate the presence of unit root for variables in natural logarithm form (Satrovic and Muslija 2017). Table 3 summarizes the obtained results. The presence of unit root is also tested at the first differences and second differences in the case of RD. The results of the test indicate that the time series of HTE isstationary at the first differences (for 5% level of significance) while RD is stationary at the second differences (for 5% level of significance).

Table 3. Augmented Dickey-Fuller (ADF) test

Variable		Test statistics	1% critical value	5% critical value	10% critical value
lnHTE	Z(t)	−1.765	−3.750	−3.000	−2.630
	MacKinnon approximate p-value Z(t) = 0.3980				
D.lnHTE	Z(t)	−2.931	−3.750	−3.000	−2.630
	MacKinnon approximate p-value Z(t) = 0.0418				
lnRD	Z(t)	−0.368	−3.750	−3.000	−2.630
	MacKinnon approximate p-value Z(t) = 0.9153				
D.lnRD	Z(t)	−1.664	−3.750	−3.000	−2.630
	MacKinnon approximate p-value Z(t) = 0.4499				
D2.lnRD	Z(t)	−3.127	−3.750	−3.000	−2.630
	MacKinnon approximate p-value Z(t) = 0.0246				

Source Authors

Table 4. Johansen tests for cointegration

Maximum rank	Parms	LL	Eigenvalue	Trace statistic	5% critical value
0	10	14.74602		28.847	15.41
1	13	25.94954	0.77548	6.44	3.76
2	14	29.16952	0.34906		
Maximum rank	Parms	LL	Eigenvalue	Max statistic	5% critical value
0	10	14.74602		22.407	14.07
1	13	25.94954	0.77548	6.44	3.76
2	14	29.16952	0.34906		

Source Authors

Moreover, econometric methodology in this paper proceeds to the application of Johansen test for cointegration (Satrovic and Muslija 2017). Table 4 summarizes the obtained results. The empirical results confirm that the values of the trace tests and those of the maximum eigenvalue tests are greater than the critical values. This confirms that the null hypothesis on no co-integration (r = 0) is rejected by both the maximum eigenvalue and trace statistics. This indicates the existence of a long-run equilibrium relationship between economic terms of interest.

Since the Johansen cointegration test does not provide information regarding the direction of causality; the Granger causality test based on the VAR model is applied. Table 5 indicates the bidirectional relationship between the economic terms of interest indicting that the research and development expenditure has a positive impact on high-technology export but also can arise as a result of achievement in high-technology export in the observed country.

Table 5. Granger causality Wald tests

Equation	Excluded	Prob > chi2
D.lnHTE	D2.lnRD	0.031
D.lnHTE	ALL	0.031
D2.lnRD	D.lnHTE	0.000
D2.lnRD	ALL	0.000

Source Authors

Table 6. ARDL/EC model

	D.lnHTE		Coef.	St. error	t	P > t	95% conf. interval	
Initial model	ADJ							
		lnHTE L1.	−0.993	0.224	−4.440	0.001	−1.476	−0.509
	LR							
		lnRD L1.	0.605	0.074	8.230	0.000	0.447	0.764
	SR							
		lnRD D1.	1.421	0.409	3.480	0.004	0.538	2.304
		_cons	7.184	1.984	3.620	0.003	2.898	11.470
Extended model	ADJ							
		lnHTE L1.	−0.941	0.169	−5.570	0.000	−1.318	−0.565
	LR							
		lnRD L1.	0.472	0.075	6.270	0.000	0.305	0.640
		lnEF L1.	0.027	0.012	2.310	0.044	0.001	0.053
	SR							
		lnRD L1.	1.551	0.328	4.730	0.001	0.820	2.282
		lnEF D1.	0.049	0.013	3.790	0.004	0.020	0.079
		_cons	8.074	1.483	5.440	0.000	4.770	11.379

Source Authors

Lastly, ARDL approach is applied to investigate the relationship between the research and development expenditure and high-technology exports in Turkey (Satrovic 2017). Reported results (Table 6) indicate a significant positive coefficient (for a 5% level of significance) with RD in both short- and long-run. Therefore, the research and development expenditure is reported to have a significant positive impact on high-technology export in Turkey indicating that an increase in RD contributes to key dimensions of high-technology exports. HTE is therefore reported to be elastic to the change in RD in both short- and long-run. The results also indicate that HTE is more responsive to the change in RD in the short- compared to the long-run. The extended model controls for the impact of economic freedom. The results of the extended model indicate a significant positive impact of economic freedom on high-technology export in the short- as well as long-run (for a 5% level of significance). However, it is important to notice that RD has stronger impact on high-technology export comparing to economic freedom. Coefficients with RD in the initial and extended model do not significantly differ.

5   Conclusion

This paper has analyzed the relationship between the research and development expenditure and high-technology export in the case of Turkey since this country has experienced exponential increase in both of the observed variables. Moreover, empirical evidence on the matter lacks. Therefore, this was the motivation to conduct this research in order to fill into the gap in literature. Due to the data availability, this research analyzes twenty years period ranging from 1995 to 2014.

Johansen test indicates that the null hypothesis on no co-integration ($r = 0$) is rejected. This indicates the existence of a long-run relationship between research and development expenditure and high-technology export over the observed period. Granger causality test indicates a bidirectional relationship between variables of interest indicting that research and development expenditure has an impact on high-technology export but also can be the result of the increased high-technology export.

Furthermore, ARDL approach is applied to investigate the relationship between the research and development expenditure and high-technology exports in Turkey. Reported results indicate a significant positive coefficient (for a 5% level of significance) with RD in both short- and long-run. Therefore, the research and development expenditure is reported to have a significant positive impact on high-technology export in Turkey indicating that an increase in RD contributes to key dimensions of high-technology exports. HTE is therefore reported to be elastic to the change in RD in both short- and long-run. The results also indicate that HTE is more responsive to the change in RD in the short- compared to the long-run. The extended model controls for the impact of economic freedom. The results of the extended model indicate a significant positive impact of economic freedom on high-technology export in the short- as well as long-run (for a 5% level of significance). However, it is important to notice that RD has stronger impact on high-technology export comparing to economic freedom. Coefficients with RD in the initial and extended model do not significantly differ.

A results indicating positive relationship between research and development and high-technology export can be of great importance for key decision makers in Turkey. The results suggest that Turkey should make an effort to improve the research and development expenditure since it has a great opportunity to contribute to key dimensions of high-technology exportand consequently to economic growth.

References

Dawson, J.W. (2003). Causality in the Freedom-Growth Relationship. *European Journal of Political Economy*, Vol. 19, pp. 479–495.

Engle, R. F. and Granger, C. W. J. (1987). Co-Integration and Error Correction: Representation, Estimation, and Testing. *Econometrica*, Vol. 55(2), pp. 251–276.

Frolov, I., and Lebedev, K. (2007). Assessing the Impact of High-Technology Exports on the Growth Rate and Structure of the Russian Economy. *Studies on Russian Economic Development*, Vol. 18(5), pp. 490–500.

Gani, A. (2009). Technological Achievement, High Technology Exports and Growth, *Journal of Comparative International Management* Vol. 12, No. 2, pp. 31–47.

Girma, S., Görg, H. and Hanley, A. (2008). R&D and Exporting: A Comparison of British and Irish Firms, Kiel Institute.

Han, C., Rhys, S., Yang, M., Ieromonachou, P. and Zhang, H. (2017). Evaluating R&D Investment Efficiency in China's High-Tech Industry. *Journal of High Technology Management Research*, Vol. 28, pp. 93–109.

Heckelman, J.C. (2000). Economic Freedom and Economic Growth: A Short-Run Causal Investigation, *Journal of Applied Economics*, pp. 71–91.

Lo Turco, A. and Maggioni, D. (2015). Dissecting the Impact of Innovation on Exporting in Turkey, *Economics of Innovation and New Technology*, Vol. 24, No. 4, pp. 309–338.

Ozcan, C.C., Aslan, M. and Nazlioglu, S. (2017). Economic Freedom, Economic Growth and International Tourism for Post-Communist (Transition) Countries: A Panel Causality Analysis. *Theoretical and Applied Economics*, Vol. XXIV, pp. 75–98.

Sandu, S., and Ciocanel, B. (2014). Impact of R&D and Innovation on High-Tech Export. *Procedia Economics and Finance*, Vol. 15, pp. 80–90.

Satrovic, E. (2017). Financial Development and Human Capital in Turkey: ARDL Approach, Cappadocia Academic Review, Vol. 1(2), pp. 1–15.

Satrovic, E. and Muslija, A. (2017). Foreign Direct Investments and Tourism: Empirical Evidence from Turkey, ICPESS Proceedings, ISBN: 978-605-68010-0-6, Vol. 2, pp. 88–100.

Usman, M. (2017). Impact of High-Tech Exports on Economic Growth: Empirical Evidence From Pakistan, *Journal on Innovation and Sustainability*, Vol. 8(1), pp. 91–105.

Ustabas, A. and Ersin, O.O. (2016). The Effects of R&D and High Technology Exports on Economic Growth: A Comparative Cointegration Analysis for Turkey and South Korea. International conference on Eurasian economies.

Yoo, S.H. (2008). High-Technology Exports and Economic Output: An Empirical Investigation, *Applied Economics Letters*, Vol. 15, pp. 523–525.

The Cyclicality of Allowance for Impairment Losses in Indonesia

Ndari Surjaningsih, Januar Hafidz[(✉)], Justina Adamanti,
Maulana Harris Muhajir, and Dhian Pradhita Sari

Bank of Indonesia, Jakarta, Indonesia
{ndari,januar,justina,maulana_hm}@bi.go.id,
dhianpradhita@yahoo.com

1 Introduction

Establishment of provision by banks aims at absorbing losses from intermediation activities, whereby losses occur in periods of economic slowdown. The loan loss provisions behaviour of banks tend to be procyclical, banks practices in increasing loan loss provisioning during the downturn economic phase while decreasing it during the upturn period. Many previous studies, among those, are done by Angklomkliew et al. (2009), Laeven and Majnoni (2003), Davis and Zhu (2005), and Bikker and Metzemakers (2005) show that banks tend to increase the loan loss provisioning during the economic downturn as their credit quality is worsening. On the other hand, there is research conducted by Packer and Zhu (2010) using a sample of 240 banks from 12 countries in Asia that shows countercyclical behaviour of loan loss provisioning. The procyclicality of loan loss provisions behaviour also occurs in Indonesian banks based on evidenced through research conducted by Wimboh et al. (2010) using Indonesian individual banking data in 1995–2009 and Agusman et al. (2012) using aggregate data of Indonesian banking in 2000–2011.

At this time, provisions establishment in banking refer to accounting standards, i.e. incurred loss model. The primary reference of incurred losses method is IAS 39 (International Accounting Standard) issued by IASB (International Accounting Standard Board), and GAAP (Generally Accepted Accounting Principles) issued by FASB (US Financial Accounting Standards Board). Critics come to IAS 39 for allowing recognition of impairment losses "too little and too late". Also, Cohen and Edward Jr. (2017) in his research mentioned results of several previous studies that found the formation of provisions based on concept incurred loss (which is backwards-looking) can contribute procyclicality of credit distribution, whereas otherwise if it is forward-looking (expected losses).

Responding to various opinions about lack of provisions formed based on incurred losses model, in July 2014, IASB issued the International Financial Reporting Standard 9 (IFRS 9). This arrangement will become effective on January 1, 2018, while FASB has issued US CECL (Current Expected Credit Loss) in 2016 and will begin to be adopted by 2019. Following this, the Financial Accounting Standards Board of the Indonesian Institute of Accountants (DSAK IAI) will adopt accounting standards consistent with IFRS 9. DSAK IAI on September 14, 2016, has issued exposure draft

N. Ozatac and K. K. Gökmenoglu (eds.), *Emerging Trends in Banking and Finance*, Springer Proceedings in Business and Economics,
https://doi.org/10.1007/978-3-030-01784-2_5

PSAK 71 (Statement of Financial Accounting Standards) on Financial Instruments which has accommodated method of expected losses. This PSAK planned to impose on January 1, 2020.

The objectives of this study are to examine how loan loss provisioning of Indonesian banks responds to their earning, credit growth, and to the changes in the business cycle (reflected by GDP growth) using panel data of 102 banks in Indonesia during the period of 2011q1–2017q1. Given research conducted by Wimboh et al. (2010) and Agusman et al. (2012) has not used data that adopt a change of provision forming method that is from PPAP to CKPN (incurred loss), it is necessary to review the behaviour using the latest data that has adopted the concept of CKPN.

2 Literatures Review

2.1 Procyclicality of Loan Loss Provisioning

In general, banks follow a procyclical pattern (or procyclicality) by increasing their loan loss provisioning during the downturn economic phase while decreasing it during the upturn. In line with that, previous studies were done by Laeven and Majnoni (2003), and Bikker and Hu (2002) state that in general the formation of provisions will be negatively correlated with economic growth and capital will correlate positively with economic growth which then leads to procyclicality. Laeven and Majnoni (2003) suggested that from a regulatory perspective, a bank's loan loss provision behaviour could be considered imprudent or procyclical. The behaviour should meet these following criteria: (i) The ratio of EBP/TA is proved to correlate negatively to the ratio of LLP/TA; (ii) Credit growth is proved to correlate negatively to the ratio of LLP/TA; and (iii) GDP growth is proved to correlate negatively to the ratio of LLP/TA. Condition (i) refers to the income smoothing hypothesis, while conditions (ii) and (iii) capture misalignments of loan loss provision with bank-specific and macroeconomic cyclical indicators.

Banks have started facing increased credit risk when the economy is in boom phase along with laxity of credit risk assessment and intense competition between banks (Borio et al. 2001; Lowe 2002). This situation potentially worsens economic condition when a recession occurs (burst period). Anticipating the situation, countercyclical provisioning will be implemented by banks with increasing provisioning in booming economic conditions and use that provision in times of worsening economic (contraction). In other words, countercyclical view holds that level of provisioning should be made positively correlated with the business cycle, and banks must identify the cyclical pattern of credit risk and allowance for losses at the right time.

Banks in Asia during the period 1996–2003 did provisioning practices that enlarged procyclicality over other regions (Craig et al. 2006). Meanwhile, Packer and Zhu (2010) studies with a sample of 240 banks in 12 countries in Asian economies during the period 2000–2009 showed the dominance of countercyclical behaviour in loan loss provisions.

Using Indonesian individual banking data during period 1995–2009, Wimboh et al. (2010) found a robust cyclical effect of the business cycle on Indonesian banks' loan loss provision behaviour. The cyclical evidenced by a negative relationship between GDP growth and loan loss provision ratio and relatively high elasticity between them which mean banks' loan loss provisions behaviour is procyclical or Indonesian banks tend to be risk sensitive. Agusman et al. (2012) conducted a similar study using aggregate Indonesian banking data over period 2000–2011 which found that Indonesian banks' loan loss provision was still procyclical.

2.2 Accounting Standards that Support Expected Credit Loss Provisioning

There are some differences between provisioning calculations based on accounting standards and regulators (Basel regime). Since the first Basel Capital Accord in 1988, the two regimes have remained different and continue to exert almost equal weights in shaping banks' loan loss provisioning practices (Gaston and Song 2014). IAS 39 recognises impairment losses based on an incurred loss based model, which only permits recognition of credit losses supported by "objective evidence". This approach has viewed as recognising impairment losses "too little and too late".

Furthermore, Gaston and Song (2014) describe the different purposes of accounting and prudential provisioning. The objective of recognition of accounting impairment loss is to ensure that balance sheet and income statement are stated reasonably in the period of accounting. While the objective of prudential provisioning requirements in Basel is to harmonise the risk-taking of banks with adequate capital and to ensure safety and sound of the banks. As a consequence of this difference, the establishment of provisions under IAS 39 is lower than that required from the perspective of credit risk analysis and capital adequacy. To overcome the gap, bank supervisor requires banks to meet its capital adequacy and also establish adequate provision.

To address lack of incurred loss model, currently, new accounting standards have been issued which establishment of provisions based on expected credit losses. IASB has issued IFRS 9—Financial Instruments: Recognition and Measurement on 24 July 2014 as a substitute for IAS 39. Likewise with United States accounting standards institute (FASB) which has issued Accounting Standards Update (ASU) No. 2016-13, Topic 326, Financial Instruments—Credit Losses, popularly referred as Current Expected Credit Losses (CECL), on June 16, 2016, as a substitute for GAAP.

The IASB is scheduling implementation of new accounting standards on January 1, 2018, and allows for early adoption. While the FASB schedules for CECL implementation for early adoption on January 1, 2019, with implementation details no later than January 1, 2020, for the PBE (Public Business Entities) which is the SEC filers (Securities and Exchange Commission) and January 1, 2021, for non-SEC filers. Although not yet entirely in line with Basel, at least the latest accounting standards will adopt expected credit loss method.

Cohen and Edward (2017) describe the similarity features owned by IFRS 9 and CECL that both are designed to provide financial statement users with more useful information about a company's ECL on financial instruments that are not accounting on fair value through profit or loss (e.g. trading portfolios). The impairment approach requires banks and other companies to recognise ECL and to update the amount of ECL recognised at each reporting date to reflect changes in the credit risk of financial assets. Both approaches are forward-looking and eliminate the threshold for the recognition of ECL so that it is no longer necessary for a "trigger event" to have occurred before reporting credit losses. Moreover, both standards require companies to base their measurements of ECL on reasonable and supportable information that includes historical, current and—for the first time—forecast information.

Table 1. The measurement of *Expected Credit Loss* (ECL)

	Performing assets	Underperforming assets[a]	Impaired assets
IASB	Stage 1 12-months ECL	Stage 2 Lifetime ECL	Stage 3 Lifetime ECL
FASB	Lifetime ECL		

[a]Underperforming assets = assets with a significant increase in credit risk

The allowances for credit losses by IASB are based on three stages, with 12 months expected credit losses recognised for stage 1 and lifetime losses for stages 2 and 3 (Stages are described in Table 1.). Because the US CECL model would require lifetime ECL recognition for financial assets at all times, it will result in more significant provisioning for financial assets which are considered Stage 1 under IFRS 9. Whereas for FASB proposed a single measurement principle that results in recognition of lifetime expected credit losses on a financial asset or group of financial assets, which is a current estimate of all contractual cash flows not expected to collect on the assets or group of assets.

Financial Accounting Standards Board of the Indonesian Institute of Accountants (DSAK IAI) has also begun to adopt accounting standards consistent with IFRS 9. DSAK IAI on September 14, 2016, has issued exposure draft PSAK 71 (Statement of Financial Accounting Standards) on Financial Instruments which has accommodated expected losses method. This PSAK planned to implement on January 1, 2020.

2.3   Loan Loss Provisioning in Indonesia

The establishment of provision regulation in Indonesia is Bank Indonesia Regulation (PBI) No. 14/15/ PBI/2012 dated October 24, 2012, concerning Assessment of Commercial Bank Asset Quality for Commercial Banks, and Financial Service Authority Regulation (POJK) No. 16/ POJK.03/2014 regarding Assessment of Bank Asset Quality for Sharia Commercial Banks and Sharia Business Units. Both of rules based on PSAK 55 Financial Instruments: Recognition and Measurement.

Indonesian banks are required to form an allowance for impairment losses (from now on shall be referred to as CKPN). CKPN is formed when there is objective evidence that the debtor is impaired. A financial asset or group of assets is impaired, and impairment losses are recognised, only if there is objective evidence as a result of one or more events that occurred after the initial recognition of the asset. An entity is required to assess at each balance sheet date whether there is any objective evidence of impairment. If any such evidence exists, the entity is required to do a detailed impairment calculation to determine whether an impairment loss should be recognised. Thus, the establishment of CKPN is based on the evaluation of each bank against its borrower so that each bank can have different policies in forming provisioning reserves for its disbursed credit.

Before adopting provisioning system based on impairment, loan loss provision is known as an allowance for earning asset losses (PPAP), which refers to the credit quality of banks. The regulator requires banks to form loan loss provision in a specified percentage by loan quality, which consists of 5 categories: (i) current, (ii) special mention, (iii) substandard, (iv) doubtful, and (v) loss. The rate of a provision that the bank must establish as follows (Table 2):

Table 2. The rate of provisions

Credit quality	Provisions	
	General reserve	Specific reserve[a]
Current	1%	
Special mention		5%
Sub standard		15%
Doubtful		50%
Loss		100%

[a]For assets with special mention, substandard, doubtful, and loss quality after being deducted with the value of the collaterals

Based on current regulations, banks are required to calculate the allowance for asset losses (PPA) which has the same concept as PPAP. The rules used to calculate PPA are same as the previous PPAP calculation rules. Furthermore, the difference between the calculation of PPA and CKPN can affect the calculation of the minimum capital adequacy requirement (KPMM). If the result of the provision for asset losses calculation on earning assets is larger than the CKPN established, banks are obliged to calculate the difference between provision for asset losses calculation and CKPN as a reduction in capital in the calculation of KPMM ratio. Whereas if the result of the provision for asset losses calculation on earning assets is the same or smaller than the CKPN established, banks do not need to make provision for asset losses into consideration in the calculation of KPMM ratio.

There are two methods to calculate the amount of CKPN that imposed in Indonesia based on Indonesian Banking Accounting Guidelines (*PAPI*) revised 2008, namely: (i) individual, and (ii) collective. The fundamental difference between two methods is that individual bank method can predict the condition of the debtor in future so that it can determine the amount of CKPN to be formed if necessary, on the contrary, collective method of the bank cannot do so. Debtors who use individual methods such as companies, meanwhile collective methods used by credit card debtors.

3 Data and Methodology

3.1 Methodology

Previous studies about procyclicality of banks loan loss provisioning in Indonesia are done by Wimboh et al. (2010) and Agusman et al. (2012). However, this research tried to fulfil the gap from the previous research regarding the more updated period of research and performed on individual data of commercial banks in Indonesia. Also, the data of loan loss provisioning has been changed as an allowance to impairment loss (CKPN) that has been imposed as per October 2012. As two previous studies, regression analysis in this study refers to Laeven and Majnoni (2003), but in previous two studies only used one model that is a static model. This research uses two estimators, namely: (i) static model with random bank-specific effect (based on Hausman Test); and (ii) dynamic model refers to Arellano and Bond (1991) using the GMM difference estimator for panel data by entering two lags of the dependent variable as a regressor. Also, this research includes interaction term (dummy slope).

The basic regression model for the first estimator is

$$\left(\frac{LLP}{TA}\right)_{it} = \alpha + \beta 1 \left(\frac{EBP}{TA}\right)_{it} + \beta 2 gCredit_{it} + \beta 3 gGDP_t + v_i + \varepsilon_{it} \tag{1}$$

where (LLP/TA) is loan loss provisions over total bank assets for bank i at time t. Moreover, *(EBP/TA)* is the profit before tax and loan loss provisions over total assets for bank i at time t. (*gCredit*) is credit growth for bank i at time t, and (*gGDP*) is the real growth of GDP at time t. Using EBP to test income smoothing behaviour, credit growth and GDP growth are used to test the behaviour of procyclicality, and also enter interaction term (dummy slope) between negative earning dummy multiplied by *EBP/TA*. Model 1 can be described in two equation in Table 3.

Table 3. Equation with GLS method

	Equation	
	1.1	1.2
Explanatory variables		
EBP$_{it}$/TA$_{i,t-1}$	✓	✓
Credit Growth	✓	✓
GDP *Growth*	✓	✓
*Negative Earning Dummy** EBP$_{it}$/TA$_{i,t-1}$		✓

As an alternative model to test the income-smoothing hypothesis, we specify a dynamic model of loan loss provisions by introducing lags of the dependent variable. The inclusion of lags of the dependent variable renders in the static model made an estimation result of the model (2) inconsistent. So later, in the model (2), we use the GMM difference estimator by Arellano and Bond (1991) to get consistent estimates of the above model. This procedure estimates the specific dynamic model in first-differences to solve the estimation problem raised by the potential presence of unobserved individual effect *vi* and gives consistent estimates under the assumption that error term ε_{it} is not serially correlated and the explanatory variables are (weakly) exogenous. We include the first and second lag to capture the speed of adjustment of loan loss provisions. We include interaction terms (dummy slopes) in this second equation which aims to test: (i) the influence of banks with negative income on loan loss provision behavior; (ii) the effect of banks size (by asset) on loan loss provisions behavior; (iii) the influence of banks types (based on ownership) on loan loss provisions behavior; (iv) the effect of high NPL ratio (above 5%) on loan loss provisions behavior; and (v) the effect of categorization of Commercial Bank based on Business Activities (BUKU) on loan loss provisions behavior.

Under these assumptions, the underlying regression model for the second estimator is:

$$\left(\frac{LLP}{TA}\right)_{it} = \alpha + \gamma 1 \left(\frac{LLP}{TA}\right)_{i,t-1} + \gamma 2 \left(\frac{LLP}{TA}\right)_{i,t-2} + \beta 1 \left(\frac{EBP}{TA}\right)_{it} + \beta 2 gCredit_{it} + \beta 3 gGDP_{t} + v_{i} + \varepsilon_{it}$$

$$(2)$$

Model 2 can be described into 17 equations in Table 4.

We use lagged values of stock variables and current values of flow variables in model 1 and 2 to avoid potential endogeneity problems. For example, loan loss provision at *t* corresponds to provisions during the year *t*, while assets at *t* −1 correspond to the stock of bank assets at the beginning of year *t*. Hence, LLP_{it}/TA_{it} is measured as $LLP_{it}/TA_{i,t-1}$.

3.2   Data

This research employs panel data of 102 commercial banks in Indonesia during the period 2011q1–2017q1, with 2550 observations. To minimise the effects of measurement errors and outliers, we have winsorized some variable based on distribution data samples at 99 and 95% percentiles.[1] As a robust test of winsorising treatment, a comparison of winsorising treatment has been done for each regression model and obtained consistent results. So the winsorising treatment used is the distribution of sample data at 99% percentile. Table 5 provides information on some descriptive statistics of the variables used in the estimation sample.

Table 6 presents correlations matrix of regression variables. The correlations indicate a statistically significant correlation between loan loss provisions and each of the explanatory variables. The correlation between loan loss provisions and profits before tax dan loan loss provisions is around 41%, suggesting banks do exercise income smoothing on average. The correlation between loan loss provisions and credit

---

[1] $LLP_{it}/TA_{i,t-1}$ dan $Credit_{it}/TA_{i,t-1}$

Table 4. Equations with GMM method

Explanatory Variables	Equations																
	2.1	2.2	2.3	2.4	2.5	2.6	2.7	2.8	2.9	2.10	2.11	2.12	2.13	2.14	2.15	2.16	2.17
LLP_t/TA_{t-1} (−1)	✓	✓	✓	✓	✓	✓	✓	✓	✓	✓	✓	✓	✓	✓	✓	✓	✓
LLP_t/TA_{t-1} (−2)	✓	✓	✓	✓	✓	✓	✓	✓	✓	✓	✓	✓	✓	✓	✓	✓	✓
EBP_t/TA_{t-1}	✓	✓	✓	✓	✓	✓	✓	✓	✓	✓	✓	✓	✓	✓	✓	✓	✓
Credit Growth$_{it}$	✓	✓	✓	✓	✓	✓	✓	✓	✓	✓	✓	✓	✓	✓	✓	✓	✓
GDP *Growth$_t$*	✓	✓	✓	✓	✓	✓	✓	✓	✓	✓	✓	✓	✓	✓	✓	✓	✓
*Negative Earning Dummy** EBP_t/TA_{t-1}		✓															
*Bank Size** EBP_t/TA_{t-1}			✓														
*Bank Size** *Credit Growth$_{it}$*				✓													
*Bank Size** GDP *Growth$_t$*					✓												
*Bank Ownership** EBP_t/TA_{t-1}						✓											
*Bank Ownership** *Credit Growth$_{it}$*							✓										
*Bank Ownership** GDP *Growth$_t$*								✓									
NPL *Gross** EBP_t/TA_{t-1}									✓								
NPL *Gross** *Credit Growth$_{it}$*										✓							
NPL *Gross** GDP *Growth$_t$*											✓						
BUKU 3* EBP_t/TA_{t-1}												✓					
BUKU 3* *Credit Growth$_{it}$*													✓				
BUKU 3* GDP *Growth$_t$*														✓			
BUKU 4* EBP_t/TA_{t-1}															✓		
BUKU 4* *Credit Growth$_{it}$*																✓	
BUKU 4* GDP *Growth$_t$*																	✓

Table 5. Summary statistics of key regression variables

Variable	Mean	Standard deviation
LLP/TA	0.49	0.69
EBP/TA	1.77	1.46
gCredit	24.08	33.96
gGDP	5.42	0.54

Note Total observations during the period 2011Q1–2017Q1 were 2550 observations for all variables. LLP/TA equals loan loss provisions over lagged total assets. EBP/TA equals profits before tax and loan loss provisions over lagged total assets. gCredit equals credit growth in real terms. gGDP equals real growth in per capita GDP

Table 6. Correlation matrix of key regression variables

Variable	LLP/TA	EBP/TA	*gCredit*	gGDP
LLP/TA	1.000			
EBP/TA	0.411***	1.000		
gCredit	−0.121***	−0.081***	1.000	
gGDP	−0.097***	0.052***	0.181***	1.000

Note Total observations during the period 2011Q1–2017Q1 were 2550 observations for all variables. LLP/TA equals loan loss provisions over lagged total assets. EBP/TA equals profits before tax and loan loss provisions over lagged total assets. gCredit equals credit growth in real terms. gGDP equals real growth of GDP

***Significance at a 1% level

growth is around −12%, suggesting imprudent behaviour by the average bank. The correlation between loan loss provisions and GDP growth is also negative around −10%, suggesting an anti-business cyclical behaviour of bank's loan loss provisioning.

4 Estimations Results

4.1 Estimation Result for *Generalized Least Squares* (GLS) Estimator

Table 7 presents the random effects regression results for GLS estimator. We find a positive and significant relationship between the ratio of loan loss provisions and bank earnings. These results suggest that banks in our sample have followed an income-smoothing pattern on average. Contrary to expectations, the real credit growth and GDP growth has an undesirable negative coefficient. These results suggest that on average behaviour of Indonesian banks loan loss provisioning still follow a procyclical pattern.

To allow for an asymmetric pattern of loan loss provisions during periods of positive and negative earnings, we interact the earnings variable with dummy variable in equations 1.2 that takes the value of one (1) when earnings are negative and zero (0) elsewhere. The results indicate that banks make statistically significantly higher

Table 7. Regression result using GLS method

	Expected sign	Equation 1.1		Equation 1.2	
		Coefficient (Std. error)	Sign	Coefficient (Std. error)	Sign
$EBP_{it}/TA_{i,t-1}$	+	0.209*** (0.033)	+	0.243*** (0.028)	+
$gCredit_{it}$	–	−0.001** (0.001)	–	−0.001** (0.001)	–
$gGDP_t$	–	−0.137*** (0.032)	–	−0.146*** (0.033)	–
Negative Earning Dummy $EBP_{it}/TA_{i,t-1}$*	–			−0.552*** (0.111)	–
Hausman test (p-value)		0.978		1.000	
R-squared		0.199		0.252	
No. of observations		2.550		2.550	
No. of banks		102		102	

Note The regressions are estimated using generalised least squares (GLS) with random bank-specific effects for the whole sample for the period 2011q1–2017q1. The dependent variable is the ratio of loan loss provisions (LLP) over lagged total assets (%). $EBP_{it}/TA_{i,t-1}$ equals profits before tax and loan loss provisions over lagged total assets (%). $gCredit_{it}$ equals credit growth, yoy (%). $gGDP_t$ is the real growth of GDP, yoy (%). The negative earning dummy takes value one (1) if profits before tax and loan loss provisions are negative, and zero (0) otherwise. The Hausman test is a test of the systematic difference between coefficients of the fixed effects and the random effects regression. We report the *p*-value of the Hausman test statistic. Constant and year dummies are included but are not reported. Standard errors are in brackets
*Significance at a 10% level
**Significance at a 5% level
***Significance at a 1% level

provisions when they incur losses than when they generate a positive level of income before provisions and tax.[2]

4.2 Estimation Result for *Generalized Method of Moments (GMM) Estimator*

Table 8 presents regression results for GMM estimator. Regression results in Table 8 equals to regression results in Table 7. The loss of a significant number of observations due to the inclusion of lagged dependent variables has not affected the estimations results in any significant way providing a good test of the robustness of our results. The coefficients on both the first lag and the second lag of the dependent variable are statistically significant, suggesting that banks are making corrections or adjustments to

---

[2] Negative earnings before provisioning times the negative regression coefficient of the interacted term, negative earnings dummy times earnings before provisioning, implies a positive effect on provisions.

their optimal path of provisioning based on their previous loan loss provisions behaviour.

Equation 2.2 add an interaction term (dummy slope) between the earnings variable and a dummy variable that takes the value of one (1) when earnings are negative and zero (0) elsewhere to allow for an asymmetric pattern of loan loss provisions during periods of positive and negative earnings. Again, we find that banks make statistically significantly higher provisions when they incur losses than when they generate a positive level of profit before provisions and tax. Based on the data, banks with negative earnings has a problem with their NPL (higher NPL). There are 76 observations during

Table 8. Regression result using GMM method

	Expected sign	Equation 2.1		Equation 2.2	
		Coefficient (Std. error)	Sign	Coefficient (Std. error)	Sign
$LLP_{i,t-1}/TA_{i,t-2}$	+	0.130*** (0.019)	+	0.119*** (0.019)	+
$LLP_{i,t-2}/TA_{i,t-3}$	+	0.140*** (0.020)	+	0.182*** (0.019)	+
$EBP_{it}/TA_{i,t-1}$	+	0.204*** (0.015)	+	0.240*** (0.017)	+
$gCredit_{it}$	−	−0.002*** (0.000)	−	−0.002*** (0.000)	−
$gGDP_t$	−	−0.069*** (0.013)	−	−0.085*** (0.014)	−
Negative Earning Dummy * $EBP_{it}/TA_{i,t-1}$	−			−0.990*** (0.180)	−
No. of observations		2.244		2.244	
No. of banks		102		102	

Note The regressions are estimated using Arellano and Bond (1991) GMM difference estimator for panel data with lagged dependent variables (we include two lags of the dependent variable). The regressions are estimated on the whole sample of banks and for the period 2011q1–2017q1. The dependent variable is the ratio of loan loss provisions (LLP) over lagged total assets (%). $LLP_{i,t-1}/TA_{i,t-2}$ equals first lag from dependent variable. $LLP_{i,t-2}/TA_{i,t-3}$ equals second lag from dependent variable. $EBP_{it}/TA_{i,t-1}$ equals profits before tax and loan loss provisions over lagged total assets (%). $gCredit_{it}$ equals credit growth, yoy (%). $gGDP_t$ is the real growth of GDP, yoy (%). The negative earning dummy takes value of one (1) if profits before tax and loan loss provisions are negative, and zero (0) otherwise. Standard errors are in brackets
*Significance at a 10% level
**Significance at a 5% level
***Significance at a 1% level

the period of 2011q1–2017q1 that has negative earnings, 46 of them have high NPL (above 5%). The facts imply that during cyclical downswings, banks use their capital to make provisions for loan losses and therefore during good times banks do not form enough provision to cover losses during bad times.

Enriching research and capture some banks behaviour, we also add another interaction term (dummy slope) as we mentioned above. The interaction term between bank size [variable taking on a value of one (1) for the banks in the top quartile by total asset value in each quarter, and zero (0) otherwise] to profit before tax and loan loss provisions over lagged total assets and GDP growth shows positive (+) and significant results. These results suggest that banks with big assets when their earnings are rising and when the economy is improving tend to increase LLP. However, based on

Table 9. Regression result using GMM method based on bank size

	Equation 2.3	Equation 2.4	Equation 2.5
	Coefficient (Std. error)	Coefficient (Std. error)	Coefficient (Std. error)
Bank Size $*$ EBP$_{it}$/TA$_{i,t-1}$	0.990** (0.490)		
Bank Size$*gCredit_{it}$		−0.036** (0.015)	
Bank Size$*gGDP_t$			0.807* (0.482)
Control variables	Yes	Yes	Yes
No. of observations	2.244	2.244	2.244
No. of banks	102	102	102

Note The regressions are estimated using Arellano and Bond (1991) GMM difference estimator for panel data with lagged dependent variables (we include two lags of the dependent variable). The regressions are estimated on the whole sample of banks and for the period 2011q1–2017q1. The dependent variable is the ratio of loan loss provisions (LLP) over lagged total assets (%). Bank Size takes value of one (1) for the banks in the top quartile by total asset value in each quarter, and zero (0) otherwise. Control variables used are (i) first lag from a dependent variable, (ii) second lag from dependent variable, (iii) profit before tax and loan loss provisions over lagged total assets, (iv) ratio of credit growth, and (v) real growth of GDP. Standard errors are in brackets

*Significance at a 10% level

**Significance at a 5% level

***Significance at a 1% level

regression results between bank size and credit growth showed negative (−) and significant results, which means that on the other hand big banks also tend to increase LLP when credit growth is down. So banks with high assets are shows the imprudent behaviour of loan loss provisioning or tend to be procyclical (Table 9).

The interaction term between bank ownership [variable taking on a value of one (1) for foreign banks, and zero (0) otherwise] to profit before tax and provision and GDP growth, show insignificant results. This fact is because probability value is above the level of significance of 10%, so the coefficient value is equal to zero (0). On the

Table 10. Regression result using GMM method based on bank ownership

	Equation 2.6	Equation 2.7	Equation 2.8
	Coefficient (Std. error)	Coefficient (Std. error)	Coefficient (Std. error)
*Bank Ownership** $EBP_{it}/TA_{i,t-1}$	0.225 (0.264)		
*Bank Ownership***gCredit*$_{it}$		−0.028*** (0.008)	
*Bank Ownership***gGDP*$_t$			−9.282 (7.158)
Control variables	Yes	Yes	Yes
No. of observations	2.244	2.244	2.244
No. of banks	102	102	102

Note The regressions are estimated using Arellano and Bond (1991) GMM difference estimator for panel data with lagged dependent variables (we include two lags of the dependent variable). The regressions are estimated on the whole sample of banks and for the period 2011q1–2017q1. The dependent variable is the ratio of loan loss provisions (LLP) over lagged total assets (%). Bank Ownership takes the value of one (1) for foreign banks, and zero (0) otherwise. Control variables used are (i) first lag from a dependent variable, (ii) second lag from dependent variable, (iii) profit before tax and loan loss provisions over lagged total assets, (iv) ratio of credit growth, and (v) real growth of GDP. Standard errors are in brackets
*Significance at a 10% level
**Significance at a 5% level
***Significance at a 1% level

other hand, the result of the interaction term, in the form of bank ownership to credit growth showed negative (−) and significant result. These results suggest that foreign banks when credit growth rises tend to lower their LLP that reflects procyclical behaviour (Table 10).

The interaction term between NPL Gross [variable taking on a value of one (1) for banks with NPL Gross above 5%] to profit before tax and loan loss provision, credit growth and GDP growth show positive (+) and significant result. These results suggest that banks with high NPL when their earnings and credit growth are rising, also economic condition is an upswing, bank tend to reserve larger provisions. Thus, banks with high NPL can be categorised as prudent LLP or tend to be countercyclical (Table 11).

The Interaction term between BUKU 3 to profit before tax and loan loss provisions indicates positive (+) and significant value which means that banks in BUKU 3 when their earnings are rising tend to reserve more significant provisions. On the other hand, as credit is rising, banks in BUKU 3 tend to lower their provisioning. This fact is evident from interaction terms between BUKU 3 with credit growth showing negative (−) and significant. These results suggest that banks in BUKU 3 are shows imprudent loan loss provisioning behaviour or tend to be procyclical (Table 12).

Table 11. Regression result using GMM method based on NPL ratio

	Equation 2.9	Equation 2.10	Equation 2.11
	Coefficient (Std. error)	Coefficient (Std. error)	Coefficient (Std. error)
NPL *Gross** $EBP_{it}/TA_{i,t-1}$	0.706*** (0.147)		
NPL *Gross**$gCredit_{it}$		0.050*** (0.012)	
NPL *Gross**$gGDP_t$			0.186*** (0.031)
Control variables	Yes	Yes	Yes
No. of observations	2.244	2.244	2.244
No. of banks	102	102	102

Note The regressions are estimated using Arellano and Bond (1991) GMM difference estimator for panel data with lagged dependent variables (we include two lags of the dependent variable). The regressions are estimated on the whole sample of banks and for the period 2011q1–2017q1. The dependent variable is the ratio of loan loss provisions (LLP) over lagged total assets (%). NPL Gross takes the value of one (1) if for banks with NPL Gross above 5%, and zero (0) otherwise. Control variables used are (i) first lag from a dependent variable, (ii) second lag from dependent variable, (iii) profit before tax and loan loss provisions over lagged total assets, (iv) ratio of credit growth, and (v) real growth of GDP. Standard errors are in brackets

*Significance at a 10% level

**Significance at a 5% level

***Significance at a 1% level

Table 12. Regression result using GMM method based on BUKU 3

	Equation 2.12	Equation 2.13	Equation 2.14
	Coefficient (Std. error)	Coefficient (Std. error)	Coefficient (Std. error)
BUKU 3* $EBP_{it}/TA_{i,t-1}$	0.835** (0.347)		
BUKU 3*$gCredit_{it}$		−0.048*** (0.012)	
BUKU 3*$gGDP_t$			−8.902 (10.734)
Control variables	Yes	Yes	Yes
No. of observations	2.244	2.244	2.244
No. of banks	102	102	102

Note The regressions are estimated using Arellano and Bond (1991) GMM difference estimator for panel data with lagged dependent variables (we include two lags of the dependent variable). The regressions are estimated on the whole sample of banks and for the period 2011q1–2017q1. The dependent variable is the ratio of loan loss provisions (LLP) over lagged total assets (%). BUKU 3 takes the value of one (1) for banks in Commercial Bank based on Business Activities 3 (BUKU 3), and zero (0) otherwise. Control variables used are (i) first lag from a dependent variable, (ii) second lag from dependent variable, (iii) profit before tax and loan loss provisions over lagged total assets, (iv) ratio of credit growth, and (v) real growth of GDP. Standard errors are in brackets

*Significance at a 10% level

**Significance at a 5% level

***Significance at a 1% level

The interaction term between BUKU 4 to profit before tax and loan loss provisions and credit growth shows a negative (−) and significant value which means that banks in BUKU 4 when their earnings are rising and when credit growth increases tend to lower their provision. So the banks in BUKU 4 shows imprudent loan loss provisioning behaviour or tend to be procyclical. Nevertheless, the behaviour of bank BUKU 4 is slightly different from the average behaviour of the banking industry that is not doing income smoothing. This fact is suspected because banks in BUKU 4 has a relatively low NPL ratio and also its income is relatively stable (not too volatile) (Table 13).

Table 13. Regression Result using GMM Method based on BUKU 4

	Equation 2.15	Equation 2.16	Equation 2.17
	Coefficient (Std. error)	Coefficient (Std. error)	Coefficient (Std. error)
BUKU 4* $EBP_{it}/TA_{i,t-1}$	−1.929* (1.085)		
BUKU 4*$gCredit_{it}$		−0.308*** (0.118)	
BUKU 4*$gGDP_t$			−25.868 (15.809)
Control variables	Yes	Yes	Yes
No. of observations	2.244	2.244	2.244
No. of banks	102	102	102

Note The regressions are estimated using Arellano and Bond (1991) GMM difference estimator for panel data with lagged dependent variables (we include two lags of the dependent variable). The regressions are estimated on the whole sample of banks and for the period 2011q1–2017q1. The dependent variable is the ratio of loan loss provisions (LLP) over lagged total assets (%). BUKU 4 takes the value of one (1) for banks in Commercial Bank based on Business Activities 4 (BUKU 4), and zero (0) otherwise. Control variables used are (i) first lag from a dependent variable, (ii) second lag from dependent variable, (iii) profit before tax and loan loss provisions over lagged total assets, (iv) ratio of credit growth, and (v) real growth of GDP. Standard errors are in brackets
*Significance at a 10% level
**Significance at a 5% level
***Significance at a 1% level

5 Conclusion and Policy Recommendation

The result above shows empirical evidence that Indonesian banks, on average, have followed an income-smoothing pattern as evidenced by the positive and significant relationship between loan loss provisions and bank earnings. On the contrary, credit growth rate and GDP growth rate has an undesirable negative coefficient which means tend to be procyclical. As a conclusion, the results suggest that, on average, Indonesian behaviour of banks loan loss provisioning follow a procyclical pattern that is potentially worsening business cycles, especially during a recession.

A forward-looking provision under a countercyclical framework that useful to curb bank's excessive risk-taking behaviour during the boom phase should be considered to enhance the more stable financial system regarding bank's intermediation role hence ensure stronger economic performance.

References

Agusman, Gunadi I., Setiyono B., Yumanita D., and Hafidz J., 2012, *"Dynamic Provisioning: The Case of Indonesia"*, Working Paper, Bank Indonesia.

Angklomkliew, S., George, J., and Packer, F., 2009. *"Issues and Developments in loan loss provisioning: the case of Asia"*, BIS Quarterly Review, December 2009.

Arellano, M., Bond, S., 1991. *"Some tests of specification for panel data: Monte Carlo evidence and an application to employment equation."* Rev. Econ. Stud. 58, 277–297.

Bikker, J.A and Metzemakers, P., 2005, *"Bank provisioning behaviour and procyclicality"*, *Journal of International Financial Markets, Institutions and Money*, vol. 15, pp. 29–51.

Bikker, J.A., H. Hu, 2002, *"Cyclical patterns in profits, provisions and lending of banks and procyclicality of the new Basel capital requirements"*, *Banca Nazionale del Lavoro Quarterly Review 55*, 143–175.

Borio, C, C Furfine and Lowe, P., 2001, *"Procyclicality of the financial system and financial stability: issues and policy options"*, BIS Papers, No. 1.

Cohen, B. H and Edwards Jr. G. A., 2017, *"The new era of expected credit loss provisioning"*. BIS Quarterly Review, March 2017, pp. 39–55.

Craig R. S., E. P. Davis, and A. G. Pascual, 2006, *"Sources of procyclicality in East Asian financial systems"*, in Packer, F and Zhu, H. (2010), *Loan loss provisioning practices of Asian banks*, pp. 1–27.

Davis, E.P and Zhu, H. 2005. *"Commercial property prices and bank performance"*, BIS Working Papers, No. 175, pp. 1–37.

Gaston E dan Song I.W., 2014, *"Supervisory Roles in Loan Loss Provisioning in Countries Implementing IFRS."*, IMF Working Paper, No. WP/14/170, pp. 1–40.

Laeven, L and Majnoni, G., 2003, *"Loan loss provisioning and economic slowdowns: too much, too late?"*, *Journal of Financial Intermediation*, vol. 12, pp. 178–197.

Lowe, Philip (2002), "Credit Risk Measurement and Procyclicality," BIS working paper 116.

Packer, F and Zhu, H., 2010, *"Loan loss provisioning practices of Asian banks"*, BIS Working Papers, No. 375, pp. 1–27.
Wimboh, S., Rulina, I., Deriantino, E., 2010, *"Procyclicality of Loan Loss Provisioning: Issues, Development and Evidence from Indonesia"*, Working Paper, Bank Indonesia.

Evalution of FDI in CE, SEE and Kosovo in Relation to Growth Rates and Other Indicators

Nakije Kida[(✉)]

Department of Banks, Finance and Accounting, AAB College, Pristina, Kosovo
nakije.kida@universitetiaab.com

1 Introduction

Impact of the Foreign Direct Investment (FDI) in economic growth in the past three decades has been hotly debated. FDI is seen as a factor of economic growth, especially in the developing countries seeing a number of benefits from the direct flow and their indirect dissemination. The focus is not only on the direct effects, it is more on their indirect effects. Some Central European (CE) countries and South Eastern Europe (SEE) have had a history of industrialized countries which inherited an outdated technology after the fall of communism. Restructuring the economy can best be done through FDI. The necessity to attract technology from the developed countries was a disturbing problem, so these countries, as well as Kosovo, created numerous measures to attract foreign investors. FDI were considered solutions to the problems of transition. The World Bank statistics also give figures that only up to 0.02% of technology, machinery and equipment comes in through import, considering FDI as the main channel of technology transfer (Jude 2012: 5).

This is complete when we see that about 70% of investment in research and development are made by a small number of large companies in the world (WB). Since Kosovo and most of the countries in the sample have been facing the shortage of finance, the best opportunity to have access to technology and advanced knowledge comes through FDI, and not through import. Therefore through the secondary data can be mentioned the measurement of technological and human diffusion, capital formation and access to foreign markets. The appearance of these elements in the endogenous theory of growth favors the long term growth. The investment growth in 2000 and 2007 (1.9 billion US $), directed the attention of researchers more towards this phenomenon, though, their decline made the rationale of investment incentives in the host countries be further discussed.

Time commitments are necessary in terms of political and economic reforms, that encourage FDI inflows, since they are considered as a catalyst for economic growth, as a factor that can reduce the effects of the global crisis (Pere and Harshova 2011).

The objective of the government of Kosovo is attracting of the foreign investments to complement the technological and knowledge gap, employee training, building of new production capacities and increasing the export. By increasing the rate of GDP per capita in Kosovo, many problems aimed by the government of the country would be

© Springer Nature Switzerland AG 2018
N. Ozatac and K. K. Gökmenoglu (eds.), *Emerging Trends in Banking and Finance*, Springer Proceedings in Business and Economics,
https://doi.org/10.1007/978-3-030-01784-2_6

addressed, and one of the challenges from official sources is the highest unemployment rate in Europe, to 30.9%, while according to informal sources, it reaches even to 45%. The contribution of FDI in terms of economic and industrial development in Kosovo has been variable, ranging between 2.6% (2005) and 12.6% (2007) of GDP.[1] While, the problem is that there is a fall in FDI relative to the GDP of 3.5% in 2016.

Therefore, the objectives of the study are to find the direct and indirect FDI impact on economic growth. In the host countries the effect of FDI on economic growth depends on conditional factors:

- The level of human capital (absorptive capacity of human capital, the threshold level, the absorptive capacity of the host economy in catching the spread of technology and knowledge that foreign firms bring).
- The level of development of local firms (domestic investment).

Are the countries considered in transition or developing countries and some Central European countries able to absorb technology and knowledge? Do they have a sufficient threshold of knowledge that enables the use of technology that FDI bring? How attractive are these countries compared to the developed countries that are part of this study? Does FDI have complementary or substitute effect on domestic investments in CE and SEE? It has also been analyzed the "catch-up" effect in the process of convergence of the developing countries towards the levels of the advanced economies.

Like the majority of the European countries, Kosovo faces shortage of capital, knowledge, management, as well as with an employment challenge. This thesis contributes to the literature in two ways: It contributes to the literature of FDI growth, focusing on the effect of technology transfer and human capital in economic growth. The contribution here is in terms of fulfilling the skills level of human capital that contributes to attracting technology through FDI in the developing and developed countries. The study extends on the existing literature about the relationship of FDI with the growth and at the same time with the other determinants of growth, determinants of human capital and domestic investments in complementariness with FDI.

There are three research questions that cover this problematic:

(i) How Foreign Direct Investment affects the economic growth in the host country, through direct effects and indirect effects, what effect the term interaction on economic growth has between FDI and human capital, or FDI and domestic investments ?

(ii) Is the FDI effect conditioned by certain factors on economic growth, and what are they ?

(iii) What effect the economic growth has on FDI increase in the host country, and what effect the human capital, domestic investments, remittances and government spending have ?

---

[1] Pere, A, Hashorva—"Western Balkans' Countries In Focus Of Global Economic Crisis" pg. 11. Economy Transdisciplinarity Cognition; www.ugb.ro/etc.

While the following hypotheses raise the issues raised:

H1: "FDI has a direct effect on the economic growth of the host countries, FDI has an indirect effect on the growth through interaction between FDI and the level of human capital and FDI with domestic investments".

H2: "Besides the economic growth, other determinants as well as human capital, domestic investments, total government spending and remittances have positive effect on the flow of FDI".

2 The Role of FDI in Economic Growth Discussions and Empirical Debates

Seeing that governments around the world are working towards creating a climate friendly for FDI, as FDI contributes directly to the formation of capital in the country through the construction of factories, machinery, transport improvement and indirectly through the creation of employment, exports, consumption and savings, and attention is focused on them. The analysis of the relationship between FDI and economic growth in our study yielded unilateral results (economic growth has positive effects on FDI as FDI does not have an increasing effect) and serves to debate this issue, taking a look at other studies to conclude that FDI and economic growth convey each other, but not always and in all cases.

However, a positive relationship between FDI and growth depends on the host country's conditions, some of which are: the level of human capital, government policies, infrastructure, location, efficiency of institutions, Balasubramanyam et al. (1996).

In other studies, there are also arguments that high levels of FDI are related to high growth rates of De Mello (1997), Borensztein et al. (1998).

Study made by Jude (2012: Chap. 6) is seen in the order of very significant studies that find the positive effect of increasing FDI. In its findings, it confirms that by combining the negative effect on accumulation of positive capital, we are able to confirm a general positive impact of FDI on economic growth in the CEEC. This shows that the IHD-growth relationship is dominated by spreading.

Unlike our study of the absorption capacity of the host economies (i.e. economic growth depends on the interaction of FDI * HC variables), it finds that the effects of FDI in the CEEC are not dependent on this threshold. Using a simultaneous equation the author in question has found that FDI causes growth and growth in turn attracts FDI.

So the connection is positive in two directions, which often does not happen. However, there are studies that identified a negative correlation between FDI and economic growth, the most important being Durham (2004), Lyroudi et al. (2004), CarkovicLevine (2005) and Lipsey (2006). The negative relationship was also reported by Lyroudi et al. (2004: 98) and Levine (2005: 197) analysis, which received negative results at the level of education, economic development and trade.

What are the circumstances that support the positive spread of FDI is best argued by Borensztein et al. (1998), Xu (2000) and Alfaro (2003),[2] which suggest that the educational level, developed financial markets and other conditions in the host economy play an important role in the positive effects of FDI. The effect of the spread is often measured indirectly through the power of interaction of FDI with human capital; this has shown to have a significant positive effect on economic growth as suggested in Borensztein et al. (1998) and Xu (2000).[3]

Mencinger (2003) analyzed the relationship between FDI and economic growth in transition countries in the 1994–2001 period and reported having a negative link. Countries in transition were in the period of their economic and political transformation; investments had entered privatization, which means that greenfield investments were scarce. While countries were in transition, the privatization tools used the most for imports and consumption, not the increase in productivity. Such a practice is almost the same in most countries in the initial transition, so the effects of increasing FDI are very small or negative.

There are studies that have found a mixed effect of increasing FDI (Alfaro 2003: 1–31). An empirical analysis that she made using cross-country data for the period 1981–1999 reports that FDI exerts a mixed effect on growth, depending on which sector analyzes. Growth in the primary sector has a significant negative effect on growth, in the manufacturing sector a positive and significant effect and in the services sector an ambiguous effect.

2.1 Relations with Economic Growth, FDI and Domestic Investment

We start from our study to measure the extent to which FDI flows have become productive investments.[4] However, we are starting from the positive view that FDI is not just an addendum to existing capital, but they can also change the existing equity structure. So we have asked the question how local investors react when entering FDI, i.e. they are substitutes or complementary[5] to domestic investments. In our study the results are consistent with several other studies,[6] FDI has followed the existing structure of the economy by going to industries where there were already many local firms and increasing competition has led to a crawling out. This analysis is done through small generalized squares using the Fixed Effects model (FE). Our analysis for the Central and Southeast European countries suggests that there is a substitution between FDI and local investment (it is characteristic that most sample countries in the

---

[2] Hirschman (1958: 109) stressed that not all sectors have the same potential to absorb foreign technology or to create links with the rest of the economy. He noted, for example, "the links are weak in agriculture and mining."

[3] The case of our study, we reported positive FDI * HC outcomes in economic growth in countries (SEE, SEE).

[4] FDI is in fact a financial flow which does not in fact guarantee its transformation into fixed capital.

[5] Jude (2012: Chap. 5), IHD may be complementary to domestic investment when intermediate goods demand stimulates the production of local suppliers and encourages them to make new investments.

[6] While similar results have found, in her study, Jude (2012: Chap. 5) which she has done instead of CCECs.

measurement period have gone through the most important stage of privatization, a stronger reason we have such results).

FDI opponents argue that the negative impact on economic growth is generated by domestic investment accumulation (Braunstein and Epstein 2002: 23); Huang (1998, 2003: 3). It is known that FDI contributes directly through the flow of capital (construction of new factories) and the introduction of new equipment (technological transfer).

However, their effect on the host economy is even greater in the form of spreading investments through indirect effects (creating links with local firms), however, it often happens that they receive their inputs from import and do not need such links. This is more so in transition countries when FDI comes in the form of acquisitions and mergers (through privatization) and often take the place of local firms through competition without contributing to economic growth in the country.

Borensztein et al. (1998) has tested the effect of FDI on economic growth by utilizing direct investment data in the 69 developing countries for the period 1970–1990 and found that FDIs "accumulate" Domestic Investment. Similar to Borensztein are the results of our study in 24 European countries have a negative and important coefficient when interacting with Domestic Investment FDI.

Finally, many authors emphasize, as a result of "learning, demonstrating, creating the effects, linking foreign and domestic firms", the effect of overseas collection weakens or even overturns in the long term, FDI will have positive effects on domestic entrepreneurship.

3 Study Methodology

Objectives enable us to apply a special methodology. Structuring the literature was difficult, coming to a conclusion that literature should be divided into two segments: firstly, the literature of FDI based on industrial organization and international production, and secondly the literature of economic growth based on the growth models. Even the paper has been structured according to this division, giving the deserved place to these two segments of literature. The macroeconomic and microeconomic analyses harmonize the differences for a more complete estimation of the FDI phenomenon. Firstly the transfer of technology basically is a microeconomic phenomenon, including identification of channels, which might not be all at this level. Therefore, having noticed that the net estimation of FDI cannot be achieved by microeconomic level, then we also have to use the macro approach, finding the determinants of the economic growth and FDI in two separate equations, too. Also the comparative method is used amongst Kosovo and the 23 countries of CE and SEE. Estimation of FDI and determinants of the economic growth has provided a real picture of the FDI performance and other indicators for 11 years (2004–2014). Also construction of a database by the World Bank (2017) (World Development Indicators—WDI) for an econometric estimation of FDI phenomenon and economic growth, has been completed with the determinants of economic growth and FDI. Econometric analysis focuses on macroeconomic dimension, to find out the effect of FDI on economic growth, the relationship between them, what effect FDI have in domestic investments, technological progress and then globally in 24 European countries and Kosovo. Meanwhile the internal instruments (7 variables with the data from the host economies) were used for the secondary data, using the method of little squares and generalized little squares too convenient and popular in the use of panel data. There were also used two methods, such as the method of Fixed Effects and Random Effects, since it is a heterogeneous sample, they can correct the dynamic panel from bias (differences) and provide efficient assessments even if endogenous the explanatory variables are present.

Methodology of secondary data—Having as objective FDI and their role in economic growth, then the literature includes two segments, growth patterns and increase productivity by using the technology and knowledge which come through FDI. Access treatment of these macro level. For an empirical explanation of problems are used these instruments in research. The study uses a panel of data on which countries are the unit of observation. Devices of multiple, linear and correlation regression used in the evaluation process are those designed specifically for panel data, such as the method of general little squares (GLS) combined with the tests of Fixed Effects (FE) and Random Effects (RE), the test of Hausman (Rho), Wald test, etc.

- *The focus group (secondary data)*, there were selected seven variables: logarithm of GDP_initial, FDI, the growth of GDP per capita, private investments, human capital (number of students enrolled in secondary level of education in relation to the population), total costs of the government and remittances. N = 24,[7] short time period (the panel has an equal amount of observations in time (years) T = 11 for each site so we have N = 24 < T = 11, while data is balanced.[8] The program STATA version 12 has served for statistical processing of secondary data.

4 Theoretical and Empirical Model

Description of the theoretical model—The assessment approach is the same as at Borensztein et al. (1998)[9] modified on several variables.

- It is used the model adopted by Borensztein et al. (1998).
- Use of LS and GLS methods through the method of fixed effects and random effects to estimate whether the transfer of technology is directed towards the growth.
- Mechanisms: The growth of the diversified capital goods (N) drives the technological progress (TP) toward growth.

---

[7] Albania, Kosovo, Macedonia, Montenegro, Croatia, Bosnia and Herzegovina, Serbia, Slovenia, Bulgaria, Romania, Hungary, Poland, Portugal, Czech Republic, Slovak Republic, Lithuania and Estonia; Germany, Switzerland, Auatria, Holland, Italy, Norway and Sweden.

[8] The unbalanced panel according to Wooldridge (2002, p. 275) causes major problems in the assessment so this is a priority in our case.

[9] The expanded model of Boreisztein et al. (1998) and its adaptation with some changes has been used in the Doctoral Thesis, Kida (2016: 169–182).

- $Y = AHt^a\,kt^{1-a}$.
- There exist the varieties N and k_t.
- $N = n - n^*$.

It is an endogenous development model that considers the technological transfer as a stimulant of growth. It follows the chain of events as: when there is an increase in the variety of capital goods or improvement in the quality of existing capital goods, then occurs the technological transfer (TP), which increases the economic growth.

N = the number of varieties of capital for an economy, n = number of varieties of capital goods produced by domestic firms, n* = number of varieties of goods produced by foreign firms. The rate of growth in developing economies that include foreign firms and domestic ones is expressed in this way:

$$g = 1/\sigma\left[A^{1/a}\psi\,F(n^*N, N/N^*)^{-1}H - \rho\right] \tag{1}$$

Equation (1), Borensztein et al. (1998: 7–9), shows that FDI, which are measured with the products manufactured by foreign firms in the total number of products (n^*/N), deduct the price of the introduction of new varieties of capital goods, increasing in this way the rate where the new capital goods are introduced. Significant terms are l: (n*/N), (N/N) and H.

In this model, growth positively depends on the percentage of goods produced from foreign firms. This is because the presence of foreign firms facilitates the production of capital goods. (H) is also positively associated with the growth. Finally, growth negatively depends on the proportion of goods produced in an economy compared to goods produced in countries with more advanced technology (N*). Thus, countries with technology behind grow faster. This is in accordance with "convergence" in the literature of growth. Empirical model of Borensztein et al. (1998):

$$g = C_0 + C_1 FDI + C_2 FDI \times H + C_3 H + C_4 Y_0 + C_5 X_1 \tag{2}$$

Ku : g = represents an annual growth rate of GDP per capita ($\hat{y}_{it}$).
FDI = FDI in relation to GDP.
H = Human capital is represented by the student enrollment rate, secondary school level in relation to the population, applied some time ago by Romer (1994, IV) who found the positive effect of human capital in FDI.
Y = initial GDP per capita is measured as the logarithm value of GDP in 2003 to capture the "Catch up" effect—it is the process of convergence towards the levels of the advanced economies (N/N*).
A or X_{it} = the group of variables introduced as determinants of economic growth.

In regression we notice that there is a coefficient for each, FDI and human capital, which cooperate together, except once when they are included separately. The same occurs with FDI variables, either, in cooperation with domestic investments, while in (X) are involved other factors, too (remittances and government spending).

Our empirical equation

$$\text{LogGDPgpc} = a_{0it} + \beta_1 \text{FDI}_{it} + \beta_2 \text{HC}_{it} + \beta_3 \text{FDI}_{it} \times \text{HC}_{it} + \beta_4 Y_{0it} + \beta_5 \text{Dom.Inv}_{it} + \beta_6 \text{Dom.Inves.} \times$$
$$\text{FDI}_{it} + \beta_7 \text{G.C.F.G.C}_{it} + \beta_8 \text{REM}_{it} + u_{it} + \varepsilon_{it}$$

$$(2a)$$

where (i) is the place, (t) is the time-period, (ai) is the specific coefficient parameter of the country (GDPgpc), a measure for the growth rate of GDP per capita, X_{it} is the matrix that represents other determinants of growth apart FDI, Human Capital ((HC) and initial GDP (Y_0), as there are the variables: Domestic Investment (Dom.Inv.), General Expenses of Government Final Consumption (GCFGC), REM.-Remittances.

μ_i—difference of specific variables in different observed countries or unverified variables; ε_i—Terms of random errors;

The second equation for FDI takes the form:

$$\log\_\text{FDI}_{it} = a_{0it} + \beta_1 \log\_\hat{y}_{yit} + \beta_2 \text{HC}_{it} + \log\_1 \beta_3 \text{HC}_{it} + \log\_2 \beta_4 \text{HC}_{it} + \beta_5 \text{Dom.Inves}_{it} + \beta_6 \text{REM}_{it}$$
$$+ \beta_7 \text{G.C.F.G.C}_{it} + u_{it} + e_{it}$$

$$(3)$$

We use the natural logarithm log_log for two variables, FDI dependent and growth of GDP per capita independent (($\log\_\text{FDI}_{it} = \log\_\text{GDPgpc}$), by country (i) in the period (t). Meanwhile we have used time delays for certain variables (lag_1 and lag_2) in equation about human capital (measurement of absorptive capacities in host countries).

The advantages of the methods and techniques used

- The estimation does not suffer from differences between countries—unnoticed prejudices because the method of the Fixed Effects eliminates these differences.

- The techniques used are reliable to control endogeneity between explanatory variables (correlation between them).

- They are useful when the database is short as in the case of our study.

- Hausman test that replaces several tests.

5   Results of the Study

Submission of Descriptive Statistics (Table 1, on appendix) from panel data—For each variable is included the number of observations, average, average distribution, and the minimum and maximum points that make the range around which the variable values fluctuate. The same conclusion is reached for all variables except for FDI, remittances and the variables that interact with any other variables (FDI * HC and FDI * Dom.Inv.) on which will be carried out the tests for normality of average distribution. Solution of the First Hypothesis and Table Results-For the output of the dependent economic growth, some tests will need to be carried out.

- Tables 2—Determination of the effects of fixed effects versus random effects,
- Table 3—Hausman's,
- Table 5—Testing for Fixed Time Effects,
- Tables 6—Testing for heteroskedasticity and the choice of the Fixed Effects Method for GDP per capita GDP,

Tables 2 and 3 from Stage A—complete, Table 4 (Appendix)-FE choice versus RE (Fixed Effects Test for Case Effects). Similarities and differences in the two models (FE/RE) of the study.

The coefficient results can be ascertained that there are similarities and differences in two regression models. Accepting that a constant (intercept) is much larger in the Fixed Effects model (40.60), it is statistically important, compared to the RE constant (10.27%), is a good start.

As mentioned in the theoretical part, individual heterogeneity is possible in the model of fixed effects and is therefore captured by a constant (that is the proof). In terms of variables the differences in coefficients in the two models are small, only in the human capital variable the change is large, and that in the FE model has a positive and insignificant coefficient while in the RE model it is negative and important.

Both models show a negative GDP_fillestare and ($p = 0.000$) statistically important and a general finding that economic growth is largely dependent on increased domestic investment. Another difference is that the R-square is much higher in the FE model compared to RE. The change occurs because in the FE model the constant captures the heterogeneity of the sites, while the random effects due to technical evaluation deficiencies cannot capture the differences. Therefore, the explanatory power in the RE model is lost.

(a) Hausman Test in Appendix complement, Table 5

To set the model's effects on fixed effects and random effects model we have used a Hausman test. The point is: If the unique (u!) Random effects are related to independent variables (regresor) in our regression. *The zero hypothesis H0 =* says the random effects are not related to the regressor, and that the RE model is preferred.

Alternative Hypothesis H1 = says u! Is associated with regressors in the model of fixed effects and is the most advanced evaluation technique.

This is <0.05 (i.e. coefficients are significant) Fixed effects used.

The result of the Hausman test is shown in Table 5 (in the Appendix) and it is convincing that the zero hypothesis is dropped to the 1% level. The result of the Hausman test says that unique effects are linked to independent variables within our model so the random effects model is biased and its coefficient (Beta) estimation will not melt to true coefficient parameters (Beta) in large samples. Therefore, the estimated coefficient gains with fixed effects are stable.

(b) **Testing for Fixed Time Effects**[10]

To see if fixed time effects are needed during a FE model, the testparm command is used. It is a common test for the forearm all years are equal to 0, if they are, then it is not necessary to use fixed time effects, press "help-testparm". After running the Fiber Effect model, write: test certificate and we have the following results (we have the table in Annex A): Prob > F is 0.8708 > 0.05,[11] so we can not reject the zero hypothesis because coefficients for all years are equal to zero, so there is no need for Fixed Time Effects in this case.

From the coefficients of table d, in Appendix, we complete the following equation: Equation Fixed Time Effects:

$$\text{Log}\Delta\text{GDPgpc}_{it} = 47.12254 - 1.449186\text{logGDPinitial.}_{it} + 0.0060911\text{FDI}_{it} + 0.0022707\text{HC}_{it}$$
$$+ 0.0635436\text{Dom.Inv.}_{it} + 0.0284214\text{REM}_{it} - 0.0315179\text{G.C.C.Ex.G}_{it}$$

(c) **Testing for heteroskedasticity**

This paragraph briefly examines the powerful robust covariance estimator of the sandwich type to provide a basis for their broader handling in a data panel.[12] The robust estimators approach has gained popularity among statisticians and econometrists since the early beginnings of econometric evaluations, Long and Ervin (2000). Assessing the most powerful standard errors creates fewer assumptions about the indivisible differences between countries as in our case (when heterogeneous data are included), but create more variance. When using this effect it is likely to be important for the accuracy of the results. In favor of their use are Stock and Watson (2003). The dose table coefficients[13] of Appendix, the "intra-regression" fixed effects, are given in the following equation:

$$\text{logGDPgpc}_{it} = 37.70864 - 1.51023\text{logGDP} - \text{initial.}_{it} + 0.006199\text{FDI}_{it} + 0.0025701\text{HC}_{it}$$
$$+ 0.0649064\text{GCFC}_{it} + 0.0286658\text{REM}_{it} - 0.0313851\,\text{G.C.C.Ex.G}_{it}$$

Hence the modification of the Wald test according to Fox and Weisberg (2011), for the heteroskedasticity group, is a good way for the Fixed Effects regression model. H0: sigma $(i)^2$ = sigma^2 for all (i); Chi2 (24) = 956.05.

Prob > Chi2 = 0.0000 (Presence of heteroskedasticity).

Zero is homoskedasticity (or constant variance).

---

[10] Note: For more details about the practical process in Condition 12, see references.
https://www.princeton.edu/ ~ otorres/Panel101.pdf.

[11] Note: testparmvitet; (1) years = 0; F(1, 179) = 0.03; Prob > F = 0.8708.

[12] The reader for a recent treatment should refer to the text Econometrics, e.g., Greene (2003), in which this paragraph is based.

[13] A heteroskedasticity test for the Fixed Effects Model is available via the command: xttest3. This is a user-written program to install and print: ssc install xttest3 (the results are given in Appendix).

We reject the null hypothesis as invalid and derive the heteroskedasticity result, Prob > CHI2 = 0.0000 < 0.05.

The use of robust regression methods complements all assumptions in a regression with panel inputs. We will use one of the robust regression approach approaches: regression with robust standard errors. As an alternative, we use the "robust" option for standard egabimus estimation using Huber-White sandwich-estimators sandwich-estimators according to Rohlfing et al. (2011: 1–10), are against heteroskedasticity, thus confirming the heteroskedasticity also known as Huber/White, (White 1980). Robust standard errors: Command-reg. xtreg. and the Robust, heteroskedastic option makes the robust standard error rating even in the linear model with the panel. There are not the same regressions as above, using the "robust" option.

So if we compare the robust FE results in regression 1, 2 and 3 in Table 7, there are differences in standard errors and t-tests (there are also variations in the coefficients) in this particular example, using robust standard errors changed the conclusions from the initial regression of Least Squares (LS). This suggests that the problems in essence were not small, meaning that there were individual differences assumed from data from the 24 countries in the study. Therefore, after this assessment the results are more convincing. The final results are calculated by Stata Software vc.12 (Table 7).

(d) *Testing for Correlation in the Series*

According to Baltagi et al. (2012: 1401–1406), the cross-correlation correlation applies to large long time series (over 20–30 years). Since corelacon is not a problem in small panels (with a few years), in our case we have only 11 years so we have no serial correlation that makes the standard error of the coefficients smaller, while R^2 is the most higher than they would actually be. Therefore, such a technique was not practiced in the panel data in our case.

5.1 The Final Results at the Rate of GDP per capita—Dependent

So after testing, the explanatory power is $R^2 = 41.6\%$, regression 4, Table 4 (Appendix) regression 1 to 4, Table 4, the explanatory power ranges from 39.8% to 41.6%, statistically are powerful. The results showed that 41.6% of the growth rate in GDP per capita can be explained by the values of the independent variables, while 58.4% of the growth rate of GDP per capita is explained by other factors that were not measured in the study. And the constant of 37.33% foresees the model as significant.

Completion of the growth equation with coefficients from Table 4:

$$\text{Log\_}\Delta\text{GDPgpc}_{it} = 37.33 - 1.496\text{log\_GDPfill.}_{it} + 0.0246\text{FDI}_{it} - 0.0213\text{HC}_{it} + 0.00407\text{FDI} * \text{HC}_{it}$$
$$+ 0.0896\text{Dom.Inv}_{it} - 0.00290\text{FDI} * \text{GCFC}_{it} + 0.0145\text{REM}_{it} - 0.0399\text{GCFGC}_{it} + e_{it}$$

(i) **InitialGDP is negative**—The variable GDP_initial is negative from p-values of the explanatory variables is clear that it is statistically important at the level 1% (i.e. p-value < 0.01) Table 4 (Appendix). Our result shows that developing countries tend to grow faster than developed countries, supported by a catching-up effect from 17 developing countries.

(ii) **Foreign Direct Investment (FDI)**, Following we measure the effect of FDI on economic growth shown in regressions 1 and 2 (Table 4), the coefficients are positive and statistically insignificant. So our findings showed that increasing effect of FDI is not found, noted that FDI does not meet domestic investment.

(iii) **Human Capital (HC)**, as a measure of human capital development, coefficients in regression 1 and 2, are statistically insignificant. Elasticity panel of the GDP growth rate per capita in regression 4, given the differences amongst countries on the panel, reveals a significantly negative sign with the coefficient –0.0213 (–0.2%) to human capital.

(iv) **Domestic Investments (Don.Inv.)**, next (Table 4, the result of the growth equation indicates that domestic investments[14] strong positive impact (significance level 1%) so growth of 1% of domestic investments stimulates economic growth to 9% (coefficient 0.0896 or 8.9%). We therefore have found that domestic investments are an important and considerable resource of the economic growth in European countries.

(v) **The term**-interaction between FDI and domestic investments (FDI * Dom.Inv),

How much have both types of investments contributed to economic growth?

The answer is that they have given negative and significant effects at 10% level i.e. increase of 10% of variables in cooperation lowers the economic growth for −0.002%. This is explained by the nature of FDI either; the period 2004–2014 is still characterized by privatization at the expense of Greenfield, similar to studies of Mencinger (2003).

(vi) **The term FDI in cooperation with human capital** (FDI * HC), the interaction term FDI * HC is positive and statistically significant at the level 10%. The growth of interactive variables for 10% has caused economic growth for 0.003%. FDI is attractive for the human capital in the country, specialization and training of human capital from FDI.

(vii) **Remittances as a percentage of GDP (REM)**, statistically they do not provide significant results at any level and in four regressions.

(viii) **The size of government** (General Expenses of Government Final Consumption %GDP) the coefficient of the size of government is presented with a negative sign −0.039 and statistically insignificant even after the powerful evaluation of standard errors (Table 4).

---

[14] Domestic investments (capital flow and technology flows) is proved that along with FDI is an endogenous variable and influenced by the economic environment. This was also explained by Durlauf et al. (2005), who states that the marginal effect of growth in domestic investment is associated with environmental effect of each country.

5.2   Solution of the Second Hypothesis Dependent FDI

In order to obtain final results for dependent FDI, we carry out the necessary tests:

(a)   Hausman test, Table 5 color blue in Annex A.

To place between the model fixed effects and random effects model we have used a Hausman test. The question is whether the unique (u!) Random effects are related to independent variables (regressors) in our regression.

Hipothesis zero = says, u! the random effects are not related to the regressor, and the RE model is preferable.

Alternative hypothesis = says, u! is associated with regressors in the model of fixed effects and is the most advanced evaluation technique.

The following hypothesis should be tested: H0: a = 0 and H1: a $\neq$ 0.

The result of the Hausman test is shown in Table 20 (in the table appendix c) and it is obvious that the alternative hypothesis is dropped to the 1% level. The Hausman Test[15] has identified who is the most accurate evaluator.

Table 5 shows that the Hausman test (1978) confirms the choice of use RE instead of FE because its p-value is greater than 0.05. Try 0.156 > 0.05 suggests that the Case Effect method should be used, so we use the method of Effective Cases, as foreseen by Clark and Linzer (2015: 2).

Statistics, Hausman and Taylor (1981: 1377), have asymptotic distribution as Hi-square with k-degrees of freedom under zero hypothesis, random effects method (RE) is more accurate. After performing the necessary tests we have followed this logic of interpretation. According to the statistics in our model, all tests—F, are less than 0.5% (<0.05). This is a test (F) to see if all the coefficients in the model are different from zero.

In all of our estimates, we have results consistent with the F-tests suggested that the coefficients are different from zero and are important to explain the growth rate of FDI as a dependent variable. Statistics also suggest that R-squares vary between 0.149 and 0.396, suggesting the high explanatory power of our two models.

This explains that more than 39% of dependent variance varies depending on independent variable variance in the RE model, while in FE it is 14.9%. We now go back to the discussion of the results separately for each of the methods used (FE/RE) in providing final conclusions for each hypothesis raised, answering research questions.

Test setting for RE versus FE (Table 6) Appendix. Random Effect Selection versus Fix Efect and result.

Similarities and differences in both models (RE/FE)

Results in coefficients can be ascertained that there are similarities and differences in two patterns of regression. Accepting that a constant (intercept coefficient) is much greater in the fixed effects model (1.233), but is not statistically significant, compared to

---

[15] For more details on how to use the Hausman test, reference.
http://www.stata.com/manuals13/rhausman.pdf.

92   N. Kida

the RE constant (−1.222), which is statistically significant even though it is negative, a confirmation that the RE model should be accepted.

As stated in the theoretical part, in the model of the fixed effects is possible the individual heterogeneity that was captured by the constant in Table 5, through the powerful versatility of standard errors. In the random effects method, the standard error estimation was not applied, and the alleged differences between 24 countries were treated as random because both the data were taken as random and therefore the results are considered more convincing in the RE.

In terms of variables, the differences in coefficients in the two models are large, only in domestic investment variables and government spending the change is smaller and that, in the RE model there is a positive and important coefficient, whereas in the FE model are negative and irrelevant except remittances, so the authentication of the second hypothesis is done through the results of the RE model. The RE model shows an increase in GDP per capita and (p = 0.027) is statistically significant at 1%, and it is concluded that FDI growth depends on GDP growth per capita, an increase of 1% of GDP growth per capita causes an increase of FDI of 2.7%.

Another difference is that the R-square is much higher in the RE model (39.6%) compared to FE (14.9%), meaning that the 39.65 of FDI growth depends on the explanatory variables used in the model, while the rest from other unknown variables. Regression of the second equation—the net inflow of FDI expressed as a percentage of GDP, determined as a dependent variable. Correlation is zero that does not indicate a strong or weak correlation between variables (r or corr (u_i, X) = 0). Prob 0.156 > 0.05 suggests that the Case Effect Method should be used.

The regression equation (in our case the logarithmic model), showed statistically significant Wald chi2 (5, 203) = 36.49, and p = 0.000, with the measure of explanatory power R-sq: within R^2 = 12.1%; R-sq between: 39.6%; R-sq Overall: 20.1% (regression 1 to 3, the explanatory power ranges from 12.1 to 39.6% (Table 7, Appendix).

The results showed that 39.6% of the growth rate in net FDI inflows can be explained by the values of independent variables, while 60.4% of their level is explained by other factors that have not been studied.

At present, the rate of GDP growth per capita in these countries plays an important role in boosting FDI growth. Overall performance, the model is pleasing, can be seen in the statistics of the model given below. The purpose of this hypothesis is to assume the determinants of FDI in some European countries. FDI determinants in our study have been found to be GDP per capita growth, domestic investment, remittances and government spending.

FDI equation, Random Effects model, Table 7 Appendix[16]:

$$\text{Log\_IHD/GDP} = -1.122 + 0.28\text{GDPgpc\_log} - 0.010\text{HC} - 0.024\text{HC\_1lag} + 0.021\text{HC\_1 lag}$$
$$+ \text{Dom.Inv}0.055 + \text{REM}.0.034 + \text{GCFGC}.0.052 + u_{it}$$

---

[16] $u_i = \alpha_i + \varepsilon_{it}$, with α_i start the random variables (being random variables—i.i.d. random-effects) and Cov(x_{it}, α_i) = 0 (vector x_{it} corresponds with independent variables which have taken place in our evaluation).

(i)   GDP growth per capita (GDPgpc), is a determinant of FDI in a significance level of 1* which means that with an increase of 1% of economic growth we have increase FDI of 2.8%.

(ii) Domestic Investment (Dom.Inv./GDP) are considered important factors in the growth of FDI in significance level of 1*, and therefore with an increase of 1% of domestic investments we have increase of FDI from 5.5%. So, domestic investments have positive effects on FDI.

(iii) Remittances (REM), appeared to be a determinant of FDI at a level of 5%, and therefore the growth 5% of remittances we have an economic growth of 3.4% FDI.

(iv) Government spending (GCFGC), are found to be important determinants of FDI in a significance level of 10%, with growth of only 1% of them, we have increase of FDI from 5.2%.

(v)   Human capital (HC) is not considered significant in either equation. Such results complete the required minimal threshold as total (14.3%) but this threshold in analytics is completed only by 7 developed countries in the sample, while the quality of education in 17 developing countries (10–12%) does not damage our ultimate outcomes very much.

5.3 Unilateral Effect of FDI and Economic Growth

In Table 8, (Appendix) the coefficients evaluated by the Wald zero test to see the effect of two variables according to the above equation and the Hausman test for the two variables as follows. In the FDI equation, Wald test refuses the zero hypothesis, but it does not have any importance.

To find the relationship between FDI and the GDP growth rate per capita we use Wald test (Abraham 1943: 11–58), Hausman test (1978)[17] and parmwise test of Granger (1988) of the causal relation. The test shows that FDI has positive irrelevant correlation to GDP growth per capita. While on the other hand the evidences prove that the growth rate of GDP per capita has strong positive links with FDI (significance level 1%). An increase to 1% in growth of GDP per capita will increase the level of FDI to around 9% (0.0867). In the Table 9, there is a positive relationship between GDP per capita and FDI. Therefore we conclude that the relationship between two variables is unilateral, economic growth has a positive effect on inflows of FDI in European countries, while FDI statistically has insignificant effects on economic growth, although it is positive.

6 Conclusion and Recommendations

First we present the results on confirmation of the first hypothesis:

---

[17] J. A. Hausman (1978). Specification Tests in Econometrics. pp. 1251–1271.
http://econweb.tamu.edu/keli/Hausman%201978.pdf.

The rate of GDP growth per capita dependent—In regression 1 of Table 4, the correlation between initial GDP and economic growth is negative and statistically significant at level of 1%. In accordance with expectations, the coefficient of the initial real GDP represents a negative signal, indicating that the convergence hypothesis is confirmed.

The coefficient of FDI is not statistically significant. FDI contains estimates "random effect" which means that FDI has not been rated for a longer period of time. This result should not be surprising because all the countries in the sample had received insignificant amount of FDI between 2004 and 2014.

The variable that represents the human capital (HC) is negatively correlated with the growth, opposing the theoretical findings (i.e., it has negative effects and statistically insignificant). The threshold level meter of knowledge on human capital (secondary education) is still negative and statistically insignificant.

In regressions 3 and 4, there have been added the interactive variables which have a positive effect, i.e. the change from interaction (FDI * HC) is positive and statistically significant at the 10% level. So a 10% increase in FDI and human capital affects the economic growth to 0.04% (Table 4).

Domestic investments are positively associated with economic growth and are statistically significant at 1% level. This means that a 1% increase of the domestic investments causes economic growth of 8.9%. So the economic base of these countries relies on domestic investments.

Meanwhile, when the domestic investments interact with FDI, the result is unexpected, significant at level of 10% and with a negative coefficient. So, the cumulative, "crowding-out" effect appears, and benefit levels are repatriated. This way, FDI has cumulative effects of domestic investments and not complementary ones.

We have a positive effect but statistically insignificant from increasing remittances, which means that expectations for an economic growth in the longer term will not be realized. While government spending has a negative coefficient and increasing statistically insignificant, which means despite the government activity, growth is not positive.

The final results for the second hypothesis—Foreign Direct Investment—Dependent.

The results (Table 7), showed that 39.6% of the growth rate in the net inflows of FDI can be explained through the values of the independent variables, while 60.4% of their level is explained through other factors.

We can find the positive effect and statistically significant growth of GDP per capita in the growth of FDI. It means that GDP per capita is an important determinant of FDI. To coefficients of growth per capita and statistically significant at 1% level. This means that 1% of the GDP growth per capita brings FDI growth of 2.8%, so FDI is dependent on economic growth.

Domestic investment is important for FDI at the level of 1% and with a positive coefficient, this way an increase of only 1% of domestic investment causes increase in FDI for 5.5%.

Remittances create positive effects in attracting FDI either because all of the coefficients in regressions 1 to 3 are positive in the level of significance for 5%, which means that a 5% increase in remittances will boost FDI to 3.4%.

The size of government has positive coefficients of 0.052% a level of importance from 1%, which means that a 1% increase in government spending leads to increase of FDI for 5.2%. In fact, a part of government spending in these countries has been used to build the infrastructure and institutions in order to attract foreign investment.

As a summary we can say that the empirical analysis of this study finds that the rate of growth of GDP per capita (the economic growth) consistently proves to be an important explanatory of FDI inflows in European countries at the level of significance of 1%.

As it is seen, there is a decreasing trend of enrollment at the secondary level of education, a great inclusion of them in education in the social sciences, an average threshold of 14% for 24 countries, while separately this level does not exceed 10% for the majority of the developing countries (especially countries of the Western Europe).

Although we find a trivial effect of FDI growing, we can say that FDI is seen as a package consisting of shares of capital and technology, as an addition to knowledge through employee training, acquisition of skills and their distribution, the introduction of new managerial and organizational practices, which together improve the quality of general investment and create the conditions for long run growth in the host countries.

Recommendations and implications of the study

- The results suggest that the absorption capacity factors of the host country are crucial for determining the economic growth. The study suggests a supportive policy in improving FDI, important investments and a higher quality of human capital. While, remittances should not be considered as an important determinant of growth in the long term even though their value is significant now.

- Policymakers should pursue the policies to attract FDI which generate overall benefits to the economy; the best way is through diversification of FDI in the sectors where the expectations are greater.

- Increasing the quality of secondary education and vocational orientation also comes as a priority.

- The paper focuses only on the positive effects of FDI on economic growth; it would be of great interest that the future studies analyze negative effects of FDI, too. The important thing is that there is no misunderstanding, though the panel defect is that the number of observations is reduced due to the major distinguishing features amongst the countries (numerous assumptions amongst individual countries).

This is one of the suggestions to be taken into account in the future studies. Regardless the obstacles that may have occurred, the study remains too important for the field of FDI.

Appendix

See Tables 1, 2, 3, 4, 5, 6, 7, 8, 9 and 10.

Table 1. Descriptive statistics of panel data (24 countries) for 2004–2014

Variable	Observations	Mean	Stand. dev.	Minimum	Maximum
log_ΔGDPgro. pc ~ a (ŷ)	210	1.006541	0.902363	−3.18799	2.51886
LogGDPinitial	264	25.24811	1.841369	21.25839	28.95328
FDI	264	6.380687	9.898636	−16.15452	88.09634
HC	264	14.45674	4.971523	7.54	26.75
FDI * HC	264	88.67297	118.342	−178.5074	999.0125
Dom.Inv. ~ f	264	23.02217	3.914311	14.55275	38.2489
FDI * Dom. Inv.	264	151.0936	228.0288	−369.1633	1904.64
REM ~ m	264	4.948647	7.092913	0.1208355	33.7
G.E.F.C.G ~ o	264	18.68272	4.217964	6.205039	29.9406

Source Data from World Development Indicators (WDI), calculated by the author

Table 2. FE Selection versus RE

(Depreciation rate depreciation GDPpc growth rate) Independent variables coefficients standard errors	Table (a) FE	Table (b) RE
logGDP_initial.$_{it}$	−1.624*** (0.208)	−0.395*** (0.082)
logGDP_initial_1$_{it}$	5.85l (4.54)	3.20 (1.89)
FDI$_{it}$	0.006 (0.005)	0.001 (0.005)
FDI * HC	0.004* (0.002)	Missing
HC$_{it}$	0.002 (0.030)	−0.058*** (0.019)
Dom.Inve$_{it}$	0.063 (0.014)	0.057 (0.015)
FDI * Dom.Invest.	−0.002* (0.001)	Missing
REM$_{it}$ Remittances	0.025 (0.021)	0.005 (0.013)
G.E.F.C.G$_{it}$ General Expenditures of Final Consumption Governments	−0.041 (0.034)	0.002*** (0.021)
Constant	40.603*** (5.34)	10.275*** (2.311)
R-squares	403	230
Correlation	−975	0

Note (In brackets are standard errors); RE: p > | z |] and [FE: p > | t |]; Significant levels: ***
1%, ** 5%, * 10%; Calculation by the author
Source World Development Indicators

Table 3. Evaluation of Hausman test on panel model for 24 seats, table c

	Coefficient (b) Fixed	Coefficient (B) Random	(b − B) Difference	Sqrt (diag (V_b − V_B)) S.E
LogGDPfill	−1.51023	−0.3906873	−1.119542	0.1727806
FDI/GDP	0.006199	0.00911549	−0.0029559	–
HC/Pop	0.0025701	−0.577948	0.0603649	0.0243275
Dom.inves/GDP ~ f	0.0649064	0.0577269	0.0071795	–

Note b = consistent under Ho and Ha; obtained from xtreg; B = inconsistent under Ha, coefficient under Ho; obtained from xtreg; Test: Ho: difference in coefficients not systematic, chi2(4) = (b − B)′[(V_b − V_B) ^ (−1)] (b − B) = 31.30, Prob > chi2 = 0.0000; (V_b − V_B is not positive definite)

Table 4. Evaluation results on the basis of fixed effects (FE): The rate of GDP growth per capita —dependent, FDI—independent along with other explanatory variables, panel over a decade (2004–2014), calculated by the author

Regression number	(1)	(2)	(3)	(4)
Independent variables	FE coefficient (Standard error)	FE robust	FE robust 2	FE robust 3
LogInitialGDP	−1.510***	−1.510***	−1.491***	−1.496***
	(0.189)	(0.179)	(0.174)	
				(0.174)
FDI	0.00620	0.00620	−0.0393	0.0246
	(0.00542)	(0.00798)	(0.0283)	(0.0405)
HC	0.00257	0.00257	−0.0198	−0.0213
	(0.0307)	(0.0235)	(0.0240)	(0.0239)
FDI_HC			0.00394*	0.00407*
			(0.00217)	(0.00223)
Dom.Inv % GDP (Dom.Inv.)	0.0649***	0.0649***	0.0608***	0.0896***
	(0.0149)	(0.0167)	(0.0156)	(0.0282)
FDI_Dom.Invest				−0.00290*
				(0.00163)
Remittances % GDP (REM)	0.0287	0.0287	0.0191	0.0145
	(0.0215)	(0.0174)	(0.0190)	(0.0197)
General Expenses of Government Final Consumption (GEGFC/GDP)	−0.0314	−0.0314	−0.0323	−0.0399
	(0.0341)	(0.0243)	(0.0239)	(0.0259)
Constant	37.71***	37.71***	37.64***	37.33***
	(4.861)	(4.670)	(4.619)	(4.462)
Observations	210	210	210	210
R-squared	0.398	0.398	0.406	0.416
Number of countries	24	24	24	24
R^2 Within	404			
R^2 Between	432			
R^2 Overall	192			
No. of countries below the threshold (start, end) = (24) 2004–2014	HC Threshold ≈ 14.3%			

Note (i) *, **, *** show level of significance* $p < 0.1$ (10%), $p < 0.05$ (5%), and $p < 0.01$ (1%). (ii) Dependent variable real growth of GDP per capita. (iii) Robust standard errors were used and reported in parentheses below each coefficient of estimation. (iv) Absorptive capacity of the country, threshold of education level (HC threshold ≈ 14.5%) for 24 countries

Table 5. Evaluation of the Hausman test table h, Appendix, in the panel model

	Coefficient (b) Fixed	Coefficient (B) Random	(b-B) Diference	Sqrt (diag (V_b-V_B)) S.E
Log_ΔGDPGPC~e	0.2676096	0.2798688	− 0.0122592	0.032659
HC	− 0.1070223	− 0.0203723	− 0.08665	0.0364594
Dom.Inv.~f	0.0430892	0.0545818	− 0.0114926	0.0081922
REM~m	− 0.0078233	0.0363206	− 0.0441439	0.0269042
G.E.F.C.G~ë	0.0257276	0.0448618	− 0.0191343	0.0403195

Calculated by the author. b = consistent under Ho and Ha; obtained from xtreg; B = inconsistent under Ha, efficient under Ho; obtained from xtreg; Test: Ho: difference in coefficients not systematic; chi2(5) = (b − B)′[(V_b − V_B) ^ (−1)](b − B) = 8.00; Prob > chi2 = 0.1560

Table 6. RE Selection versus FE (Tables, Appendix), result

Variables coefficients stand. errors p-value	FE	RE
$\log\_\Delta\hat{y}_{it}$	−0.267 (0.092)	0.027*** (0.086)
HC_{it}	−0.107 (0.042)	−0.02** (0.022)
Dom.Inves.$_{it}$	0.043*** (0.022)	0.054*** (0.020)
REM_{it}	−0.01*** (0.031)	0.036*** (0.015)
$G.E.F.C.G_{it}$	0.025*** (0.048)	0.044*** (0.026)
Constant	1.233 (1.233)	−1.222 (0.836)
R-squares	149	396
Corr.	−975	0

In brackets are standard errors; [RE: p > | z |] and [FE: p > | t |]; Significant levels: *** 1%, ** 5%, * 10%; Calculated by the author

The sample of the countries included in the study

See Table 11.

Definition of data

Empirical literature provides different opinions on the influence of independent variables (growth determinants) on economic growth. In our study, the determinants of growth are simultaneously determinants of FDI.

Table 7. FDI and economic growth (The result through the Random Effects method)

Regression number		(1)	(2)	(3)
Independent variable	Coefficient (Standard errors)	Random 1	RE 2	RE 3
log_GDPgrowthcapita		0.280***	0.281***	0.286***
		(0.0860)	(0.0860)	(0.0867)
HC		−0.0204	−0.00936	−0.0104
		(0.0221)	(0.0310)	(0.0314)
lag1_HC			−0.0103	−0.0240
			(0.0283)	(0.0341)
lag2_HC				0.0212
				(0.0284)
GCFC/GDP		0.0546***	0.0542***	0.0553***
		(0.0207)	(0.0209)	(0.0210)
Remittances/GDP		0.0363**	0.0366**	0.0343**
		(0.0157)	(0.0160)	(0.0164)
(General Expenses of Government Final Consumption %GDP)		0.0449*	0.0514*	0.0520*
		(0.0267)	(0.0274)	(0.0282)
Constant		−0.881	−0.998	−1.122
		(0.836)	(0.865)	(0.887)
R-Squares (within, Between, Overall)		121	396	215
Observations		203	202	201
Number of countries		24	24	24
No. of countries below the threshold (start, end) = (24) 2004–2014		HC threshold ≈ 14.3%		

Note The dependent variable is GDP growth rate per capita. Evaluation is done by GLS. (Standard errors are in parenthesis). *** $p < 0.01$, ** $p < 0.05$, * $p < 0.1$; (1%, 5%, 10%). Calculated by the author

Table 8. Evaluation of the Hausman test (1978) for FE and RE

Test cross-section Fix effects			
Test summary	Chi-Sq. Statistic	Chi-Sq. d.f.	Prob.
Cross-section Fixes	31.30	4	0.0000
Test cross-section random effects			
Test summary	Chi-Sq. Statistic	Chi-Sq. d.f.	Prob.
Cross-section random	8.00	5	0.156

Note Hausman test-calculated with STATA, vs. 12 (from the author)

Table 9. Testi Parwise i Granger Causality (Granger 1988)

Koeficientet e vlersuar - Variabla të Varuara (x-y)	
ΔGDPGpc(lag)	FDI(lag)
ΔGDPGpcit (0.0867)	0.286***
FDI$_{it}$ (0.0405)	0.0246
Granger Causality parwise Test	
Wald Causality Test	
Null Hypothesis: GDP causes FDI FDI does not cause GDPGCP	

Note In parentheses is the standard deviation *** Significant at level 1%. Calculated by the author

Table 10. Regression variables

Variables	Definition	Argument, importance
Annual GDP growth rate per capita (GDPGPC)	Annual GDP growth per capita in percentage. GDP per capita is the gross domestic product in relation to the population	
FDI$_{it}$-in relation to GDP	lag^aFDI^b: Foreign Direct Investment, net inflows (% of GDP).. FDI/GDP*100	**Positive** (Borensztein et al. 1998; Ram and Zhang 2002); Negative (Alfaro 2003)
Initial GDP (T_1) with a year time lag	GDP (current in US $)	**Negative** (Barro 2013; Mankiw et al. 1992)
Log_Initial GDP (Y_0)—logarithm of initial GDP	GDP (current in US $). For the indicator; 0 log of y is considered the natural logarithm of GDP per capita (2003) of the country (i), as the initial level of our analysis. The study includes 24 countries; $i \epsilon$ [1;24]. STATA_12 is represented by $logY_0$	
HC-human capital in relation to the population without time lag	(lagHC): The gross registration ratio in secondary schools is used as a representative of human capital development in the host country in relation to the population (used with lag)	**Positive** (Borenztein 1998)
HC_1 human capital with one year lag	(lagHC): Secondary education with one year lag, registration in the high secondary education^c/population	
HC_2 human capital with two year lag	Registration in the high secondary level of education with two years lag/Population (secondary education, students)	
FDI_HC	(lagFDI * HC): FDI in interaction with human capital. The conditions of FDI interaction with the factors of absorption capacity of the host country multiply FDI	
FDI_DOM.INV.	Direct Foreign Investments as a percentage of GDP in interaction with Domestic Investment (as a percentage of GDP). FDI * FDI_DOM.INV	
DOM.INV	Domestic investment (% of GDP)	**Positive** (Barro 2013)
Remittances	Personal remittances, taken (% of GDP)	

(continued)

Table 10. (*continued*)

Variables	Definition	Argument, importance
EGFC	Total Expenditure of Government Final Consumption (% of GDP): This variable is used to capture the impact of the government's size on the economic growth of the host country as suggested in the literature	**Positive** (Ram 1986)

[a]The time factor (lag) is used to measure the effect in the initial period due to unfavorable conditions in the host country (inherited from the planned economy, political conflicts or wars, and delayed effects) where is suggested a return back (lag) of one or two years after the entry of a foreign firm (this study, for 2003 measures the effect in 2004 (lag_1 and Lag_2) and in 2005). Failure to apply the time factor often argues the negative effects of FDI. For example, Stancik (2007)

[b]Net FDI flows as a percentage of GDP are used as a measure for the investments of Multinational Companies (and foreign firms) in the host country (UNCTAD 1999). Asia Pacific J. Manage (2008) 25:573–593. https://doi.org/10.1007/s10490-007-9074-z. http://papers.ssrn.com/sol3/papers.cfm?abstract_id= 1490986

[c]According to Aleksynska et al. (2003), the level of high (tertiary) education of human capital in a host country is expected to make FDI more effective in stimulating economic growth

1. *Economic growth*—represented by real annual GDP growth per capita (GDPgpc).

2. *Gross Domestic Product (GDP$_{it}$) at the beginning of 2003 (Y$_0$)*: Log_InitialGDP (Y$_0$) or the natural logarithm of real GDP (logY$_0$) at the beginning of each period, so that it is equal to the initial year of one and two year intervals. For the Initial_GDP per capita, the scale of 2003 is chosen, i.e. the year before the start of the sample. GDP is taken at purchase prices, or the amount of the added value of all resident producers in an economy, plus product taxes and minus subsidies. So, the initial GDP variable (Y$_0$) in the study is expected to reach the catching-up effect (N/N*).[18]

3. *Foreign Direct Investment (FDI as % of GDP)* are used as a standard in literature (Asiedu 2002; Choi 2009), in the model is conceptually analogous to parts of goods produced by foreign firms, (n * /N).[19] The FDI net inflow was used for measurement of FDI. It includes the amount of capital, reinvestment of profits, long-term capital and short-term capital as shown in the balance of payments.

4. *FDI in interaction with human capital (FDI/GDP$_{it}$ * HC/Population$_{it}$)*: FDI in interaction with the variable of absorption capacity (HC) of the host country, i.e. gross registration in the secondary education as a percentage of the country's population, expresses the term of interaction or the indirect impact of FDI on economic growth. This will also determine the level of education threshold.

5. *Domestic Investment (DOM.INV./GDP$_{it}$)*: Is represented by formation of the fixed gross capital minus FDI. GCFCs are expenditures or additions to fixed assets of the economy minus net changes in the inventory level.

---

[18]There are empirical evidence from the studies of Barro (2013) and Mankiw et al. (1992). This was also applied by Carkovic and Levine (2002) but in a five year period.

[19]We assume that the ratio of Foreign Direct Investment to GDP, which, for over a decade, has been an independent variable, is a good representation for (n * / N). FDI is available in this study only from 2004–2013.

Table 11. The sample of the countries included in the study (developed countries, developing countries, transition countries)

European countries (24)		
Developed Countries	Developing countries	Countries in transition
SWE	CVN	KVS
NLD	BGR	ALB
AUT	ROM	FYROM
DEU	HUN	MNE
CHE	POL	HVR
NOR	PRT	BIH
ITA	CZK	SRB
	SVK	
	LTU	
	EST	
7	10	7

Source World Bank (World Development Indicators 2015). By the author

6. *Variables in interaction with each other: [(FDI/GDP$_{it}$) × (DOM.INV./GDP$_{it}$)]*, in our case, is an interaction variable between FDI and domestic investment.

7. *Secondary level of education (lag_HC/pop$_{it}$)*: The gross registration rate is the total census report, regardless of age, of the age group that officially corresponds to the level of education (secondary education—the high secondary school level) in relation to the population of the country.

8. *Remittances (REM/GDP$_{it}$)*: are remittances to their homes by emigrants working abroad (through formal channels).

9. *Total expenditure of government final consumption (Exp.Gov.Fin.Conc../GDP$_{it}$)*: The government expenditure ratio to GDP is taken by WDI as a measure of government involvement in the economy. The general government consumption includes all current government expenditure on purchase of goods and services (including employee compensation and government transfers). It also includes most of the expenses for national defense and security, but excludes government military expenses that is part of government capital formation.

The description of command (xtreg[20]), in Stata vs. 12,[21] to the use of methods (FE/RE).

---

[20] (http://www.stata.com/manuals13/xtxtreg.pdf#xtxtreg).

[21] To Stock and Watson (2008), STATA version 12 uses, NT - N - K - M degrees of freedom to the tests in small samples. Cluster-robust Huber/White standard errors are reported by the option Vce: xtreg ln_GDPgrow.p.c ttl_exp ttl_exp2, fe Vce (idcode grup). STATA reports T- small samples and F-tests with N − 1 degrees of freedom. Moreover, STATA multiplies cluster-robust covariance by N/(N − 1) to correct for degrees of freedom in small samples. Stock and Watson (2008), Heteroskedasticity-Robust Standard Errors for Fixed Effects Panel Data Regression, Econometrica, 76(1), 155–174. [advanced]

The <u>xtreg</u> command is suitable to the regressions into models with panel data. In particular, <u>xtreg</u> is more suitable to assess the regression of the random effect model (RE), using the estimator (GLS estimator), the results given by the matrix-weighted average of the between and within. The selection of the model (RE) requires that the evaluation is done with the GLS method by specifying the small samples with the Swamy-Arora evaluation and by evaluating the variance component at the individual level as a choice for evaluation.[22] The vce type of assessment (Robust) reports the type of standard error that derives from the conventional theory (asymptotic) and is a powerful evaluation when, within the group, there is a correlation (cluster) due to the lack of specificities, therefore the supportive methodology or the Jackknife method has been used.[23] Even FE requires regression to be evaluated with fixed-effects (within) and the GLS method. These two methods (fe, re) are considered more appropriate[24] for evaluating the panel data through Stata, in our case STATA vs. 12.

The Wald test: <u>xttest3</u>

Modified Wald test for heteroskedasticity GroupWise in the FE regression model

$$H0 : sigma(i)^{\wedge}2 = sigma^{\wedge}2 \text{ for all } i$$
$$chi2(24) = \quad 956.05'; \quad Prob > chi2 = \quad 0.0000$$

Testing for the correlation in the series:

The series correlation tests are applied in macro panels in long time series (over 20–30 years). It is not a problem in micro panels (just a few years). In our case we have only 11 years, so there is no serial correlation. The serial correlation causes the standard error of the coefficients to be smaller, while R^2 are currently higher.

FE model is used in the data panel for GDPgpc growth rate, dependent:

The Hausman test, Table 18, suggests if: Prob ch2 = 0.0000, smaller than 0.05 (<0.05), is considered important and suggests the Fixed Effects methods to be used. Therefore, in Table 19 (Chapter Four), the Fixed Effects (FE) method is used.

The Random Effects model is used in the data panel for FDI—dependent:

The Hausman test, Table 20, suggests if: Prob 0.156 > 0.05, bigger than 0.05 (>0.05), is considered important and suggests the Random Effects methods to be used. Therefore, in Table 22, our Case Study has used the Random Effects method (RE).

---

[22] See the additional attachment: xtreg, random effects (re), methods and formulas in more detail.

[23] Vce specification (Robust) chooses to use GLS.

[24] See Baltagi (2013, Chap. 2), reference: Baltagi, B.H., and L. Liu, Alternative Ways of Obtaining Hausman's Test Using Artificial Regressions, Statistics and Probability Letters, 77, 2007, 1413–1417; and Allison (2009), offers many examples that in the estimates are used fixed effects versus random effects.

Table 12. cor. Log_GDPpc., FDI, HC, FDI * HC, Dom.Inve., FDI * Dom. Inves., Remittances (obs = 210)

log_GDPgro~ë, logGDP~l, IHD, HC, IHD_HC, GCFC~f IHD_GCFC remita~m								
log_GDPgro~ë	1.0000							
logGDP_initial	−0.4141	1.0000						
FDI	0.1602	−0.1198	1.0000					
HC	−0.0182	−0.4776	−0.0586	1.0000				
FDI_HC	0.1962	−0.2552	0.9578	0.1771	1.0000			
Dom..Inv~f	0.3390	−0.2953	0.1318	−0.0382	0.1430	1.0000		
FDI_Dom.Inv.	0.2062	−0.1643	0.9801	−0.0640	0.9425	0.2815	1.0000	
Remitances~m	0.1709	−0.4186	0.1645	0.1809	0.2194	0.0782	0.1771	1.0000

Table 13. corlog_GDPgpc, logGDP_initial, FDI, HC, FDI * HC, Dom.Invest., FDI * Dom.Invest, Remitances (obs = 210)

log_GDPgrow ~ e, logGDP ~ l, FDI, HC, FDI_HC, Dom.Inv ~ f, FDI * Domestic Investment, REM ~ m

	log_GDPgrow ~ e	logGDP_initial	FDI	HC	FDI * HC	Dom.Inves ~ f	FDI * Dom.Invest.	Remitances ~ m
log_GDPgrow ~ e	1.0000							
logGDP_initial	−0.4141*	1.0000						
	0.0000							
FDI	0.1602	−0.1168	1.0000					
	0.0202	0.0581						
HC	−0.0182	−0.4731*	−0.0728	1.0000				
	0.7930	0.0000	0.2382					
FDI * HC	0.1962	−0.2490*	0.9618*	0.1464	1.0000			
	0.0043	0.0000	0.0000	0.0173				
Dom.Inves ~ f	0.3390*	−0.3168*	0.1087	−0.0506	0.1229	1.0000		
	0.0000	0.0000	0.0779	0.4126	0.0460			
FDI * Dom.Invest.	0.2062	−0.1704	0.9785*	−0.0763	0.9478*	0.2580*	1.0000	
	0.0027	0.0055	0.0000	0.2168	0.0000	0.0000		
Remitances ~ m	0.1709	−0.4259*	0.1361	0.1774	0.1903	0.1184	0.1572	1.0000
	0.0131	0.0000	0.0271	0.0038	0.0019	0.0546	0.0105	

Results after the final certification of the tests are presented in chapter IV, Tables 16, descriptive statistics, Table 19 FE method, and Table 22 RE method.

Correlation Matrices

See Tables 12 and 13.

Chart representation of variables used in a 24 country—panel (graphical-scatter plot, Stata. vs. 12). Source: WDI, 2015, Graphic 1–14, by the author.

See Charts 1, 2, 3, 4, 5 and 6 and Graph 7.

Interaktion between variables (Y-X):

See Charts 8 and 9 and Graph 10.

Interaction between log, _GDPpc log and initial log_GDP (negative)

See Graph 11.

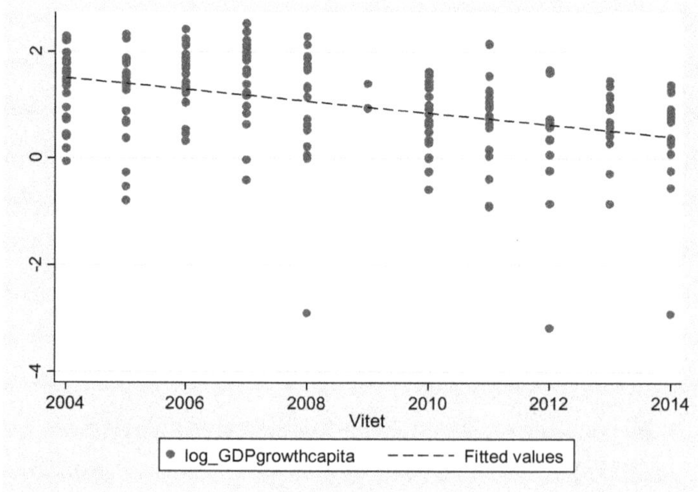

Chart 1. Growth rate of GDP per capita in 24 European countries in 2004–2014

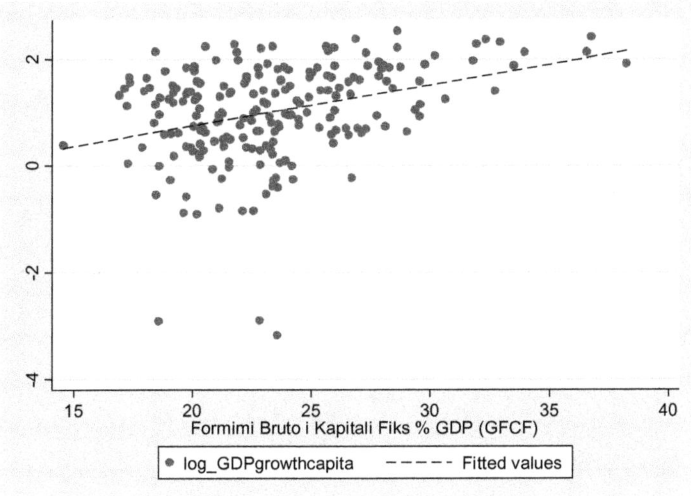

Chart 2. LoG_GDPgpc/domestic investments/GDP

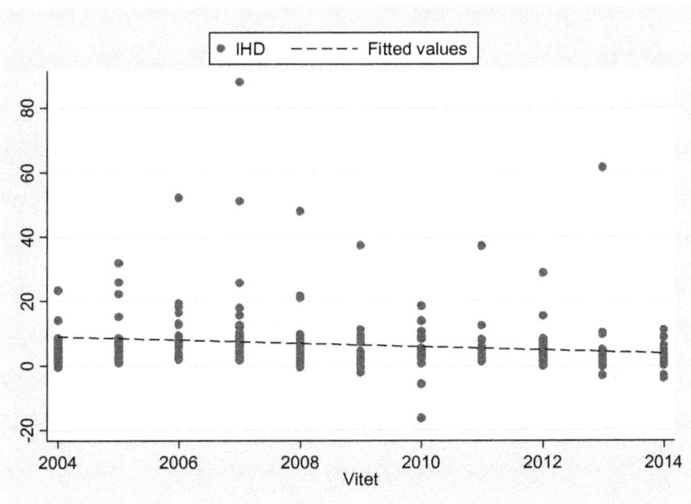

Chart 3. FDI/GDP in US $ (2004–2014)

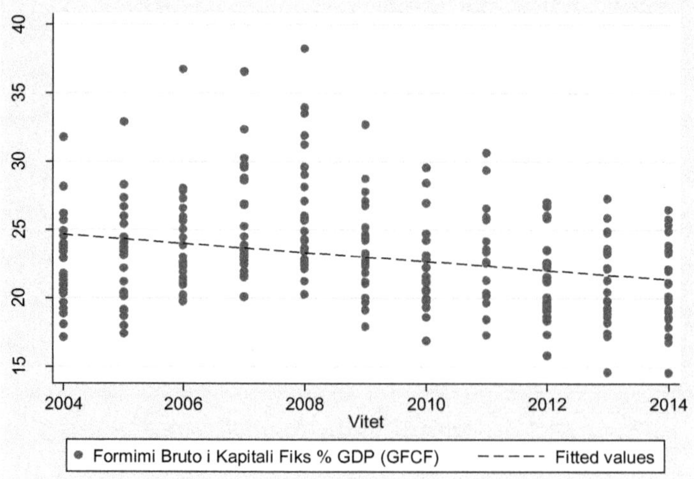

Chart 4. Domestic investments/GDP

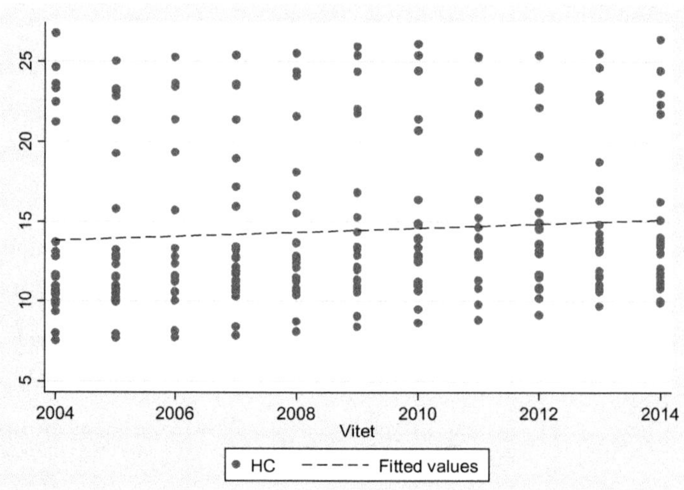

Chart 5. Human capital/population

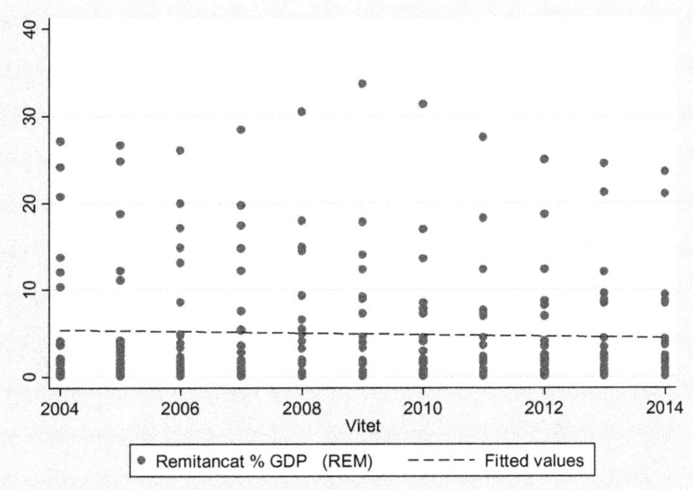

Chart 6. Remittances/GDP

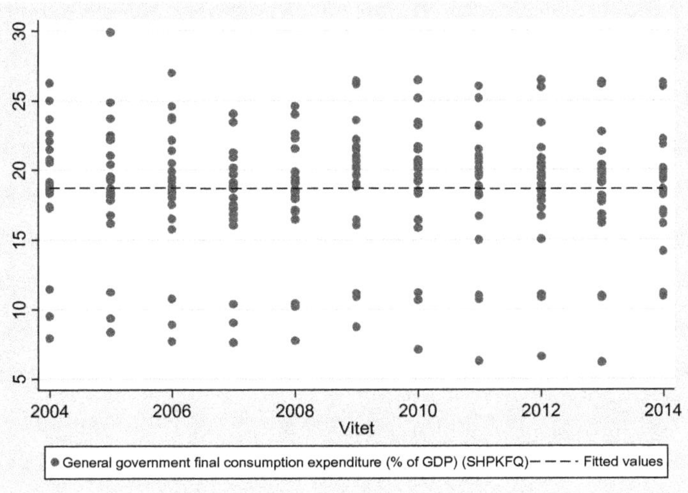

Graph 7. General government consumption final expenditures/GDP

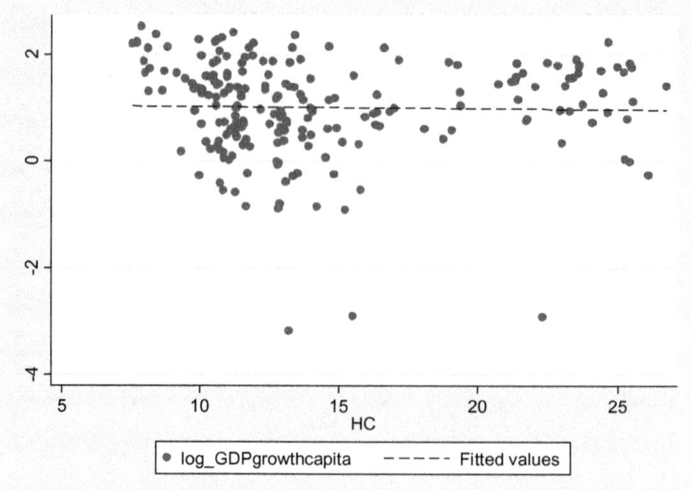

Chart 8. GDP growth rate per capita and human capital

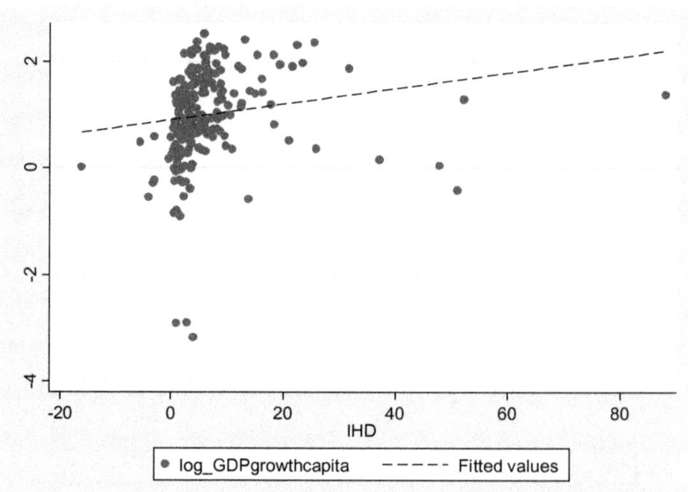

Chart 9. FDI/GDP (dependent) and Log_GDPGpc (independent)

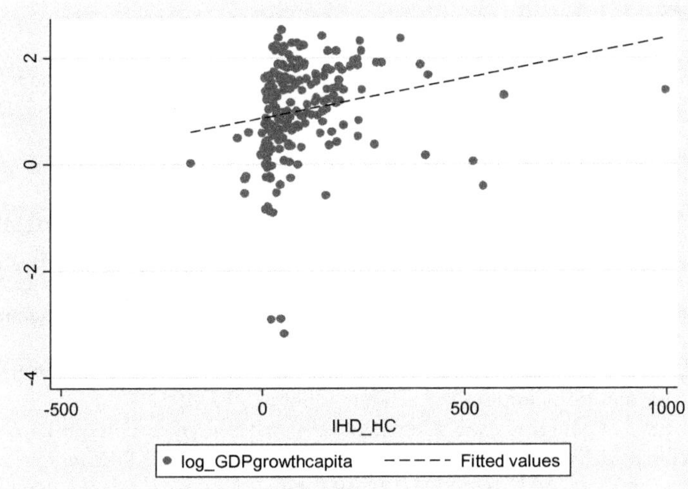

Graph 10. Log_GDP pc and FDI in interaction with HC

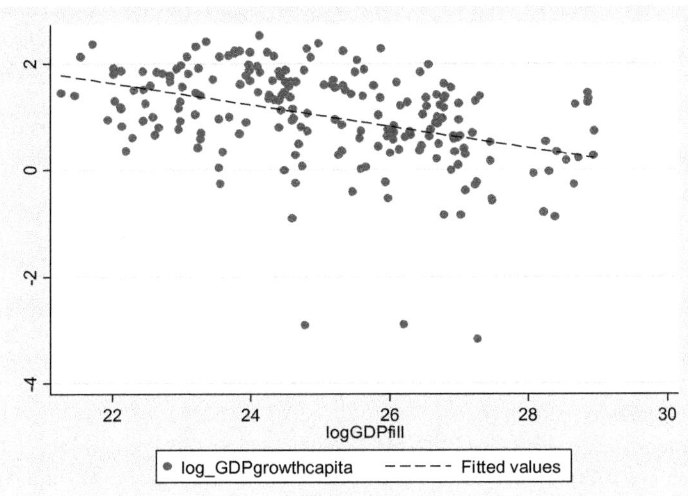

Graph 11. Logging GDPgpc per capita and log_GDP_initial)\(lfitlog_GDPgpc logGDP_initial)

References

Abraham Wald (1943). Tests of Statistical Hypotheses Concerning Several Parameters When the Number of Observations is Large.pp. 11–58. Source: Transactions of the American Mathematical Society, Vol. 54, No.

Aleksynska, M., Gaisford, J., & Kerr, W. (2003). Foreign direct investment and growth in transition economies.

Alfaro, L. (2003). Foreign Direct Investment and Growth: Does the Sector Matter? *Harvard Business School. pp. 2–3. http://www.people.hbs.edu/lalfaro/fdisectorial.pdf.

Allison, P. D. (2009). Fixed effects regression models (Vol. 160). SAGE publications.

Asiedu, E. (2002). On the determinants of foreign direct investment to developing countries: is Africa different?. World development, 30(1), 107–119.

Balasubramanyam, V. N., Salisu, M., & Sapsford, D. (1996). Foreign direct investment and growth in EP and IS countries. The economic journal, 92–105.

Borensztein, E.; J.D. Gregorio and J.W. Lee. (1998). How Does Foreign Direct Investment Affect Economic Growth?. pp. 121. *Journal of International Economics*, vol. 45, 115–135. https://doi.org/10.1016/s0022-1996(97)00033-0. www.sciencedirect.com/science/article/pii.

Barro Robert J., (2013), "Education and Economic Growth," Annals of Economics and Finance, Society for AEF, vol. 14(2), pages 301–328.

Baltagi, Badi H., Liu, Long, (2012). "The Hausman–Taylor panel data model with serial correlation," Statistics & Probability Letters, Elsevier, vol. 82(7), pages 1401–1406.

Carkovic, M. and Levine, R. (2005). *"Does foreign direct investment accelerate economic growth?'*, în Moran T., Graham E. and Blomstrom M. (eds), Does Foreign Direct Investment Promote Development? Institute for International Economics and Center for Global Development, Washington, DC, pp. 195–220.

Choi, S. W. (2009). The effect of outliers on regression analysis: regime type and foreign direct investment. Quarterly Journal of Political Science, 4(2), 153–165.

Clark, T. S., & Linzer, D. A. (2015). Should I use fixed or random effects? Political Science Research and Methods, 3(2), 399–408.

De Mello Jr., Luiz R. (1997) "Foreign direct investment în developing countries and growth: A selective survey', Journal of Development Studies, 34: 1, 1–34.

Durham, J. B. (2004). Absorptive capacity and the effects of foreign direct investment and equity foreign portfolio investment on economic growth. European economic review, 48(2), 285–306

Durlauf, S. N., Johnson, P. A., & Temple, J. R. (2005). Growth econometrics. Handbook of economic growth, 1, 555–677.

Elissa Braunstein Gerald Epstein (2002). Bargaining Power and Foreign Direct Investment in China: Can 1.3 Billion Consumers Tame the Multinationals?. pp. 1–41. http://scholarworks.umass.edu/cgi/viewcontent.cgi?.

Fox, J., & Weisberg, S. (2011). Multivariate linear models in R. An R Companion to Applied Regression. Los Angeles: Thousand Oaks.

Granger, C. W. (1988). Some recent development in a concept of causality. Journal of econometrics, 39(1–2), 199–211.

Hausman, J. A. (1978). Specification tests in econometrics. Econometrica: Journal of the econometric society, 1251–1271.

Hausman, J.A. and W.E. Taylor (1981). Panel Data and Unobservable Individual Effects, pp. 1–23, http://web.mit.edu/14.33/www/hausman.pdf ose si ne Econometrics, journals 49, 1981, pp. 1377–1398.

Jude C, (2012). *Investissement direct étranger, transfert de technologie et croissance économique en Europe Centrale et Orientale*. pp. 1–222. Écolre Doctorale Sciences De l'Homme et de la Societe Laboratoire d'économie d'Orléans/Fsegathese en Cottutelle Internationale. https://halshs.archives-ouvertes.fr/tel-01127259/document.

Kida N., (2016). The impact of Foreign Direct Investment on Gross Domestic Product in Kosovo. pp. 1–367. http://www.uet.edu.al/images/doktoratura/NAKIJE_KIDA.pdf.

Lipsey, R. E. (2006). Measuring international trade in services (No. w12271). National Bureau of Economic Research.

Long, J. S., & Ervin, L. H. (2000). Using heteroscedasticity consistent standard errors in the linear regression model. The American Statistician, 54(3), 217–224.

Lyroudi, K., Papanastasiou, J., & Vamvakidis, A. (2004). Foreign direct investment and economic growth in transition economies. South-Eastern Europe Journal of Economics, 2(1), 97–110

Mankiw, N. G., Romer, D., & Weil, D. N. (1992). A contribution to the empirics of economic growth. The quarterly journal of economics, 107(2), 407–437.

Mencinger, J. (2003). Does foreign direct investment always enhance economic growth? Kyklos, 56(4), 491–508.

Pere E., A, Hashorva (2011). "WesternBalkans' Countries In Focus Of Global Economic Crisis" pg. 11. Economy Transdisciplinarity Cognition; www.ugb.ro/etc.

Ram R (1986) Government size and economic growth: A new framework and some evidence from cross-section and time-series data. American Economic Review 76 (1): 191–203

Ram, R., & Zhang, K. H. (2002). Foreign direct investment and economic growth: Evidence from cross-country data for the 1990s. Economic Development and Cultural Change, 51(1), 205–215.

Rohlfing, J., Gardonio, P., & Thompson, D. J. (2011). Comparison of decentralized velocity feedback control for thin homogeneous and stiff sandwich panels using electrodynamic proof-mass actuators. Journal of Sound and Vibration, 330(5), 843–867.

Romer, P. (1994). The Origins of Endogenous Growth. pp. 1–20. http://www.development.wne.uw.edu.pl/uploads/Courses/de_jt_romer1.pdf.

Stancik, J. (2007). Horizontal and vertical FDI spillovers: recent evidence from the Czech Republic.

Stock, J. H., & W Watson, M. (2003). Forecasting output and inflation: The role of asset prices. Journal of Economic Literature, 41(3), 788–829.

Stock, J. H., & Watson, M. W. (2008). Heteroskedasticity-robust standard errors for fixed effects panel data regression. Econometrica, 76(1), 155–174.

UNCTAD (1999) World Investment Report, Foreign Direct Investment and the Challenge of Development, UN, New York, Geneva.

Wooldridge J (2002). Econometric Analysis of Cross-section and Panel Data. pp. 1–735. https://jrvargas.files.wordpress.com/2011/01/wooldridge_j-_2002_ecoometric.

World Bank. (2017). World development indicators. (2017). Retrieved from http://databank.
    worldbank.org
White H (1980). "A Heteroskedasticity-Consistent Covariance Matrix and a Direct Test for
    Hwhitweteroskedasticity." Econometrica, 48, 817–838.
Xu, B., & Wang, J. (2000). Trade, FDI, and international technology diffusion. Journal of
    Economic Integration, 585–601.

Forecasting Economic Activity of East Asia Through the Yield Curve (Predicting East Asia's Economic Growth and Recession)

Osman Altay and Kelvin Onyibor[✉]

Department of International Economics and Finance, European University
of Lefke, Lefke, North Cyprus, Turkey
oaltay@eul.edu.tr, kelvinonyibor@gmail.com

1 Introduction

The ability to predict the future is a very fascinating process for people, especially the ability to predict economic outcomes, as this has a tendency of increasing profitability and efficiency. The interest rate term spread; specifically the difference between the long and short term yield on bond has predictive power for future economic forecasting. Among all other economic and financial forecasting tools, the yield curve stands as the best tool in forecasting economic growth and recession of an economy few quarters ahead.

Typically plotting the yield against maturity portrays an upward sloping curve, however, a possible recession can be said to be erupting when the yield curve is seen in a flat or downward sloping position, meaning an anticipated recession has a possibility of occurrence within few quarter lag.

The interest rate term spread which is estimated as the margin that exist between the long and short term interest rates has been the ultimate measure for recession forecasting. This statement is backed up theoretically by the fact that short term interest rate is a monetary policy instrument while long term interest rate essentially portrays future expectation on economic conditions in the future; as a result of this fact the difference between both of them may carry essential information for individuals, and policy makers.

Theoretically, two dimension exist in this area of study; first, the use of the Ordinary Least Estimator in an attempt to forecast future economic growth. Secondly, the use of Probit Regression Model to predict future erupting recessions. However, the primary aim of this research is to inculcate this two approach to analyse the general fluctuation of the economic activity in East Asia through the help of the interest rate term spread, and to the best of my knowledge, no study has been done on it so far for this region.

There has been many research aimed at predicting the economic growth through the yield curve with little or no positive stand to prove comprehensively that there exists a correlation between the yield curve and economic development in any country.

The main question posed by this research is, how long into the future in quarters can the term spread of interest rate predict future economic activity. According to

N. Ozatac and K. K. Gökmenoglu (eds.), *Emerging Trends in Banking
and Finance*, Springer Proceedings in Business and Economics,
https://doi.org/10.1007/978-3-030-01784-2_7

Bonser-Neal and Morley (1997) economic activity one year into the future can be predicted using the term spread.

Hence, this work will seek to find out how many quarters into future economic growth would be predicted by the term spread in selected major East Asia countries. The fact that a forecaster can predict the future economic activity such as recession, does not necessarily mean it has the potential to avert this recession but it stands as a basis in minimising future loss from the recession and help manage risk by private agents such as risk managers, practitioners and portfolio managers whose profits and earnings depends on the current economic and financial state of an economy.

Besides the fact that our research would be based on a new region, the East Asian economy, this study would also be focused on examining the impact of interest rate term spread on economic activity from a different perspective by including additional explanatory variables (Broad Money Supply and Stock Market Index) to the model in an attempt to help increase the predictive nature of the yield curve and finally, both panel data analysis and probit model regression would be used to test for correlation and predictiveness respectively.

While the relationship between term spread and economic activity have been broadly studied by several researchers for well-developed countries such as US, UK and other European countries with a hand-full of results and conclusions been drawn out of their findings, evidence from research on this area for developing and underdeveloped economies of the world, especially East Asia, have so far been limited. And this is as a result of the fact that the stock market of these emerging markets have only deepened significantly in the late 1990s, Mehl (2006).

1.1   Background

It is of no doubt that informations on future economic outcomes is essential for the consumers, production sectors, investors and even the policy makers of every nation. The association between economic activity and interest rate came into light when Ederington (2005) explains how interest rate term spread fluctuate with respect to the business cycle.

Subsequent research, Bonser-Neal and Morley (1997) has tried to establish a relationship between term spread and economic growth but there have been no generally agreed-up theory to justify how the relationship exist. Yet researchers still believe that unconscious actions to stabilize economic outputs by monetary authorities have been the engineering move that gives the term spread the predictive powers over economic growth. That is, when a contractionary monetary policy is in play, this causes the short term interest rates to rise more than the long term therefore shrinking the gap between the two yield, and as a result this forces the yield curve to flatten even more.

It is worthy of note, that monetary policies towards this relationship have been outlined with little economic and financial theoretical backings. However, according to Feroli (2004), Estrella (2005), and Estrella and Turbin (2006), the objectives and reaction functions of policies made by monetary policy makers defines the degree to which the term spread of interest rates possess predictive power towards economic activity of any nation. For example the term spread would have lesser predictive ability if the monetary policies are targeted exclusively in controlling inflation rather than the deviations of output growth from its potential.

The paper continues as follows; Chap. 2 would consist of a brief examination of existing literature in this area of study. Chapter 3 would show the methods to be used in other to analyse the relationship between the term spread and economic activity also it would cover every detail about how and where we intend to collect and analysis data for this study. All results and discoveries would be stated clearly in Chap. 4. Chapter 5 would carry the possible conclusion to be drawn from this research. Then finally recommendations would be made for policy makers to look into.

2 Literature Review

Many empirical studies have been carried out in this area to test the authenticity of this claim that the term spread have predictive power over economic activity and the results of some of this studies shows that higher spread cripples economic growth of an economy while some came up with the conclusion that, as a matter of fact, there exists little or no relationship between interest rate term spread and economic growth of an economy. It is worthwhile to outline some of this empirical studies.

The relationship between term spread of interest rate and economic activity was formalized by Hu (1993). In his empirical analysis he proposed, that an increase in the term spread would lead to economic growth for industrialized countries which falls into the G7 grouping.

According to Bonser-Neal and Morley (1997), who examined nine well developed economies, which include; Germany, France, Italy, United Kingdom, Spain, USA, Canada, Australia and Sweden, and discovered that economic activities in these countries are well predicted by the term spread using the probability unit (probit) model in estimating the recession trend in these countries. In the same vein, Kim and Limpaphayom (1997) carried out a similar study for Japan and the results indicated that only the short term interest rate predicts the economic trend of Japan not the term spread.

Goodfriend, Marvin (1993), in their study on the predictive power of term spread on economic activity on 12 Euro-area countries discovered that the yield curve slope contains good empirical evidences that shows predictive ability on the economic activity in this Euro-Zone countries.

Contrary to earlier researches, Feitosa and Tabak (2007) found out that the economic activities of Brazil is not explained by the movement of the yield curve using the probit model to predict Brazil's recession trends.

Furthermore, Laurent (1988), added a piece into the area, when she examined the relationship between the yield curve and economic growth of the EU-15 which includes; Austria, Spain, Denmark, Portugal, Ireland, Greece, Luxemburg, Italy, the Netherlands, Belgium, France, Germany, Sweden and the United Kingdom. Using the spread between 3 month and 10 years government bond, which was modelled through panel data analysis, the results show positive relationship in Ireland, Belgium, Luxemburg and France but negative in the rest of the countries.

In a more detailed analysis, Gogas and Pragidis (2010), examined 5 European Countries both EMU and non EMU member countries from the period of 1991–2009 quarterly adjusted. They went further by augmenting non monetary variable to the model, using Probit Model of the inverse cumulative distribution function of the standard distribution, coupled with several test of goodness of fit of the model. Gogas and Pragidis found out that the yield curve coupled with the augmented non monetary variables explains the trends in economic activities in these countries under study.

Similarly, Dueker (1997), examined the case of the United Kingdom using a different model which according to him outperform the standard probit model. Using the B-Spline in-sample and out-sample model, he was able to closely predict economic downsides of the United Kingdom compared to other conclusions derived from earlier researchers. This was facilitated through the use of the entire yield curve rather than just the difference between the long term and short term interest rates.

Finally, Mehl (2006), who investigated the impact of the yield curve on the economic growth and inflation in Nigeria, with the singular purpose of expanding the scope of the relationship by including inflation as an independent variable. His study covered seasonally adjusted data from the period between 1986 and 2006 using the dynamic ordinary least square estimation technique (DOLS). Mehl estimated valid reliable results that interest rate term spread has a positive and long run relationship between inflation and economic growth, indicating that term spread is a good indicator for economic activity predictions.

2.1 Study Area

A number of selected East Asian countries would be used in the course of this study. These countries and the time horizon was selected based on the reasons below;

Countries Selected:

Japan, China and South Korea. From (2003:Q1–2016:Q4).

Reasons:

1. These countries are rapidly growing relative to many other countries in the region and no study has yet been done on them with respect to this topic.

2. Since this 3 countries have the highest share of stock transactions in the whole East Asia, (About 80% of total stock volume) trading in these stock markets majorly influence the entire stock market in East Asia. Mehl (2006).

3 Methodology

3.1 Model Specifications

Following the basic standard relationship between the term spread and economic growth the Ordinary Least Square Regression model below is estimated:

$$\text{Real GDP}_{t+n} = \alpha_0 + \beta_1 \text{SPREAD}_t + \varepsilon_t \tag{1}$$

Now, including the monetary and non-monetary explanatory variables into the regression;

$$\text{Real GDP}_{t+n} = \alpha_0 + \beta_1 \text{SPREAD}_t + \beta_2 \text{M2}_t + \beta_3 \text{SMI}_t + \varepsilon_t \tag{2}$$

where:

Real Gdp t + n is denoted as Future real GDp predicted at time n (n months ahead).

N = is the lag of spread, this lag can assume values ranging from 2, 3, 4, 5, or 6.

SPREAD$_t$ = is denoted as the difference between the 10 years and 3 months government bonds at time t.

M2$_t$ = This is the broad money supply.

SMI$_t$ = Stock Market Index.

ε_t is the error term of the regression.

3.2   Further Specifications

Since our sole aim is to predict recession through the term spread, we would be employing a non-linear estimator, the Probit Regression Model which would be used to predict future negative trend within the long run cyclical component of Real GDP according to (Estrella and Mishkin 1997):

$$\text{Probit}\,(\text{BS}_t = 1) = \Phi\left[\tilde{\alpha}_0 + \tilde{\alpha}_1\left(i_{\text{LR},t-1} - i_{\text{SR},t-1}\right)\right], i = 1 \tag{3}$$

where:

BS$_t$ = The estimated dummy (categorical) value which assume value 1 whenever the cyclical component of GDP falls below long run trend.

Φ = This is the standard normal cumulative distribution function.

$\tilde{\alpha}_0 + \tilde{\alpha}_1$ = This denotes the estimated parameters; intercept and slope of the model respectively.

$(i_{\text{LR},t-1} - i_{\text{SR},t-1})$ = This represents the term spread which is the difference between the 3 months and 10 years government bond of the respective country.

To accommodate the non monetary explanatory variables included in the model, the Probit Model would be reconstructed to accommodate the changes, hence;

$$\textbf{Probit}\left(\textbf{BS}_t = 1\right) = \Phi\left[\tilde{\alpha}_0 + \tilde{\alpha}_1\left(i_{LR,t-1} - i_{SR,t-1}\right)\right] + \tilde{a}_s S_{t-1} \tag{4}$$

$$\textbf{Probit}\left(\textbf{BS}_t = 1\right) = \Phi\left[\tilde{\alpha}_0 + \tilde{\alpha}_1\left(i_{LR,t-1} - i_{SR,t-1}\right)\right] + \tilde{a}_m M_{t-1} \tag{5}$$

where:

S_{t-1} = % change in stock market index, Dueker (1997).

M_{t-1} = Broad Money Supply.

3.3 Data Collection and Analysis

Seasonally adjusted data would be collected for GDP from the period of 2000:Q1 to 2013:Q4. This time horizon was selected based on the availability of data as earlier data display trend breaks and low consistency. This GDP data would be converted into seasonal real GDP by taking year 2000 as base year. Since the purpose of this study is to predict real GDP deviations from long-run trend, we would now decompose our Seasonally Adjusted Real GDP data of each country to the cyclical component by using the Hodrick-Prescott (1997) filter known as the (HP Filter). The purpose of this is to project our Real GDP data in a smooth and non linear trend which would only be affected by long-run fluctuations rather than short-run. In addition, to eliminate the bias caused by the HP filter discussed in the literature, we would be examining the robustness of the estimated business cycle by using alternative specifications for the Hodrick-Prescott Filter parameter λ (lambda), this parameters would include; λ = 1000, 1600, 2200 (Diebold et al. 1995).

In this paper, it is worthy of note that economic recession is considered as the negative deviation of real GDP from the long run trend. With the constructed business cycle, each countries cyclical component of real GDP would be extracted from which our dummy (categorical) variable (BS) would be constructed. Our dummy variable would take the value one (1) whenever our business cycle falls in the negative trend and the value zero (0) elsewhere, keeping in mind that our sole aim for this study is to use the term spread to predict negative deviations in our seasonally adjusted real GDP which has been constructed into cyclical component.

On the other hand, our independent variables would consist of the interest rate term spread which would be the difference between 3 month and 10 years government bond of each of the three countries, which according to Estrella and Mishkin (1997) best predict economic activity. This data would be seasonally adjusted as well to fit our seasonally adjusted Real GDP.

Stock Market Index and Broad Money Supply (M2) were also included in the study as monetary and non monetary explanatory variables to help improve the predictability power of the yield curve as proposed by Gogas and Pragidis (2012). These variables just as the others were also seasonally adjusted to fit into the model. Real GDP data for each country would be collected from the World Bank Database, Government Bond yield of maturity 3 months and 10 years would be collected from the Central Bank

Statistical Bulletin of each respective country while Market price index and broad money supply (M2) data would be extracted from the respective countries IMF and other financial databases.

4   Forecasting Results

4.1   Descriptive Statistics

For the aim of evaluating the impact of term spread on economic growth, we first analyse the descriptive statistics of our employed time series variables. These descriptive statistics displays valuable information like the mean, Median, min and max values, the skewness which gives information about the distribution of our sample and also the Jarque-Bera statistic. Table 3 contains the descriptive statistics of our variables for Japan employed in this study. Other countries' results are represented in the appendix section.

Since our mean and median values of our series falls between our minimum and maximum values, we can boldly conclude that our series follows a high level of consistency Hamilton and Kim (2002). Furthermore, we can also add that, since, our estimated standard deviation is low, deviations of our mean from actual values is very small. Finally, statistical values from the skewness and kurtosis, provides tangible information as regards to the symmetry of the probability distribution of our series as well as the distribution tail thickness respectively. The importance of the above two statistics, helps in the computation of the Jarqua-Bera which evaluates the normality of our time series data (Table 1).

Table 1. This table represents the descriptive statistics of the regression variables

	Japan				China			
	M2	Spread	SPI	RGDP	M2	SPREAD	SPI	RGDP
Mean	7.84	0.93	1.32	5.76	7.04	0.87	5.95	5.95
Median	7.65	0.97	1.31	5.75	6.24	0.82	5.80	5.80
Maximum	9.67	1.90	1.95	6.07	1.49	1.89	9.73	9.73
Minimum	6.71	0.09	0.83	5.41	1.93	0.39	2.82	2.82
Std. Dev.	0.63	0.43	0.34	1.74	1.10	0.33	2.12	2.12
Skewness	0.58	−0.04	0.24	−0.18	0.42	0.83	0.15	0.15
Kurtosis	2.15	2.29	1.82	2.25	1.81	3.65	1.76	1.76
Jarque-Bera	4.89	1.18	3.82	1.59	4.97	7.49	3.77	3.77
Probability	0.08	0.55	0.14	0.45	0.08	0.02	0.15	0.15
Sum	4.39	52.6	74.1	3.22	3.94	48.88	3.33	3.33
Sum Sq. Dev.	4.10	10.4	6.4	1.66	9.25	6.21	2.47	2.47
Observations	56	56	56	56	56	56	56	56

4.2   Time Series Properties of Data

In other to analyse the predictive power of interest rate term spread on economic growth we would first, test for the time series properties of our variables, hence, testing for stationarity of our variables used in the course of this study. Displayed in Table 2 is the stationarity test for Japan), conducted using both ADF and PP unit root test, results shows that, only Spread was stationary at level, while all variables could be seen to be stationary at first difference. Hence, we can conclude that our variables were integrated at both level and first difference. Other countries' results are represented in the appendix section.

Table 2. Shows the unit root test of the variables

Japan					
Variable	Levels/diff	ADF		PP test	
		C	C & T	C	C & T
SPREAD	Level	−3.52***	−3.689**	−2.27***	−3.287
	1st difference	−5.52497*	−4.21587*	−7.2152*	−6.529884
RGDP	Level	−0.541425	−5.879215	−1.63241	−2.8912454
	1st difference	−2.25963*	−5.4086*	−5.3779*	−5.429825
SPI	Level	−0.183375	−1.158545	−0.84365	−1.632415
	1st difference	−4.8412	−4.842079	−4.354	−4.8372
M2	Level	−1.4177	−1.54154	−0.215874	−0.215874
	1st difference	−6.632	−7.556412	−6.5624	−11.521

Noted (*), (**), (***) represents 1, 5, 10% significant level of unit root rejection

Since our variables are statistically strong and also displayed a high and sufficient level of stationarity, we then moved on to carry out our probit estimation, and as such we first employ the HP filter to our seasonally adjusted Real GDP to get the cyclical component of GDP. The purpose of this is to project our Real GDP data in a smooth and non linear trend which would only be affected by long-run fluctuations rather than short-run. In addition, to eliminate the bias caused by the HP filter discussed in the literature, we would be examining the robustness of the estimated business cycle by using alternative specifications for the Hodrick-Prescott Filter parameter λ (lambda), this parameters would include; $\lambda = 1000, 1600, 2200$ (Diebold et al. 1995).

From Fig. 1, we could clearly conclude that the extracted cyclical component displayed insignificant deviation from each other; hence it is robust to various to alternative lambdas (λ). Same result was gotten for both China and South Korea. Figures for cyclical component for China and South Korea are represented in the appendix section.

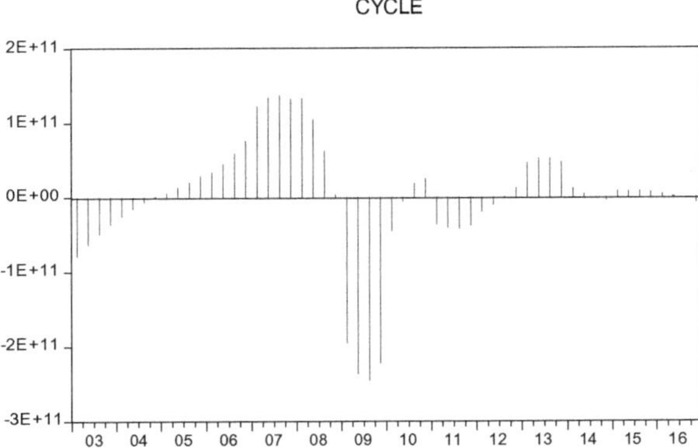

Fig. 1. Extracted cyclical component of real GDP sensitivity to alternative parameter specifications for Japan

We then move on to construct our dummy variable which take the value one (1) whenever our business cycle falls in the negative trend and the value zero (0) elsewhere. While keeping in mind that our sole aim for this study is to use the term spread to predcit negative deviations in our seasonally adjusted real GDP which has been constructed into cyclical component.

Next we estimate the earlier outlined Probit model to see whether the term spread possess predictive power over the economic growth trend using the constructed dummy variable as the dependent variable and also at what lag selection level (quarter) those the interest rate term spread predict.

The standard cumulative distribution probit model was estimated at 5 different lag selection level as shown in Table 3, The selected lag level is S_t-5 since at lag 5 the z-statistics proved significant and the McFadden R^2 is relatively the highest making it the best fit model for the recession forecast ing following the stated McFadden R^2 minimum and maximum bound level of 0.2–0.4. where a value to 4 interprets a high probability of a recession while values closer to 2 shows no evidence of recession, however values out of this constructed bounds is considered inconclusive. McFadden (1974) Next, we include the other explanatory variables into the regression in other to detect if this variables adds any informational or predictive power to the interest rate term spread, hence we estimate (Table 4);

Table 3. Probit estimation with Spread as the only explanatory variable

Japan					
Variable	Coefficient	Std. error	z-Statistic	Prob.	McFadden R^2
St−1	−0.02923	0.405702	−0.072047	0.9426	0.00007
St−2	−0.28562	0.429511	−0.664988	0.5061	0.21418
St−3	−0.496326	0.453531	−1.094359	0.2738	0.14739
St−4	−0.740042	0.485147	−1.525397	0.1272	0.29435
St−5	−0.910128	0.513029	−1.774029	0.0161	0.34016

Table 4. Probit estimation with Spread and SPI as explanatory variables in Japan

Variable	Coefficient	Std. error	z-Statistic	Prob.	McFadden R^2
St−5	−2.361762	1.147471	−2.058233	0.0396	0.368195
SPI	−3.636078	1.25685	−2.893008	0.0038	

Table 5. Probit estimation with Spread and M2 as explanatory variables in Japan

Variable	Coefficient	Std. error	z-Statistic	Prob.	McFadden R^2
St−5	−1.874927	0.956573	−1.960046	0.05	0.086285
M2	−6.09E-15	4.13E-15	−1.474471	0.1404	

$$\text{Probit}\,(BS_t = 1) = \Phi\left[\tilde{\alpha}_0 + \tilde{\alpha}_1\left(i_{LR,t-1} - i_{SR,t-1}\right)\right] + \tilde{a}_s SPI_{t-1} \qquad (6)$$

$$\text{Probit}\,(BS_t = 1) = \Phi\left[\tilde{\alpha}_0 + \tilde{\alpha}_1\left(i_{LR,t-1} - i_{SR,t-1}\right)\right] + \tilde{a}_m M2_{t-1} \qquad (7)$$

When Stock market index was included in the model, the McFadden R^2 increased drawing closer to the upper bound 0.4 and also the z-statistics of our included explanatory variable came out significant at 1% significant level.

In the same vain, M2 was included as shown in Table 5, unfortunately, it proved insignificant and also push the the McFadden R^2 down showing a less likelihood of a possible recession prediction traits in the model (Table 6).

Table 6. Probit estimation with Spread, SPI and M2 as explanatory variables in Japan

Variable	Coefficient	Std. error	z-Statistic	Prob.	McFadden R2
St−5	−1.310181	1.004008	−1.304951	0.1919	
SPI	−1.662807	0.668228	−2.488381	0.0128	
					0.266695
M2	−4.02E-15	4.15E-15	−0.969879	0.3321	

Finally, both Stock market price index and Broad money supply was inculcated together into the model to test for joint effect on the predictive power of interest rate term spread on economic growth and as expected, less predictive content can be seen as compared to the model having just stock price index.

Hence, we conclude that the best fit model for recession prediction following the results from alternative specifications is;

$$\text{Probit}\,(BS_{t+5} = 1) = \Phi\left[\tilde{\alpha}_0 + \tilde{\alpha}_1\left(i_{LR,t+5} - i_{SR,t+5}\right)\right] + \tilde{a}_s SPI_t \qquad (8)$$

4.3   Future GDP Growth Trend Predicted by the Term Spread

In other to further justify our finding, we went ahead to plot extracted business circle alongside the interest rate term spread lagged 5 quarters to see if the spread actually predicts GDP trend movement.

The plotted graph in Figs. 2 and 3, shows the GDP growth trend plotted against the difference between the 3 month and 10 years government bond of China and Japan lagged 3 and 5 quarters ahead respectively (Figs. 4 and 5).

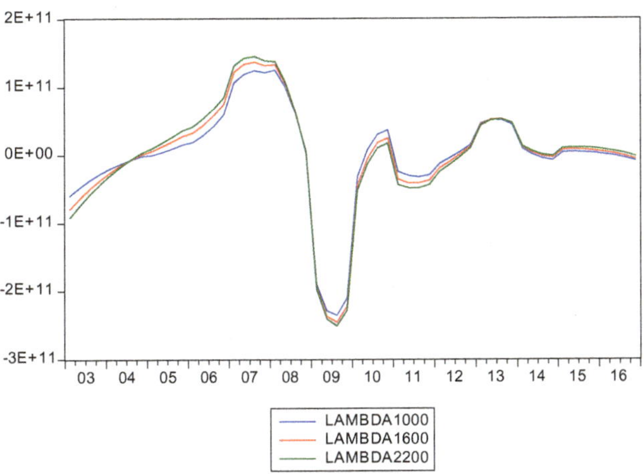

Fig. 2. Cyclical component sensitivity to alternative parameter specifications for Japan

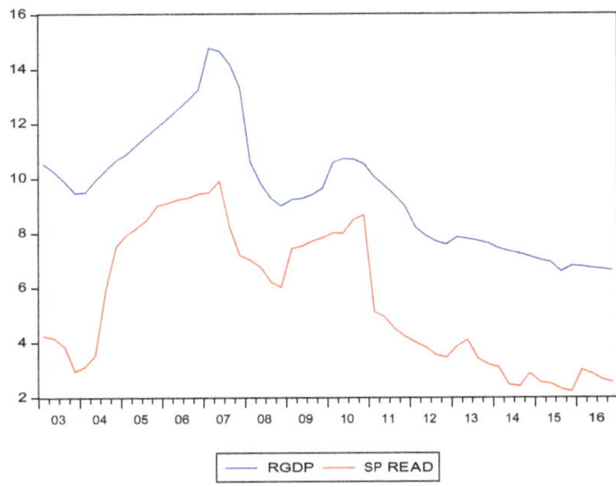

Fig. 3. GDP growth trend plotted alongside the term spread lagged 3 quarters ahead in China

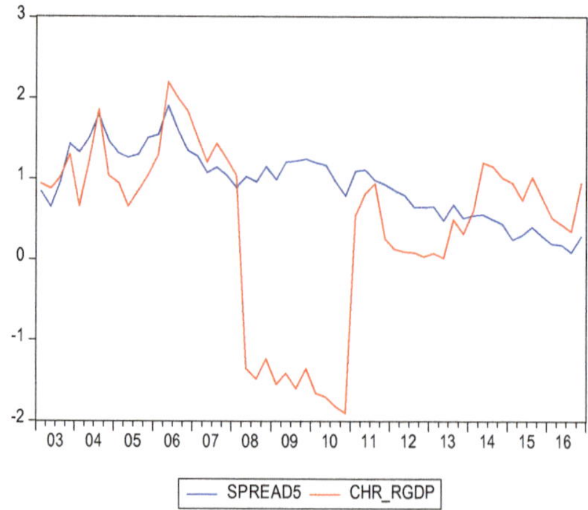

Fig. 4. GDP growth trend plotted alongside the term spread lagged 5 quarters ahead in Japan

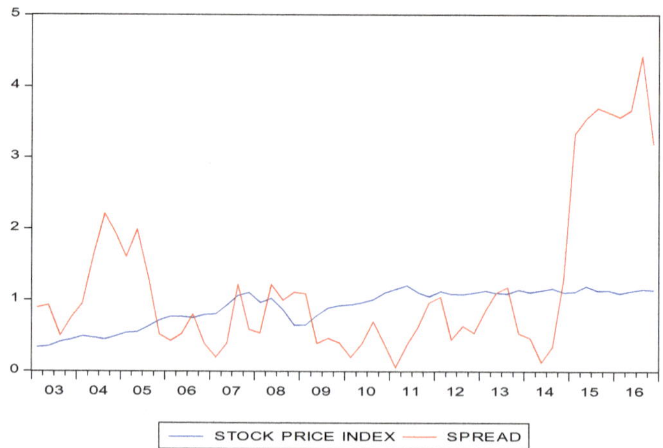

Fig. 5. GDP growth trend plotted alongside the term spread lagged 2 quarters ahead in South Korea

From the graphs, we can see that a decline in the spread value is always preceded by a decline in the Real GDP of Japan. Hence, concurring to Dueker (1997), that the term spread actually has a positive relative with Real GDP growth trend.

However, no predictive trend could be detected in South Korean estimation which goes in line with the results gotten from the table of its Probit regression estimations.

Table 7. OLS results for individual countries with respective fitted lags

OLS regression result of all countries using individual selected lag

Country (Lags)	Constant	Spread	P-value	R2
Japan n = 5	5.64E+12	2.65E+11	9.507379***	0.42161
China n = 3	0.131215	9.52E-15	11.21884***	0.57985
South Korea n = 2	0.079866	1.96E-14	3.302655*	0.026873

This is as a result of the damages they suffer from its stock market rating caused by the hostility of North Korea during military crises, which as a matter of fact affected the South Korea financial market negatively and also the high volatility of the interest rate on government bonds which is caused by risk associated with government investment since there has always been political unrest arising from the northern part of Korea. Laurent (1988).

4.4 Ordinary Least Square Estimation Results Using Optimum Lag Length Selection

We further run an OLS estimation of our whole sample using term spread and economic growth as independent and dependent variables respectively, and the results are displayed below in Table 7.

From the above table we can conclude that both Japan and China displayed positive and statistically significant P-values at (2.65) and (9.52) respectively, with a 1% significant level and also having an R^2 of (0.42161) and (0.57985). This interprets as 42% and 57.9% of the changes that occur in RGDP was explained by the interest rate term spread for Japan and China respectively.

However, as expected, Interest rate term spread proved insignificant in explaining the changes that occur in RGDP which is also backed up by the extremely low value of its R^2 (0.026873).

5 Conclusion Remarks and Future Research

The question of interest rate being able to accurately predict real economic growth have in it a lot of preliminary work to answer. The spread between the 3 months 10 years government bond contains predictive informations in forecasting real economic growth 2 to 5 quarters ahead, our result is in line with Jallah (2004) who found that interest rate term spread predicts real economic growth 5 quarters ahead in Germany. if this technique is well employed similar results can be gotten from other countries of the world. From our analysis, we depict that the best predictive lags are 5, and 3 for Japan and China respectively. Unfortunately, interest rate term spread could not accurately predict the direction of future economic growth trend.

Despite, the importance of term spread in forecasting economic growth, it shouldn't be a direct replacement for the predictions made by financial companies since there are other economic and financial indicators which affects economic growth, however it does provide a useful and quick check in addition to more technical and sophisticated prediction tools.

This study despite being robust in alternative specifications and modeling, suffered from some certain limitations which include; first, long stream of time series data could not be obtain as a result of multiple random structural data breaks in data sources, also this study was singularly designed to capture the direction of economic growth trend movement while ignoring the degree and depth of increase or decrease of the trend. Lastly, further research could put more effort in including other explanatory variables that could help improve the predictive power of the interest rate term spread on economic growth.

Appendix

See Figs. 6, 7 and Tables 8, 9.

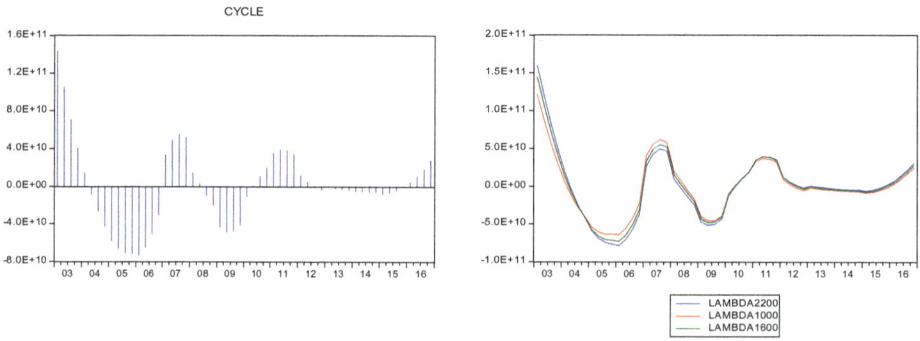

Fig. 6. Extracted cyclical component of real GDP sensitivity to alternative parameter specifications for China

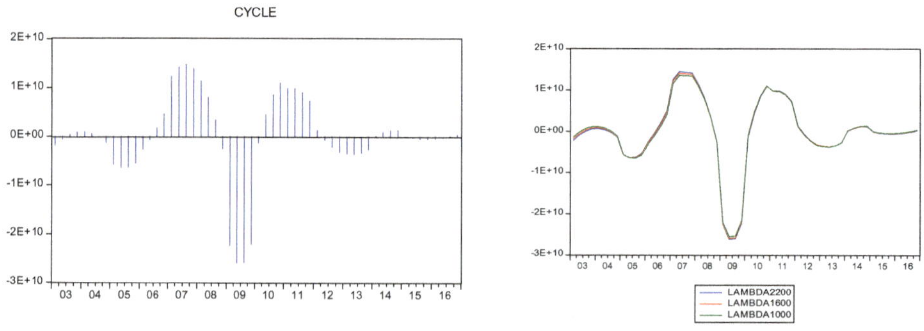

Fig. 7. Extracted cyclical component of real GDP sensitivity to alternative parameter specifications for South Korea

CHINA

Probit estimation with Spread as the only explanatory variable

Variable	Coefficient	Std. error	z-Statistic	Prob.	McFadden
Ut−1	3.39E-15	8.28E-14	4.24093	0.0074	0.324575
Ut−2	−1.99E-14	8.58E-14	−0.231916	0.0066	0.351127
Ut−3	−4.47E-14	8.92E-14	−0.501031	0.0063	0.370636
Ut−4	−7.21E-14	9.31E-14	−0.774496	0.4386	0.24188

Probit estimation with Spread and SPI as explanatory variables

variable	Coefficient	Std. error	z-Statistic	Prob.	McFadden
Ut−3	3.95E-14		0.352683	0.0043	0.394896
SPI	−2.129939	0.752617	−2.830044	0.0047	

Probit estimation with Spread and M2 as explanatory variables

variable	Coefficient	Std. error	z-Statistic	Prob.	McFadden
Ut−3	−2.04E-12	9.88E-13	−2.060957	0.0393	0.054867
M2	9.55E-14	4.73E-14	2.019006	0.4435	

Probit estimation with Spread, SPI and M2 as explanatory variables

variable	Coefficient	Std. error	z-Statistic	Prob.	McFadden
Ut−3	−5.28E-13	1.12E-12	−0.470244	0.0082	
SPI	−1.993532	0.801988	−2.485739	0.0129	0.189862
M2	2.81E-14	5.29E-14	0.531409	0.5951	

South Korea

Probit estimation with Spread as the only explanatory variable

variable	Coefficient	Std. error	z-Statistic	Prob.	McFadden
Ut−1	0.38186	0.167243	2.283271	0.0224	0.072325
Ut−2	0.464091	0.190391	2.437563	0.0148	0.154091
Ut−3	0.37696	0.194896	1.93416	0.0531	0.053473
Ut−4	0.228711	0.199935	1.143926	0.2527	0.018345

Probit estimation with Spread and SPI as explanatory variable

variable	Coefficient	Std. error	z-Statistic	Prob.	McFadden
Ut−2	0.471892	0.189747	2.486952	0.0129	0.097593
SPI	−0.677071	0.7431	−0.911143	0.3622	

Probit estimation with Spread and M2 as explanatory variable

variable	Coefficient	Std. error	z-Statistic	Prob.	McFadden
Ut−2	0.510818	0.201626	2.533496	0.0113	0.086515
M2	−8.86E-17	4.29E-16	−0.20643	0.8365	

Probit estimation with Spread SPI and M2 as explanatory variable

variable	Coefficient	Std. error	z-Statistic	Prob.	McFadden
Ut−2	0.325097	0.225823	1.439611	0.15	
SPI	1.39E-15	1.02E-15	1.369161	0.1709	0.124164
M2	−0.907302	1.785937	1.627886	0.1035	

Table 8. This table represents the descriptive statistics of the regression variables

South Korea			
M2	SPI	Spread	RGDP
1.07	0.90	1.54	1.19
1.06	1.01	1.59	0.82
1.32	1.20	2.31	4.42
8.04	0.33	8.80	0.05
1.51	0.26	4.54	1.11
−0.05	−0.8	0.03	1.48
1.81	2.21	1.71	4.02
3.30	6.97	3.87	2.91
0.19	0.03	0.14	0.05
5.98	50.48	8.62	6.54
1.26	3.73	1.13	4.32
56	56	56	56

Table 9. Shows the unit root test of the variables

China		ADF		PP test	
Variables	Levels/first diff	C	C & T	C	C & T
Spread	Level	−2.254871***	−3.658412**	−2.965487	−3.254875**
	1st difference	−5.635987*	−4.552487*	−7.232314*	−6.012478*
RGDP	Level	−0.257849	−5.257745	−1.012458	−2.894215
	1st difference	−2.878541*	−5.256451*	−5.231485	−5.429825*
SPI	Level	−0.201124	−1.87542	−0.213587	−1.962145
	1st difference	−4.5248754*	−4.635245	−4.829354*	−4.635874*
M2	Level	−1.231487	−0.632545	−1.965487	−0.325874
	1st difference	−6.52487	−7.339344*	−6.054871*	11.562485*

South Korea		ADF		PP test	
Variables	Levels/first diff	C	C & T	C	C & T
Spread	Level	−2.551247***	−3.63541**	−2.568475***	−3.632548**
	1st difference	−5.639874*	−4.524698*	−7.548974*	−6.552147*
RGDP	Level	−0.54871	−5.96874	−1.023147	−2.800214
	1st difference	−2.147852*	−5.369854*	−5.232314*	−5.295487*
SPI	Level	−0.383451	−1.31754	−0.575484	−1.94751
	1st difference	−4.564145*	−4.079548*	−4.639854*	−4.879755*
M2	Level	1.638545	−0.036548	−1.783996	−0.56874
	1st difference	−6.85451*	−7.965487*	−6.56457*	11.87985*

References

Bonser-Neal, Catherine, and Timothy R. Morley. (1997) "Does the Yield Spread Predict Real Economic Activity? A Multicountry Analysis," *Federal Reserve Bank of Kansas City Economic Review,* vol. 82, pp. 37–53.

Diebold, Francis X., and Roberto S. Mariano. (1995) "Comparing Predictive Accuracy," *Journal of Business and Economic Statistics,* vol. 13, pp. 253–63.

Dueker, Michael J. (1997) "Strengthening the Case for the Yield Curve as a Predictor of U.S. Recessions," *Federal Reserve Bank of St. Louis Review,* vol. 79 (March/April), pp. 41–51.

Ederington, A. (2005) "The Predictive Power of the Term Structure of Interest Rates in Europe and the United States: Implications for the European Central Bank," *European Economic Review,* vol. 41 (July), pp. 1375–1401.

Estrella, A. (2005). Why does the yield curve predict output and inflation?. The Economic Journal, 115(505), 722–744.

Estrella, Arturo, and Turbin A.H. (2006), "The Term Structure as a Predictor of Real Economic Activity," *Journal of Finance,* vol. 46 (pp. 555–76).

Estrella, Arturo, and Frederic S. Mishkin. (1997), "Predicting U.S. Recessions: Financial Variables as Leading Indicators," *Review of Economics and Statistics,* vol. 80 (pp. 45–61).

Feitosa, M.A. and Tabak, B.N. (2007). "Predictability of Economic Activity Using Yield Spreads: The Case of Brazil. Anais Do XXXV Encontro Nacional De Economia" *Proceedings of the 35th Brazilian Economics Meeting,* 029.

Feroli, M. (2004) "Monetary Policy and Informational Content of the Yield Spread", *Federal Reserve Board Division of Research and Statistics.* pp. 39–57.

Gogas, P., & Pragidis, I. (2010). Does the interest risk premium predict housing prices. DUTH Research Papers in Economics 1–2010, Democritus University of Thrace, Department of Economics.

Gogas, P. and Pragidis, I. (2012). "GDP trend deviations and The Yield Spread: The Case of Eight E.U Countries". *Journal of Economics and Finance* 36: 226–237.

Goodfriend, Marvin. (1993) "Interest Rate Policy and the Inflation Scare Problem," *Federal Reserve Bank of Richmond Economic Quarterly,* vol. 79 pp. 1–24.

Hodrick, R. J., & Prescott, E. C. (1997). Postwar US business cycles: an empirical investigation. Journal of Money, credit, and Banking, 1–16.

Hamilton, J.D. and Kim D.H, (2002). "A Re-examination of the predictability of economic activity using the yield spread. Journal of money", *Credit and Banking* 34(2): 340–360.

Hu, Z. (1993). "The Yield curve and Real Activity". *IMF Staff Papers* 40(4):781–806.

Jallah, S. (2004). "A VAR analysis of the effects of monetary policy in Malaysia". *Master of Economics Research Report,* University of Malaya, Kuala Lumpur.

Kim, A. and Limpaphayom, P. (1997). "The Effect of Economic Regimes on the Relation between Term Structure and Real Activity in Japan". *Journal of Economics and Business,* 49(4), 379–392.

Laurent, Robert. (1988) "An Interest Rate-Based Indicator of Monetary Policy," *Federal Reserve Bank of Chicago Economic Perspectives,* vol. 12 (January/February), pp. 3–14.

Mehl, A. (2006) "The Yield Curve as a Predictor and Emerging Economies" *Bofit Discussion Paper* No. 18/2006.

McFadden, D. (1974) "Quantitative Methods for Analyzing Travel Behaviour on Individuals: Some Recent Developments". *Discussion of model evaluation (in the context of multinomial logit models)* p. 306.

Risk Information of Stock Market Using Quantum Potential Constraints

Sina Nasiri[1(⊠)], Eralp Bektas[1], and Gholamreza Jafari[2]

[1] Department of Banking and Finance, Eastern Mediterranean University,
Famagusta, North Cyprus, Turkey
`sinanasiri.sbu@gmail.com, eralp.bektas@emu.edu.tr`
[2] Department of Physics, Shahid Beheshti University, G.C., Tehran, Iran
`gjafari@gmail.com`

1   Introduction

Financial markets, as one of the most complex interacting systems, and their high frequency data availability have become attractive for several other disciplines such as computational finance, environmental finance and information management and finance. As a clear example, powerful approaches from statistical physics have been used for modelling the markets. In his pioneer work, Bachelier (1900), for instance, focused on pricing of options, using the formalization of random walk to obtain an appropriate differential equation for the probability function of price changing. This innovative statistical approach became the starting point for alternative models such as the Mandelbrot hypothesis (1963) and the Black and Scholes (1973). Furthermore, Chakraborti et al. (2009) and Chen (2014) used the chaos theory to analyze the state of a financial system. Nowadays, due to the strong correlations and subsequent entanglement of the markets, quantum mechanics can be used as a suitable toolkit for studying the evolution of these entangled systems. Khrennikov (1999), a pioneer in this area, applied Quantum Mechanics into modeling some financial systems. In a series of papers, Choustova (2002, 2004, 2009) introduced a mathematical modeling based on Classical and Quantum Mechanics to investigate the dynamics of the financial systems. They argued that the real financial conditions are comprised of hard as well as soft components. The former component may be governed by the classical Hamiltonian mechanics, while the latter is described by Bohmian quantum mechanics.

Using empirical data, Tahmasebi and his associates (2015) employed the quantum potential method to describe the mechanism of the fluctuations of price returns. They found that the existence of vertical potential walls could be responsible for this issue through the time entanglement of the price return. In addition, their findings showed that the probability distribution function of the price return of the markets obeys a power law behavior indicating a scale invariance of the price return, which, in turn, enables one to get information about the behavior of the emerging and mature markets. Very recently, Shen and Haven (2017) estimated the classical as well as the quantum potential function, using the empirical data for the commodity markets. They could confirm confirmed the existence of the potential walls and the scaling behavior of the return variations. Emphasizing different information contents of the classical and

© Springer Nature Switzerland AG 2018
N. Ozatac and K. K. Gökmenoglu (eds.), *Emerging Trends in Banking and Finance*, Springer Proceedings in Business and Economics,
https://doi.org/10.1007/978-3-030-01784-2_8

quantum potentials, which reflect the hard and soft market conditions respectively, they pointed out the correlation between these two potentials.

The present study, by following the same logic adopted by Tahmasebi et al. (2015) and Shen and Haven (2017), aimed to investigate the risk of different stock markets as a main point in the portfolio theory. The paper is organized as follows. In Sect. 2, a brief review of quantum potential is presented, and then data description and their analyses are proposed in Sect. 3. In Sect. 4, the proposed model is applied to stock markets. Finally, Sect. 5 is devoted to concluding remarks.

2 A Review on Quantum Potentials

In 1952, David Bohm presented a theory that is known as the Bohmian quantum mechanics (Bohm 1952). In Bohm's model, the particles move on well-defined classical paths, while the quantum effects are explained by a 'quantum force' emerging from the wave-like behaviors of the particles.

In Bohmian quantum mechanics, the dynamics of the system is described by inserting the wave function $\psi(q,t) = R(q,t)\exp\left(i\frac{S(q,t)}{\hbar}\right)$ in the Schrodinger equation $i\hbar\frac{\partial\psi}{\partial t} = -\frac{\hbar^2}{2m}\frac{\partial^2\psi}{\partial q^2} + V\psi$ and obtaining two coupled equations for $R(q,t)$ and $S(q,t)$ as follows (see Holland 2000).

$$\frac{\partial R^2}{\partial t} + \frac{1}{m}\frac{\partial}{\partial q}\left(R^2\frac{\partial S}{\partial q}\right) = 0, \tag{1}$$

$$\frac{\partial S}{\partial t} + \frac{1}{2m}\left(\frac{\partial S}{\partial q}\right)^2 + \left(V - \frac{\hbar^2}{2mR}\frac{\partial^2 R}{\partial q^2}\right) = 0, \tag{2}$$

where, $R(q,t)$ and $S(q,t)$ represent the amplitude and the phase of the wave function and h, q and m are the Plank constant, position and mass of the particle, respectively. In Eq. (2), in addition to the classical potential, V, there is another potential:

$$U(q,t) = \frac{\hbar^2}{2mR}\frac{\partial^2 R}{\partial q^2}, \tag{3}$$

which is called the quantum potential.

3 Data Description and Analysis

The data used in the present study were extracted from Thomson Router database for the Dow Jones Industrial Average (DJIA), The Standard and Poor's 500 (S&P 500), Deutsche Boerse AG German Stock Index (DAX), Tokyo Stock Price Index (TOPIX) as the developed markets, and Shanghai Index (SSEC) as the emerging market indices, from January 2010 to December 2017, to investigate the collective behavior of their price returns.

4 Application of the Quantum Potential Method to the Financial Markets

In applying the above method to a given stock market, $q(t)$ denotes the price return, m and $\hbar$ indicate the market value and the uncertainty in price and price change, respectively, and $S(q,t)$ represents the phase of the market quantities. When a single market is concerned, m and $S(q,t)/\hbar$ are assumed to be constant, however, when the interconnection of at least two different markets is concerned, the value of S becomes important.

Let $q(t) = \ln p(t+dt) - \ln p(t)$, where $p(t)$ and dt are the price and time interval of the price change, respectively. Let $R(q,t)$ denote the probability distribution function (PDF) for the price return, which could be extracted using the data described in Sect. 3 for all indices. The typical results for the price, price return and PDF of the Dow Jones index are plotted in Fig. 1a–c, respectively.

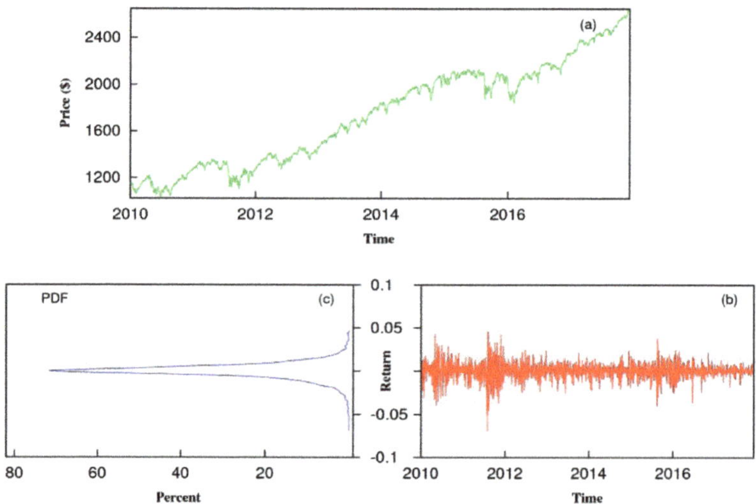

Fig. 1. **a** The price of Dow Jones index versus time; **b** the sketch of the price return versus time for the same index; **c** the PDF of the price return for the same index

Following Tahmasebi et al. (2015) and Shen and Haven (2017), we calculated the quantum potential for each index by applying the corresponding PDF in Eq. (3). The results for the quantum potentials for all indices were calculated on daily, weekly, seasonal and yearly basis. The typical quantum potential for Dow Jones index is shown in Fig. (2).

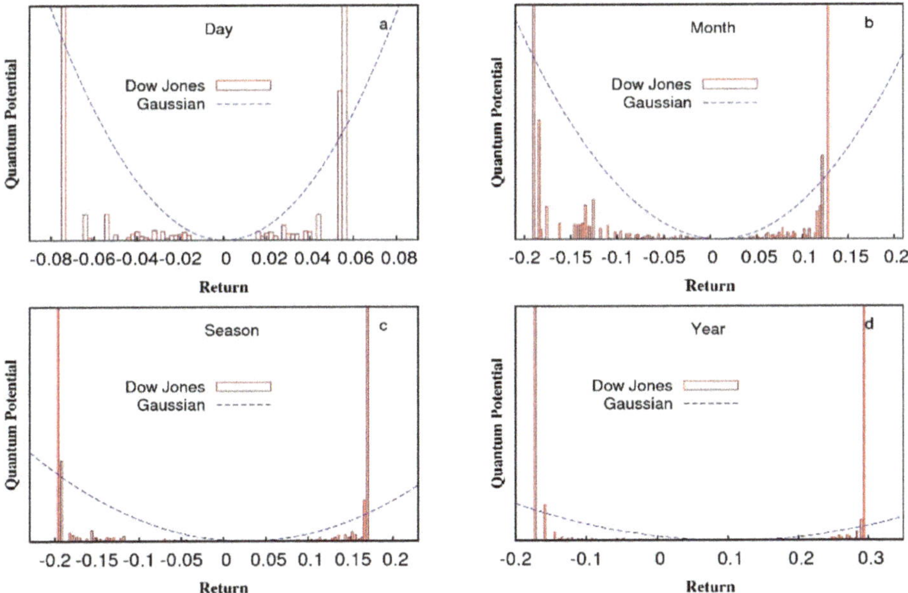

Fig. 2. The plot of **a** daily, **b** monthly, **c** seasonal and **d** yearly quantum potential versus the price returns; the dashed line corresponds to the white noise quantum potential

To check the model, the quantum potential of the Gaussian white noise, which is unbiased in prices at different times correlation, was compared with the quantum potential of Dow Jones index with the same variance. In order to derive the quantum potential for the Gaussian white noise of the respective index, one may insert the corresponding function, R, represented by $\exp(-(q-q_0)^2)/2\sigma^2$, into Eq. (3), and after some mathematical calculations obtain

$$U(q,t) = \frac{4(q-q_0)^2}{4\sigma^4} - \frac{2q}{2\sigma^2}, \tag{4}$$

where σ represents the variance and q_0 is the average variation of price returns for the market under examination.

In Fig. 2, the quantum potential of the real data (solid line) is compared with the quantum potential of the Gaussian white noise (dashed curve). It can be seen from the above four panels that there exist quantum potential walls which confine the returns into a specified domain. The variations of the returns increase from 6%, on a daily basis, to 30% on an annual timescale, where the Bohmian quantum potential walls tend to be Gaussian like. This is expected to occur in real situations, where the stock market prices do not change considerably during a day in contrast to the yearly variations.

Investing, as a financial decision, has always entailed two components of 'risk' and 'return' whose trade-off offers different investment combinations. On the one hand, investors seek to maximize their profits from an investment and, on the other hand, they are faced with the uncertainty surrounding the financial markets, which in turn, creates an uncertainty in the access to the investment returns. In other words, all investment decisions are based on the relationship between the two inevitable elements of risk and return. According to a clear consensus observed for the existence of positive relations between the risk and return, the quantum potential can be used as a useful indicator for comparing the risks of different indices against each other. As shown in Fig. 3, where the daily and yearly quantum potentials for different indices are plotted, a wider range of the potential walls means a higher return, and consequently, a higher risk.

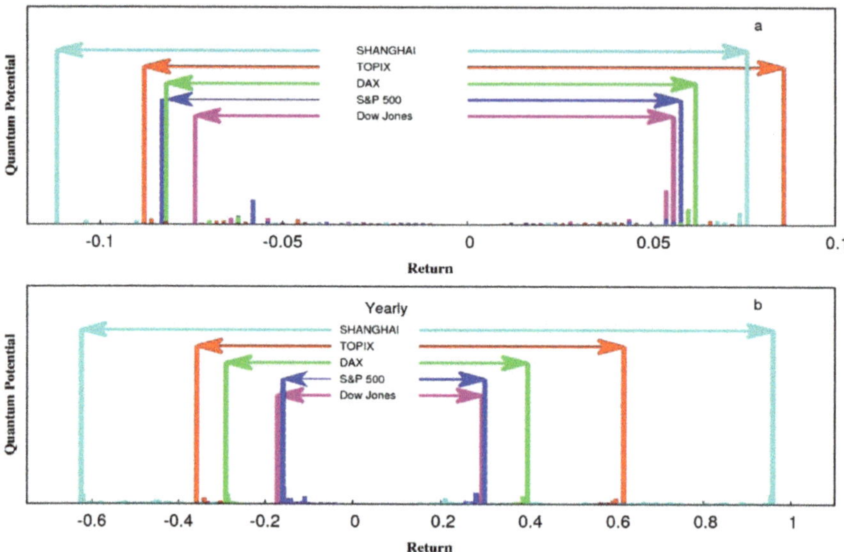

Fig. 3. **a** The daily and **b** yearly quantum potentials for the selected indices

Shanghai index as an emerging market has a relatively wide range of returns. Therefore, the corresponding wide ranges of the quantum potential walls indicate a higher risk both in daily and yearly time scales. In contrast, the relatively short ranges of the quantum potential walls indicate a lower risk for the Dow Jones and S&P 500, as the developed markets indices. These results are consistent with those of Derrabi and Leseure (2005) who showed that the emerging markets have higher returns in comparison to the developed markets, while being more risky.

Tables 1 and 2 show the results of the risk and the average return based on the quantum potential permissions, respectively. As shown in Table 1, it is found that the amount of the risk is highest for Shanghai as compared to other indices. The lowest and highest risks are in bold and italic values, respectively.

According to Table 2, the daily average returns of all indices, from 2010 to 2017, are negative as also shown in Fig. 3. This is due to the fact that the quantum potentials for all indices are left-oriented with respect to the mean value. The situation is reversed

Table 1. Risk of the selected indices based on the quantum potential permissions (between walls) in the period of January 2010–December 2017

	Daily	Monthly	Seasonally	Yearly
S&P 500	0.1421	**0.3167**	0.3924	**0.4600**
Dow Jones	**0.129**	**0.3183**	**0.3662**	**0.465**
Shanghai	*0.1876*	*0.6114*	*1.0048*	*1.5855*
Topix	0.175	0.43744	0.6236	0.9766
Dax	0.1461	0.4905	0.6596	0.6880

The lowest and highest risks are in bold and italic values, respectively

Table 2. Quantum potential restrictions on the price return is not symmetric for positive and negative values

	Daily	Monthly	Seasonally	Yearly
S&P 500	−0.00167	0.0156	0.0453	0.1664
Dow Jones	−0.00185	0.01618	0.04772	0.1578
Shanghai	−0.00268	−0.00072	0.001515	0.01059
Topix	−0.00164	0.00969	0.02527	0.07397
Dax	−0.00184	0.0108	0.03088	0.11903

This table shows the average returns of the selected indices based on these restrictions (January 2010–December 2017)

for the yearly time scale, where the average returns become positive for all indices and the corresponding quantum potential walls behave as right-oriented. This is due to the collective behavior of the stock markets that reveals the lower price return for the short run than for the long run.

5   Conclusions

In this study, we have employed the Bohmian quantum mechanics for investigating five selected stock indices of the emerging and developed markets. Calculating their quantum potentials, we compared them with the corresponding quantum potentials of the Gaussian white noise having the same variances. We have found that in the short-run, where the entanglement in prices is higher, the quantum potential walls are robust and narrower than those of the long-run pattern, where the entanglement is lower.

In order to maximize the expected returns of the selected portfolio, one may need to diversify the risk through selecting different stocks from different markets. The relation between the risk and average return shows that the long-run investments in the developed stock markets could be more safe and profitable than short-run investments.

Presumably, the trading strategy in an individual investor scale is a personal decision. However, it seems that in the collective scales there is a global pattern that governs the behavior of the stock markets. This global strategy pattern which is reflected as an average outcome in the real data, though not known in detail, is embedded in the quantum potential. In other words, the variance of the individual scale decisions is not much far from that of the other investors and follows a global pattern, which confines the events into a domain wall.

References

Bachelier, L. (1900). Théorie de la spéculation. *Annales scientifiques de lÉcole normale supérieure, 17*, 21–86. https://doi.org/10.24033/asens.476

Black, F., & Scholes, M. (1973). The Pricing of Options and Corporate Liabilities. *Journal of Political Economy, 81*(3), 637–654. http://dx.doi.org/10.1086/260062

Bohm, D. (1952). A Suggested Interpretation of the Quantum Theory in Terms of "Hidden" Variables. *I. Physical Review, 85*(2), 166–179. https://doi.org/10.1103/physrev.85.166

Chakraborti, A., Muni Toke, I., Patriarca, M., & Abergel, F. (2009). *Econophysics: Empirical facts and agent-based models.* ArXiv e-prints

Chen, J. (2014). The Unity of Science and Economics: A New Foundation of Economic Theory. *SSRN Electronic Journal.* http://dx.doi.org/10.2139/ssrn.2516607

Choustova, O. A. (2002). Pilot wave quantum model for the stock market. In: Khrennikov, A. Yu. (ed.) Quantum Theory: Reconsideration of Foundations, *Ser. Math. Model, 2*, 41–58. http://www.arxiv.org/abs/quant-ph/0109122

Choustova, O. (2004). Bohmian mechanics for financial processes. *Journal of Modern Optics, 51* (6–7), 1111–1111. https://doi.org/10.1080/09500340408233645

Choustova, O. (2009). Quantum probability and financial market. *Information Sciences, 179*(5), 478–484. https://doi.org/10.1016/j.ins.2008.07.001

Derrabi, M. & Leseure, M. (2005). Global Asset Allocation: Risk and Return Trade-off on Emerging Stockmarkets. Risk Management in Emerging Markets, 35–55. https://doi.org/10.1057/9780230596368_4

Holland, P. (2000). The quantum theory of motion: an account of the de broglie-bohm causal interpretation of quantum mechanics. University Press, Cambridge

Khrennikov, A. (1999). Classical and quantum mechanics on information spaces with applications to cognitive, psychological, social and anomalous phenomena. *Foundations of Physics, 29* (7), 1065–1068. arXiv:quant-ph/0003016

Mandelbrot, B. (1963). The Stable Paretian Income Distribution when the Apparent Exponent is Near Two. *International Economic Review, 4*(1), 111. https://doi.org/10.2307/2525463

Shen, C., & Haven, E. (2017). Using Empirical Data to Estimate Potential Functions in Commodity Markets: Some Initial Results. *International Journal of Theoretical Physics, 56* (12), 4092–4104. https://doi.org/10.1007/s10773-017-3446-z

Tahmasebi, F., Meskinimood, S., Namaki, A., Farahani, S. V., Jalalzadeh, S., & Jafari, G. R. (2015). Financial market images: A practical approach owing to the secret quantum potential. *EPL (Europhysics Letters), 109*(3), 30001. https://doi.org/10.1209/0295-5075/109/30001

Migration Influence on Human Capital Under Globalization

Olga Lashkareva, Sofya Abetova[(⊠)], and Gulnar Kozhahmetova

Faculty of Economics, L.Gumilyov Eurasian National University of Astana,
Astana, Kazakhstan
abetovasofa@gmail.com

1   Introduction

Economic globalization comprehensively influences on human development of a country and global community and breeds international competition at world commodity market increasing mobility of capital and labor force. Within the conditions of extensive world economic relations among countries, economic cooperation is based on increase of exports and imports, including the regional economics into the system of international division of labor. At the same time, there are intensive trade liberalization, strengthening international competition in exchange of commodities and services, attraction of investments and capital as well as equally important labor power. Migration is the key factor of development. Survival of the world developed economies depends on migration.

1.1   The Degree of Scientific Development of the Issue

Nowadays, millions of people are departing their countries in search of better lives. This is due to poor economic situation at home and religious or political problems. These migration movements are defined as migration of labor force and labor resources. At the present time, international migration has become worldwide, the countries included in the Organization for economic co-operation and development (OECD), 35 most developed countries in the world are reviewed in this article. In recent years, in many OECD countries investments of enterprises in intellectual capital has been growing faster than investments in physical capital, such as equipment and real estate, and this trend persists even under difficult economic conditions. Exactly migration processes, currently, are the force that has an effect on economics, politics and all components of human capital. A large number of scientific studies prove a problem and the urgency of the research.

1.2   The Aim of the Article

The aim of the article is to review migration impact on human capital in world economies, to present the problems of migration in the OECD countries in a detailed form, and to identify possible strategies for behavior in the world arena.

© Springer Nature Switzerland AG 2018
N. Ozatac and K. K. Gökmenoglu (eds.), *Emerging Trends in Banking
and Finance*, Springer Proceedings in Business and Economics,
https://doi.org/10.1007/978-3-030-01784-2_9

1.3   Statement of Basic Materials

The modern global economy is represented by interaction and competition of countries with the main development models, namely, innovation-driven growth model, technology, raw materials and agrarian models. The innovation-driven growth model is characterized by production of knowledge, export of technology, science-intensive products (USA, Germany). The technological model is peculiar to countries importing technology, high technology products (Japan, Singapore, and South Korea). The raw materials model is export of raw materials, import of products (Iran, Russia). The agrarian model is export of agricultural products, import of manufactured goods (Greece, Mongolia). Some countries are at an intermediate stage of development between these types, combining the characteristics of several models. However, the most countries at this stage of globalization are focused on technological development and further development of an innovative economy. It is primarily related to those countries that have such a strategic resource of economic growth and increased competitiveness, as a significant scientific and educational potential. So, for example, the main competitive advantage of the USA is high-quality accumulated human capital for which favorable conditions have been created to operate as the development driver. And high-quality human capital enables that the USA meet periodically all emerging issues and difficulties. Moreover, they enable that the country won geopolitical completion with the USSR. Within the conditions of globalization of the world economy and division of labor in it, the USA re-established all its traditional and secondary production facilities of industrial economy in the developing countries with cheap labor force. The USA for instance almost renounced manufacturing consumer electronics for these reasons. But, in addition, to provide food and general safety they support and develop the most cost-effective agriculture in the world. Sweden in the post-war period due to heavy unproductive expenses in social sphere and reduction of the level of competition at all levels because of the large unproductive costs in the social sphere and the decline in competition at all levels lagged behind leading countries (USA, Japan, Germany, Luxembourg, etc.) in GDP per capita and high technology. To improve the economy and society, development programs were developed on the basis of the theory of human capital, including computer programs for calculating the quality and efficiency of human capital at the level of organizations (here the Swedes are ahead other countries). This helped them to use resources more effectively, to increase competition, to reduce dependency, and again enter the top five countries with the most competitive economies in the world.

2   Relevant Studies

When assessing human capital in the terms of industrial and innovative development of the country, the characteristic criterion is creation of own human capital on the basis of modern high-tech technologies, human access to education and training, allowing him to become a competitive specialist both in the domestic and foreign labor markets. At the same time, the need to achieve competitive advantages of human capital based on international comparability of indicators of other countries increases. In accordance with the ILO Recommendation No. 195 "On Human Development: Education, Staff Training and Continuous Learning" adopted by the ILO General Conference (June 2004, Geneva), new quality of human capital as a result of continuing education can be described as acquisition of competence, qualification, potential for employment by an employee.

The nature of a new quality of human capital should be characterized based on quality shifts in demographic indices (population size, gainfully employed population, sex-age structure, average life expectancy), economic (GDP per capita, employment rate and unemployment rate, wages), social (rate of literacy and education of population, employed and unemployed). The new quality of human capital, in our opinion, means the realization of opportunities and in ensuring the security of human life, his political and civil rights, freedom of the individual. The new quality of human capital is determined by achievement of high standards of quality of life. Assessment of a new quality of human capital is possible as a result of the quantitative measurement of new qualitative changes achieved. This requires selection of indicators to assess the level of human capital development at this stage.

As the base values and the most real indicators of human development is the choice of three basic capabilities proved in the UNDP Human Development Reports: long and healthy life, education and decent standard of living. They form integrated indicators of HDI and allow assessing the achieved level of human development and capital of the country and making international comparisons. Enterprise innovation involves investments in a variety of intangible assets, such as data, software, patents, design, and new organizational processes. These non-physical assets make up together the knowledge-based capital or intellectual capital. Enterprise investment in intellectual capital accommodates to growth and productivity.

Studies in the European Union and the United States show that the contribution that enterprise investment in intellectual capital contributes to average productivity growth is between 20% and 34%. Intellectual capital is transforming what makes firms competitive. In the automobile construction and manufacture sector, for example, software plays an increasingly important role in the cost of developing new cars, with millions of lines of computer programs at the heart of high-tech cars. As we noted above, there is a close relationship between investment and the reproduction of human capital. Investment contributes to creation of favorable conditions for the reproductive movement of human capital. These conditions provide new opportunities, which, when effectively are used, can lead to an increase in the welfare of society and the socio-economic development of the country.

Investments are an important means of reproduction of human capital, as they provide favorable conditions for this process, improve the quality of life. Investment should be permanent, sustainable, increasing and carried out at every stage of the reproduction of human capital. Investment is the driving force behind the process of human capital formation. Initially human capital is accumulated through investments in health, education and culture. Due to investment, human capital is simply reproduced and expanded.

The main criteria for assessing the effective functioning of human capital can be presented as follows:

- sustainable post-crisis economic development of the country;
- creation of new jobs on a permanent basis with high technology innovation;
- achievement of high-performance labor in the main sectors of the economy;
- making human capital relevant and competitive in labor markets and reducing unemployment;

– ensuring high quality of life according to international standards.

They are closely interlinked and create opportunities for increased public investment as well as foreign investment in human capital. Sustainable economic development and the stable state of the economy makes it possible to increase the prime costs of the country for education, health care, increase in funds' investment and family spending on training and vocational training of skilled workers.

Most of the factors of effective functioning of human capital can be measured by quantitative indicators. Some of them can be evaluated only by expert. Their impact on human capital varies, and it is difficult to measure. At the same time, it is important to distinguish the main, priority and determining at the moment and in the future among them. In this regard, it is important to study the role of human capital in ensuring post-crisis recovery of the economy, its stability and economic growth of the country. Moreover, the prospects for the development of many countries of the world economy and expectations are constantly considered in conjunction with sustainable economic development.

Income inequality has almost doubled in most OECD countries over the past two decades. In many countries, long-term trends of rising inequality are observed, in others—there is a sudden and transient increase in the level of inequality. Inequality trends in different countries are uneven. Today, the lowest level of inequality is observed in Sweden, Denmark, Iceland, Slovenia, and the highest one is in China, Indonesia and South Africa. In average, 10% of the richest families in the OECD countries own half of the total wealth, 50% of the less wealthy families own almost 50%, and the remaining 40% own no more than 3% of the wealth. In the US, 1% of the population owns 35% of wealth, in Austria and the Netherlands 1% of the population owns 25%, and in Canada 1% of the inhabitants account for about 16% of wealth.

Inequality in the OECD countries is far beyond the limits of income and affects many vital areas. Inequality arises, for example, in access to education, health care. The OECD notes that, in addition to income, parents' education has a strong impact on the ability of children to obtain quality education. On average, in the OECD countries, children with low-educated parents will receive higher education with a probability of 15%. But they almost four times oftener (63%) enter the university, if at least one of the parents has a higher education. Children with a more educated parent are 6 times less likely to drop out of school than children whose parents have a lower level of education. Health care advances in the OECD countries over the last century have led to that expected lifespan has been steadily increased in all the OECD countries, increasing by average 3 months per year since 1970 due to reduction of some important health risks (in particular, smoking) and improvement of health care systems, which steadily improve the quality of care. However, these achievements in the field of health care were not equally distributed.

For example, a twenty-five-year-old man with a low level of education can live at least 4 years less than a man with higher education in all the OECD countries. A person with a low level of education in the US is likely to live 7 years less than a person with a higher education. In Sweden, this indicator is 6 years, and in Hungary—14 years. Income inequality is higher in cities than in other localities, and, as a rule, even higher in megalopolises, as they attract highly skilled workers and the most productive firms.

In many OECD countries, there are significant differences in the income of regions, especially between urban and rural regions. People living in cities earn by an average of 18% more than residents of other settlements, although these differences do not take into account the discrepancies in the cost of living that can significantly change the picture. In the United States, Italy and Japan, the average income in the richest megalopolises is almost twice as high as in ordinary cities.

The digital revolution, big data, the data collection processes themselves have become important for economic activity. Therefore, the question arises as to the method of data collection, possession and use. The ability to extract information and apply data for commercial purposes stimulates the economic activities. Data analysis facilitates to make decisions efficiently and quickly, to increase performance through the use of fast and inexpensive automated technologies. If you do not control innovation and data management, then the market basis of society can be undermined. The OECD highlights the increase in income inequality after technological changes in Germany, Italy, the USA, Denmark, Portugal, Sweden and Brazil. Nevertheless, the sphere of ICT becomes a separate market force, which also allows you to receive income. ICT increases labor productivity, demand for skilled workers and jobs with non-standard tasks. There is a difference in income between less and more skilled workers.

The spread of temporary, part-time employment and self-employment influences on labor productivity. In France and Switzerland, Poland, Portugal and Spain, these types of employment grew by 10%. In the OECD countries, part-time employment increased from 15.4% in 2007 to 16.8% in 2015. The reason for this phenomenon is digitalization, changes in the requirements for the qualification of workers, an increase in the proportion of non-standard jobs where interpersonal skills or creativity are needed.

In the OECD countries, employees in the financial sector make up 4% of the workforce. In Luxembourg and the UK—more than 30% of financial officers work in the best financial firms. According to the OECD, such firms pay higher salary than salaries of workers with similar profiles in other sectors, which also lead to inequality. Income inequality affects on productivity and limits the ability of people with low incomes to contribute to economic growth by hindering the accumulation of human capital. States should invest in human capital, for example, to provide low-income people with the opportunity to receive education and personal development, which raises the level of family income. According to OECD research, people with a low level of education are 2 times more likely to go to hospitals with lung diseases and diabetes than people with a high level of education. In regions with the most unequal income distribution, GDP growth decelerates. According to OECD research, after the 2008 crisis, regions with a more even distribution of income turned out to be more resilient to economic consequences. Inequality puts pressure on government social budgets. Since 1990, the government social expenditures have increased from 17.1% in 1990 to 21.2% in 2014 on average for the OECD countries. At the same time, social security is aimed not at supporting incomes of the able-bodied population, but more at paying sickness benefit pensions, old age pension and survivor's pension.

The World Bank (WB) report "The Changing Wealth of Nations 2018", presented on January 30, 2018 in Washington, provides interesting statistics on the growth of global welfare from 1995 to 2014 while increasing global inequality, the gap between the richest and the poorest countries has reached 5200%.

The authors of the study caution governments against enthusiasm in increase of financing human capital development by any means, including depletion of resources. The report reviews the level of welfare in 141 countries for the period from 1995 to 2014 based on the assessment of aggregate indicators of natural resources (forests and minerals), human capital (income of citizens throughout their lives), material capital (construction, infrastructure, etc.) and net foreign assets. According to the report, human capital is the most significant component of welfare in general, whereas in low-income countries, natural resources account for almost half of this indicator. Inequality between countries is growing. The standard of living has increased by about 66%, from $690 trillion to 1143 trillion (in fixed market prices in US dollars for 2014). At the same time, the level of inequality remained significant. Thus, the authors of the report note, Welfare value in the OECD countries with a high level of income was 52 times higher than in the low-income countries. The decline in the level of well-being per capita is observed in a number of large countries with low incomes. In addition, in some countries of the Middle East with a high level of carbon stocks. This decline was also noted in several high-income OECD countries affected by the 2009 financial crisis. A decline in well-being per capita indicates a possible depletion of the critical resources needed to generate future revenues, and "this fact is rarely reflected in GDP growth indicators in countries".

The World Bank once again in this regard calls for paying more attention to development of human capital, but now also warns against the identified risks of this process. Human capital should not be built at any cost. On a world-wide scale, today, already 70% of the wealth accrues to human capital, about 25%—to material, and 10% —to natural resources. In the states with average incomes the natural component can reach 25%, in the poor—47%. In OECD high-income countries, natural capital per capita in 2014 was three times higher than that of poor countries, although its share in the total wealth structure was only 3%. "Through the formation and additions to human capital and natural resources, countries around the world can achieve a higher level of prosperity and stronger economic growth. The World Bank Group bolsters its efforts supporting the countries to improve the level and efficiency of investment in human capital", says World Bank Group President Jim Yong Kim.

The report describes that more than two dozens of low-income countries, in which natural resources played a leading role in welfare development in 1995, have moved into the category of middle-income countries over the past 20 years. And this was partly due to the investment of income from natural resources in such industries as infrastructure, education and health care, which boost additions to human capital. But the authors of the report emphasize that "achievement of well-being is by no means to increase capital by depleting natural reserves." "If growth is due to the depletion of natural resources, such as forest land and fisheries, it will be short-term. As our studies have shown, the cost of natural resources per capita, as a rule, increases with income growth. This contradicts the traditional notion that development invariably entails the depletion of natural reserves", says Karin Kemper, Senior Director of the Environment and Natural Resources Global Practice at the World Bank.

The report also provides such curious assessments. For the period from 1995 to 2014, the cost of natural resources in the world has doubled. Among other factors, this is due to higher raw material prices, as well as an increase in economically proven reserves. On the contrary, the cost of productive forests decreased by 9%, and in many regions the increase in agricultural land was due to the reduction of forests.

The report, which was a continuation of similar assessments, contains estimates of human capital. This human capital is estimated as the amount of income received during the remaining period of a person's working life, so this indicator takes into account health care and education. The World Bank notes that women account for less than 40% of the world's human capital due to lower income levels throughout life. And this is a potential unused in full. Ensuring gender equality can lead to an increase in welfare at the expense of human capital by 18%.

Thus, all components are important for the integrated effectiveness of human capital. Low quality of any of them reduces its overall quality. Negative synergetic and multiplicative effects of the weakening of the effectiveness of human capital begin to act while declining efficiency or reducing quality of any component.

It should be noted that the basic component of human capital is the mentality of the people, including traditions and culture, attitudes toward work, family, law-abidance, religion. The determinants of human capital are upbringing, education, health, accumulated knowledge, science, quality of life, competition and economic freedom, the rule of law and rights, security, mobility and creativity of business and citizens—a synthetic and complex socio-economic category at the intersection of various disciplines and sciences: economics, psychology, sociology, information technologies, history, medicine, pedagogy, philosophy, political science and others.

More than 258 million migrants live in the world. Such statistics were cited by the UN Department for Economic and Social Affairs, "this is more by 14 million people compared to 2015, when the number of international migrants in the world—people living in a state that is not their birthplace—was the highest from ever registered—244 million people" in accordance with the Report of the International Organization for Migration (IOM).

At the same time, the share of migrants in the population composition is especially high in some countries of the Persian Gulf—the UAE (88.4%), Qatar (75.7%) and Kuwait (73.6%). In 2015, Germany ranked first in the world by number of requests for asylum—442 thousand in 2015. In total in the European Union, last year it was registered more than 1.2 million of such requests, that twice more than data of 2014. The IOM points out that the main part of the Syrian refugees is hosted by neighboring countries with Syria, in particular, Turkey (2.2 million), Lebanon (1.2 million) and Jordan (nearly 630,000). Women make up on average less than half of all migrants in the world, although in North America and Europe these figures are higher than the worldwide average by 3–4%.

Thus, 3.4% of the world's population left their countries. Each tenth of them is a displaced person, that is, a refugee. At the same time, the number of such people increased by 49% compared to the beginning of the 21st century.

Most of all migrants live in the US—almost 50 million people, that is, every fifth person who left his home country. In Russia, there are about 12 million migrants; the same number is in Germany and Saudi Arabia.

Despite the stereotypes about migrants living exclusively on the allowance, 74% of them are of working age (from 20 to 64 years)—this is more than the percentage of the world's working-age population (57%).

Most of all those who left their country were born in India—17 million people. Mexicans are at the second place—13 million people. From 6 to 11 million people also left China, Bangladesh, Ukraine, Syria, Pakistan and Russia.

We will carry out a more detailed analysis of migration in the OECD countries, since migration processes are currently a force that have impact on the economy, politics and all components of human capital.

For this purpose, all the OECD countries are divided into eight groups by total inflow of migrants for the period from 2010 to 2015:

Group 1—countries with the number of migrants up to 50,000 people (Slovak Republic, Latvia, Iceland, Estonia, Slovenia, Finland, Luxembourg, Hungary, Israel, Czech Republic, Mexico, Portugal)

Group 2—countries with the number of migrants from 50,000 to 100,000 people (Denmark, Ireland, Norway, Poland, New Zealand)

Group 3—countries with the number of migrants from 100,000 to 150,000 people (Sweden, Belgium, Switzerland)

Group 4—countries with the number of migrants from 150,000 to 200,000 people (Netherlands, Austria, Chile)

Group 5—countries with the number of migrants from 200,000 to 250,000 people (Australia, Italy)

Group 6—countries with the number of migrants from 250,000 to 300,000 people (France, Canada, Spain)

Group 7—countries with the number of migrants from 300,000 to 400,000 people (Korea, Japan)

Group 8—countries with more than 400,000 migrants (UK, USA, Germany).

Select a country with the largest volume of migration from each group (except Japan, data are not available) (Fig. 1).

Most of migrants for the period 2000–2015 are in Germany, the total number was 3,047,006 people. Germany is a popular country for migration, because of its loyalty. While Japan, which is in the seventh group—countries with the number of migrants from 300,000 to 400,000 people, is a country of stable migration, with a total of 5,355,166 migrants for the period of 2000–2015.

Spain, with a total of 7,325,227 migrants, employed migrants in the informal sector of the economy (construction and home-based job). This country is attractive from the ethnocultural point of view for immigrants from various Spanish-speaking Latin American countries, who are easier to adapt. Spain is a country of new immigration.

Despite the fact that Switzerland is in the third group, the total number of migrants was 1,985,774 people. The countries of this group have been the most attractive for migrants for all the years. As can be seen, between 2000 and 2012, Austria hosted up to 100,000 migrants per year, and in 2015 the inflow of migrants increased twice. The need to receive and distribute refugees and illegal migrants to the EU from the countries of North Africa, the Middle East and South Asia played an important role. Italy, with a total number of migrants of 5,180,739 people, has undergone significant changes, turning from a country of emigrants (as of today 4 million Italians live abroad)

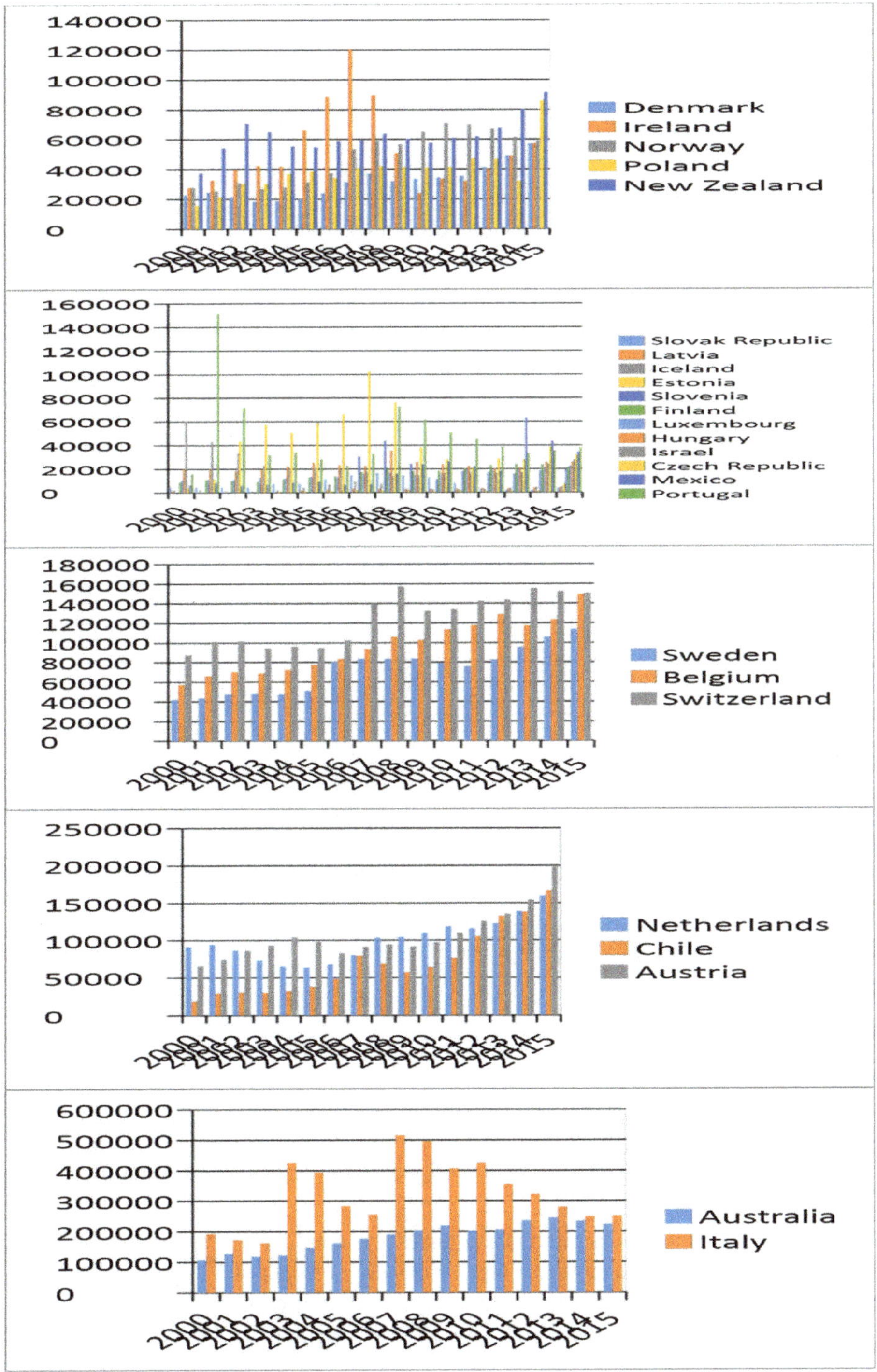

Fig. 1. Overall figures on migration on the OECD countries

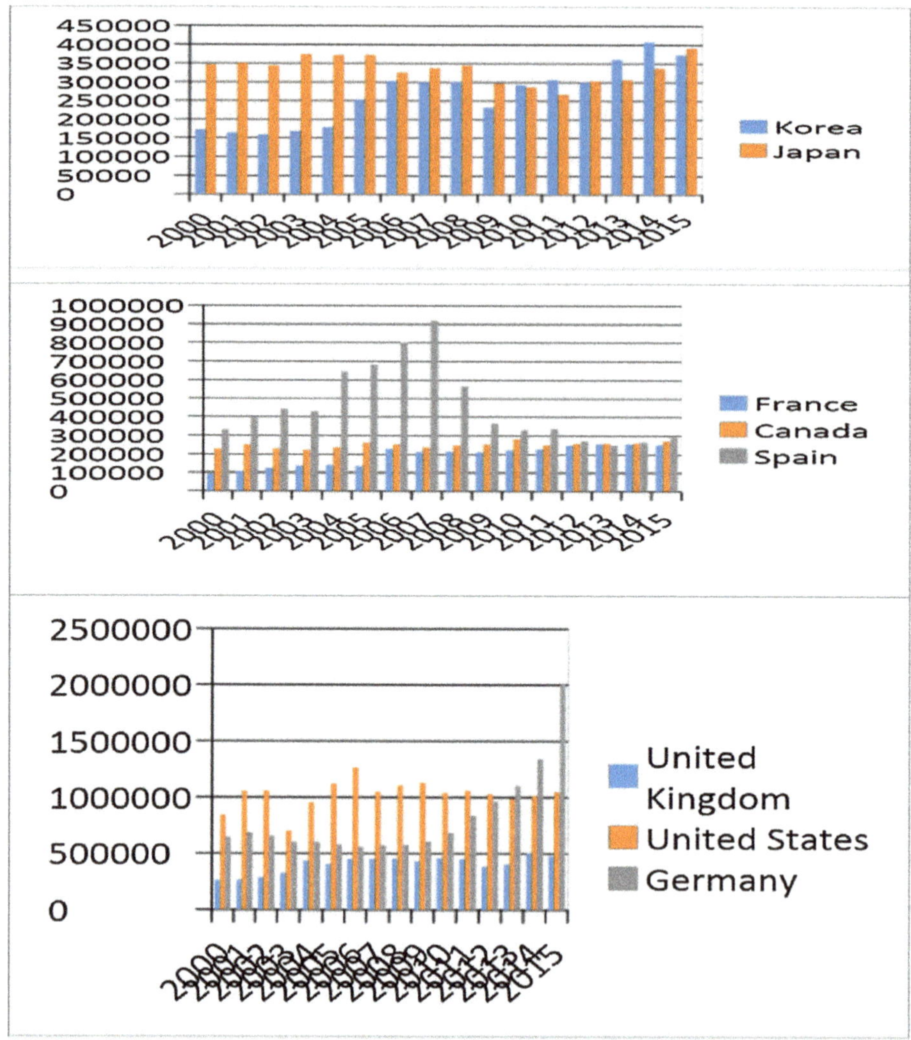

Fig. 1. (*continued*)

to the object of active immigration. This country is attractive more because of geographical location than economic activity.

At the same time, migrants seeking a better life show interest to economically more active countries (Fig. 2).

Analyzing the above-mentioned countries by employment indicators, it can be concluded that the percentage of the employed is generally higher in almost all countries except Portugal, but at the same time, more migrants are employed with a low level of education, as they more often agree to a lower salary. However, it should be

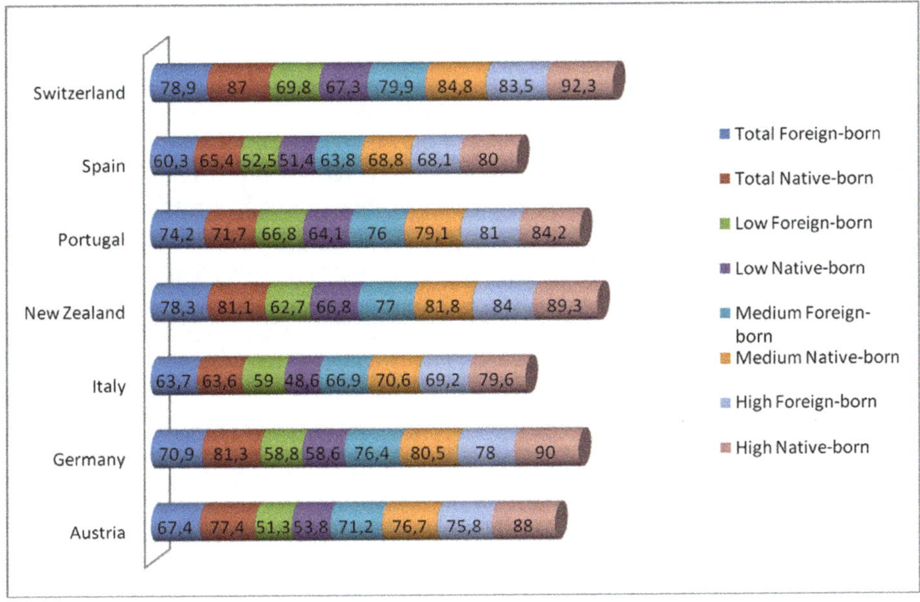

Fig. 2. Employment rates by place of birth and educational attainment (25–64), percentage

taken into account that not only labor migrants with high qualifications depart. Refugees, as a rule, do not have education, qualifications, work skills required in the host countries. The level of human capital in these countries tends to decrease, since migrants according to recent data make up 14% of the population of host countries. Migrants are oftener employed in the informal economy, which distinctive features are lack of legal protection and lack of information on the rights they need in order not to become victims of exploitation and other violations by the employer, intermediaries and officials. Most migrants occupy niches in the labor market, which are not filled by local workers. The lack of information on real employment opportunities and working conditions in the host countries opens up opportunities for the exploitation of migrant labor, resulting in compulsory labor, the worst forms of child labor, human trafficking and other forms of violence. Women are much more likely than men to become victims of trafficking. Those migrants with unregulated status who are exiled to the country of citizenship, at home receive very little social and economic aid. In many cases, these people are stigmatized, and they need to make a lot of efforts to return to their old life.

Among people with higher and secondary education, the percentage of the employed is higher among the local population; the difference can be as high as 12%. At the same time, experts, speaking about the positive experience of labor migration, in the case of the return of migrants to their homeland after studying, work, speak about improvement of the quality of human capital. In addition, it is important to note that labor migration and migrant remittances to their home countries become a way of survival for their families and ensure that they are their financial independent and increase their opportunities.

Recently, the share of highly qualified specialists in world flows has significantly increased. Migration of highly qualified specialists is a pledge of mutually beneficial development of the member countries of various international unions. As it is about enriching with ideas, sharing knowledge, professional skills, which determine the effectiveness of modern economic development, the migration of these specialists is of common interest. But only in the case when it refers to temporary, return migration. If migration assumes irrevocable character, then in this case it is already a question of "brain drain", which causes extremely negative consequences for the countries from which it occurs. Unfortunately, in the case of refugees or illegal migration, it is a question of low-skilled labor force.

If we consider the flow of migrants by place of birth in the countries selected, the following picture is obtained (Fig. 3).

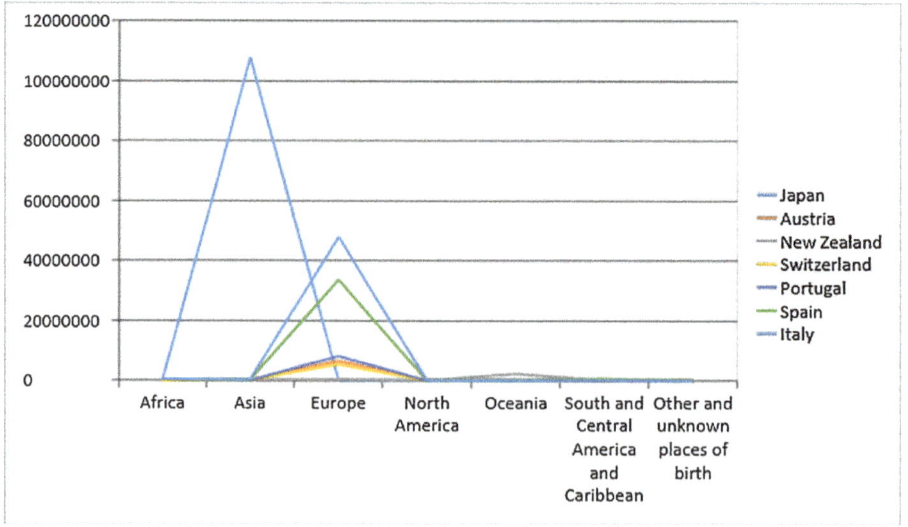

Fig. 3. The flow of migrants by place of birth

As seen, modern migration processes are characterized by the inflow of unskilled and, consequently, cheap labor force to Canada, the USA and Western Europe from the countries of Africa, the Middle East, Eastern Europe, etc. The main reason for this migration process is the reorientation of the "indigenous" population of developed countries to more prestigious professions of modernity in the conditions of the demographic crisis. And, in spite of a number of political and economic measures taken regarding the influx of immigrants, the influx of unskilled labor force into the countries of Western Europe and North America remains. Then, we consider it expedient to estimate the unemployment rate by place of birth and sex in the countries chosen for the research (Fig. 4).

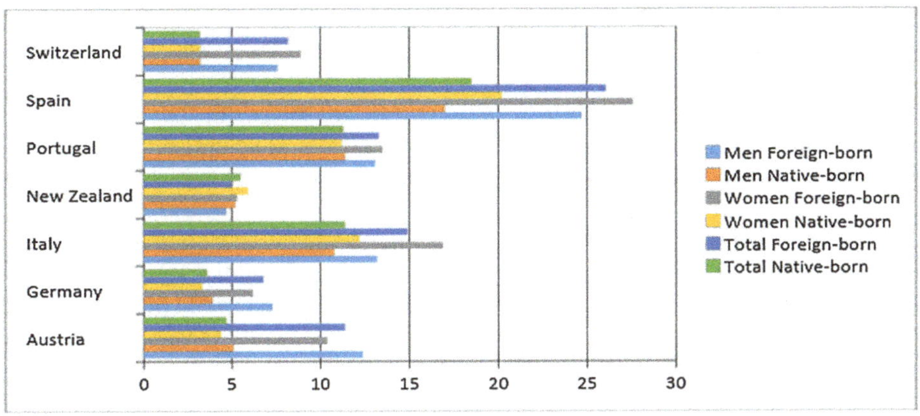

Fig. 4. Unemployment rate by place of birth and sex

The situation is quite clear, the unemployed are migrant to a great extent, and in many countries the number of unemployed females exceeds the number of unemployed males. According to some estimates, 50% of economic growth in the OECD countries over the last 50 years is due to increase of education level and more than half of this increase is resulted from women's greater access to education and a reduction in gender inequality.

In the conditions of development of the economy of a post-industrial society (a knowledge-based economy), the "flow of (brain drain) of talents" into the most developed countries of the world gains global dimensions. Now young researchers and specialists (and not just old and prominent scientists) are the subject of this migration. In order to attract the largest number of intellectuals (priority is given to specialists in the natural sciences and computer technologies), special state programs are developed and implemented in developed countries.

Findings and directions for future research.

Thus, due to the processes of intercountry labor migration, distribution of human capital in the world economy is changing. In the terms of globalization of the modern social structure, maintaining and building own human capital, as well as attracting human resources from other countries, become a strategic task for each state.

The agreed measures in the field of education and skills development can serve to provide individuals with opportunities to increase their potential and create favorable conditions for development. Education and skills development should begin at an early age and continue throughout whole life. According to the OECD, countries that help deprived children in this area have a smaller gap in the effectiveness of training between students in a profitable and disadvantaged position. The OECD proposes a concept that needs to be developed—early childhood education and care services (ECEC). The work includes 3 directions: removal of barriers to access to education, including for migrants; support for family and external interventions to help parents; providing opportunities for the development of socio-economic and cultural skills. Similarly, support should be provided to school-age children, it also includes 3 areas:

combating poor progress; providing opportunities for the development of socio-economic skills. In England, personal, social, medical and economic skills have been already developed in the junior school for early personality becoming and help in choosing a profession; Support for schools at a disadvantage. In the UK, there is a program to hire the best directors in such schools. In New Zealand and in France, the directors of such schools receive higher wages than their colleagues, even from the best schools.

In addition to formal education, measures are also required to provide for further training and development, especially among low- and middle-skilled adults and migrants. For this purpose, it is recommended: to improve basic skills for involvement in further education; to provide funding for training adults at a disadvantage (in Japan, for these purposes, the government provides subsidies to employers); to provide innovative and flexible training opportunities to overcome access barriers for the most vulnerable groups (for example, uneducated youth, people without work experience, single parents, migrants); to combine adult education, professional training and career guidance for the reintegration of adults into the labor market; and to develop new lifelong learning schemes in particular aimed at people with low and medium qualifications.

Fiscal policy should also be aimed at helping the population. In many countries (France, Portugal, the United States, etc.) unemployment benefits are common. Support can be more narrow-minded, for example, subsidies for free meals for children in school (USA, UK, France). To reduce the level of income inequality of contributions to pension funds or mortgage costs can be released from paying taxes.

Governments should play an important role in supporting people adapt to changes in the labor market. For this, social protection mechanisms and a comprehensive activation policy should be used. For example, the concept of unconditional basic income implies fixed regular payments to all members of society. Although this concept is very controversial, it has been tested in some countries. For example, in Finland, since January 2017, 2000 beneficiaries of unemployment benefits are paid with a basic income of 560 euros per month, equivalent to about a quarter of the average income of one person.

The policy should be flexible and adapted to new changes, aimed at long-term results. An important element is support of young people, which is the group that is least adapted to the labor market. Support should be aimed at developing skills of entrepreneurship, mentoring, granting, micro-credit and credit guarantees, creating entrepreneurship networks. For example, the Prince's Trust Enterprise program in the UK offers a support package for disadvantaged youth, including grants, loans, coaching and online support. In 2005, it created about 150 startups.

Japan is an example of a policy aimed at supporting laid-off workers to reintegrate into the labor market, where in 2012, following Sharp's announcement of reduction of the employees over the age of 40, the state employment services created a coordinating committee whose tasks included delivery of advisory services, arrangement of meetings and interviews, psychological help, support in acquiring new skills. The committee's work allowed the former employees of the company to find a new job quickly without significant losses in the quality of life level.

Any policy aimed at developing the labor market should also take into account the need for integration of women. Although the women participation rates are gradually increasing, nevertheless, in the OECD countries only 67.4% of women participated in the labor market in 2015, compared to 80% of men, and the pay gap was 15%. In 2016, only 4.8% of senior positions were occupied by women.

In order to increase gender equality in different areas, the OECD member countries and a number of non-member countries adopted the OECD 2013 Gender Recommendation and the Recommendation on Gender Equality in Public Life in 2015 with call for countries to promote gender equality through various actions, including legislation, policies, monitoring and special campaigns. Important initiatives are related to alleviating the inequalities that result from the need to care for the child. So, in 2013, public spending on pre-school education and care exceeded 1% of GDP in Denmark, Finland, France, Iceland, Norway and Sweden.

The state should help to create an environment that gives business a chance to survive. The policy should be aimed at increasing productivity, bridging the gap between the most and least productive firms, improving business dynamics, and supporting SMEs.

According to the OECD, reforms in insolvency regime promote the productivity growth. Reforms in Belgium and Italy made it possible to halve the volume of capital paid by laggard firms.

Often the serious barriers to firms, especially SMEs, are taxes. To overcome them, asymmetric taxation of profits and losses, distribution of taxes between capital and labor income, tax credits and discounts for research and development, etc. can be introduced.

The policy should be focused on developing skills and reducing the gap between people for growth in productivity. According to the OECD, more effective work in this area can contribute to an increase in labor productivity by an average of 10%.

The policy should be aimed at improving the working conditions in regions, cities, communities, including lagging regions. In many countries, 20% of the population (the upper quintile) lives in regions with productivity three times higher than 20% of the population in the lower quintile. To mitigate this situation, the policy should be multidirectional. For example, approaches to rural development policies in most OECD countries continue to focus mainly on agriculture and, therefore, it is necessary to increase productivity in non-agricultural economic activities. Cross-sectoral, horizontal and vertical policy coordination is also needed. One of the key elements of the regional development policy is affordable housing and access to public transport. It is necessary to take into account the factors of globalization when making political decisions. This includes both the United Nations Sustainable Development Goals, the Paris Agreement, and the countries' agreements on the automatic exchange of information and the exchange of information on request. To take into account all the factors, various methods can be used, from dialogue to supranational regulation.

Increase in competitiveness of human capital in post-crisis conditions for development of the national economy based on innovative industrialization is a complicated problem that requires a comprehensive integrated approach. It is interrelated with solution of many priority tasks in activities of the relevant ministries, departments and other management structures on the basis of interaction and cooperation. Development of arrangement and effective measures to improve competitiveness of human capital will contribute to the overall successful implementation of the concept of the formation and development of competitive human capital around the world.

References

Adukov R., Adukova A. New model of executive governmental structure as a human capital development factor // Економічний часопис - XXI. 2015. Т. 1. № 7-8. p. 24–27.

http://stats.oecd.org.

https://cyberleninka.ru/article/n/rol-chelovecheskogo-kapitala-v-usloviyah-globalizatsii-postindustrialnogo-obschestva.

Lashkareva O.V. Development of human capital in Kazakhstan: trends, priorities and arrangement. Monograph. Almaty: Astana, LLP Master Po, 2017 – 139 p. ISBN 978-601-326-030-3.

Schwab K. The Global Competitiveness Report 2011–2012 // World Economic Forum. – Швейцария: Davos, 2011. – P. 528.

Destination Marketing and Tourism Entrepreneurship in Ghana

Selira Kotoua[✉], Mustafa Ilkan, and Maryam Abdullahi

School of Computing and Technology, Eastern Mediterranean University,
Famagusta, North Cyprus, Turkey
{kotoua.selira,maryamabdullahi550}@gmail.com,
mustafa.ilkan@emu.edu.tr

1 Introduction

Majority of tourism marketing activities take place in the tourism destination market settings (Day 2017; Veasna et al. 2013). Tourism destinations form the strong foundations of the models of the tourism systems (Lisowska 2017; Tussyadiah et al. 2017). The tourism industry in Ghana is currently emerging as the rudimentary pillar of analysis in the tourism market (Pino and Peluso 2015; Camilleri 2017a, b, c, d; Liu et al. 2018). Nevertheless, tourism destination marketing and management is a complicated problem that needs methodical approach and comprehensive understanding to deal with potential tourists' attraction and destination organizations (Pattanaro 2014; Pike and Page 2014; Marasco et al. 2018). Tourists have diversification choices available from the various destination marketing institutions and different supply of tourism products and services around the world (Li et al. 2017; Weldearegay 2017; Veasna et al. 2013). Many tourism institutions at different destination compete for tourists' attention due to the various competitive marketplaces (Utama 2016). The destinations desire to be more successful and attractive required productivity and the incorporation of destination marketing, managerial policies and robust comprehension of the destination marketing conditions to entice tourists' visitation intentions (Mijoč et al. 2017; Santini et al. 2018) (Fig. 1).

The developing of the destination marketing and management activities are in accordance with the process of developing destination markets globally (Stylidis and Cherifi 2018; Avraham and Ketter 2016). The tourism industry has the biggest potential to continue to expand and grow with the growth of the world populations, expansions of businesses and age related travel structure that includes social factors like the use of the internet and culture of globalization (Kim 2016; Hipsher 2017) The United Nations World Tourism Organization (UNTWO 2016) reveals that international arrivals global could be up to 1.5 billion by the year 2020 and may generate a revenue of more than US\$ 1 trillion (UNTWO 2017). This indicates that thousands of businesses can be generated in large and small quantity by selling and providing services to tourists around the world at various tourism destinations (Li and Ryan 2018; Fronek 2018).

Entrepreneurship in the form of small medium sized has been receiving popularity within the tourism industry in various ways that include research and new company set ups within the tourism industry for innovative reasons and the creation of value

© Springer Nature Switzerland AG 2018
N. Ozatac and K. K. Gökmenoglu (eds.), *Emerging Trends in Banking
and Finance*, Springer Proceedings in Business and Economics,
https://doi.org/10.1007/978-3-030-01784-2_10

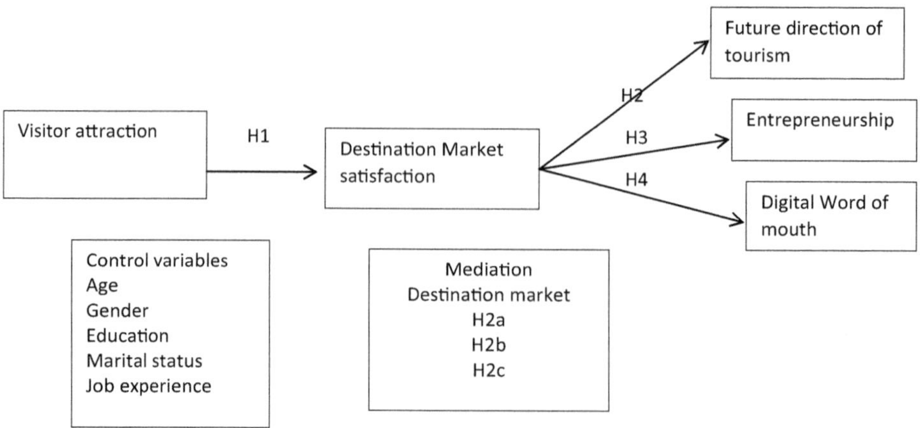

Fig. 1. Conceptual research model

(Fong et al. 2018; Henderson et al. 2018). Despite this emerging of tourism from the entrepreneurship industry, the relevant literature on tourism entrepreneurship is not much (Daniele and Quezada 2016; Dredge 2016). The entrepreneurship industry with the amalgamation of tourism has various issues related with certain perspectives and approaches. This research therefore seeks to address the void that exists in the literature of tourism and entrepreneurship through a research model development to examine the relationships between tourism and entrepreneurship through questionnaire and to high light the contribution of the study (Day and Mody 2016; Franchetti and Page 2008). It is generally accepted by tourism research academicians that the amalgamation of tourism and entrepreneurship play important role in dealing with consumer needs and provide unexpected quality of services to consumers at various destination marketing.

2   Visitors' Attraction

Attractions at destination markets are the most important elements of tourism. This study explores the different types of attractions that have impact on tourists' behavior (Mckercher 2016; Hasan et al. 2018). The types of attractions are human made attraction, natural attraction, events related attractions and activity based attractions (Moscardo and Murphy 2016; Burke and Hughes 2018). Majority of the attractions are significant to comprehend and encompass their managerial structure and ownership, target marketing and the orientation of the attractions (Rodrigues et al. 2017). The whereabouts of attractions such as fixed place, special occasion taking place at a location is beneficial to tourism managers and planners to perceive the intended meaning of potential demands for the attraction and the most important effective marketing strategy to adopt (Hahm and Severt 2018; Camilleri 2017a, b, c, d).

Other characteristics of attractions that planners and managers view include accessibility and not just the destination but the transportation system involved in the location and how this can be helpful to consumers with disabilities. The authenticity of a destination marketing attractions and the need to provide interpretation of services and special commercial signs play a major role in tourists' attraction to destinations (Pearce and Schänzel 2013; Maeda et al. 2018). Tourists' attractions are natural destinations, attributes, items or human made constructions that have important special appeal to tourism consumers and the local people (Lindberg and Veisten 2012; Kapiki and Jaksic 2015). Various tourists' attractions at verity of destinations suggest that certain particular attractions play motivational role as major indicators for tourism consumers to select the destinations to visit (Lesjak et al. 2015; Sertkan et al. 2017). Tourists' attractions are arguably the main components of the tourism industry. They are the most essential motivators for travelers and are the core of tourism products and services globally (Mckercher 2016).

Tourism without destination attractions, would have a profound negative impact in tourism and there will be no need for tourism services (Marinao 2018; Yoo et al. 2018). There are different ways to classify tourism destination attraction but this study identifies only four main groups of attractions. (i) Different attributes that exist from nature, (ii) manmade buildings, sites and structures that are developed and designed to attract tourism such as worship centers based on religious believes to attract and use as leisure amenities, (iii) manmade building structures that are designed to accommodate visitors' needs. Samples of such structures include theme parks and (iv) the organization of special events to attract tourists. Based on these studies the hypothesis 1 is formed.

H1: Visitor attraction has positive relationship with destination marketing satisfaction.

3 Future Direction of Tourism

Some of the negative problems that will affect tourism in the future in Ghana are climate change and population increase (Mackay and Spencer 2017; Saniotis et al. 2011). UNWTO (2017) and UNWTO World Tourism Barometer (2018) predicts that the world population will increase by 1.3 billion people in 2020. It is proposed that this will have enormous effect on tourism if climate change affects countries of popular tourism destinations and reduce tourists' arrival to certain destinations though out the years to come. Tourism in Ghana is growing at a rapid rate and as a new destination of tourism the economy has experienced a major improvement in 2017 due to large tourists' arrival (UNWTO/WTCF City Tourism Performance Research 2018). However, if there is a climate change in Ghana tourists arrivals may decline and the economy will be affected (Jopp et al. 2014; Grigorieva 2018). Other problems that are likely to affect tourism in Ghana is the rate at which the government increase fuel prices. An increase in fuel price will make flying to Ghana expensive and tourists may select alternative destination to visit instead of Ghana (Morlotti et al. 2017; Camilleri 2017a, b, c, d). Renting cars could also be expensive for visitors thereby limiting the amount of tourists to the country.

There could also be positive effects that may increase tourism in Ghana in the future. Ghana was a center for slave trade and thousands and millions of slaves were carried through the shores of Ghana to Europe and other parts of the world (Taskin and Rashid 2018; Sertkan et al. 2017). The slave trade centers still exist as exhibitions for people of slave decedents and each year many tourists visit Ghana to see those centers (Suzuki 2017a, b). This amount of target history in Ghana is enough to attract tourists into the country (Yankholmes et al. 2009). Many tourists around the world search to learn about ancient history and because Ghana is a perfect state for ancient history many people could still visit if the country experience climate change and over population(). Due to these theories the hypothesis 3 is formed.

H2: Destination Market satisfaction has positive relations with Future direction of tourism.

3.1   Entrepreneurship

Tourism and entrepreneurship are intermixed and growing together rapidly. This makes entrepreneurship a strong contributor to tourism destination marketing (Sheldon et al. 2016; Triantafillidou and Tsiaras 2018). Entrepreneurship is diversifying tourism products and services in various destination markets and influencing opportunities in small scale medium size businesses (Firat et al. 2014; Chandrikapure et al. 2017). The activities of entrepreneurship have discoveries, evaluations and exploitations to initiate new goods and services into tourism destination marketing with the notion to make profits (Hritz and Franzidis 2018). The innovation of tourism and entrepreneurship involves the organization, the processing of raw materials and efforts to target tourists that did not exist previously (Franchetti and Page 2009; Bertrand and Schoar 2006). The entrepreneurs are individual business persons who are alert of business opportunities for trading. They have the capabilities to easily identify suppliers and customers and act as intermediaries to maximize profits (Triantafillidou and Tsiaras 2018). The mixture of entrepreneurship and tourism is a new business or combination of businesses developed in the face of uncertainty and risk to grow and receive advantages (Rogerson 2007). The most important factors that strongly differentiate entrepreneurship and tourism are the viable managerial innovations, the opportunity to identify process and grow businesses with effective managerial strategical tools (Triantafillidou and Tsiaras 2018).

H3:   Destination   Market   satisfaction   has   positive   relationship   with entrepreneurship.

3.2   Digital Word of Mouth

Travelers search for information before making decision to buy tourism products and service to tourism settings (Fritzsche 2017; Riaz et al. 2018). One of such information search is digital word of mouth (Alon and Brunel 2018). Marketing scholars have indicated that digital word of mouth communication has an effect on tourist behavior and purchase decision based on choice (Huete-Alcocer 2017; Ismagilova et al. 2017a, b). It is also testified that since digital word of mouth is tourist dominated, it is perceived as more dependable and well-grounded than organizational generated communications (Weitzl 2016). Furthermore, this also suggest that traditional word of mouth form of advertisement and communication is losing its effectiveness to digital word of mouth because of lack of reliability and doubt of trustworthiness (Ismagilova et al. 2017; Yang et al. 2018). An increase number of tourists are turning to the internet as source of information to purchase tourism products and services (Chetthamrongchai 2017; Marchiori and Cantoni 2016). Travelers benefits from using the internet to search for information because there is much information available to search at all times (Xiang 2018; Cavada et al. 2017). The information from the internet is frequently provided by the tourism organizational sponsored websites and advertisements while digital word of mouth comes from internet communities like internet forums, news groups, bulletin boards provide travelers with the ability to share their stories, experience, opinions and knowledge with potential tourists on the internet (Nyangwe and Buhalis 2017). These kinds of participations of audience in the media does not just make tourists receivers of information but also distributors and creators of contents such as texts, photos, video and many more (Alzua-Sorzabal et al. 2013). Based on the theory of digital word of mouth, this hypothesis is formulated.

H4: Destination Market satisfaction has positive relationship with Digital Word of mouth.

4 Literature Review

There are various dialogues in tourisn about the conceptualization of tourism literature and destination marketing but a standard defintion with regards to destination has been difficult to obtain (Hanna et al. 2017). There are divergents in permutations and inference link to such an effort (Scantlebury 2012). The study of (Pike 2008) proposed that a destination market is a geographical extent to which clusters of tourism resources are available for use but are completely different from political boundries (Mckercher 2016). Rubies (2001) and Murdy et al. (2018) suggest that tourism clusters are accumulated visitors resources, infrastructures, attractions that provide services to tourists from various backgrounds, destinations and administrative institutions. Chang (2018) reveals that the integration and coordination of tourism clusters provide consumers with the experience they expect from the destinations they select to visit.

The coordination of tourists' attractions can be complicated such that there need to be a stimulation of broad collaboration in the tourism industry to entice potential tourists (Camilleri 2018; Deale 2016). The most significant entrepreneurship problem is the creation of new tourism products and service to attract and market to visitors. Tourists' personal experience at distinct destinations play important role in revisit intention (Woosnam et al. 2018; Camilleri 2017a, b, c, d). Due to the present amalgamation of tourism and entrepreneurship skills, managers can easily understand and predict tourist behavior and mould their products and services to catch their attention to influence their visitation intentions (Stylidis et al. 2018). Understanding travelers' vacations dreams based on sun lust, comfort, relaxation, fun, nature, peacefulness and convenience, products and services can be prepared to target this market. Koh and Hatten (2002) suggest that the availability of entrepreneurship in society impact tourism innovation that can be transformed to tourists' attraction. Similarly, Sthapit and

Coudounaris (2017) propose that tourism scholars should promote tourism in a manner that can create memorable experience among travelers. The features of nature, landscapes such as climate, cultural food, and amenities can create captivating memorable memories in consumers (Tukamushaba et al. 2016; Mahdzar et al. 2015).

Destination marketing is important for tourism scholars working or nursing the idea to work in entrepreneurship career in travel and tourism (Song and Bae 2017; Sertkan et al. 2017). The success of hospitality business depends largely on competition. In the same way, various opportunities can manifest and develop to the mutual benefit of both the destination and the tourism business untapped by the two groups (Pulido-Fernandez and Merinero-Rodríguez 2018; Abou-Shouk 2017). The constraints confronted by tourism destination markets such as policies, are often distinct from those confronted by individual tourism businesses. The comprehension of such problems between the two parties goes a long way to assist stakeholders to develop new promotions, new tourism products and distribution channels to their own advantages.

The growing attention of sustainability and consumers lifestyles decisions making processes have strong impacts on tourism destination marketing in the future (Abedin 2015; Chuang 2018). Tourism destination markets are thrilling areas of continuous growth and expect skills noted as major contributors of economic growth with job creation across the world (Lee and Kim 2018; Chi et al. 2018). Travel and Tourism created 108,741 million jobs directly in 2016 that was an increase of 3.6% of total employment in the world (Sreejesh and Abhilash 2017). Similarly, a forecast of 2.1% growth in 2017 was made to 111,013 million jobs that was also an increase of 3.6% of total employment worldwide (Lo et al. 2014). This include jobs by travel agents, hotels, airlines and other passenger transportation services (Li et al. 2017; Haynes and Egan 2015). These jobs also include activities of the restaurant and leisure industries directly supported by tourists (WTTC 2017). Tourism destinations are generally accepted as the most challenging products to market due to competition. In the coming years, the difficulties facing destination marketing are likely to worsen on the impact of the future destination marketing (Aarstad et al. 2018; Pulido-Fernández and Merinero-Rodríguez (2018). The issues facing tourism businesses are unique and cannot be advanced in isolation from other competitive and supportive products.

The development of tourism destination markets through entrepreneurship plays important role in the success of economic growth in various nations. Ferri and Aiello (2017) demonstrates that entrepreneurship has been popular within the tourism industry in recent years. Entrepreneurship is an important factor in tourism and a pivotal factor that has persistent growth and success around the world. However, despite the emerging prospects of tourism and hospitality, relevant amalgamation of tourism and entrepreneurship literature is scanty and has numerous problems of certain degree of perspectives and approaches (Novais et al. 2018). Tourism is essential to the economy of Ghana and the development of the entrepreneurship as a whole but needs absolute comprehension of the complicated interaction and the interrelations among the various environmental components that play important role in tourism and hospitality development (Tervo-Kankare 2018; Triantafillidou and Tsiaras 2018).

It is comprehensive to suggest that the tourism industry is not a closed system but depends on the support of other industries to develop and grow to maturity (Räikkönen and Grénman 2017; Pavia and Fioričić 2017). Tourism destinations satisfaction are defined as the settings of groups of attractions, visitors' facilities and services that combine to constitute tourism destination products to create satisfaction for tourists (Vučetić 2018; Novais et al. 2018). The research of Žabkar et al. (2010) proposed the attributes of destination satisfaction as available packages, access to the destinations, modern amenities, activities that include night life and attractions as a general classification for tourism destination satisfaction. In spite of this general classification, the features of destination marketing are very contextual and the evaluation of destination marketing satisfaction should reflect the particular attributes that distinguish the destination (Ali et al. 2018; Kiatkawsin and Han 2017) and Milman and Tasci (2017) used the expectancy disconfirmation theory and various other attributes to identify and define destination marketing satisfaction. The expectancy disconfirmation theory is a cognitive theory which is utilized to define post buying or the post adoption of destination satisfaction, expectations, and perception of destination performance and disconfirmation beliefs (Ryzin 2013; Filtenborg et al. 2017). The cognitive theory of psychology reveals that mental processes such tourists' intentions, visitors' memory and perceptions play a significant role in determining destination satisfaction (Altarawneh et al. 2018).

The traditional word of mouth is just about face to face communication between social relations (Zhang and Daugherty 2009). In the offline messaging, one word of mouth message can influence a sizable number of receivers by passing through several chain of respondents (Guadalupi 2017). Digital word of mouth or online word of mouth on the other hand goes though faster and they could reach a large number of people receiving the message and potentially spreading them to other receivers via emails, WhatsApp and other internet based media (Reichelt 2013). Despite the fact that captivating news may spread like wild fire, the decision as to whether to spread the news or the captivating information lies with the person receiving the information (Amadeo et al. 2018; Karunakaran et al. 2018). Digital word of mouth therefore spread faster than the traditional word of mouth because of the internet strong capabilities. Social comparison theory and the theory of reason and action were involved in this research.

5 Methodology

The relationships in the research model were tested using data collected from a target population sample of 250 full time and part time employees from entrepreneur and tourism businesses in Kumasi, Ghana. These discerned from the Kumasi metropolitan authority which is a government based institution where businesses are registered in the region. The businesses that were included in the study were selected based on the research of Thomas (2016) where the sampling frames were accommodation (e.g. hotels, guests' houses and motels), restaurants, pubs, tour operators, tourists' attractions, travel agents and handicraft shops. These business organizations were selected in order to reduce non coverage errors where the participants were excluded from the sampling frame and were not provided with the chance to be selected into the sample

(Cornish and Jones 2017). Entrepreneurs based in Kumasi were selected because about 90% of the tourists that come to Ghana visit Kumasi and spend several nights. Majority of small business owners dwell in the region and a total of 375 businesses were involved in this research.

Permission was requested from the above stated institutions to collect data. As the permission was obtained, questionnaire were distributed directly to the respondents through the self-administered approach to gather data for the research. The respondents were assured of their confidentiality and were requested to complete the questionnaire. A total of 300 questionnaires were distributed to the target participants and by the accepted date for collecting the data, 250 questionnaires were obtained representing response rate of 83.33%. 35% of the respondents were between the ages of 20 and 25 and 52% were between the ages of 30 and 35 while the rest were more than 35 years of age. The female respondents were 48% and the male were 52% indicating the male as the overall majority. 35% of the respondent had secondary school leaving certificates. 32% had University degrees and the rest were associate degree holders. 26% of the participants have work experience of more than 1 year. 35% had job tenure between 2 and 7 years and the rest job experience of more than 8 year. 72% of the participants were not married, divorced or single while the rest were married.

6 Measurement

Five items from Leask et al. (2013) and Matthews et al. (2018) were used to measure visitor attraction. The sample items were "attraction exceed expectation", "I am happy I visited this place". The participants were asked to show the rate at which they feel happy to be in the attractions on a 5 point Likert scale (1 = strongly disagree to 5 = strongly agree). The high scores showed a great propensity of exceeded expectation of the traveler's attractions. The Cronbach's alpha was 0.92. Destination market satisfaction was guarded using 5 items Likert scale of (1 = I not important to 5 = very important). The sample constructs were ("opportunity to rest", "possibility of shopping") from the study of Kumar and Kaushik (2017). The results indicate strong tourists' affectivity for the destination. The Cronbach's alpha value was 0.89. The future direction of tourism were assessed by five constructs from the research of Shoval (2018) and Gursoy (2018). On the response of 5 point Likert scale from (1 = strongly disagree to 5 = strongly agree) where the sample constructs were ("promotion on the internet", and "paperless hotel rooms"). The results of the cronbach's alpha were 0.78. Entrepreneurship based on medium sized small business was measured through the study of Boateng (2017) and Mutandwa et al. (2015). 4 items point Likert scale of (1 = I strongly disagree to 5 = I strongly agree) were utilized. The sample constructs were ("free to pursue own dream in business", "The opportunity to learn and gain knowledge through entrepreneurship"). The outcome of the cronbach's alpha was 0.76. Digital word of mouth based on the study of Reichelt (2013) and Chen et al. (2015) used three items to measure their validity. On the response of 4 Likert scale (1 = I completely disagree to 5 = I completely agree). The sample items were ("use of the internet to search for information", electronic word of mouth from bloggers") and the results of the Cronbach's alpha was 0.88.

7 Main Results

The control variables are presented in the respondent profile in Table 1. Hypothesis 1 forecasted that visitors' attraction has strong influence on destination marketing satisfaction. Hierarchical regression analysis was conducted on the control variables representing age, gender, marital status, education, works experience and employees status were put as the first step.

The relationship between the independent variable which is the visitor attraction and the destination market satisfaction as a mediator were introduced in the second step. In the third step, the mediator and the dependent variables representing future direction of tourism, entrepreneurship and the digital word of mouth were entered. In the fourth step, the mediator variable was introduced into the relationship between the independent variable and the dependent variables, to test for partial or full mediation. These tests were conducted to minimize multicollinearity and to increase the interpretability in the relationships between the hypothesis and the t-test results as shown on Table 2. The measures were firstly tested for exploratory factor analysis through the principal components and varimax rotation. The constructs had overall loadings above 0.50 as the general acceptable cutoff level for factor loadings and there was no need to drop any items. The final output of the five factor analysis indicates that all the t-values were significant. A confirmatory factor analysis was also conducted with SPSS software 22 on Table 2 to assure the fit statistics of the five factor model (X^2/df = 1.36; GFI = 0.86; IFI = 0.91; RMSEA = 0.068; SRMR = 0.058; AGFI = 0.89; NFI = 0.82; NNFI = 0.79; CFI = 0.90). Table 2 shows that all the observed latent variables were between the range of 0.71 to 0.88 and the t values were greater 2.00 averagely (Table 3).

8 Hypothesis Testing

The output of the hierarchical regression analysis suggest in Table 4 that when the mediator variable was introduced between visitor attraction and future direction of tourism (β = 0.43, P < 0.001) there was a direct impact on destination market satisfaction. As a result, the hypothesis H1 is supported.

The results in Table 4 further indicates that the including of decision market satisfaction as a mediator in the relationship between visitor attraction and entrepreneurship (β = 0.31, P < 0.01) had a significant influence on destination satisfaction among tourists. Similarly, the inclusion of the mediator variable, decision market satisfaction in the relations between visitor attraction and digital word of mouth (β = 0.25, P < 0.05) show positive significance on tourists intending to visit. Based on the values of these variables demonstrated above, hypotheses H2, H3 and H4 are all

Table 1. Respondent profile

Demographics	Frequency	Percentage variance
Age		
18years and below	70	25
20–28	84	30
30–38	78	28
40–58	48	17
Total	280	100
Gender		
Male	175	62.5
Female	105	37.5
Total	280	100
Marital status		
Single/widow/divorce	182	65
Married	98	35
Total	280	100
Education		
Secondary school	104	37
University	96	34
Masters	80	29
Total	280	100
Work experience		
2 year and below	76	27
4-6 years	86	31
10-12	93	33
14 years and above	25	9
Total	280	100
Employees status		
Full time employees	164	59
Part time employees	116	41
Total	280	100

Note In the profile sample respondents were requested to indicate their age, gender, marital status, educational level, works experience and employees status. The N = 280. Gender was coded as binary variable where female = 0 and male = 1. Marital status was also coded as two variables married or divorce

supported. A separate regression analysis test conducted between the visitor attraction and decision market satisfaction ($\beta = 0.21$, 0.05) suggest that the two variables have significant relationship. The relationship between visitor attraction and future direction of tourism was significant ($\beta = 0.49$, $P < 0.001$). However, the mediation effects between visitor attraction and the future direction was reduced in magnitude and no more significant when decision market satisfaction as a mediator was introduced between the two variables.

Table 2. Scale items and confirmatory factor analysis results

Constructs items	Standardized factor loading	t-values	P-values	Alpha value	AVE value
Visitor attraction				0.92	0.78
Majority of tourists have positive ideas about destinations they intend to visit	0.81	20,333	0.000		
The employees are friendly	0.74	56,598	0.000		
The destination has a unique image that attracts visitors	0.84	67,158	0.000		
Tourists appreciate the natural environment	0.77	48,911	0.000		
The destination is popular among travelers	0.71	39,104	0.000		
Destination market satisfaction				0.89	0.81
Tourists feel happy and secured about their personal safety	0.88	76,445	0.000		
The destination is always kept clean	0.85	50,833	0.000		
Night life and entertainment is great	0.86	60,994	0.000		
Booking to visit is easy	0.87	60,994	0.000		
The prices of hotel in the destination are affordable	0.72	33,753	0.000		
Future direction of tourism				0.78	0.77
Promotions and selling of tourists available products	0.78	45,000	0.000		
Software application allows you to pick the best and the nearest restaurant	0.80	60,994	0.000		
Online travel technology may change quite dramatically	0.79	76,445	0.000		
Foreign languages will disappear, making it easier to immerse into an unfamiliar culture	0.73	48,911	0.000		
creative strategies adopted by tourists	0.78	60,994	0.000		

(continued)

Table 2. (*continued*)

Constructs items	Standardized factor loading	t-values	P-values	Alpha value	AVE value
Entrepreneurship				0.76	0.82
Small handicraft business	0.89	53,327	0.000		
Small size road side restaurants for tourists	0.86	48,911	0.000		
Shopping centers for tourists popular destinations	0.76	48,911	0.000		
Beads stall close to popular tourists hotels	0.87	38,735	0.000		
Digital word of mouth				0.88	0.89
Information satisfaction and intentions to visit	0.85	60,994	0.000		
Information collection from the internet	0.75	64,000	0.000		
Evaluation of other substitute destinations	0.78	54.234	0.000		

AVE = Average variance extracted

Table 3. Descriptive statistics of study the correlation variables

Variables	1	2	3	4	5	6	7	8	9	10	11
Age											
Gender	0.20										
Marital status	0.07	0.02									
Education	0.03	0.06	0.01								
Work experience	0.05	0.10	0.04	0.21							
Employee status	0.01	0.09	0.05	0.18	0.20						
Visitor attraction	0.21	−0.16	0.11	0.15	0.18	0.33**					
Destination market satisfaction	0.20	0.13	0.09	0.10	0.05	0.29*	0.26*				
Future direction of tourism	−0.10	0.20	0.12	−0.17	0.09	0.25*	0.38**	0.28*			
Entrepreneurship	0.13	0.14	0.08	−0.12	0.06	0.34**	0.43**	0.44**	0.46**		
Digital word of mouth	0.02	0.04	0.03	0.05	0.14	0.35**	0.39**	0.38**	0.36**	0.45**	
Mean	1.53	1.45	1.39	1.45	1.32	1.43	1.38	1.56	1.63	1.69	1.72
Standard deviation	4.43	5.32	5.41	4.92	4.83	4.56	4.63	5.44	4.87	4.38	4.58

Note The composite results for each group of items were evaluated to find the average items results. The results for visitor attraction, destination market satisfaction, and future direction of tourism, entrepreneurship and digital word of mouth were scale from 1 to 5. Gender was code as binary and male = 1 and female = 0

*Correlations are significant at the 0.05 level

**Correlations are significant at the 0.01 level

Table 4. Hierarchical constructs regression analysis output: mediating effects

Dependent constructs and standardized regression output

Independent variables	Future direction of tourism			Entrepreneurship			Digital word of mouth		
	Step 1	Step 2	Step 3	Step 1	Step 2	Step 3	Step 1	Step 2	Step 3
(1) Control variable									
Age	0.02	0.04	0.08	0	0.03	0.09	0.01	0.05	0.11
Gender	0.01	0.06	0.05	0.02	0.04	0.06	0.1	0.05	0.03
Education	0.1	0.01	0.09	0.07	0.02	0.01	0.12	0.13	0.14
Work experience	0.07	0.03	0.09	0.05	0.03	0.08	0.09	0.01	0.04
Employment status	0.11	0.02	0.04	0.09	0.12	0.07	0.01	0.06	0.07
(II) Visitor attraction	–	0.43***	0.18	–	0.31**	0.09	–	0.25*	0.12
(III) Destination market satisfaction	–	–	0.49***	–	–	0.36**	–	–	0.28*
F	12.69***	15.06***	26.01***				10.56***	18.22***	14.82**
R^2 at every step	0.12	0.32	0.38				0.04	0.12	0.15
ΔR^2	–	0.1	0.06				–	0.08	0.03
VA → DMS → FDT = 3.28***									
VA → DMS → EN = 2.07**									
VA → DMS → DWM = 2.01*									

Note Gender was coded as binary. Male = 1 and female = 0. VA-Visitor attraction, DMS-Destination market satisfaction, FDT-future direction of tourism EN-Entrepreneurship, DWM-Digital word of mouth. *p < 0.05, **p < 0.01, ***p < 0.001. The overall results did not show any issue of multicollinearity. This means there was no problem of variance inflation factor

Table 4 also shows augmentation and significance in the R^2 of the conceptual research model ($\Delta R^2 = 0.06$, $p < 0.01$). A Sobel test conducted between visitor attraction, decision market satisfaction and future direction of tourism shows ($t = 3.28$, $P < 0.001$). The outcome proposes that decision market satisfaction as a mediator has full mediation output with visitor attractions and H2a is supported. The results of the variables indicated on Table 4 also proposes that the relations between destination market satisfaction and entrepreneurship was significant ($\beta = 0.36$, $P < 0.01$). However, the mediation effects between visitor attraction and the entrepreneurship was reduced in magnitude and no more significant when decision market satisfaction as a mediator was introduced between the two variables. Table 4 also shows significance increase in the R^2 of the conceptual research model ($\Delta R^2 = 0.08$, $p < 0.05$). A Sobel test performed between visitor attraction, decision market satisfaction and entrepreneurship shows ($t = 2.07$, $P < 0.01$). The results propose that decision market satisfaction as a mediator has full mediation output with visitor attractions and H2b is supported. The results of the variables shown on Table 4 demonstrates the relations between visitor attraction and digital word of mouth was significant ($\beta = 0.28$, $P < 0.05$). It was also noted that the mediation effects was reduced in size and no more significant when decision market satisfaction as a mediator was put between the two variables. Table 4 also shows important increase and significance in the R^2 of the conceptual research model ($\Delta R^2 = 0.03$, $p < 0.05$). A Sobel test conducted between visitor attraction, decision market satisfaction and digital word of mouth shows ($t = 2.01$, $P < 0.05$). The outcome indicates that decision market satisfaction as a mediator has full mediation output with visitor attractions and H2c is supported.

9 Discussion

The tourism industry and entrepreneurship are intermingled such that the entrepreneurship plays important roles in the modification of tourism leisure supply and recreational activities (Rosen 2010). Majority of tourism businesses in Ghana are small medium size enterprises that depend solely on entrepreneurship and the research on this subject has not been much explored in Ghana (Chung and D'Annunzio-Green 2018). There has been exceptional increase in homes and family stay, family type of restaurants, guest houses, home stay, cafes and retailing shops that cater for tourists in the destination (Heryán 2017). Based on the reason that Ghanaians have a great value for family unity and collectivism, majority of family own businesses have become essential components in tourism and are passed on from one family generation to another (Asero and Skonieczny 2018). Aside family own business, entrepreneurship has also played outstanding role in tourism development such as hotel chains to take care of tourists accommodational needs, bars and general excellent night life to create beautiful memories among tourists (Nicolau and Masiero 2013).

This study provides important contributions to the tourism relevant literature in three basic ways. Full mediation test was conducted on the part of decision market satisfaction as a mediator (i) between the relations of visitor attraction and the future direction of tourism (ii) visitor attraction and entrepreneurship and (iii) visitor attraction and digital word of mouth. The second important contribution to knowledge about this research is that, it is conducted in Ghana as a developing country in the Western part of Africa where the mediation effects are being examined and lastly, the data was obtained from a target population sample of full time and part time employees from entrepreneurs and tourism businesses in Kumasi, Ghana for a duration of two weeks. The findings related to visitor attraction on decision market satisfaction are in line with the research of Mckercher (2016). The theory of visitor attraction was involved in this study (Borm 2012). The theory of visitor attraction suggests that tourism destination attractions have huge influence on decision market satisfaction and visitors attraction which are the most important components in the tourism industry (Matthews et al. 2018; Ballantyne et al. 2018). Without attractions to entice tourists to destinations, there will be no need for tourism services such as airlines transport, accommodational facilities like hotels, guest house, motels, food and many more (Tiarto 2018). The major concern about attraction of tourism destination decision making to visit is the expenditure. It is noted that a small part of tourists' disbursement is spent in the local community in Ghana while the rest of the expenditure goes on airline, food and hotel accommodation (Socorro et al. 2018). The findings therefore propose that visitor attraction on decision market satisfaction has a valuable impact on tourists' visitation but how much money is left in the destination by tourists should be a concern to the destination. Furthermore, the result also suggest that the full mediation between decision market satisfaction and future direction of tourism, entrepreneurship and digital word of mouth have positive involvement in tourists satisfaction and motivational intention to visit and see tourists attractions.

10   Managerial Implications

There are various significant implications for managers emerging from the outcome of this research. The managers of destination organizations dealing with tourists' attractions and full time and part time employees from entrepreneurship institutions and tourism businesses should be encouraged to be friendly to visitors (Fitzpatrick 2018). This is significant because full or part time employees with high views of tourists' attractions influence tourists' satisfaction to spend a reasonable duration of period to enjoy in tourists' destination attractions (Choe and Kim 2018). Managers can also occasionally organize training programs for employees to learn how to deal with visitors. Training employees to deal with customers will highly influence the employees to be engaged in their individual work activities and to be effective on visitor attraction and decision market satisfaction towards entrepreneurship and digital word of mouth. Furthermore, training to deal with tourists will increase the knowledge of employees and their abilities to work independently without supervision and through empowerment. The two most important daily problems with regards to the tourism sector are the reasons why tourists travel and what do they expect to see from the settings (Sohn and Yoon 2016; Sertkan et al. 2017). Tourists' number one priority is always the motivation of destination satisfaction. In the present competitive destination marketing, providing visitor attraction is enormously associated with the reasons why tourists travel (Pennington-Gray and Schroeder 2018; Chi et al. 2018; Jiang et al. 2015). It is therefore of paramount importance to pay strong attention to destination attractions development in order to beat the world competition and to attract more tourists to visit (Pulido-Fernández and Merinero-Rodríguez 2018; Gajdosik et al. 2018). The concept of authenticity in visitor attraction depends on the comprehension of tourists' motivation towards destination market satisfaction.

11 Limitation and Futuristic Study

This study has some few limitations just like any other research and suggestions for future research directions. The primary limitation is the time frame under which the research was conducted. Duration of two weeks was used to collect data for this study in the near future more time should be allocated to interview more respondents (Kilubi 2017). Secondly, data was obtained directly from respondents and the common method bias problems were avoided. It was also observed that obtaining data through this process eliminates the idea of selection bias. A similar research conducted reveals that data distribution and collection in this manner is the best medication to remove potential data issues in empirical research (Darmawan et al. 2014; Chapuis et al. 2017). For destination to play important role and become competitive in the attraction sector in the tourism industry, there will be a need to improve and develop attractions such as sightseeing, shopping centers and cultural activities, casinos for gambling and recreational activities at the various tourism setting (Chen and Li 2018). Strategies to attract tourists from abroad and visitors from the residents within the destination to provide fun and memorable experience should be encouraged.

References

Aarstad, J., Ness, H., Haugland, S. A., & Kvitastein, O. A. (2018). Imitation strategies and interfirm networks in the tourism industry: A structure–agency approach. Journal of Destination Marketing & Management. https://doi.org/10.1016/j.jdmm.2018.01.003

Abedin, A. (2015). Value Priorities and Consumer Behavior of Turkish Immigrants in Germany. Marketing Dynamism & Sustainability: Things Change, Things Stay the Same… Developments in Marketing Science: Proceedings of the Academy of Marketing Science, 97–108. https://doi.org/10.1007/978-3-319-10912-1_29

Abou-Shouk, M. A. (2017). Destination management organizations and destination marketing: adopting the business model of e-portals in engaging travel agents. Journal of Travel & Tourism Marketing, 35(2), 178–188. https://doi.org/10.1080/10548408.2017.1350254

Ali, F., Kim, W. G., Li, J., & Jeon, H. (2018). Make it delightful: Customers experience, satisfaction and loyalty in Malaysian theme parks. Journal of Destination Marketing & Management, 7, 1–11. https://doi.org/10.1016/j.jdmm.2016.05.003

Alon, A., & Brunel, F. (2018). Peer-to-peer word-of-mouth: word-of-mouth extended to group online exchange. *Online Information Review, 42*(2), 176–190

Altarawneh, L., Mackee, J., & Gajendran, T. (2018). The influence of cognitive and affective risk perceptions on flood preparedness intentions: A dual-process approach. Procedia Engineering, 212, 1203–1210. https://doi.org/10.1016/j.proeng.2018.01.155

Alzua-Sorzabal, A., Gerrikagoitia, J. K., Torres-Manzanera, E., & Domínguez-Menchero, J. S. (2013). A Methodology to Collect Information on Future Hotel Prices Using Internet Distribution Systems. Information and Communication Technologies in Tourism 2013, 543–553. https://doi.org/10.1007/978-3-642-36309-2_46

Amadeo, M., Campolo, C., & Molinaro, A. (2018). Empowering 5G network softwarization through information centric networking. Internet Technology Letters. https://doi.org/10.1002/itl2.30

Asero, V., & Skonieczny, S. (2018). Cruise Tourism and Sustainability in the Mediterranean. Destination Venice. Mobilities, Tourism and Travel Behavior - Contexts and Boundaries. https://doi.org/10.5772/intechopen.71459

Avraham, E., & Ketter, E. (2016). Marketing and Destination Branding. Tourism Marketing for Developing Countries, 39–66. https://doi.org/10.1057/9781137342157_4

Ballantyne, R., Hughes, K., Lee, J., Packer, J., & Sneddon, J. (2018). Visitors values and environmental learning outcomes at wildlife attractions: Implications for interpretive practice. Tourism Management, 64, 190–201. https://doi.org/10.1016/j.tourman.2017.07.015tiarto

Bertrand, M., & Schoar, A. (2006). The role of family in family firms. *Journal of economic perspectives*, *20*(2), 73–96

Boateng, A. (2017). Social Entrepreneurship and the Possible Intersect with Female Entrepreneurship. African Female Entrepreneurship, 103–125. https://doi.org/10.1007/978-3-319-65846-9_4

Bordas Rubies, E. (2001). Improving public-private sectors cooperation in tourism: A new paradigm for destinations. Tourism Review, 56(3/4), 38–41.

Borm, J. (2012). The Attractions of England, or Albion under German Eyes. In Travel Writing and Tourism in Britain and Ireland (pp. 85–96). Palgrave Macmillan, London

Burke, R., & Hughes, J. (2018). Handbook of Human Resource Management in the Tourism and Hospitality Industries. https://doi.org/10.4337/9781786431370

Camilleri, M. A. (2017). Integrated Marketing Communications. Tourism, Hospitality & Event Management Travel Marketing, Tourism Economics and the Airline Product, 85–103. https://doi.org/10.1007/978-3-319-49849-2_5

Camilleri, M. A. (2017). Market Segmentation, Targeting and Positioning. Tourism, Hospitality & Event Management Travel Marketing, Tourism Economics and the Airline Product, 69–83. https://doi.org/10.1007/978-3-319-49849-2_4

Camilleri, M. A. (2017). The Airline Business. Tourism, Hospitality & Event Management Travel Marketing, Tourism Economics and the Airline Product, 167–177. https://doi.org/10.1007/978-3-319-49849-2_10

Camilleri, M. A. (2017). Tourism Distribution Channels. Tourism, Hospitality & Event Management Travel Marketing, Tourism Economics and the Airline Product, 105–115. https://doi.org/10.1007/978-3-319-49849-2_6

Camilleri, M. A. (2018). Travel Marketing, Tourism Economics and the Airline Product. Tourism, Hospitality & Event Management. https://doi.org/10.1007/978-3-319-49849

Cavada, D., Elahi, M., Massimo, D., Maule, S., Not, E., Ricci, F., & Venturini, A. (2017). Tangible Tourism with the Internet of Things. Information and Communication Technologies in Tourism 2018, 349–361. https://doi.org/10.1007/978-3-319-72923-7_27

Chandrikapure, R., Bandewar, M., & Mulchandani, M. (2017). Paperless Billing for Small and Medium Scale Businesses. Icsesd-2017. https://doi.org/10.24001/ijaems.icsesd2017.52

Chang, S. (2018). Experience economy in hospitality and tourism: Gain and loss values for service and experience. Tourism Management, 64, 55–63. https://doi.org/10.1016/j.tourman.2017.08.004

Chapuis, B., Calmon, P., & Jenson, F. (2017). Best Practice Principles and Guidance for the Exploitation of Simulated POD Data in Relation with Experimental Data. IIW Collection Best Practices for the Use of Simulation in POD Curves Estimation, 45–49. https://doi.org/10.1007/978-3-319-62659-8_10

Chen, C., Nguyen, B., Klaus, P., & Wu, M. (2015). Exploring Electronic Word-of-Mouth (eWOM) in The Consumer Purchase Decision-Making Process: The Case of Online Holidays – Evidence from United Kingdom (UK) Consumers. Journal of Travel & Tourism Marketing, 32(8), 953–970. https://doi.org/10.1080/10548408.2014.956165

Chen, Y., & Li, X. (. (2018). Does a happy destination bring you happiness? Evidence from Swiss inbound tourism. Tourism Management, 65, 256–266. https://doi.org/10.1016/j.tourman.2017.10.009

Chetthamrongchai, P. (2017). The Influence of Travel Motivation, Information Sources and Tourism Crisison Tourists' Destination Image. Journal of Tourism & Hospitality, 06(02). https://doi.org/10.4172/2167-0269.1000278

Chi, C. G., Pan, L., & Chiappa, G. D. (2018). Examining destination personality: Its antecedents and outcomes. Journal of Destination Marketing & Management. https://doi.org/10.1016/j.jdmm.2018.01.001

Choe, J. Y., & Kim, S. (2018). Effects of tourists' local food consumption value on attitude, food destination image, and behavioral intention. International Journal of Hospitality Management, 71, 1–10. https://doi.org/10.1016/j.ijhm.2017.11.007

Chuang, S. (2018). Facilitating the chain of market orientation to value co-creation: The mediating role of e-marketing adoption. Journal of Destination Marketing & Management, 7, 39–49. https://doi.org/10.1016/j.jdmm.2016.08.007

Chung, K. L., & D'Annunzio-Green, N. (2018). Talent management practices in small- and medium-sized enterprises in the hospitality sector. Worldwide Hospitality and Tourism Themes, 10(1), 101–116. https://doi.org/10.1108/whatt-10-2017-0065

Cornish, T., & Jones, P. (2017). Recruitment, Selection and Unconscious Bias. The Psychology of Ethnicity in Organisations, 36–57. https://doi.org/10.1057/978-1-137-33014-7_3

Daniele, R., & Quezada, I. (2016). Business Models for Social Entrepreneurship in Tourism. Social Entrepreneurship and Tourism Tourism on the Verge, 81–100. https://doi.org/10.1007/978-3-319-46518-0_5

Darmawan, D., Kurniadi, D., & S. (2014). Boundary potential distribution in rectangular object based on data collection system. https://doi.org/10.1063/1.4897097

Day, J. (2017). Collaborative Economy and Destination Marketing Organisations: A Systems Approach. Collaborative Economy and Tourism on the Verge, 185–202. https://doi.org/10.1007/978-3-319-51799-5_11

Day, J., & Mody, M. (2016). Social Entrepreneurship Typologies and Tourism: Conceptual Frameworks. Social Entrepreneurship and Tourism on the Verge, 57–80. https://doi.org/10.1007/978-3-319-46518-0_4

Deale, C. S. (2016). Entrepreneurship education in hospitality and tourism: insights from entrepreneurs. Journal of Teaching in Travel & Tourism,16(1), 20–39. https://doi.org/10.1080/15313220.2015.1117957

Dredge, D. (2016). Institutional and Policy Support for Tourism Social Entrepreneurship. Social Entrepreneurship and Tourism Tourism on the Verge, 35–55. https://doi.org/10.1007/978-3-319-46518-0_3

Ferri, M. A., & Aiello, L. (2017). Tourism destination management in sustainability development perspective, the role of entrepreneurship and networking ability: Tourist Kit. World Review of Entrepreneurship, Management and Sustainable Development, 13(5/6), 647. https://doi. org/10.1504/wremsd.2017.086334

Filtenborg, A. F., Gaardboe, F., & Sigsgaard-Rasmussen, J. (2017). Experimental replication: an experimental test of the expectancy disconfirmation theory of citizen satisfaction. Public Management Review, 19(9), 1235–1250. https://doi.org/10.1080/14719037.2017.1295099

Firat, A., Turker, G. O., & Metin, I. (2014). Specification of target market in small and medium scale accomadation businesses: A study on boutique hotels operating in city of Mugla. International Journal of Academic Research,6(1), 82–88. https://doi.org/10.7813/2075-4124.2014/6-1/b.12

Fitzpatrick, L. (2018). Practical strategies to help develop dementia-friendly hospital wards. Nursing Older People, 30(2), 30–34. https://doi.org/10.7748/nop.2018.e982

Fong, V. H., Wong, I. A., & Hong, J. F. (2018). Developing institutional logics in the tourism industry through coopetition. Tourism Management,66, 244–262. https://doi.org/10.1016/j.tourman.2017.12.005

Franchetti, J., & Page, S. J. (2008). Entrepreneurship and Innovation in Tourism. Tourism and Entrepreneurship, 107–130. https://doi.org/10.1016/b978-0-7506-8635-8.00007-1

Franchetti, J., & Page, S. J. (2009). Entrepreneurship and innovation in tourism: Public sector experiences of innovation activity in tourism in Scandinavia and Scotland. *Tourism and entrepreneurship: International perspectives*, 107–130

Fritzsche, A. (2017). Spreading Innovations: Models, Designs and Research Directions. Diffusive Spreading in Nature, Technology and Society, 277–294. https://doi.org/10.1007/978-3-319-67798-9_14

Fronek, P. (2018). Current perspectives on the ethics of selling international surrogacy support services. Medicolegal and Bioethics, Volume 8, 11–20. https://doi.org/10.2147/mb.s134090

Gajdošík, T., Gajdošíková, Z., & Stražanová, R. (2018). Residents' perception of sustainable tourism destination development - A destination governance issue. Global Business & Finance Review, 23(1), 24–35.

Grigorieva, E. (2018). The impact of home-to-destination climate differences for tourism. Current Issues in Tourism, 1–6. https://doi.org/10.1080/13683500.2018.1428287

Guadalupi, C. (2017). Learning quality through prices and word-of-mouth communication. Journal of Economics & Management Strategy, 27(1), 53–70

Gursoy, D. (2018). Future of hospitality marketing and management research. Tourism Management Perspectives, 25, 185–188. https://doi.org/10.1016/j.tmp.2017.11.008

Hahm, J., & Severt, K. (2018). Importance of destination marketing on image and familiarity. Journal of Hospitality and Tourism Insights, 1(1), 37–53. https://doi.org/10.1108/jhti-10-2017-0002

Hanna, P., Font, X., Scarles, C., Weeden, C., & Harrison, C. (2017). Tourist destination marketing: From sustainability myopia to memorable experiences. Journal of Destination Marketing & Management. https://doi.org/10.1016/j.jdmm.2017.10.002

Hasan, M. R., Jha, A. K., & Liu, Y. (2018). Excessive use of online video streaming services: Impact of recommender system use, psychological factors, and motives. Computers in Human Behavior, 80, 220–228. https://doi.org/10.1016/j.chb.2017.11.020

Haynes, N., & Egan, D. (2015). The Future Impact of Changes in Rate Parity Agreements on Hotel Chains: The long-term implications of the removal of rate parity agreements between hotels and online travel agents using closed consumer group booking models. Journal of Travel & Tourism Marketing, 32(7), 923–933. https://doi.org/10.1080/10548408.2015.1063897

Henderson, I. L., Avis, M., & Tsui, W. H. (2018). Testing discontinuous innovations in the tourism industry: The case of scenic airship services. Tourism Management, 66, 167–179. https://doi.org/10.1016/j.tourman.2017.12.007

Heryán, T. (2017). Insolvency of the Hotels Among Visegrad-Plus Countries. Eurasian Business Perspectives Eurasian Studies in Business and Economics, 39–48. https://doi.org/10.1007/978-3-319-67913-6_3

Hipsher, S. (2017). Tourism: Job Creation, Entrepreneurship, and Quality of Life. Poverty Reduction, the Private Sector, and Tourism in Mainland Southeast Asia, 231–251. https://doi.org/10.1007/978-981-10-5948-3_11

Hritz, N., & Franzidis, A. F. (2018). Exploring the economic significance of the surf tourism market by experience level. Journal of Destination Marketing & Management, 7, 164–169. https://doi.org/10.1016/j.jdmm.2016.09.009

Huete-Alcocer, N. (2017). A Literature Review of Word of Mouth and Electronic Word of Mouth: Implications for Consumer Behavior. Frontiers in Psychology, 8. https://doi.org/10.3389/fpsyg.2017.01256

Ismagilova, E., Dwivedi, Y. K., Slade, E., & Williams, M. D. (2017). Traditional Word-of-Mouth (WOM). Electronic Word of Mouth (eWOM) in the Marketing Context SpringerBriefs in Business, 5–15. https://doi.org/10.1007/978-3-319-52459-7_2

Ismagilova, E., Dwivedi, Y. K., Slade, E., & Williams, M. D. (2017). Electronic Word-of-Mouth (eWOM). Electronic Word of Mouth (eWOM) in the Marketing Context SpringerBriefs in Business, 17–30. https://doi.org/10.1007/978-3-319-52459-7_3

Jiang, S., Scott, N., & Ding, P. (2015). Using means-end chain theory to explore travel motivation: An examination of Chinese outbound tourists. Journal of vacation marketing, 21 (1), 87–100.

Jopp, R., Mair, J., Delacy, T., & Fluker, M. (2014). Climate Change Adaptation: Destination Management and the Green Tourist. Tourism Planning & Development, 12(3), 300–320. https://doi.org/10.1080/21568316.2014.988879

Kapiki, S. T., & Jaksic, D. (2015). Consumers perceptions of the local hotel recreation facilities: the case of Greek and Serbian young people. International Journal of Tourism Policy, 6(1), 46. https://doi.org/10.1504/ijtp.2015.075143

Karunakaran, R. K., Manuel, S., & Satheesh, E. N. (2018). Spreading Information in Complex Networks: An Overview and Some Modified Methods. Graph Theory - Advanced Algorithms and Applications. https://doi.org/10.5772/intechopen.69204

Kiatkawsin, K., & Han, H. (2017). Young travelers intention to behave pro-environmentally: Merging the value-belief-norm theory and the expectancy theory. Tourism Management, 59, 76–88. https://doi.org/10.1016/j.tourman.2016.06.018

Kilubi, I. (2017). Research methodology and data collection. Strategic Technology Partnering and Supply Chain Risk Management, 79–89. https://doi.org/10.1007/978-3-658-19918-0_8

Kim, H. S. (2016). A Feasibility Study of Mountain Tourism-Related Business with Job Creation Opportunity In View of Mountain Tourism Promotion Act. International Journal of Tourism and Hospitality Research, 30(2), 211. https://doi.org/10.21298/ijthr.2016.02.30.2.211

Koh, K. Y., & Hatten, T. S. (2002). The tourism entrepreneur: The overlooked player in tourism development studies. International Journal of Hospitality & Tourism Administration, 3(1), 21–48.

Kumar, V., & Kaushik, A. K. (2017). Destination brand experience and visitor behavior: The mediating role of destination brand identification. Journal of Travel & Tourism Marketing, 1–15. https://doi.org/10.1080/10548408.2017.1401032

Leask, A., Fyall, A., & Barron, P. (2013). Generation Y: An Agenda for Future Visitor Attraction Research. International Journal of Tourism Research, 16(5), 462–471. https://doi.org/10.1002/jtr.1940

Lee, Y., & Kim, I. (2018). Change and stability in shopping tourist destination networks: The case of Seoul in Korea. Journal of Destination Marketing & Management. https://doi.org/10.1016/j.jdmm.2018.02.004

Lesjak, M., Navrátil, J., Pícha, K., & Gilliam, V. L. (2015). The Predictors of the Willingness to Recommend a Visit for Diversified Tourism Attractions. Czech Journal of Tourism, 4(2). https://doi.org/10.1515/cjot-2015-0005

Li & Ryan, C. (2018). Souvenir shopping experiences: A case study of Chinese tourists in North Korea. Tourism Management, 64, 142–153. https://doi.org/10.1016/j.tourman.2017.08.006

Li, F., Wen, J., & Ying, T. (2017). The influence of crisis on tourists' perceived destination image and revisit intention: An exploratory study of Chinese tourists to North Korea. Journal of Destination Marketing & Management. https://doi.org/10.1016/j.jdmm.2017.11.006

Li, S., Yao, Y., & Xu, L. (2017). Evolutionary game analysis of online travel agency and hotels pricing strategy. 2017 International Conference on Grey Systems and Intelligent Services (GSIS). https://doi.org/10.1109/gsis.2017.8077723

Lindberg, K., & Veisten, K. (2012). Local and non-local preferences for nature tourism facility development. Tourism Management Perspectives,4, 215–222. https://doi.org/10.1016/j.tmp.2012.08.004

Lisowska, A. (2017). Crime in tourism destinations: Research review. Tourism, 27(1). https://doi.org/10.18778/0867-5856.27.1.12

Liu, Y., Li, Y., & Parkpian, P. (2018). Inbound tourism in Thailand: Market form and scale differentiation in ASEAN source countries. Tourism Management, 64, 22–36. https://doi.org/10.1016/j.tourman.2017.07.016

Lo, A. S., Mak, B., & Chen, Y. (2014). Do travel agency jobs appeal to university students? A case of tourism management students in Hong Kong. *Journal of Teaching in Travel & Tourism*, *14*(1), 87–121

Mackay, E. A., & Spencer, A. (2017). The future of Caribbean tourism: competition and climate change implications. Worldwide Hospitality and Tourism Themes, 9(1), 44–59. https://doi.org/10.1108/whatt-11-2016-0069

Maeda, T., Yoshida, M., Toriumi, F., & Ohashi, H. (2018). Extraction of Tourist Destinations and Comparative Analysis of Preferences Between Foreign Tourists and Domestic Tourists on the Basis of Geotagged Social Media Data. ISPRS International Journal of Geo-Information, 7(3), 99. https://doi.org/10.3390/ijgi7030099

Mahdzar, M., Shuib, A., Herman, M., & Ramachandran, S. (2015). Perceive quality, memorable experience and behavioral intentions: An examination of tourists in National Park. Hospitality and Tourism 2015, 25–27. https://doi.org/10.1201/b19162-7

Marasco, A., Buonincontri, P., Niekerk, M. V., Orlowski, M., & Okumus, F. (2018). Exploring the role of next-generation virtual technologies in destination marketing. Journal of Destination Marketing & Management. https://doi.org/10.1016/j.jdmm.2017.12.002

Marchiori, E., & Cantoni, L. (2016). Evaluating Destination Communications on the Internet. Analytics in Smart Tourism Design Tourism on the Verge, 253–279. https://doi.org/10.1007/978-3-319-44263-1_15

Marinao, E. (2018). Determinants of Satisfaction with the Tourist Destination. Mobilities, Tourism and Travel Behavior - Contexts and Boundaries. https://doi.org/10.5772/intechopen.70343

Matthews, Y., Scarpa, R., & Marsh, D. (2018). Cumulative attraction and spatial dependence in a destination choice model for beach recreation. Tourism Management, 66, 318–328. https://doi.org/10.1016/j.tourman.2017.12.009

Mckercher, B. (2016). Do Attractions Attract Tourists? A Framework to Assess the Importance of Attractions in Driving Demand. International Journal of Tourism Research, 19(1), 120–125. https://doi.org/10.1002/jtr.2091

Mijoč, J., Marković, S., & Horvat, J. (2017). The Role of Local Authenticity In Forming Tourists Intentions. https://doi.org/10.20867/tosee.04.46

Milman, A., & Tasci, A. D. (2017). Exploring the experiential and sociodemographic drivers of satisfaction and loyalty in the theme park context. Journal of Destination Marketing & Management. https://doi.org/10.1016/j.jdmm.2017.06.005

Morlotti, C., Cattaneo, M., Malighetti, P., & Redondi, R. (2017). Multi-dimensional price elasticity for leisure and business destinations in the low-cost air transport market: Evidence from easyJet. Tourism Management, 61, 23–34. https://doi.org/10.1016/j.tourman.2017.01.009

Moscardo, G., & Murphy, L. (2016). Using destination community wellbeing to assess tourist markets: A case study of Magnetic Island, Australia. Journal of Destination Marketing & Management, 5(1), 55–64. https://doi.org/10.1016/j.jdmm.2016.01.003

Murdy, S., Alexander, M., & Bryce, D. (2018). What pulls ancestral tourists 'home'? An analysis of ancestral tourist motivations. Tourism Management, 64, 13–19. https://doi.org/10.1016/j.tourman.2017.07.011

Mutandwa, E., Taremwa, N. K., & Tubanambazi, T. (2015). Determinants Of Business Performance Of Small And Medium Size Enterprises In Rwanda. Journal of Developmental Entrepreneurship, 20(01), 1550001. https://doi.org/10.1142/s1084946715500016

Nicolau, J. L., & Masiero, L. (2013). Relationship between Price Sensitivity and Expenditures in the Choice of Tourism Activities at the Destination. Tourism Economics, 19(1), 101–114. https://doi.org/10.5367/te.2013.0192

Novais, M. A., Ruhanen, L., & Arcodia, C. (2018). Destination competitiveness: A phenomenographic study. Tourism Management, 64, 324–334. https://doi.org/10.1016/j.tourman.2017.08.014

Nyangwe, S., & Buhalis, D. (2017). Branding Transformation Through Social Media and Co-creation: Lessons from Marriott International. Information and Communication Technologies in Tourism 2018, 257–269. https://doi.org/10.1007/978-3-319-72923-7_20

Pattanaro, G. (2014). Success Factors for Collaborative Destination Marketing. Tourism Management, Marketing, and Development, 221–237. https://doi.org/10.1057/9781137354358_12

Pavia, N., & Floričić, T. (2017). Innovative Accommodation Facilities In Tourism And Hospitality Industry – Integrated Hotels. https://doi.org/10.20867/tosee.04.16

Pearce, D. G., & Schänzel, H. A. (2013). Destinations: Tourists Perspectives from New Zealand. International Journal of Tourism Research, 17(1), 4–12. https://doi.org/10.1002/jtr.1955

Pennington-Gray, L., & Schroeder, A. (2018). Crisis concierge: The role of the DMO in visitor incident assistance. Journal of Destination Marketing & Management. 9, 381–383.

Pike, S., & Page, S. J. (2014). Destination Marketing Organizations and destination marketing: A narrative analysis of the literature. Tourism Management, 41, 202–227. https://doi.org/10.1016/j.tourman.2013.09.009

Pino, G., & Peluso, A. M. (2015). The development of cruise tourism in emerging destinations: Evidence from Salento, Italy. Tourism and Hospitality Research, 18(1), 15–27. https://doi.org/10.1177/1467358415619672

Pulido-Fernández, J. I., & Merinero-Rodríguez, R. (2018). Destinations relational dynamic and tourism development. Journal of Destination Marketing & Management, 7, 140–152. https://doi.org/10.1016/j.jdmm.2016.09.008

Räikkönen, J., & Grénman, M. (2017). The Experience Economy Logic in the Wellness Tourism Industry. Co-Creation and Well-Being in Tourism Tourism on the Verge, 3–18. https://doi.org/10.1007/978-3-319-44108-5_1

Reichelt, J. (2013). Modell zur Erklärung der Bedeutung von Online Word-of-Mouth für Konsumenten. Informationssuche Und Online Word-of-Mouth, 13–41. https://doi.org/10.1007/978-3-658-01373-8_2

Riaz, A., Gregor, S., & Lin, A. (2018). Biophilia and biophobia in website design: Improving internet information dissemination. Information & Management, 55(2), 199–214. https://doi.org/10.1016/j.im.2017.05.006

Rodrigues, D., Lopes, D., Alexopoulos, T., & Goldenberg, L. (2017). A new look at online attraction: Unilateral initial attraction and the pivotal role of perceived similarity. Computers in Human Behavior, 74, 16–25. https://doi.org/10.1016/j.chb.2017.04.009

Rogerson, C. M. (2007). Supporting small firm development in tourism: South Africa's Tourism Enterprise Programme. *The International Journal of Entrepreneurship and Innovation*, 8(1), 6–14

Rosen, H. (2010). Entrepreneurship and Leadership in HospitalityInsights and Implications for Hospitality and Tourism Education1. Strategic Management for Hospitality and Tourism, 299–327. https://doi.org/10.1016/b978-0-7506-6522-3.00015-8

Ryzin, G. G. (2013). An Experimental Test of the Expectancy-Disconfirmation Theory of Citizen Satisfaction. Journal of Policy Analysis and Management, 32(3), 597–614. https://doi.org/10.1002/pam.21702

Saniotis, A., Hansen, A., & Bi, P. (2011). Climate Change and Population Health: Possible Future Scenarios. Climate Change - Socioeconomic Effects. https://doi.org/10.5772/23175

Santini, F. D., Ladeira, W. J., & Sampaio, C. H. (2018). Tourists perceived value and destination revisit intentions: The moderating effect of domain-specific innovativeness. International Journal of Tourism Research. https://doi.org/10.1002/jtr.2178

Scantlebury, M. M. (2012). Attractions - The Beating Heart of The Tourism Industry, Are You Ready For More Change? Journal of Tourism & Hospitality, 01(03). https://doi.org/10.4172/2167-0269.1000e116

Sertkan, M., Neidhardt, J., & Werthner, H. (2017). Mapping of Tourism Destinations to Travel Behavioural Patterns. Information and Communication Technologies in Tourism 2018, 422–434. https://doi.org/10.1007/978-3-319-72923-7_32

Sheldon, P. J., Pollock, A., & Daniele, R. (2016). Social Entrepreneurship and Tourism: Setting the Stage. Social Entrepreneurship and Tourism on the Verge, 1–18. https://doi.org/10.1007/978-3-319-46518-0_1

Shoval, N. (2018). Sensing tourists: Geoinformatics and the future of tourism geography research. Tourism Geographies, 1–3. https://doi.org/10.1080/14616688.2018.1437768

Sohn, H., & Yoon, Y. (2016). Verification of Destination Attachment and Moderating Effects in the Relationship Between the Perception of and Satisfaction with Tourism Destinations: A Focus on Japanese Tourists. Journal of Travel & Tourism Marketing, 33(5), 757–769. https://doi.org/10.1080/10548408.2016.1167394

Socorro, M. P., Betancor, O., & Rus, G. D. (2018). Feasibility and desirability of airport competition: The role of product substitutability and airlines nationality. Journal of Air Transport Management, 67, 224–231. https://doi.org/10.1016/j.jairtraman.2017.03.004

Song, H., & Bae, S. Y. (2017). Understanding the travel motivation and patterns of international students in Korea: using the theory of travel career pattern. Asia Pacific Journal of Tourism Research, 23(2), 133–145. https://doi.org/10.1080/10941665.2017.1410193

Sreejesh, S., & Abhilash, P. (2017). Investigating the process through which e-servicescape creates e-loyalty in travel and tourism websites. *Journal of Travel & Tourism Marketing, 34* (1), 20–39

Sthapit, E., & Coudounaris, D. N. (2017). Memorable tourism experiences: antecedents and outcomes. Scandinavian Journal of Hospitality and Tourism, 18(1), 72–94. https://doi.org/10.1080/15022250.2017.1287003

Stylidis, D., & Cherifi, B. (2018). Characteristics of destination image: visitors and non-visitors' images of London. Tourism Review. https://doi.org/10.1108/tr-05-2017-0090

Stylidis, D., Sit, J. K., & Biran, A. (2018). Residents' place image: a meaningful psychographic variable for tourism segmentation? Journal of Travel & Tourism Marketing, 1–11. https://doi.org/10.1080/10548408.2018.1425176

Suzuki, H. (2017). "They are Raising the Devil with the Trading Dows:" Reconsidering the Royal Navy's Anti-Slave Trade Campaign from the Slave Trader Perspective. *Slave Trade Profiteers in the Western Indian Ocean,* 59–72. https://doi.org/10.1007/978-3-319-59803-1_4

Suzuki, H. (2017). The Slave Trade in the Nineteenth-Century Western Indian Ocean: An Overview. *Slave Trade Profiteers in the Western Indian Ocean,* 19–40. https://doi.org/10.1007/978-3-319-59803-1_2

Taskin, R., & Rashid, M. M. (2018). Tourism in Kuakata, Bangladesh:Understanding Current Status and Future Prospects. *Ottoman Journal of Tourism and Management Research, 3*(1), 235–244. https://doi.org/10.26465/ojtmr.2018319507

Tervo-Kankare, K. (2018). Entrepreneurship in nature-based tourism under a changing climate. Current Issues in Tourism, 1–13. https://doi.org/10.1080/13683500.2018.1439457

Thomas, R. (2016). Entrepreneurship in hospitality and tourism: A global perspective. Tourism Management, 55, 309. https://doi.org/10.1016/j.tourman.2016.03.005

Tiarto (2018). The Implication Of Airlines Deregulation In The End Of The 20Th Century On Industrial Development Of Commercial Air Transport Schedule In Indonesia. Proceedings of the Conference on Global Research on Sustainable Transport (GROST 2017). https://doi.org/10.2991/grost-17.2018.29

Triantafillidou, E., & Tsiaras, S. (2018). Exploring entrepreneurship, innovation and tourism development from a sustainable perspective: evidence from Greece. *Journal for International Business and Entrepreneurship Development, 11*(1), 53–64.

Tukamushaba, E. K., Xiao, H., & Ladkin, A. (2016). The effect of tourists' perceptions of a tourism product on memorable travel experience: Implications for destination branding. European Journal of Tourism, Hospitality and Recreation, 7(1). https://doi.org/10.1515/ejthr-2016-0001

Tussyadiah, I. P., Wang, D., & Jia, C. (2017). Virtual Reality and Attitudes Toward Tourism Destinations. Information and Communication Technologies in Tourism 2017, 229–239. https://doi.org/10.1007/978-3-319-51168-9_17

UNWTO Tourism Highlights: 2017 Edition. (2017). https://doi.org/10.18111/9789284419029

UNWTO World Tourism Barometer, 16(1). (2018). https://doi.org/10.18111/wtobaromatereng.2018.16.issue

UNWTO/WTCF City Tourism Performance Research. (2018). https://doi.org/10.18111/9789284419616

Utama, I. G. (2016). Destination Loyalty Model of Senior Foreign Tourists Visiting Bali Tourism Destination. Managing the Asian Century Development of Tourism and the Hospitality Industry in Southeast Asia, 37–49. https://doi.org/10.1007/978-981-287-606-5_3

Veasna, S., Wu, W., & Huang, C. (2013). The impact of destination source credibility on destination satisfaction: The mediating effects of destination attachment and destination image. Tourism Management, 36, 511–526. https://doi.org/10.1016/j.tourman.2012.09.007

Vučetić, A. (2018). Importance of environmental indicators of sustainable development in the transitional selective tourism destination. International Journal of Tourism Research. https://doi.org/10.1002/jtr.2183

Weitzl, W. (2016). Research Methods. Measuring Electronic Word-of-Mouth Effectiveness, 163–207. https://doi.org/10.1007/978-3-658-15889-7_4

Weldearegay, H. G. (2017). The Determinants of Tourism Destination Competitiveness (TDC): PLSPath Model of Structural Equation Modeling. Journal of Tourism & Hospitality, 06(05). https://doi.org/10.4172/2167-0269.1000315

Woosnam, K. M., Draper, J., Jiang, J., Aleshinloye, K. D., & Erul, E. (2018). Applying self-perception theory to explain residents attitudes about tourism development through travel histories. Tourism Management, 64, 357–368. https://doi.org/10.1016/j.tourman.2017.09.015

Xiang, Z. (2018). From digitization to the age of acceleration: On information technology and tourism. Tourism Management Perspectives, 25, 147–150. https://doi.org/10.1016/j.tmp.2017.11.023

Yang, Y., Park, S., & Hu, X. (2018). Electronic word of mouth and hotel performance: A meta-analysis. Tourism Management, 67, 248–260. https://doi.org/10.1016/j.tourman.2018.01.015

Yankholmes, A. K., Akyeampong, O. A., & Dei, L. A. (2009). Residents perceptions of Transatlantic Slave Trade attractions for heritage tourism in Danish-Osu, Ghana. *Journal of Heritage Tourism, 4*(4), 315–329. https://doi.org/10.1080/17438730903186441

Yoo, C., Yoon, D., & Park, E. (2018). Tourist motivation: an integral approach to destination choices. Tourism Review. https://doi.org/10.1108/tr-04-2017-0085

Žabkar, V., Brenčič, M. M., & Dmitrović, T. (2010). Modelling perceived quality, visitor satisfaction and behavioural intentions at the destination level. Tourism management, 31(4), 537–546.

Zhang, J., & Daugherty, T. (2009). Third-Person Effect and Social Networking: Implications for Online Marketing and Word-of-Mouth Communication. American Journal of Business, 24(2), 53–64. https://doi.org/10.1108/19355181200900011

Assessing the Factors Militating Against Microfinance in Alleviating Chronic Poverty and Food Insecurity in Rural Northern Ghana

Bibiana Koglinuu Batinge[1(✉)] and Hatice Jenkins[2]

[1] Department of Secretaryship and Management Studies, Sunyani Technical University, Sunyani, Ghana
porsabia123456@yahoo.com
[2] Department of Banking and Finance, Eastern Mediterranean University, Famagusta, North Cyprus, Turkey
hatice.jenkins@emu.edu.tr

1 Introduction

Poverty is one major concern in many developing countries of the world. In this millennium age, where most continents continue to register sustainable economic growth and development, Africa is not only lagging behind but is trapped in a vicious circle of borrowing and donor dependency syndrome which some critics such as Mhango (2017), Gukurume (2012), Okosun et al. (2010) point out as one of the causes practically sabotaging real development. Truly, Africa has perpetually failed to focus its development efforts on the optimum utilization of the immense natural resources that many countries in Africa are endowed with to turn it into wealth to propel their economies and people towards a high level of economic and social development, and as a consequence eliminate pervasive poverty. Females in emerging countries are confronted on a day-to-day basis by several traditional prejudices that brand them and thwart their efforts from improving on their wellbeing; especially women from deep-rooted patriarchal sub-Saharan Africa are prevented from developing their talents to take opportunities that reduce poverty and food insecurity, Ghana inclusive and the rural northern Ghanaian woman worst victim. Writings have it that, Agriculture alone backs 20% of Ghanaian's Gross Domestic Product (GDP), and Ghana Living Standards Survey (2016), asserted that 71% of the rural populace rely on agriculture as the basis of livelihood, either farming crops or rearing animals with a very high percentage of 85–95% of both urban and rural people in the northern regions completely dependence on agriculture. Also, according to Ghana's Statistical Service Population and Housing Census (2010) reports Ghana's overall poverty rate as declining, yet, the three regions in the north have seen only negligible decreases, with the poverty rates in the north, two to three times the national average. As a result of these, chronic food insecurity remains a critical challenge. Many of the people especially women and children live each day in abject poverty; children go at times without food, their bodies stunted with signs of malnutrition. One of the authors is a native of northern Ghana.

© Springer Nature Switzerland AG 2018
N. Ozatac and K. K. Gökmenoglu (eds.), *Emerging Trends in Banking and Finance*, Springer Proceedings in Business and Economics,
https://doi.org/10.1007/978-3-030-01784-2_11

In an attempt to alleviate this serious poverty prevalence in the three regions, past and present Ghana Governments and well-meaning institutions around the world have instituted interventions such as microfinance and other poverty related programs to curtail the problem, interventions include; *Millennium Development Goal 1 (MDG1), Food and Nutrition Security (FNS), Medium-Term Agriculture Sector Investment Plan (METASIP) (2011–2015), Sustainable Development Goals (SDG 1 & 2), World food program (WFP), United Nations Development Program (UNDP), Danish International Development Assistance (DANIDA), and Germany for International Cooperation (GIC), Ghana's vision 2020* and many more poverty and food security measures to curtail this problem in the northern territory of Ghana especially women, yet to no avail.

1.1 Statement of the Problem

All of the above inventions established in northern Ghana are to help the women take opportunities to liberate them from poverty and improve at least, their basic needs. Predominantly, in the rural areas of the northern regions of Ghana, outmoded cultural beliefs, traditions and customs, allows only males to completely take birthrights of important assets such land and cattle and the women are made to belief that men are superior to them. However, the men are unable to cope with the meager responsibility of providing the basic needs for their families. Hence, there is perpetual poverty and food shortage in the area and the most affected, the vulnerable- women and children go at times without food, their bodies stunted with signs of malnutrition, compelling the continuous migration of families to the rural areas particularly, the Bono Ahofo Region of Ghana-Sunyani.

However, researches findings indicate that microfinance services are tools for alleviating the active poor from poverty and empowerment, especially women in both developed and emerging nations (Bakhtiari 2011; Boateng et al. 2015; Ashta et al. 2015; Miled and Rejeb 2015; Kumah and Boachie 2016). In contrasts, this paper anticipates that, the success of microfinance as women's economic and social empowering tool in the area of this study depends on several issues. Such issues are the, existing cultural beliefs, general attitudes and the tribal customs within this group. These issues interrupt the women's expertise about themselves and limit their capability in handling microfinance services to improve their financial situation. The customary ideologies and egotisms barriers that the rural northern women face in their male dominated areas are quite scanty in literature. Hence the basis of this paper is to examine the traditional restrictions confronting northern rural families, especially females in accessing the opportunities microfinance services renders to solve the poverty prevalence, rather than migrating to another rural set ups.

1.2 Research Objectives

The main objective of this paper was to examine the traditional restrictions confronting rural families especially women in accessing microfinance services to aid in alleviating poverty and the chronic food insecurity.

These specific objectives were raised:

(a) To investigate local customs and attitudes that militates against the enhancement of microfinance services in reducing poverty and chronic food insecurity.

(b) To examine the agricultural tools and skills used in cropping and keeping of the livestock in their original homes-rural areas in northern Ghana.

(c) To find out what policies Ghana Government put in place to minimize these food and poverty challenges in northern rural Ghana.

2 Literature Review

To put this article in its proper context, the Embeddedness Theory was adapted. The Embeddedness Theory is formed on sociological, rules and open market concept to propagate one of the numerous potential clarifications of how collective construction delivers supremacy and controls to aids in inter- organizational structures (Uzzi and Gillespie 2002). It contends that the procedure of implanting profitable contacts in mutual affections inspires into upcoming connections, prospects of faith and support that endorses sole assets formation in the association.

Though there are numerous microfinance institutions Ghana, not every active poor can get access to the government or formal-registered microfinance institutions. Hence in rural northern Ghana many of the microfinance institutions are informal, with Susu as the most accessible one. Susu, lending from family and friends are among the oldest informal financial services in Africa. Susu is an informal financial means of which people securely save and access their money, and gain access to credit. The accumulated savings is returned to the clients and the circle continues. The characteristic of Susu (an informal loan club) is skewed towards trust (Ledgerwood et al. 2013; Tripathi 2015). Embeddedness philosophy estimates that profitable dealings develop entrenched in mesh of collective attachments that alternates the distributive haggling decisions by which fair dealings yield. These prospects raised since the embeddedness of lucrative businesses in societal affections influences that viable deal, with prospects of give-and-take that individuals usually practice in managing with folks they come to identify well, opportunities that bargain a dependable design for supervising dealings since they are erudite in previous understandings and equally agreed over socialization. Also, since give-and-take dwells on multidimensional collective affairs that are tough for competitors to mimic and to curtail the expenditures of printed agreements, than early additional confidence are acknowledged and responded to. Thus, embeddedness delivers the vital preparing device for original agreements of confidence and common trust that, is acknowledged and reimbursed, harden over mutual reserves and self-perseverance. By divergence, prospects of greedy acts inside provision's span links are possible to apt suspicion, even if an achievement is trustworthy, excluding in separate circumstances where financial enticements are associated or third parties apply equality (Uzzi and Gillespie 2002).

Convincingly, embeddedness philosophy is founded on prospects of reliance that rise since embeddedness embroils dealings by persons who recognize each other success beyond socialization and mutuality that stimulate exceptional wealth formation. In the dealings of Susu, is similarly grounded on common convictions, sincerity and trustworthiness for the members to support everyone's investment and offer advances to everyone. Short of conviction, linkages and verve, innovativeness would flop. The concept is a signal of the talents of connotation which would ascend when persons in a viable acts belief in one another, and sense the importance and willingness to toil collectively. This procedure of confidence creates links and businesses smoother and additional self-motivation, so the members and their assets are emotionally guaranteed. Therefore, members who are in bond discover mutuality that endorses wealth in their collaboration and connotation. According to Block 2003; Hodgson 2017; *"Karl Polanyi and the writing of the Great Transformation Theory and society"*, asserted that, relations both mutual and commercial, would typically be a consequence of conviction that has advanced from the singular member. Karl's philosophy botched to identify the circumstance that there is rivalry, harmonization and assessment of bazaar properties that has the control to force collaboration as well as societal conviction. It permits souk discussion to be assumed as a partisan and public brawl above official rules. The embeddedness of monetary achievement as a resolution to an exact problematic bazaar performer's expression, Value, excellence of possessions and resourcefulness of performers are issues well perceiving which might convey around collective collaboration as well as conviction (Beckert 2007; Grunig and White 2011). Embeddedness philosophy stimulus this search in appreciating exactly how traditional opinions and methodologies destroy womenfolk in grasping chances in microfinance services particularly, rural women in northern part of Ghana, who migrate to the villages of Bono Ahafo.

2.1 Overview of the Microfinance Sector in Ghana and Government Policies

According to literature the concept of microfinance is very old in Ghana. Available evidence suggests that the first credit union in West Africa was established in northern Ghana in 1955 by Roman Catholic missionaries, (Abor and Quartey 2010; Martín-Tapia et al. 2010). However, Rotating Saving and Credit Associations (Susu), is known to be one of the oldest microfinance schemes in Ghana. Susu is thought to have originated from Nigeria and spread to Ghana in the early twentieth century, with the main objective of supporting micro-enterprises owned by the active poor who has no access to traditional banking, especially women (Schindler 2010). According to World Bank statistics, micro, small and medium enterprises-MSMEs, are largely owned by women and have also contributed greatly to the informal sector businesses. On the contrary, almost all the women in rural areas, especially in northern Ghana continue to encounter difficulties in accessing credit compared to their female's counterparts in the urban centers (Dalitso and Peter 2000). This lack of access to credit for women from the rural communities is one of the economic setbacks to the country's development. Marlow and Swail 2014, in their paper titlted, *'Gender, risk and finance: why can't a woman be more like a man?'* avowed that many women are disadvantaged in financing their business growth. They face a number of difficulties and cultural barriers such as the traditional land tenure system, inheritance system, ignorance of business laws and ethnics, lack of formal education, and lack of knowledge of financial transactions and their riskiness (Ghana Statistically Survey 1999). The International Finance Corporation (IFC), survey conducted in 2012, indicated that approximately 58% of women owned MSMEs, but lack of access to credit is a severe barrier to growth. However, Ghana had a large number of micro-credit programs that were implemented to support female owned MSMEs' access to credit since 1991 (Goyal and Yadav 2014). Economically, it is noted that about 70% of Ghana's Gross Domestic Product (GDP), is produced by MSMEs, of which 44% of these enterprises are female owned (Yeboah 2015). Although such figures are impressive, for the Sub-Saharan Region there is still a visible gender gap in women's economic participation and opportunities. According to the World Economic Forum Gender Gap Report, Ghana ranked 71st out of 135 countries in 2012 in gender inequality not only in the world but also in the Sub-Saharan Africa of 25 countries, Ghana ranked number 10, still indicating a bigger gender gap. However, the 2010 Ghana Population and Housing Census indicate that, out of the 28 million people living in the country, 51% are female and majority of them are poor, living in the rural setups. Previous population and housing Censuses in Ghana also confirmed this.

Ghana Governments in awareness of these great disparities in gender, especially in the north territory of Ghana, have put countless number of poverty inventions to bridge this gap. Some of these interventions include; structural adjustment programme (SAP), known as the Economic Recovery Programme (ERP). This policy targeted to improve resource allocation, increase economic efficiency and improve the country's ability to manage domestic and global problems, The Financial Sector Adjustment Program (FINSAP) since 1986, with the sole objective of liberalizing interest rates, Microfinance and Small Scale Loans Centre (MASLOC), a government microfinance institution, to provide credit facilities to the active poor, the Savanna Accelerated Development Plan (SADP), to improve the poverty situation in northern Ghana, the Disproportional of Civil Society Plan and Malnutrition (DSPM), to look into children nutritional conditions, Disproportional Burden on the Poor Plan (DBPP), aimed at helping the very poor, and the Rapid Achievements Survival Millennium Development Goal (RASMD), an agenda for growth and prosperity and the Hunger Vision 2020, the list is not exhausted. All these interventions are mostly having the same objectives, including equal in human dignity and rights, the right to food, health, work and education (IMF 1998; Wronka 2016). Yet the northern rural poverty and food insecurity still continue, and children and women are the most effected. Though, the country has enough resources to help fight this prevalence, it seems the right channel to curtail this is missing. These women have to be given the opportunity to their basic right, self-confidence, encourage, support and their views respected first, choose and pick decisions that affect them, before any meaningful invention can be achieved (Harding 2016). Unfortunately, most of the females are completely under the direction of their patriarchal counterparts, their dos and don'ts are in the hands of the men, without any questions coming from them, especially in the rural setups of northern Ghana (Dapila 1995). Molyneux 2016 maintained that, women bear the major responsibility for meeting basic needs, yet are systematically denied the freedom of action and voice in decision-making to fulfill this responsibility. For the number of interventions established by past and present Ghana Governments are numerous, yet this rural northern folk's poverty cycle continuous.

2.2 The Indigenes of Northern Ghana and Their Livelihood Roles

According to History, the northern Ghanaian is well known for his honesty, bravely, hardworking and above all sober and respectful (Lentz 1994; Lentz 2006). These attributes of the northerners according to literature, prompt the British-Ghana's Colonial Masters to decide that the Northerners of Ghana, at that time do not need formal education to function. Hence, British reserved the country's security, the cultivating of the cocoa plantation, the non- mechanized minerals mining fields, the construction of railways and all other infrastructures needed at that time to the Northerners. For instance, the clearing of the forest to plant the cocoa at the time need a brave and hardworking persons with wisdom, for the forests were full of all kind of dangerous animals and very poisonous classes of reptilian. Also the underground Gold, bauxite and manganese mining fields were not mechanized, hence very dangerous, and construction of the railways needed such strong and brave persons, for almost every job that was labor-intensive, the Northerner at that time was fit for these jobs and was cut off from formal education (Brukum 1997; Saaka 1987). The negative effect of this decision by the British is one of the main contributing factors of the majority illiterates in the northern part of Ghana today, and the poverty prevalence and chronic food insecurity in the northern part of Ghana. The Ghana's Statistical Service (2010) asserted that, while Ghana's overall poverty rate has declined, the three regions in the north have seen only marginal decreases. Poverty rates in the north are two to three times the national average, and chronic food insecurity remains a critical challenge there. As a result, many of the people live each day in abject poverty.

The rural northerners of today are mostly peasant farmers (crops and animals). Ghana's rural areas, especially the three regions in the north of Ghana, have very limited access to the productive assets that would facilitate a shift from subsistence farming and livestock farming to modern, and commercialized agriculture (Konings 1994; Kuu-Ire 2009; Lobnibe 2010; Nyewie 2010). The major constraints to their livelihoods include; illiteracy, lack of water, very poor infrastructure and with no or little vocational and technical skills (Hartl 2011; Bisariya and Mishra 2015). As a result, many rural young men and young women leave their villages in the northern territory for urban centers of Ghana in search for non-existing or menial jobs (Agyei-Mensah and Owusu Agyei-Mensah and Owusu 2010). Hence, the poorest of the poor in Ghana, is the rural northern Ghanaian woman.

In the context of this paper, awareness is articulated concerning cultures, morals, assertiveness and beliefs that affect microfinance services. The overall approaches in the direction of these magnitudes to a certain extent differentiate exact standards, customs or opinions that stimulus the overall perceived consequences of financial liberation as well as self-confidence (Field et al. 2016; Joseph and Imhanlahimi 2011;

Wanyoike 2012). As the improvement of visions of own-independence, self-assurance portrayed by improved awareness around own ability and experiences, by way of life of the imminent and pensiveness (Trommsdorff 2012; Verbeek et al. 2012). Communal actions which describe disparities within womanhood and manhood in civilizations, usually assigning diverse duties and household tasks and allocating inferior values to schedules related to females, have damagingly influenced womenfolk in their pursuit for achievement. Certain standards comprise the task of merely the gender part/obligation for reproductive effort inside the home to womanhood and the main income realizing obligation to menfolks. In numerous circumstances, this has led unfortunately to females taking very inadequate chances to exploit their abilities confidently. Ghalib and Hossain (2010). Cultures would play qualms on women substances and likely decrease their conjugal predictions in certain places of the social order. Females grieve from stresses coming from outmoded methods of conventional cultures, where they are estimated mainly to provide on their domestic responsibilities in advance, they reflect about refining their pecuniary happiness (Jamali et al. 2009). Owing to the dogmatic defiance of males and extra traditional obstacles, females are constrained to execute their productive quotas and domestic routines (Yasmeen and Karim 2014). Women are an assortment to be obedient and altruistic, and are barred from relating with the public (Fakir and Nicol 2012).

Further restraints such as damaging societal defiance and narrow-mindedness against womanhood typically in emerging nations ascend from inequitable ethnic beliefs and mores of the male-controlled nations. Chauvinism is articulated over disparity attitudes in the direction of womenfolk entirely and usual in diverse morals and projections for women's collective demeanor in precise (Woldie and Adersua 2004). Initially, females are trained to be obedient and altruistic and as a consequence of this, women are deprived of membership in revenue making undertakings as well as admission to microfinance and bazaar amenities (Narteh et al. 2017; Ogbeide and Ele 2015; Simba et al. 2016). Traditional dynamic forces importantly prejudiced the progress of women-ran MSEs. They established that indigenous societies, standards, approaches and chain of command have robust effect on females-owned MSEs. Conversely, certain females in the villages in the north of Ghana had effectively accomplished to disentangle themselves from these shameful influences (Mbiti et al. 2015). Traditional physiognomies such as sexual category require countless influence on the defiance and conduct of personalities and their background in life. Whether particular person would progress and grow into a businessperson or not would rest on his or her environment and worth demeanors. Hence outmoded influences such as religion, ethnic links, conviction amongst associates in an establishment, business principles and approaches, customs and opinions related by means of sex and obligations ensure biased enactment of microfinance and other poverty alleviating tools amongst womanhood. Sexual category matters have a resilient effect on women undertakings. Females continue in difficulty to unravel themselves from that humiliation of existence as 'customary woman'. The traditional conviction that womankind have a responsibility 'take in' and do not ask questions is still foremost in several groups. Women continue to require the consent of their men to access credit. Rustic ladies are trained to trust that gentlemen's ideas are trustworthy than theirs, and as a consequence they incline to drive alongside per conclusions taken by their men.

Therefore, almost all females consider it hard to link corporate associations owing to these customs and common egotisms on their way. Characteristically, rural females seem to begin trades for existence nonetheless per no objective to develop (Mbiti et al. 2015).

Regardless of the volume of articles on microfinance services support in alleviating poverty and chronic food shortage in the rural northern Ghana, their experiential works did not clearly convey the traditional influences troubling the womenfolk involved in microfinance. Indigenous communal mores, dogmas and defiance and their bearing on females and creation of females sets remained inadequately considered. Record of the existing texts on customs, doctrines and impudence are founded on urban women and their microfinance activities and microfinance institutions work. Their foremost worry was on women empowerment through microfinance related activities. These perceptions are not included in this paper and texts connected to them required not been revised in this article. Customs, creeds and defiance are different to every one's area and kingdom. Islamic cultures have completely diverse beliefs that interrupt females' undertakings. Ghana, a nation with diverse ethnic groups has dissimilar traditional approaches to sexual category and sexual roles. The rural northern society continues to grasps resolutely onto their customs. Encounters confronting them are different as likened to others. Few previous studies have revealed the northern culture on women empowerment, however not on the rural northern woman. Scholars have also not search on; in what manner the mixture of several traditions might affect microfinance success on the rustic woman of northern Ghana. Ghana in its peculiar structure is established on numerous traditions and beliefs; with rural northern Ghana been very prominent in this. This research paper investigates into the traditions, doctrines and customs that might have an divergent effects on females' community ties, accomplishment of improvement and in what ways entirely, this as a group interrupt microfinance positive impact on these ladies' chronic poverty and food insecurity.

3   Methodology

3.1   Sample Procedure

The study area of this article is the rural Northern Regions of Ghana-Upper West, upper East and Northern Region. But sample is drawn from the rural northern migrants leaving in the villages of Bono Ahafo Region of Ghana-Sunyani. A non-probability (snowball) sampling procedure was used to collect primary data from 300 individuals' rural northern settles in the villages of Bono Ahafo. According to (García-Pérez et al. 2014; Hing and Nisbet 2010), a non-probability sampling procedure is required when data features are irregular such as these.This research questionnaire contains two major parts; multiple choice questions and the Likert scale items. The first part of the questionnaire was designed to collect information on the demographic characteristics of the respondents such as gender, age, education, marriage and occupation. The second part, respondents were asked a number of Likert scale items to investigate the traditional convictions that militate against microfinance positive impact on women chronic poverty and food insecurity. In these Likert scale material, respondents were asked to give their opinions on a number of statements indicating, whether poverty and chronic food insecurity is cause by traditions and gender roles or poor government interventions. Respondents' opinions ranked as highly disagree (1), disagree (2), neutral (3), agree (4), and highly agree (5).

3.2 Research Design

This study design adapted a descriptive and causative investigation established on the clarification by Hair et al. (2008), that descriptive research strategy is suitable when the study aims include the drive of the amount to which the selected variables are linked and how a variable source controls the observations of other variables. Also a quantitative method was used owing to its neutrality; it also enables data to be transformed into distinct units that can be compared with others by the use of statistical investigation which is a vital measure of numerical study. Scientific Package for Social Science, 18 (SPSS, 18) statistically software was used to analyze the data.

4   Findings

According to Afrane (2002), Leinbach (2003), social demographics profile of microfinance services recipients is a significant influence that could have consequences on their poverty tendency. Therefore, sex, age, marital status, level of education and the types of occupations are the features used to analysis their effects on the chronic poverty and the food insecurity in rural northern settlers in Bono Ahafo villages of southern Ghana.

From the Table 1, bulk of the sample, 200 (66.7%) are females with only 100 (33.3%) males. The age distribution revealed that most of the respondents 82.0% fall in the active working class, between 18–45 years old, and the rest 18. % is in the 46–62 age groups. 65.7% of the sample are married, while 25.3% are single, 6.3% are widows or widowers only 2.7% are either divorce or separated. The education level of the respondents; 31.3% of the respondents are complete illiterates, 60.4% had first cycle education (primary and junior schools), 8.3% had technical and vocational training. Therefore majority of the respondents had primary and junior schools education, while 8.3% had technical and vocational skills. Under type of occupation; 76.7 of the respondents are peasant crops and animals farmers, while 15.0% are petty traders, only and 8.3% do government and other jobs. The results on the number of children in a household of a respondent shows that, 16.7% of the respondents had eleven (11) or more dependents, 28.7% had eight (8) or ten (10) children, 8.0% had 2 or 4 children, while only 9.7%, had no child.

Table 2 indicates the challenges of the poverty prevalence and food insecurity confronting the rural northern indigenes; these vary from the old systems of farming, lack of knowledge on mechanize farming, sole dependency on a single reason rain fall with no source of irrigation, absence of agricultural experts to offer advice, lack of basic family needs, poor storage system and non-existing markets for perishable farm

Table 1. Demographic characteristics of respondents

Gender	Frequency	Percent	Cumulative percent
Male	100	33.3	33.3
Female	200	66.7	100.0
Total	300	100.0	
Age			
18–25	82	27.3	27.3
26–35	164	54.7	82.0
36–45	37	12.3	94.3
46–62	17	5.7	100.0
Total			
Marital status			
Single	76	25.3	25.3
Married	197	65.7	91.0
Widow/widower	19	6.3	97.3
Divorce/separate	8	2.7	100.0
Total	300	100.0	
Level of education			
Illiterate	94	31.3	31.3
Primary school	107	35.7	67.0
Junior high school	74	24.7	91.7
Technical and vocational skills	25	8.3	100.0
Total	300	100.0	
Type of occupation			
Farming/animals	230	76.7	76.7
Petty trading	45	15.0	91.7
Gov't/other work	25	8.3	100.0
Total	300	100.0	
Number of children			
No child	29	9.7	9.7
2 or 4 children	24	8.0	17.7
5 or 7 children	111	37.0	54.7
8 or 11 children	86	28.7	83.3
12 and above children	50	16.7	100.0
Total	300	100.0	

Field work; December, 2016

produce. Almost all recorded very high percentages scores, indicating that if the above measures are available poverty and food shortage would be minimized, except two items on mechanize farming that recorded low percentages and low averages 28.7% (1.51) and 50.0% (1.92) respectively.

Table 3 shows the degree of responses of negative cultural influences on poverty and food insecurity effecting indigenes of rural northern Ghanaians. The results show

Table 2. Responses on Traditional farming practices

No_	Traditional farming practices causes of poverty and food insecurity	1	2	3	4	5	%	Mean
1	I still practice the traditional way of farming	1.3	1.3	25.0	31.0	41.3	72.0	4.0000
2	I practice mechanized farming	2.3	28.7	40.3	22.0	6.7	28.7	1.5167
3	I practice both traditional and mechanized	0.7	4.0	45.3	24.7	25.3	50.0	1.9200
4	If farming is mechanized food insecurity will reduce	1.0	2.0	12.7	25.0	59.3	84.4	4.1067
5	I rely solely on natural rainfall for farming	2.3	1.2	14.7	19.0	62.7	81.7	4.2633
6	There is no source of irrigation for farming	2.0	1.0	24.0	42.0	30.7	72.7	3.9667
7	If agricultural experts offer advice farm produce will increase	1.0	0.7	24.0	31.7	42.7	74.4	3.9900
8	On average there are enough resources to cater for the family's basic needs	0.7	1.3	26.7	37.0	34.3	71.3	3.7100
9	The poor storage system and non-existing markets, is the cause of food insecurity	0.3	2.3	21.7	40.0	35.7	75.7	3.9667
10	There is no ready market for the perishable crops	1.3	2.7	51.0	20.7	24.3	45.3	4.1700

Field work; 2016

Note Respondents' opinions ranked as highly disagree (1), disagree (2), neutral (3), agree (4), and highly agree (5). The percentage (%) column is the addition of agree and highly agree (4 and 5), respectively

higher percentages and average scores, confirming that microfinance services cannot succeed in alleviating poverty and the chronic food shortage, if the negative cultural, unproductive, outmoded practices such as; woman is confirmed to the kitchen and bedroom (73.0%, 4.27), Women require much time for family responsibilities (73.0%, 4.27), force girl marriages (65.7%, 3.93), women mobility is restricted (72.0%, 2.99), women seek permission access loans (67.7%, 3.24), men control the loans (68.0%, 3.62), men are supposed to be the wage earners (71.0%, 3.95), migration of northern youth to southern cities (72.3%, 3.68), numerous chieftaincy disputes (65.3%, 3.99) and scrapping of scrap all the unproductive outmoded practices (68.7%, 4.076).

Table 4, findings on the impact of Ghana government policies in solving the poverty and food insecurity in this study area, indicate that if the government could put interventions such as; Ghana Governments have established MFI (70.6%, 4.08), government MFIs loans are flexible with low interest rate (72.3%, 4.2), provides available and affordable health centers (29.7%, 3.98), subside some farm inputs (73.7%, 4.26), provides efficient storage system (71.6%, 4.23), guarantees prices for farm perishable produce (75.6%, 4.14), provides irrigation system (76.0%, 4.25), trains enough agricultural experts (75.3%, 4.30), encourages the youth by creating jobs (74.4%, 4.34), and easily access credit facility at the government MFIs which recorded a low percentage and mean score of (3.0%, 2.00) respectively.

Table 3. Degree of responses of cultural factors negatively influence on poverty and food insecurity

No_	Negative cultural influence on women performance	1	2	3	4	5	%	Mean
1	Northern rural woman is confirmed to the kitchen	1.7	2.7	29.0	22.7	44.0	66.7	3.4867
2	Women require too much time in family responsibilities	0.7	4.7	21.7	44.7	28.3	73.0	4.2700
3	The force girl marriages are some of the causes of food insecurity and poverty	0.7	7.7	26.0	37.7	28.0	65.7	2.9867
4	The women mobility is restricted by men	2.3	3.0	22.7	48.0	24.0	72.0	3.9267
5	The women seek permission access loans	4.0	12.7	15.7	49.0	18.7	67.7	3.2367
6	The men control the loans	4.7	10.7	16.7	51.3	16.7	68.0	3.6233
7	The men are supposed to be the wage earners	0.3	0.7	22.3	47.3	23.7	71.0	3.9500
8	The migration of northern youth to southern cities	2.0	2.3	23.3	40.0	32.3	72.3	3.6800
9	The numerous chieftaincy disputes are the some of the causes	1.3	1.3	31.0	25.0	41.3	65.3	3.9900
10	Ghana government should scrap all the unproductive outmoded practices	2.3	6.7	22.0	40.0	28.7	68.7	4.0767

Survey work; 2016, Percentages and averages in parentheses

Note Respondents' opinions ranked as highly disagree (1), disagree (2), neutral (3), agree (4), and highly agree (5). The percentage (%) column is the addition of agree and highly agree (4 and 5), respectively

Discussions

According to (Afrane 2002; Leinbach 2003; Hes 2013) the demographic profile of microfinance clients is a significant issue that may have repercussions on their financial developmental tendencies. Some of these features include gender, age, marital status, level of education, type of Occupation and the number of children, were examined to determine their influence the on microfinance services in alleviation poverty and food insecurity. For instance, duties, responsibilities, and type of occupations of respondents, may have an influence on the household tasks and work-related issues of respondents and their households, as well as effect on the family budget (Meinzen-Dick and Quisumbing 2012). This is shown on table one where most of the respondents are females, majority in active working class, with many children, very low levels of education, with non or little vocational or technical skills, leading to their engagement mainly on outmoded farming practices, based on the customs beliefs.

Respondents are still practicing the traditional method of farming, with just a handful of them claimed to be practicing both traditional and mechanized farming, with the claim belief that, if the farming methodology is changed, with availability of irrigation, agricultural experts to offer advice, combined with effective storage system and ready market for the perishables products, the rural northern chronic poverty

Table 4. Degree of responses of government policies on poverty and food insecurity

No_	Government policies the causes of poverty and food insecurity	1	2	3	4	5	%	Mean
1	Ghana Gov't has established MFIs	0.7	4.0	24.7	45.3	25.3	70.6	4.0767
2	I can easily access credit facility at the government MFIs	33.0	36.0	27.7	2.0	1.0	3.0	2.0000
3	If the government MFIs loans are flexible with low interest rate	3.0	1.7	23.0	43.3	29.0	72.3	4.2100
4	If gov't provides available and affordable health centers poverty will reduce	0.7	4.7	66.0	17.7	11.0	29.7	3.9767
5	Gov't subside some farm input	3.3	1.0	22.0	42.0	31.7	73.7	4.2633
6	Gov't provides no efficient storage system	1.0	0.7	26.7	37.0	34.6	71.6	4.2267
7	No guarantees prices for produce	1.4	1.7	21.3	49.3	26.3	75.6	4.1400
8	No irrigation system	0.7	2.7	20.7	52.7	23.3	76.0	4.2500
9	No trained agricultural experts to advice the farmers	1.3	2.7	20.7	51.0	24.3	75.3	4.3000
10	No jobs to prevent the northern youth from migrating to southern Ghana	1.7	3.0	21.0	53.7	20.7	74.4	4.3367

Survey work; 2016, Percentages and means in parentheses

Note Respondents' opinions ranked as highly disagree (1), disagree (2), neutral (3), agree (4), and highly agree (5). The percentage (%) column is the addition of agree and highly agree (4 and 5), respectively

prevalence will reduce. This results is in line with (Below et al. 2012; Baig and Aldosari 2013) that development and educative procedures need an expressive and genuine provisions be put in place to improve and answer the requirements of farmers with the aim of reducing poverty and food insecurity. However, this contradicts (Lambisia et al. 2016) that with traditions and outmodedness the poverty prevenlence cannot be reduced. Also, important is the confirmation by majority of the respondents that, a three square meal throughout the year is difficult to come by hence children go at times without food. Consequently the rural northern Ghanaian especially the vulnerable lacks the basic necessities of live. This fact had been recorded by the Ghana statistical Service 2010 Population and housing census, that the three northern regions of Ghana poverty rate is as twice as much of the southern part leading to chronic food insecurity and high levels of poverty. Also, respondents in this study still attach great importance to; cultural values, morals and beliefs that describe differences amid females and males in communities, usually assigning diverse duties, routines and allocating inferior actions related with females which adversely affects females in their search for achievement. These findings approved that of Weiss and Montgomery 2015; Teame 2016 studies, that almost all these customs comprise the task of simply gender duties or responsibilities, for instead kitchenette to females and the main income-earning responsibility to males. Assigning and titling the inferior duties and responsibilities to the female persons impairs their abilities to full take advantages of the opportunities around them to liberate themselves and their households from food insecurity and poverty. Widely held views of the respondents were that customs and outmoded principles have a very negative influence on the female person in access and utilizing microfinance services to improve their wellbeing. Again, majority of the respondent asserted that, though the income earning responsibilities are supposedly allocated to the men, they are not able to fulfill this responsibility in times of severe food crisis, and the women have to manage with whatever that is available, but making sure the children survive (Atiyat 2015; Wray 2007). Higher percentages of the respondents confirmed that, though women's movement is restricted; the men mostly decide, direct and dictate the use of the loan and finally misuse it. This is in accordance with studies by Houweling et al. (2015a, b), Suh (2011) that men may coerce their women to give up their loans preventing them from expanding businesses. In a nut shell, the article finding averred that, the major cause of the chronic food insecurity and poverty in the area is patriarchal philosophies in the area. However, 31% of the respondents do not think that the chieftaincy disputes in some part of the area under this study had any effect on the poverty prevalence in the area. The policies that Ghana gov't put in place to eradicate the rural northern poverty menace, through effective microfinance services, is engrossed dishonesty and bureaucracies, compounding the clients' poverty plight. However, the generalization of this paper would not be fair due to the difficulty in knowing the population of all rural women that are involved in Susu.

5   Conclusions

The Outcomes of this article-"*Assessing the Driving Forces Militating against Microfinance in Alleviating the Chronic Poverty and Food Insecurity in Rural Northern Ghana*" show that, many rural northern Ghanaian women are still battling under their deep-rooted patriarchal system that prevent them from developing their talents to take opportunities to reduce poverty and food insecurity. Findings of (Fakir and Nicol 2012; Jamali et al. 2009; Yasmeen and Karim 2014) are guides to the trials many rural Sub-Saharan Africa women face. Non-formal financial institutions, such as microfinance services are poverty tools that are giving opportunities to empowerment. Unfortunately, females in male-controlled cultures, for instance northern rural Ghanaian woman are far from seeing this financial liberty. The findings revealed that traditional women have a responsibility 'take in' and do not ask questions are still foremost in several groups in the areas of this study. The rural northern lady of Ghana is trained to trust that gentlemen's ideas are trustworthy than theirs, and as a consequence they incline to drive alongside per conclusions taken by their men. Hence they continue to take permission from their menfolk to contact loans to trades for existence nonetheless, per no objective to develop. Also, the illiteracy canker, lack of technical and vocational skills, bureaucracies and corruptions in assessing Ghana Government microfinance services, non-ready markets and bad storage facilities for perishable farm produce, compounded with the outmoded methods of agriculture have been revealed. Although, not all aspects of the culture is bad, most of the mores in the rural northern set-up of Ghana is gradually weakening many humanities currently, and rural womenfolk still suffer great deal of ethnic prejudice. So, is significant to construct a viable environment that identifies the unexploited talents of womankind in rural northern

Ghana. This is only achievable through conscious efforts of the males in the area, with understanding that the female person has equal human rights and privileges.

Recommendations:

(a) The districts assembles should enforce the by-laws that for bit any outmoded unproductive cultural activity currently in the areas.

(b) The traditional farming methods should be replaced with mechanizes farming, assistance of agricultural experts, storage facilities and guarantee prices.

(c) Sensitization about the female equal rights and privileges should be re-enforced, with yearly wards to parents who girl child score 85–90% School attendance.

(d) The men should be encouraged to attend with the female micro financial services gatherings, assist the females to develop and expand their businesses.

References

Abor, J., & Quartey, P. (2010). Issues in SME development in Ghana and South Africa. *International Research Journal of Finance and Economics*, 215–228. 39(6).

Afrane, S. (2002). Impact assessment of microfinance interventions in Ghana and South Africa: A synthesis of major impacts and lessons. *Journal of Microfinance/ESR Review, 4(1), 4.*, 4, 4 (1).

Agyei-Mensah, S., & Owusu, G. (2010). Segregated by neighbourhoods? A portrait of ethnic diversity in the neighbourhoods of the Accra Metropolitan Area, Ghana. Population, Space and Place. 499–516, 16(6).

Ashta, A., Khan, S., & Otto, P. (2015). Does microfinance cause or reduce suicides? Policy recommendations for reducing borrower stress. Strategic Change. *Wiley Online Library*, 165–190, 24(2).

Atiyat, R. (2015). NO REDRESS? INVESTIGATING WIFE ABUSE THROUGH THE LENS OF FEMINIST THEORY AND RESOURCE THEORY IN JORDAN. *Doctoral dissertation, University of York).*

Baig, M. B., & Aldosari, F. (2013). Agricultural extension in Asia: Constraints and options for improvemen. *The Journal of Animal & Plant Sciences*, 619–632, 23(2).

Bakhtiari, S. (2011). Microfinance and poverty reduction: some international evidence. *nternational Business & Economics Research Journal (IBER)*, 5(12).

Beckert, T. E. (2007). Cognitive Autonomy and Self-Evaluation in Adolescence: A Conceptual Investigation and Instrument Development. *North American Journal of Psychology*, 9(3).

Below, T. B., Mutabazi, K. D., Kirschke, D., Franke, C., Sieber, S., Siebert, R., & Tscherning, K. (2012). Can farmers' adaptation to climate change be explained by socio-economic household-level variables?. *Global Environmental Change*, 223–235, 22 (1).

Bisariya, R. S., & Mishra, A. (2015). Vocational Skills and Training to Empower Citizens of India. *Vindhya Int. J. Manage*, 2395–2059. 1(1).

Block, F. (2003). Karl Polanyi and the writing of the Great Transformation. *Theory and society, 32(3), 275–306.*, 275–306, 32(3).

Boateng, G. O., Boateng, A. A., & Bampoe, H. S. (2015). Microfinance and poverty reduction in Ghana: Evidence from policy beneficiaries. *REVIEW OF BUSINESS AND FINANCE STUDIES*, 1 (6).

Brukum, N. K. (1997). The Northern Territories of the Gold Coast under British colonial rule, 1897–1956, a study in political change (Doctoral dissertation). *National Library of Canada*.

Dalitso, K., & Peter, Q. (2000). The policy environment for promoting small and medium-sized enterprises in Ghana and Malawi. *University of Manchester*.

Dapila, F. N. (1995). Inculturation and ancestor veneration: The case of the Dagaaba Catholics. *University of Ottawa (Canada)*.

Fakir, S., & Nicol, D. (2012). Investigation: Obstacles and Barriers to Renewable Energy in South Africa: A Study. Department of Environmental Affairs and Tourism.

Field, E., Martinez, J., & Pande, R. (2016). Does Women's Banking Matter for Women? Evidence from Urban India. *Working Paper, November, S-35306-INC-1*.

Ghalib, A. k., & Hossain, F. (2010). How Effective are Microfinance Programmes in Serving the Poorest? Empirical Perspectives on Outreach and Impact from Survey-based Research. University of Manchester.

Goyal, P., & Yadav, V. (2014). To be or not to be a woman entrepreneur in a developing country. *Psychosociological Issues in Human Resource Management, 68–78, 2(2)*.

Grunig, J. E., & White, J. (2011). The effect of worldviews on public relations theory and practice. *Excellence in public relations and communication management, 31–64*.

Gukurume, S. (2012). Interrogating Foreign Aid and the Sustainable Development Conundrum in African Countries: A Zimbabwean Experience of Debt Trap and Service Delivery. *International Journal of Politics and Good Governance, 3(3.4), 1–20.*, 1–20, 3(3,4).

Hair, J. F., Celsi, M., Ortinau, D. J., & Bush, R. P. (2008). Essentials of marketing research. New York, NY: McGraw-Hill/Higher Education.

Harding, S. (2016). Whose science? Whose knowledge?: Thinking from women's lives. *Cornell University Press*.

Hartl, M. (2011). Technical and vocational education and training (TVET) and skills development for poverty reduction–do rural women benef. *Journal of Education and Practice*.

Hes, T. N. (2013). International Letters of Social and Humanistic Sciences. *Socio-economic profile of village bank member in suburban Ankara: microcredit mannequin and assumptions on microfinance market of Turkey, 55–75, 7*.

Hing, N., & Nisbet, S. (2010). A qualitative perspective on physical, social and cognitive accessibility to gambling. Journal of Gambling Issues, (24), 101–120.

Hodgson, G. M. (2017). Karl Polanyi on economy and society: a critical analysis of core concepts. *Review of Social Economy, 1–25, 75(1)*.

Houweling, T. A., Morrison, J., Alcock, G., Azad, K., Das, S., Hossen, M., & Manandhar, D. S. (2015). Reaching the poor with health interventions: programme-incidence analysis of seven randomised trials of women's groups to reduce newborn mortality in Asia and Africa. *Epidemiol Community Health, jech-2014*.

Houweling, T. A., Morrison, J., Alcock, G., Azad, K., Das, S., Hossen, M., & Manandhar, D. S. (2015). Reaching the poor with health interventions: programme-incidence analysis of seven randomised trials of women's groups to reduce newborn mortality in Asia and Africa. *J Epidemiol Community Health, jech-2014*.

Jamali, D., Zanhour, M., & Keshishian, T. (2009). Peculiar strengths and relational attributes of SMEs in the context of CSR. *Journal of Business Ethics, 87(3), 355–377, 355–377, 87(3)*.

Joseph, I. E., & Imhanlahimi, J. E. (2011). Access and impact assessment of micro finance banks on rural poor in Nigeria: a case study of Edo state. *Indian Journal of Economics and Business, 10(2).*, 10(2).

Konings, P. (1994). Capitalist rice farming and land allocation in Northern Ghana. *he Journal of Legal Pluralism and Unofficial Law, 89–119, 16(22)*.

Kumah, A., & Boachie, W. K. (2016). An Investigation into the Impact of Microfinance in Poverty Reduction in Less Developed Countries (LDCs): A Case of Ghana. *American Scientific Research Journal for Engineering, Technology, and Sciences (ASRJETS)*, 26(3), 188–201.

Kuu-Ire, S. A. (2009). Poverty reduction in Northern Ghana-A review of Colonial and Post-Independence Development Strategies. *Ghana Journal of Development Studies*, 6(1).

Lambisia, L. A., Ngahu, S., & Wagoki, J. (2016). EFFECT OF TABLE BANKING ON ECONOMIC EMPOWERMENT OF SELF-HELP GROUPS IN RONGAI SUB-COUNTY, KENYA. *International Journal for Economics, Commerce and Management*, vol, iv, issue, 2.

Ledgerwood, J., Earne, J., & Nelson, C. (2013). The new microfinance handbook: A financial market system perspective. *World Bank Publications*.

Leinbach, T. R. (2003). Small enterprises, fungibility and Indonesian rural family livelihood strategies. *sia Pacific Viewpoint, 44(1), 7–34.*, 7–34, 44 (1).

Lentz, C. (1994). They must be Dagaba first and any other thing second The colonial and post-colonial creation of ethnic identities in North-Western Ghana. *African Studies*, 57–91, 52(2).

Lentz, C. (2006). Ethnicity and the making of history in Northern Ghana. *Edinburgh University Press.*

Lobnibe, I. (2010). Of Jong Migrants and Jongsecans: understanding contemporary rural out-migration from Northwest Ghana. *Journal of Dagaare Studies*, 7(10).

Marlow, S., & Swail, J. (2014). Gender, risk and finance: why can't a woman be more like a man ? *Entrepreneurship & Regional Development*, 80–96, 26(1–2).

Martín-Tapia, I., Aragón-Correa, J., & Rueda-Manzanares, A. (2010). Environmental strategy and exports in medium, small and micro-enterprises. *Journal of World Business*, 266–275, 45(3).

Mbiti, F. M., Mukulu, E., Mung'atu, J., & Kyalo, D. (2015). The Influence of Access to Credit on Growth of Women-Owned Micro and Small Enterprises in Kitui County, Kenye. *Public Policy and Administration*, 61–70, 3(1).

Meinzen-Dick, R., & Quisumbing, A. (2012). Global Food Policy Report: Chapter 4-Closing the Gender Gap. *International Food Policy Research Institute, Washington, DC.,[Google Scholar]*, 21–45, 4 (2).

Mhango, N. N. (2017). Africa's Dependency Syndrome: Can Africa Still Turn Things around for the Better? *Langaa RPCIG*, 14–25 (1).

Miled, K. B. H., & Rejeb, J. E. B. (2015). Microfinance and poverty reduction: a review and synthesis of empirical evidence. Procedia-Social and Behavioral Sciences, 195, 705–712.

Molyneux, M. (2016). Women's movements in international perspective: Latin America and beyond. *Springer.*

Narteh, B., Mahmoud, M. A., & Amoh, S. (2017). Customer behavioural intentions towards mobile money services adoption in Ghana. *The Service Industries Journal*, 1–22.

Nyewie, B. (2010). The Relationship Between Migration and Poverty: The Case of Peasant Dagaaba Farmers in the Upper West Region of Ghana. *Erasmus University.*

Ogbeide, O. A., & Ele, I. (2015). Smallholder farmers and mobile phone technology in Sub-Sahara Agriculture. *Mayfair Journal of Information and Technology Management in Agriculture, 1*, 1–19, 1(1).

Okosun, I., Siwar, C., Hadi, A. S., & Nor, A. M. (2010). The urban poverty dilemma in Nigeria and attempts towards poverty alleviation. *Journal of Sustainable Development in Africa*, 165–181, 12(2).

Saaka, Y. (1987). Some linkages between the north and the south in the evolution of national consciousness in Ghana. *Journal of Black Studies*, 3–19, 18(1).

Schindler, K. (2010). Credit for what? Informal credit as a coping strategy of market women in Northern Ghana. *The Journal of Development Studies*, 234–253, 46(2).

Simba, N. O., Agak, J. O., & Kabuka, E. K. (2016). Impact of Discipline on Academic Performance of Pupils in Public Primary Schools in Muhoroni Sub-County, Kenya. *Journal of Education and Practice*, 164–17, 37(6).

Suh, D. (2011). Institutionalizing social movements: the dual strategy of the Korean women's. *The Sociological Quarterly*, 442–471, 52(3).

Teame, G. (2016). The Socio-Economic Impact of Female Employment on Intimate Partner Violence; A study on Female Employees of Yirgalem Addis Textile Factory. *(Doctoral dissertation, Addis Ababa University)*.

Tripathi, V. K. (2015). Micro finance in India-growth, and evolution in India. *International Journal of Information, Business and Management, 7(3), 291.*, 291, 7 (3).

Trommsdorff, G. (2012). Development of "agentic" regulation in cultural context: the role of self and world views. *Child Development Perspectives*, 19–26, 6(1).

Uzzi, B., & Gillespie, J. J. (2002). Knowledge spillover in corporate financing networks: Embeddedness and the firm's debt performance. *Strategic Management Journal*, 595–618, 23(8).

Verbeek, H., Zwakhalen, S. M., van Rossum, E., Kempen, G. I., & Hamers, J. P. (2012). Small-scale, homelike facilities in dementia care: a process evaluation into the experiences of family caregivers and nursing staff. *International journal of nursing studies*, 21–29, 49(1).

Wanyoike, K. D. (2012). FACTORS WHICH DETERMINE THE USE OF MOBILE BANKING BY MICRO AND SMALL ENTERPRISES IN NAIROBI, KENYA. *(Doctoral dissertation, SCHOOL OF BUSINESS, UNIVERSITY OF NAIROBI)*.

Weiss, J., & Montgomery, H. (2015). Great expectations: microfinance and poverty reduction in Asia and Latin America. *Oxford Development Studies, 33(3–4), 391–416.*, 391–416, 33 (3–4).

Woldie, A., & Adersua, A. (2004). Female entrepreneurs in a transitional economy: Businesswomen in Nigeria. *International Journal of Social Economics*, 78–93. 31(1/2).

Wray, S. (2007). omen making sense of midlife: Ethnic and cultural diversity. *Journal of aging studies*, 31–42, 21(1).

Wronka, J. (2016). Human rights and social justice: Social action and service for the helping and health professions. *Sage Publications*.

Yasmeen, K., & Karim, M. A. (2014). Impact of interaction term between education and loan size on women's decision making. *Journal of Entrepreneurship and Business Innovation*, 123–141, 1(1).

Yeboah, M. A. (2015). Determinants of SME growth: An empirical perspective of SMEs in the Cape Coast Metropolis, Ghana. *The journal of business in developing nations*, 14–24.

Improving the Mobile Payment Experience and Removing the Barriers

Ersin Unsal[(✉)]

Fibabanka R&D Center, Istanbul, Turkey
`ersin.unsal@fibabanka.com.tr`

1 Introduction

Internet revolution, mobile revolution and finally fintech (financial technology) era has changed the financial industry deeply and nowadays this transformation is so deep that the word "disruption" rather than "change" is more preferred. As technology advanced, financial institutions are stepping up their technological investments incrementally to achieve productivity and customer engagement. These technological investments result in new products and service channels for customers. At first internet banking and soon later mobile banking has become the dominant financial channel for especially the customers in developed countries. Besides omni-channel approaches, emergence of internet/mobile only (branchless—digital only) banking institutions was one of the first radical results of this technological revolution. And the current outcome of this revolution is the entrance of technology-based companies into the finance market (fintech revolution i.e.).

Fintech revolution has started to transform the finance sector in various domains such as money transfers, payments, loans etc. Payments, especially mobile payments, can be named as one of the hottest fintech domains, since the technology titans like Apple and Google are entering into the mobile payments domain through their services (Apple Pay and Google Pay respectively) with huge expectations. On the other hand, financial institutions (especially banks and card networks/schemes) are developing various different strategies and products to compete with fintech rivals.

This paper, in accordance with review of current advancements in mobile payment domain, aims to propose an innovative mobile payment solution which provides an easier, secure and faster payment experience. To provide a better understanding of the proposed model, a brief literature review with current mobile wallet solutions and their pros and cons (pro et contra) is presented in Sect. 2. Section 3 discusses the barriers and frictions of mobile payment experience in detail. Section 4 proposes a new mobile payment solution to overcome the addressed downsides of existing mobile wallets. Finally, the conclusion section will include summary, inferences and future work.

N. Ozatac and K. K. Gökmenoglu (eds.), *Emerging Trends in Banking and Finance*, Springer Proceedings in Business and Economics,
https://doi.org/10.1007/978-3-030-01784-2_12

2 Mobile Payments

2.1 Mobile Payments: A Short Introduction and Definition of Terms

Mobile payments can be defined as "any payment where a mobile device is used in order to initiate, activate and/or confirm this payment" (Karnouskos 2004). Another similar definition from the literature is as follows; "payments for goods, services, and bills with a mobile device by taking advantage of wireless technology and other communication technologies" (Dahlberg et al. 2008). Mobile payments can be differentiated based on various characteristics, including the technology used and the transaction size, location, service type, stakeholder structure and funding mechanism (Dahlberg et al. 2008; Raina et al. 2012; Staykova et al. 2015; Au and Kauffman 2008; De Bel and Gâza 2012; Dennehy and Sammon 2015).

Depending on the payment location and service type mobile payments can be divided into two types; (1) remote payments and (2) near field payments (proximity payments). Proximity payments require physical interactions between both parties involved whereas remote payments are made when money transfers are done over a distance and do not require physical interaction of both parties. Payment via POS (Point-of-Service) device is an example for proximity payments whereas electronic and mobile commerce payments are examples of remote payments. When it comes to technological differences; remote payments are based on technologies such as 3G/4G, Wi-Fi, SMS, WAP etc. whereas proximity payments are based on technologies such as RFID, Infrared, NFC, HCE, etc. (Hao and Siyu 1698). QR Code payments are an emerging mobile payment technology which is employed for both proximity payments and remote payments.

Mobile payments can also be categorized based on funding mechanism such as credit/debit card payments, application payments, operator billing and NFC payments (Hao and Siyu 1698). Also, nowadays cryptocurrencies are shining out as a new emerging funding mechanism. Finally, transaction size (payment amount i.e.) may also be used to categorize mobile payments.

Mobile payments history goes back to 1997, when Coca Cola first introduced vending machines that accept SMS based payments (Mallat 2007; Dahlberg et al. 2015). NFC based payments were the next big thing in mobile payments history. To develop NFC based mobile payment solutions, banks came together with telecom operators and SIM card manufacturers which resulted in complex business models and disappointing market results. Development of Host Card Emulation (2012) for Android based devices and announcement of Apple Pay (2014) with NFC support for IOS based devices have two very important milestones for NFC based payments.

Today, mobile payments have become a very hot domain with frequent introduction of new mobile wallets and other innovative mobile solutions almost every day. In the following sections; prominent mobile payment solutions will be discussed to provide a better understanding of current mobile payment market.

2.2 Mobile Wallets: State of the Art

A mobile wallet is an "app" for your smart phone or tablet that allows you to organize your payment cards, coupons, vouchers and identification to facilitate financial transactions (Au and Kauffman 2008). At the beginning of mobile wallet era, the main idea was to replace the plastic payment cards with digital applications; but now mobile wallets are aiming to enhance the shopping experience for consumers. Mobile wallets can now facilitate various financial transactions such as money transfers, personal finance management, campaigns, promotions and loyalty management besides mobile payment transactions. To give a better understanding of mobile wallet market; emerging and popular mobile wallets can be categorized depending on the provider/owner of wallet as (1) tech-titan wallets, (2) marketplace wallets, (3) bank/card scheme wallets, (4) merchant wallets, (5) telecom wallets and (6) others:

It is possible to categorize mobile wallets in different ways depending on their functionalities, underlying technologies, target market, etc. The categorization of mobile wallets presented in Table 1 is built on provider/owner of mobile wallets. Since business value proposition and business functionalities of mobile wallets are highly dependent on its provider, provider-based categorization results in a more lucid view of mobile wallet market.

Table 1. Categorization of mobile wallets

Mobile wallet types					
Tech titan wallets	Marketplace wallets	Bank/card scheme wallets	Merchant wallets	Telecom wallets	Others
Google pay	Amazon pay	BBVA wallet	Walmart pay	Vodafone	PayPal
Apple pay	Alipay	Visa V.me		Orange	
Samsung pay		MasterCard PayPass			

2.3 Alternative Mobile Payment Solutions

Mobile wallets are well known, most popular mobile payment solutions; but there are different products in mobile payments domain and some of them have demonstrated impressively successful and promising results. In general, mobile wallet concept is highly dependent on existing credit card schemes and infrastructures; whereas alternative products focus on different payment schemes and infrastructures for mobile payment transactions. To give a better understanding of mobile payment domain; the following alternative mobile payment solutions will be introduced shortly.

(1) M-Pesa is a popular SMS (Short Message Service) based mobile payment and money transfer service which is widely adopted in Tanzania and Kenya (https://www.mpesa.in/portal/). Similar SMS based payments or direct operator billing payment services are available in different countries but case studies show that

these solutions are mostly preferred by unbanked customers especially in developing countries such as African countries.

(2) Cryptocurrencies (Skinner 2014, 2016), especially Bitcoin, is an emerging concept which provides crypto currencies that can operate independently of a central bank regulation (Hayes et al. 2016). People can buy, sell and transfer Bitcoins via Bitcoin wallets. Cryptocurrency concept has gained a lot of popularity but is in its infant stages and has a lot to do with governmental and financial regulations before becoming a widely accepted currency.

(3) Direct banking payment solutions have been around for years and allow to pay online purchases via internet banking applications and bank accounts. Direct banking payment products are mostly browser-based payment products (https://www.sveawebpay.com). The main drawback of direct banking payments is that, they only support banking accounts as payment method.

3 Barriers and Frictions in Mobile Wallet Experience

Mobile payments domain is an emerging and innovative domain and every other day a new mobile wallet solution comes up with innovative and attractive features. On the other hand, each new product comes with different downsides which prevent market adoption. Hardware dependency, bank or merchant limitations, technical problems, high fraud rates and user experience problems may be listed as the major deficits that prevent higher market adoption for new mobile wallets. Since each mobile wallet may have unique features and downsides; it can be difficult to find a systematic approach to evaluate the overall mobile wallet experience in the market. Consultancy and research firms have limited wallet market analysis reports to give an overview of the mobile wallet market and most of these reports are not available to public (Carlisle et al. 2013; Allied Market Research 2017; Berg Insight 2014; RnR Market Research 2016; Grand View Research 2024). Carlisle & Gallagher Group's mobile wallet market analysis report is a unique report which is available to public and contains a comprehensive and systematic review of mobile wallet market. According to Carlisle & Gallagher Group's report, mobile wallets can be evaluated using the following criteria (Carlisle et al. 2013).

Customer Experience:

- Device Compatibility: Ability to work on multiple devices types: iPhone, Android, BlackBerry and Windows.

- Wallet Set-Up: Customer set-up/Management Experience—Ease of use, setup and intuitive management of the app.

- Consumer Shopper Experience: Features designed to improve the overall shopping experience. (e.g., merchant locate, product information, shopping lists, posting to social media).

- Additional Functionality: Other "WOW" features. (e.g., rewards, coupons).

Payment Capabilities:

- Merchant Acceptance: Number of merchants that accept mobile wallet as a payment device at POS.

- Payment Options: The breadth of available payment options available at the point of sale to a consumer through his or her mobile device.

- Check-Out Experience: Ease of making a purchase transaction and resulting activities including refund and transaction history.

- Transaction Range: Range of transaction types that can be facilitated with the wallet (Peer-To-Peer/P2P, Online purchase, Point of Sale/POS).

Carlisle & Gallagher Group's report has also an assessment of 18 different mobile wallets in 4 different wallet provider categories using these criteria. The summary of assessment depending on the wallet provider category is presented in Table 2.

Carlisle & Gallagher Group's report employs a 5-point scale to assess each mobile wallet functionality. "Overall" row contains average values for each functionality. At first glimpse, it is obvious that the results are unsatisfying and disappointing. For example, in terms of shopping experience and payment options; current wallets are far away from satisfying customers (1.3/5). Merchant acceptance and transaction range functionalities are also very limited and disappointing (2/5). Average results show that current mobile wallet products are failing to provide most desired functionalities such as frictionless payment experience, flexible payment options and easy checkout experience. In other words, there seems to be fundamental problems in our view of mobile wallet concept and a new different point of perspective shall be employed to improve mobile payment experience.

Another important inference of Table 2 is that; bank wallets are missing the main functionality of a mobile wallet; payment. In terms of device capability, set-up and additional functionality; bank wallets have the highest assessment, whereas in terms of payment capabilities bank wallets are non-existing (0/5). If bank wallets were to support seamless payment capabilities and satisfying customer experience; they would be more promising mobile wallet solutions.

Interestingly, there are recent research reports which show that most of the customers would prefer to use a bank based mobile wallet solution (BI 2013; First Annapolis Consulting 2017). In other words, the customers were asked "if you were two choose one provider of a mobile wallet app, which would be your preferred provider?" and customer choice was "my bank". The results of these two researches are summarized in Table 3.

Table 3 shows that customers are increasingly preferring their bank for mobile wallet provider as the first choice and card brands (Visa, MasterCard) are customers second choice for mobile wallet providers. These results also show that customers prefer financial institutions as mobile wallet providers and customers demand for banks as mobile wallet providers is increasing dramatically. The other interesting result is that, giant technology firms (Apple and Google) are becoming rivals for banks for the near future. There for mobile wallet products may be considered as a strategic option for banks in this competitive market.

Table 2. Assessment of mobile wallets

Wallet provider	Device capability	Set-Up	Shopping Experience	Additional functionality	Merchant acceptance	Payment options	Checkout experience	Transaction range
Tech titans	3, 0	3, 2	1, 6	2, 4	3, 2	3, 0	2, 2	2, 8
Merchants	3, 4	3, 6	3, 4	1, 8	2, 8	1, 0	4, 0	2, 6
Card associations	1, 7	3, 3	0, 3	2, 0	2, 0		2, 7	1, 7
Banks	5, 0	4, 0	0, 0	3, 0	0, 0	0, 0	0, 0	1, 0
Overall	3, 3	3, 5	1, 3	2, 3	2, 0	1, 3	2, 2	2, 0

Table 3. Customer choice for mobile wallet provider

Research question	If mobile wallet was available from each of the following companies, whose mobile wallet would you be most likely to use? (%)	If you were two choose one provider of a mobile wallet app, which would be your preferred provider? (%)
1st choice	My bank 27	My bank 48
2nd choice	PayPal 16	My card brand 16
3rd choice	Visa 12	Apple 13
4th choice	Chase 5	PayPal 10
5th choice	Master card 5	Google 4
Source	BI Intelligence reports	First annapolis consulting
Year	2013	2017

4 Improving Mobile Payment Experience

In this section, proposed mobile payment solution will be explained starting from roots of the idea followed by the proposed user experience. Proposed solution emerged from the idea that current mobile payment solutions are failing to fulfill basic user expectations as stated in previous section. Instead of developing brand-new mobile wallet products, adding seamless payment capabilities and frictionless payment experience to existing mobile banking products is proposed.

4.1 Pay by Your Bank: A New Mobile Payment Approach

Current mobile wallets, although equipped with latest innovative technologies and developed by most competent IT organizations, surprisingly face severe customer and merchant adoption problems and cannot attract critical levels for mass adoption. On the other hand, traditional banks experience victorious results in terms of customer engagement with their emerging mobile banking applications. It is not reasonable to associate these distinctive results with technical incompetency, lack of product development experience or misconfigured marketing strategies. Customer perception, heritage, legacy, branding, knowledge repository and existing infrastructure of banks may better explain the success of mobile banking applications.

Those mobile banking applications offer countless financial capabilities except basic payment functionalities. NFC and emerging HCE technologies are employed for proximity payments; but remote payment functionality is missing in mobile banking applications. Banks have introduced virtual credit cards and e-commerce special prepaid cards for remote payments. These products may help solving security problems but still customer experience is cumbersome and has frictions. The complex business model in credit card payment systems (acquirers, merchants, issuers, card schemes, commission rates) is resilient to change and the best approach may be leveraging existing business models with new perspectives. With the help of emerging tokenization standard, mobile banking applications can support remote payment functionality and become fully functional mobile wallets.

Introduction of remote payment functionality to banking applications will result in increased usefulness of banking applications. Two different research studies held in different countries show that usefulness of mobile wallets is the main factor increasing the adoption of mobile wallets. Various tech giants or telco operators are introducing innovative and secure wallet solutions but when it comes to the user adoption, ease of use and usefulness of the wallet is the most critical factor (Aydın and Burnaz 2016; Yadav 2017).

4.2   Pay by Your Bank: User Experience and Payment Flow

Proposed remote payment solution, PYB (Pay by Your Bank), provides necessary technical infrastructure and services for banks and merchants to form a frictionless mobile payment flow. When merchants and banks register to the PYB services; customers can use PYB payment flow to complete their payments as in Fig. 1.

1. Customer selects products/services to purchase and merchant app's check-out page is displayed to customer
2. When customer selects to pay by PYB; customer is directed to Bank App's login page

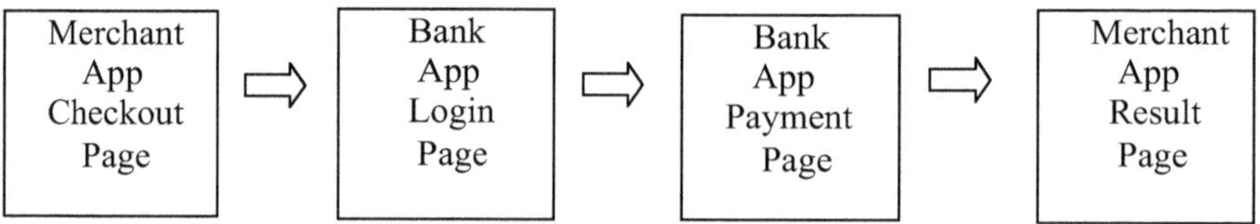

Fig. 1. PYB payment flow

3. After successful authentication; bank app's payment page is displayed and available payment options are presented to customer
4. Customer selects payment method and after completion of payment transaction; customer is directed to Merchant App's result page.

4.3   Pay by Your Bank: Advantages for Customers, Merchants and Banks

PYB payment flow aims to provide frictionless and secure payment experience for customers but that is not all. PYB payment flow provides important advantages for all the participating partners of a payment transaction as below:

Advantages for Customers:

- Ease of use: Well-known, secure and daily used banking apps will be used for remote payments. Customers don't have to trust, download and set up third party mobile wallets for remote payments.

- Security: Confidential financial information will always be kept only in banks domain. Customers don't have to enter their credit card information to third party wallet applications or merchants' applications.

- Multiple Payment Options: Customers can complete their payment with either their account, debit card or credit card. Moreover, banks can provide special loans or other funding options for specific payment transactions.

- Frictionless Payment: Bank wallets will eliminate payment authorization errors such as insufficient funds and error-prone manual entered credit card information. Bank wallets can pre-authorize payments at first and guarantee successful payment transaction which will eliminate all payment authorization problems. Depending on the customers' financial situation, bank wallets can guide customer to use different funding options.

Advantages for Merchants:

- Multiple Payment Options: Merchants can accept both money orders, debit and credit card payments with only one integration.

- Increase Sales: A significant amount of payment transactions fail due to errors such as incorrect credit card information and insufficient fund errors. Bank wallets can pre-authorize payments at first and guarantee successful payment transaction. Depending on the customers' financial situation, bank wallets can guide customer to use a different payment option. These functionalities will increase sales volume for merchants.

- Fraud Prevention: Bank wallets will authenticate customer before payment transaction via their highly secure mobile authentication process which means less fraud rates for merchants.

Advantages for Banks:

- Competitive Advantage: Competition against fintech companies and especially tech giants (Apple, Google, etc.) will be very challenging and therefore innovative mobile payment products which can increase customer satisfaction will provide competitive advantage for banks.

- Customer Engagement: Banks will be able to touch their customers during payment transaction via their banking apps. Banks can offer new products, services and promotions to their customers. Moreover, banking apps will be used more frequently when remote payment capability is included.

- Security: With the help of tokenization; sensitive financial information will not be disclosed to third parties which means a higher level of security. Moreover, with help of advanced authentication functionalities of banking apps; payment fraud rates will decrease radically.

Table 4 summaries the advantages of the PYB Mobile Payment Solution for customers, merchants and banks.

5 Conclusion and Future Work

Technological advancements and customer expectations has been transforming banking industry deeply for a long time. Mobile payments domain is one of the hottest areas of this deep technological transformation in finance sector. In addition to banks and financial institutions, numerous telecommunication firms and leading technology giants

Table 4. Advantages of PYB mobile payment solution

Advantages for customers	Advantages for merchants	Advantages for banks
Ease of use	Multiple payment options	Competitive advantage
Security	Increase sales	Customer engagement
Multiple payment options	Fraud prevention	Security
Frictionless payment		

have been introducing innovative mobile payment products and solutions to achieve high market adoption and customer engagement. Nevertheless, mobile payment experience is still cumbersome and frictional and therefore open to innovative, frictionless and secure solutions. This paper proposes a patented, innovative, frictionless and secure payment solution which provides significant advantages to customers, merchants and banks. The proposed solution is currently developed within Fibabanka Intrapreneurship Program. Although proposed solution is coherent with academic studies and market research reports and also provides important advantages to all parties—customers, the merchants and the banks; the market response, customer engagement and adoption rates will be the most important and determiner factors to evaluate the success of proposed solution.

References

Allied Market Research, "Mobile Payment Market by Mode of Transaction, Type of Mobile Payment, and Application: Global Opportunity Analysis and Industry Forecast, 2017–2023"

Au, A. & Kauffman, R., "The economics of mobile payments: Understanding stakeholder issues for an emerging financial technology application", Electronic Commerce Research and Applications, 7(2), 141–164, 2008

Aydın, G., Burnaz, S.: "Adoption of Mobile Payment Systems: A Case Study on Mobile Wallets", Journal of Business, Economics and Finance, vol. 5, no. 1, pp. 73–92, 2016

Berg Insight, "Mobile Payment Services, 2014"

BI Business Insider, "The State of the mobile Payments Race Report, 2013"

Carlisle & Gallagher Consulting Group, "Mobile Wallet Market Analysis", pp. 1–5, 2013

Dahlberg, T., Guo, J., Ondrus, J., "A Critical Review of Mobile Payment Research", Electronic Commerce Research and Applications, vol. 14, 2015, pp. 265–284

Dahlberg, T., Mallat, N., Ondrus, J., Zmijewska, A., "Past, present and future of mobile payments research: A literature Review", Electronic Commerce Research and Applications, vol 7, 2008, pp. 165–181

De Bel, J., & Gâza, M., "Mobile Payments 2012 - My mobile, my wallet? Innopay Version 1.01.", 2012

Dennehy, D., Sammon, M., "Trends in mobile payment research: A literature review, Journal of Innovation Management," JIM, 3, 1, 49–61, 2015

EMV Payment Tokenization Specification, https://www.emvco.com

First Annapolis Consulting, "Mobile Wallet Report, 2017"

Grand View Research, "Mobile Wallet Market Analysis By Product, By Application and Segment Forecasts Till 2024"

Hao, Y., Siyu, G.: The Research on Mobile Payments in the Theory of Electronic Commerce. International Conference on Mechatronics, Industrial and Control Engineering, pp. 1698–1701. Atlantis Press (2014)

Hayes, A. S., "Cryptocurrency value information: An empirical study leading to a cost of production model for valuing bitcoin", Telematics and Informatics, 2016

Karnouskos, S., "Mobile payment: A journey through existing procedures and standardization initiatives", IEEE Communications Surveys and Tutorials, vol. 6, no. 1–4, 2004, pp. 44–66

Mallat, N., "Exploring consumer adoption of mobile payments - A qualitative study", Journal of Strategic Information Systems, 16(4), 413–432, 2007

Raina V. K., Pandey U. S., and Makkad M., "A User Friendly Transaction Model of Mobile Payment with reference to Mobile Banking in India," International Journal of Information Technology, vol. 18, no. 2, pp 1–6, 2012

RnR Market Research, "Global and China Mobile Payment Industry Report, 2016–2020"

Skinner, C.: "Digital Bank: Strategies to Launch or Become a Digital Bank", Marshall Cavendish International, 2014

Skinner, C.: Value Web, "How Fintech Firms are Using Bitcoin, Blockchain and Mobile Technologies to Create the Internet of Value", Marshall Cavendish International", 2016

Staykova, K. S., Damsgaard, J., "The race to dominate the mobile payments platform: Entry and expansion strategies", Electronic Commerce Research and Applications, 2015

Yadav, P., "Active Determinants for Adoption of Mobile Wallet", I-manager's Journal on Management", vol. 12, no. 1, 2017

Financial Sector-Based Analysis of the G20 Economies Using the Integrated Decision-Making Approach with DEMATEL and TOPSIS

Hasan Dinçer[✉] and Serhat Yüksel

İstanbul Medipol University, Istanbul, Turkey
{hdincer, serhatyuksel}@medipol.edu.tr

1 Introduction

Financial sector plays a very significant role for the economic improvement of the countries. The main reason is that they bring together the parties that have saving and need fund (Capponi et al. 2017; Hugonnier and Morellec 2017). In other words, with the help of financial system, the parties that have funds can have a chance to increase their savings. On the other side, the parties that need fund can satisfy this demand easily owing to the effective financial system. Consequently, it can be understood that financial system has a contributing effect on the economic improvement (Narteh 2015; Joseph et al. 2015).

G20 economies refer to the countries which have the highest economic growth in the world. According to World Bank report, it constitutes 85% of the world economy and 80% of the trade in the world. Therefore, it can be seen that economic performance of these countries has an essential effect in world economies. That is to say, any problems in the economies of these countries may affect many different countries negatively. Due to that aspect, the effectiveness of the financial sector in G20 economies contributes the world economic performance.

While considering the issues emphasized above, it can be understood that the studies which focus on the financial performance are very beneficial. Similarly, in this study, it is aimed to evaluate the performance of G20 economies by considering financial sector-based factors. By analyzing the similar studies in the literature, 9 different criteria are identified for these economies. These criteria are weighted with the help of DEMATEL approach. In addition to this condition, G20 economies are evaluated by using TOPSIS methodology.

This study consists of 5 different sections. After this introduction section, in the second part, similar studies in the literature are analyzed. In addition to them, the third section gives information about the methodology. In this part, DEMATEL and TOPSIS methods are explained. Moreover, the fourth section includes the application on G20 economies. Finally, analysis results and recommendations are presented in the last section.

© Springer Nature Switzerland AG 2018
N. Ozatac and K. K. Gökmenoglu (eds.), *Emerging Trends in Banking and Finance*, Springer Proceedings in Business and Economics,
https://doi.org/10.1007/978-3-030-01784-2_13

2 Literature Review

Financial sector is the subject that attracted the attention of the many researchers in the literature. For example, Honohan (2008) made a study about the indicators of the financial performance. It is identified that the number of account holders plays a key role in this process. Similar to this study, Allen et al. (2002), Wu and Olson (2010), Prasad and Madhavi (2012) and Drummond (2003) also emphasized this aspect in their studies. In addition to these studies, it is also defined that some studies emphasized the importance of automated teller machines in the financial performance. For instance, Narteh (2015) underlined the importance of automated teller machines in customer satisfaction of the financial sector. Furthermore, Konheim (2016), Sridharan et al. (2014), Jegede (2014) and Joseph et al. (2015) also reached this conclusion in their studies.

It is also defined that some studies emphasized the importance of bank capital to asset ratio in financial performance. Akins et al. (2016) underlined the importance of this ratio in bank competition and financial stability. Capponi et al. (2017), Hugonnier and Morellec (2017) and Bashir and Hassan (2017) focused on this topic in their studies. On the other side, Polodoo et al. (2015) stated the importance of non-performing loans in order to understand the effectiveness of financial system. Rajha (2016), Dimitrios et al. (2016), Ghosh (2015) and Yüksel (2017) also underlined this issue in their studies.

Additionally, LaPlante and Paradi (2015) made a study to understand the indicators of the performance in financial sector and concluded that the number of branches plays a key role in this aspect. Similarly, Herrera-Restrepo et al. (2016), Paradi et al. (2018) and Oh and Park (2015) also identified the same topic in their studies. Furthermore, Lane and McQuade (2014), Samarina and Bezemer (2016), Grintzalis et al. (2017) and Tobe (2017) emphasized the importance of domestic credits for this situation.

While making analysis, it is also concluded that the amount of portfolio investment is the key factor of the performance of financial sector. As an example, Düll et al. (2017) made a study about the financial sector effectiveness and determined that portfolio investment amount gives important information about this situation. Cao and Ward (2014), Bhatta et al. (2017) and Albulescu (2015) also identified this condition. Moreover, Kocaarslan et al. (2017), Bayar et al. (2014), Joseph and Fernandez (2016) identified that the value of the stocks traded in the market is an important indicator of this issue.

3 Methodology

3.1 DEMATEL

The Battelle Research Center defined the concept of The DEMATEL (Decision Making Trial and Evaluation Laboratory) initially in 1970s for understanding the causality problems in the real-world applications. For this purpose, it is structured in a hierarchical form for the interrelation and interaction among the criteria (Hu et al. 2014; Hsu and Liou 2013; Hsu et al. 2013; Liu et al. 2014). The DEMATEL can be summarized as (Yang et al. 2008; Hu et al. 2014; Hsu et al. 2012; Chiu et al. 2013):

The first step is to build the direction matrix using the defined scales. Decision makers select the best scale which defines the relationship between the criteria for each direction. The linguistic evaluations are defined in the five-point scales from as no influence (0), low influence (1), middle influence (2), high influence (3), and extreme influence (4).

The second step continues by computing the initial influence matrix A by scores. $A = \left[a_{ij}\right]_{n \times n}$ is obtained from the convergence of the expert scores with the direct relation matrix, where a_{ij} is the degree of the influence of the factor i on factor j.

$$A = \begin{bmatrix} a_{11} & a_{21} & a_{13} & \cdots & a_{1n} \\ a_{21} & a_{22} & a_{23} & \cdots & a_{2n} \\ a_{31} & a_{32} & a_{33} & \cdots & a_{3n} \\ \vdots & \vdots & \vdots & \ddots & \vdots \\ a_{n1} & a_{n2} & a_{n3} & \cdots & a_{nn} \end{bmatrix}$$

The following step is to normalize the direct effect matrix N. The values can be attained by normalizing the initial influence matrix as seen below.

$$N = A/s$$

$$s = max\left[\max_{1 \leq i \leq n} \sum_{j=1}^{n} a_{ij}, \max_{1 \leq j \leq n} \sum_{i=1}^{n} a_{ij}\right]$$

The fourth step is to build the total influence matrix T. I is an identity matrix and $\lim_{h \to \infty} N^h = [0]_{n \times n}$.

$$T = N + N^2 + N^2 + \cdots + N^h = N\left(I + N + N^2 + \cdots + N^{h-1}\right)(I - N)(I - N)^{-1}$$

$$T = N\left(I - N^h\right)(I - N)^{-1} = N(I - N)^{-1}, \text{ when } \lim_{h \to \infty} N^h = [0]_{n \times n}$$

The fifth step is to compute the influential network relation map. For this purpose, the sum of each row and column for T can be provided by the following equations, where vector r represents the sum of all vector rows $r = (r_1, \ldots, r_i, \ldots, r_n)$, and vector y indicates the sum of all vector columns $y = (y_1, \ldots, y_i, \ldots, y_n)$. i equals j, $i, j \in \{1, 2, \ldots, n\}$, $(r_i + y_i)$ defines the total degree of the influence among criteria, and the higher its value, the closer the criterion is to object's central point. $(r_i - y_i)$ is the degree of causality among criteria. When $(r_i - y_i)$ is positive, it means that criterion i influences other criteria. Otherwise, the criterion is influenced by other criteria.

$$T = \left[t_{ij}\right]_{n\times n}, \quad i,j = 1,2,\ldots,n$$

$$r = \left[\sum_{j=1}^{n} t_{ij}\right]_{n\times 1} = (r_i)_{n\times 1} = (r_1,\ldots,r_i,\ldots,r_n)$$

$$y = \left[\sum_{i=1}^{n} t_{ij}\right]'_{1\times n} = (y_j)'_{1\times n} = (y_1,\ldots,y_i,\ldots,y_n)$$

The last step is to determine a threshold value for pointing out whether a criterion influences the other factor. Generally, the threshold is defined as an averaged value of the total relation matrix.

3.2 TOPSIS

TOPSIS (Technique for Order Preference by Similarity to Ideal Solution) is firstly introduced as a type of multi criteria decision making approach in 1980s (Hwang and Yoon 1981). The method aims to rank the alternatives by constructing the finite set in the maximized distance from the negative ideal solutions and the minimized distance from the positive ideal solutions. The main steps of the method are detailed in below:

The first step defines the normalized values using the vector normalization procedure.

$$r_{ij} = \frac{x_{ij}}{\sqrt{\sum_{i=1}^{m} x_{ij}^2}} \quad i = 1, 2, 3, \ldots, m \text{ and } j = 1, 2, 3, \ldots, n$$

The second step follows by weighting the values as

$$v_{ij} = w_{ij} \times r_{ij} \text{ where } i = 1, 2, \ldots, m \text{ and } j = 1, 2, \ldots, n$$

The third step defines the positive (A^+) and negative (A^-) ideal solutions due to the benefit and cost criteria.

$$A^+ = \{v_{1j}, v_{2j}, \ldots, v_{mj}\} = \{\max v_{1j} \, for \, \forall j \in n\}$$
$$A^- = \{v_{1j}, v_{2j}, \ldots, v_{mj}\} = \{\min v_{1j} \, for \, \forall j \in n\}$$

The following step considers the distances to the best (D_i^+) and the worst alternative (D_i^-) for each criterion

$$D_i^+ = \sqrt{\sum_{j=1}^{n} \left(v_{ij} - A_j^+\right)^2}$$

$$D_i^- = \sqrt{\sum_{j=1}^{n} \left(v_{ij} - A_j^-\right)^2}$$

The final step computes the relative closeness to the ideal solution for ranking alternatives as follows

$$RC_i = \frac{D_i^-}{D_i^+ + D_i^-} \text{ for i} = 1, 2, \ldots, \text{m and } 0 \le RC_i \le 1.$$

4 An Application on the G20 Economies

Financial sector-based indicators have been used for ranking the G20 economies with the integrated decision-making approach. For this purpose, the weights of the indicators have been computed by the DEMATEL method and the ranked results have been obtained by using the TOPSIS method.

In the first stage, DEMATEL method have been applied. Table 1 shows that selected financial sector-based criteria of performance measurement for the G20 economies. As seen in Table 1, 9 criteria—Accounts at the financial institutions (C1), Automated teller machines (C2), Bank Capital to Assets Ratio (C3), Bank nonperforming loans to total gross loans (C4), Commercial bank branches (C5), Domestic credit provided by financial sector (C6), Domestic credit to private sector by banks (C7), Portfolio investments (C8), Total value of Stocks traded (C9)—have been selected with the supported literature.

Table 2 represents the financial sector-based indicators of the G20 economies. The data has been obtained from the official website of the World Bank and constructed by considering the latest years that the full data of the G20 countries are available on the database.

Five decision makers have been appointed to evaluate the financial sector indicators with the DEMATEL method and the decisions have been provided in the consensus. The direct relation matrix has been constructed. The evaluation results have been presented in Table 3.

Normalized values of direct relation matrix have been seen in Table 4.

After the normalization procedure, the total relation matrix has been calculated and the results are seen in Table 5.

In the final step of the first stage, total cause and effect of criteria have been pointed out by computing the values of ri and yi. The results are in Table 6.

C4 is the most influenced factor as C9 is the most effective criterion in the financial sector indicators. However, C6 has the highest importance in the criteria while C2 has the weakest importance in financial sector-based performance of the G20 economies.

The second stage in the application continues by the TOPSIS method. In the first step, financial sector-based input data of the G20 economies have been attained from the World Bank Database and the values have been normalized as seen in Table 7.

Normalized values have been weighted in Table 8.

In the final step of the second stage, the values of relative closeness have been calculated and ranking results have been illustrated in Table 9.

Table 1. Selected financial sector indicators for the G20 economies

Financial sector-based criteria	Definition	Supported literature	Source organization
Accounts at the financial institutions (C1)	Denotes the percentage of the account holders who are greater than age 15, by themselves or together with someone else, at a bank or another type of financial institution	Honohan (2008), Allen et al. (2002), Wu and Olson (2010), Prasad and Madhavi (2012), Drummond (2003)	Demirguc-Kunt et al. 2015
Automated teller machines (C2)	Defines the automated teller machines that provide clients of a financial institution with access to financial transactions in a public place, per 100.000 adults	Konheim (2016), Sridharan et al. (2014), Jegede (2014), Joseph et al. (2015), Narteh (2015)	International Monetary Fund, Financial Access Survey
Bank Capital to Assets Ratio (C3)	Includes the funds contributed by owners, retained earnings, general and special reserves, provisions, and valuation adjustments in the bank capital to assets (%)	Capponi et al. (2017), Hugonnier and Morellec (2017), Bashir and Hassan (2017), Akins et al. (2016)	International Monetary Fund, Global Financial Stability Report
Bank nonperforming loans to total gross loans (C4)	Represents the value of nonperforming loans divided by the total value of the loan portfolio including nonperforming loans before the deduction of specific loan-loss provisions (%)	Polodoo et al. (2015), Rajha (2016), Dimitrios et al. (2016), Ghosh (2015), Yüksel (2017)	International Monetary Fund, Global Financial Stability Report
Commercial bank branches (C5)	Defines the retail locations of resident commercial banks and other resident banks (per 100.000 adults)	LaPlante and Paradi (2015), Herrera-Restrepo et al. (2016), Paradi et al. (2018), Oh and Park (2015)	International Monetary Fund, Financial Access Survey

(continued)

Table 1. (*continued*)

Financial sector-based criteria	Definition	Supported literature	Source organization
Domestic credit provided by financial sector (C6)	Implies the all credit except the credit to the central government provided by the all of financial sector such as deposit money banks and other financial corporations (% of GDP)	Lane and McQuade (2014), Samarina and Bezemer (2016), Grintzalis et al. (2017)	International Monetary Fund, International Financial Statistics and data files, and World Bank and OECD GDP estimates
Domestic credit to private sector by banks (C7)	Refers to the credits of the private sector provided by the deposit taking corporations except central banks (% of GDP)	Tobe (2017), Thierry et al. (2016), Gozgor (2014), Claessens and Horen (2014)	International Monetary Fund, International Financial Statistics and data files, and World Bank and OECD GDP estimates
Portfolio investments (C8)	Presents the transactions of the equity and debt securities in the billions of U.S. dollar	Düll et al. (2017), Cao and Ward (2014), Bhatta et al. (2017), Albulescu (2015)	International Monetary Fund, Balance of Payments Statistics Yearbook and data files
Total value of Stocks traded (C9)	Defines the total number of domestic and foreign shares are multiplied by their market prices by the end of the year (% of GDP)	Kocaarslan et al. (2017), Bayar et al. (2014), Joseph and Fernandez (2016)	World Federation of Exchanges database

Source Adapted from The World Bank Database

Analysis results demonstrate that Italy has the best performance. In addition to this country, Japan, United States and Korea are other countries that have high performance. On the other side, Argentina is listed in the last rank due to the financial sector-based performance indices. Moreover, Mexico, Indonesia and Turkey are other countries which have low performance results.

5   Discussion and Conclusions

G20 countries play a very key role for world economy because they have a very significant percentage of GDP and trade in the world. Therefore, performance analysis of these countries should be made periodically. Parallel to this aspect, in this study, it is aimed to evaluate the performance of G20 countries. Within this context, financial sector-based factors are taken into the consideration. For this purpose, 9 different

Table 2. Financial dataset of the G20 economies

Countries/Criteria	C1	C2	C3	C4	C5	C6	C7	C8	C9
Argentina	50.2	36.9	12.5	2.0	13.1	22.0	12	−35.3	0.7
Australia	98.9	154.3	5.2	1.0	30.1	159.2	122	27.3	48.2
Brazil	68.1	113.9	9.0	2.9	20.3	85.9	46	19.2	26.2
Canada	99.1	216.2	4.9	0.5	24.2	172.3	124.4	−113.9	75.0
China	78.9	19.7	7.2	1.2	7.8	118.7	102	62.2	114.1
France	96.6	104.0	5.3	4.2	38.6	143.0	92.3	−5.3	41.0
Germany	98.8	112.3	5.6	2.3	14.9	122.3	96.4	230.4	32.6
India	52.8	5.3	7.1	4.3	11.9	69.8	50	4.7	35.9
Indonesia	35.9	14.1	12.8	2.1	17.7	34.5	25	−19.0	10.2
Italy	87.3	106.9	5.9	18.0	53.3	137.6	83.8	177.7	95.5
Japan	96.6	132.8	5.5	1.7	33.9	295.6	98.0	274.5	99.9
Korea, Rep.	94.4	247.1	8.1	0.5	18.0	158.7	148	66.3	91.0
Mexico	38.7	42.0	10.8	3.0	15.0	37.0	17	−32.1	9.9
Russian Federation	67.4	72.4	8.5	6.7	38.5	24.4	41.6	−2.4	7.8
Saudi Arabia	69.4	53.7	13.7	1.1	8.2	−3.7	38	−8.2	75.0
South Africa	68.8	51.8	7.6	3.2	10.2	167.9	77	−16.4	70.0
Turkey	56.5	46.1	11.6	2.7	19.7	52.2	31	−6.3	39.6
United Kingdom	98.9	121.2	5.6	1.7	25.1	194.7	192.7	−195.5	78.0
United States	93.6	173.9	11.7	1.9	33.6	216.8	59.8	−196.7	224.1

Source The World Bank Database

Table 3. Direct relation matrix for financial sector indicators

Criteria	C1	C2	C3	C4	C5	C6	C7	C8	C9
Accounts at the financial institutions (C1)	0	3	2	3	3	4	3	3	1
Automated teller machines (C2)	2	0	1	2	2	2	2	2	1
Bank capital to assets ratio (C3)	3	1	0	2	2	2	2	2	2
Bank nonperforming loans to total gross loans (C4)	3	1	2	0	2	3	3	2	1
Commercial bank branches (C5)	4	4	3	2	0	3	3	3	2
Domestic credit provided by financial sector (C6)	4	1	2	4	3	0	4	2	2
Domestic credit to private sector by banks (C7)	4	1	2	4	3	4	0	2	2
Portfolio investments (C8)	3	2	2	3	3	3	3	0	4
Total value of stocks traded (C9)	1	1	2	2	3	3	4	4	0

Table 4. The normalized direct relation matrix

	C1	C2	C3	C4	C5	C6	C7	C8	C9
C1	0.000	0.125	0.083	0.125	0.125	0.167	0.125	0.125	0.042
C2	0.083	0.000	0.042	0.083	0.083	0.083	0.083	0.083	0.042
C3	0.125	0.042	0.000	0.083	0.083	0.083	0.083	0.083	0.083
C4	0.125	0.042	0.083	0.000	0.083	0.125	0.125	0.083	0.042
C5	0.167	0.167	0.125	0.083	0.000	0.125	0.125	0.125	0.083
C6	0.167	0.042	0.083	0.167	0.125	0.000	0.167	0.083	0.083
C7	0.167	0.042	0.083	0.167	0.125	0.167	0.000	0.083	0.083
C8	0.125	0.083	0.083	0.125	0.125	0.125	0.125	0.000	0.167
C9	0.042	0.042	0.083	0.083	0.125	0.125	0.167	0.167	0.000

Table 5. The total relation matrix

	C1	C2	C3	C4	C5	C6	C7	C8	C9
C1	0.694	0.525	0.543	0.750	0.706	0.826	0.782	0.664	0.472
C2	0.536	0.276	0.351	0.500	0.472	0.530	0.523	0.446	0.327
C3	0.632	0.354	0.353	0.558	0.528	0.594	0.585	0.499	0.402
C4	0.670	0.373	0.453	0.516	0.557	0.662	0.652	0.523	0.387
C5	0.880	0.590	0.608	0.757	0.636	0.839	0.826	0.706	0.536
C6	0.848	0.461	0.552	0.793	0.716	0.696	0.827	0.641	0.510
C7	0.848	0.461	0.552	0.793	0.716	0.839	0.684	0.641	0.510
C8	0.831	0.509	0.567	0.778	0.737	0.827	0.819	0.587	0.599
C9	0.697	0.429	0.519	0.680	0.676	0.756	0.781	0.671	0.415

Table 6. Total cause-effect and weights of the financial sector indicators

Criteria	r_i	y_i	$(r_i + y_i)$	$(r_i - y_i)$	Weights
C1	5.9623	6.6365	12.5988	−0.6742	0.127
C2	3.9615	3.9779	7.9393	−0.0164	0.080
C3	4.5049	4.4959	9.0008	0.0090	0.091
C4	4.7920	6.1245	10.9164	−1.3325	0.110
C5	6.3777	5.7442	12.1219	0.6336	0.122
C6	6.0438	6.5679	12.6117	−0.5240	0.127
C7	6.0438	6.4794	12.5232	−0.4356	0.126
C8	6.2536	5.3779	11.6316	0.8757	0.117
C9	5.6238	4.1594	9.7832	1.4644	0.099

indicators are identified. Additionally, in order to reach this objective, DEMATEL and TOPSIS methods are taken into the consideration.

As a result of DEMATEL analysis, it is determined that bank nonperforming loans to total gross loans (C4) is the most influenced factor whereas total value of stocks

Table 7. Normalized criterion matrix

Countries/Criteria	C1	C2	C3	C4	C5	C6	C7	C8	C9
Argentina	0.145	0.073	0.325	0.093	0.117	0.041	0.031	0.155	0.002
Australia	0.286	0.303	0.135	0.046	0.268	0.263	0.311	0.215	0.138
Brazil	0.197	0.224	0.234	0.134	0.181	0.145	0.117	0.207	0.075
Canada	0.287	0.425	0.127	0.023	0.215	0.284	0.317	0.079	0.215
China	0.228	0.039	0.187	0.056	0.069	0.197	0.260	0.248	0.327
France	0.280	0.204	0.138	0.194	0.343	0.237	0.236	0.183	0.118
Germany	0.286	0.221	0.145	0.106	0.133	0.203	0.246	0.409	0.093
India	0.153	0.010	0.184	0.199	0.106	0.119	0.128	0.193	0.103
Indonesia	0.104	0.028	0.333	0.097	0.157	0.062	0.064	0.170	0.029
Italy	0.253	0.210	0.153	0.833	0.474	0.228	0.214	0.359	0.274
Japan	0.280	0.261	0.143	0.079	0.301	0.483	0.250	0.452	0.286
Korea, Rep.	0.273	0.486	0.210	0.023	0.160	0.262	0.378	0.252	0.261
Mexico	0.112	0.083	0.281	0.139	0.133	0.066	0.043	0.158	0.028
Russian Federation	0.195	0.142	0.221	0.310	0.342	0.045	0.106	0.186	0.022
Saudi Arabia	0.201	0.106	0.356	0.051	0.073	0.000	0.097	0.181	0.215
South Africa	0.199	0.102	0.197	0.148	0.091	0.277	0.196	0.173	0.201
Turkey	0.164	0.091	0.301	0.125	0.175	0.090	0.079	0.183	0.114
United Kingdom	0.286	0.238	0.145	0.079	0.223	0.320	0.492	0.001	0.224
United States	0.271	0.342	0.304	0.088	0.299	0.356	0.153	0.000	0.642

Table 8. Weighted criterion matrix

Countries/Criteria	C1	C2	C3	C4	C5	C6	C7	C8	C9
Argentina	0.018	0.006	0.029	0.010	0.014	0.005	0.004	0.018	0.000
Australia	0.036	0.024	0.012	0.005	0.033	0.033	0.039	0.025	0.014
Brazil	0.025	0.018	0.021	0.015	0.022	0.018	0.015	0.024	0.007
Canada	0.036	0.034	0.012	0.003	0.026	0.036	0.040	0.009	0.021
China	0.029	0.003	0.017	0.006	0.008	0.025	0.033	0.029	0.032
France	0.036	0.016	0.013	0.021	0.042	0.030	0.030	0.022	0.012
Germany	0.036	0.018	0.013	0.012	0.016	0.026	0.031	0.048	0.009
India	0.019	0.001	0.017	0.022	0.013	0.015	0.016	0.023	0.010
Indonesia	0.013	0.002	0.030	0.011	0.019	0.008	0.008	0.020	0.003
Italy	0.032	0.017	0.014	0.092	0.058	0.029	0.027	0.042	0.027
Japan	0.036	0.021	0.013	0.009	0.037	0.061	0.032	0.053	0.028
Korea, Rep.	0.035	0.039	0.019	0.003	0.020	0.033	0.048	0.030	0.026
Mexico	0.014	0.007	0.025	0.015	0.016	0.008	0.005	0.019	0.003
Russian Federation	0.025	0.011	0.020	0.034	0.042	0.006	0.013	0.022	0.002
Saudi Arabia	0.026	0.008	0.032	0.006	0.009	0.000	0.012	0.021	0.021
South Africa	0.025	0.008	0.018	0.016	0.011	0.035	0.025	0.020	0.020
Turkey	0.021	0.007	0.027	0.014	0.021	0.011	0.010	0.021	0.011
United Kingdom	0.036	0.019	0.013	0.009	0.027	0.041	0.062	0.000	0.022
United States	0.034	0.027	0.028	0.010	0.037	0.045	0.019	0.000	0.063

Table 9. The values of RCi and ranking the G20 economies

Countries/Criteria	Di+	Di−	CCi	Ranking
Argentina	0.147	0.029	0.163	19
Australia	0.115	0.070	0.377	7
Brazil	0.126	0.044	0.260	13
Canada	0.119	0.071	0.375	8
China	0.123	0.060	0.330	10
France	0.109	0.066	0.379	6
Germany	0.119	0.069	0.367	9
India	0.130	0.038	0.227	14
Indonesia	0.143	0.032	0.182	17
Italy	0.068	0.122	0.643	1
Japan	0.101	0.099	0.496	2
Korea, Rep.	0.112	0.082	0.421	4
Mexico	0.142	0.030	0.173	18
Russian Federation	0.122	0.055	0.312	11
Saudi Arabia	0.141	0.040	0.221	15
South Africa	0.119	0.054	0.312	11
Turkey	0.133	0.037	0.219	16
United Kingdom	0.116	0.082	0.415	5
United States	0.111	0.092	0.455	3

traded (C9) is the most effective criterion in the financial sector indicators. On the other side, it is also identified that domestic credit provided by financial sector (C6) has the highest importance in the criteria while automated teller machines (C2) has the weakest importance in financial sector-based performance of the G20 economies.

After DEMATEL analysis, G20 economies are evaluated by using TOPSIS methodology. According to the results, it is defined that Italy is the best country. Moreover, Japan, United States and Korea are other successful countries in comparison with the others. In addition to this result, it is also concluded that Argentina is the country that has the lowest performance. Furthermore, Mexico, Indonesia and Turkey are also other countries that have lower performance.

By considering the analysis results, it is recommended that G20 countries should focus on the indicators which are defined as the significant in this study. Thus, these countries can have a chance to improve their economies. In this study, it is aimed to make an important contribution to the literature by focusing on the essential topic. However, a new study, which evaluates this subject with different methodology, will also be very beneficial.

References

Akins, B., Li, L., Ng, J., & Rusticus, T. O. (2016). Bank competition and financial stability: evidence from the financial crisis. *Journal of Financial and Quantitative Analysis, 51*(1), 1–28.

Albulescu, C. T. (2015). Do Foreign Direct and Portfolio Investments Affect Long-term Economic Growth in Central and Eastern Europe?. *Procedia Economics and Finance, 23*, 507–512.

Allen, F., McAndrews, J., & Strahan, P. (2002). E-finance: an introduction. *Journal of Financial Services Research, 22*(1–2), 5–27.

Bashir, A., & Hassan, A. (2017). Interrelationship Among Basel Capital Regulation, Risk, and Efficiency in Pakistani Commercial Banks. *Business & Economic Review, 9*(2), 165–186.

Bayar, Y., Kaya, A., & Yildirim, M. (2014). Effects of stock market development on economic growth: Evidence from Turkey. *International Journal of Financial Research, 5*(1), 93.

Bhatta, B., Marshall, A., & Thapa, C. (2017). Foreign bias in bond portfolio investments: the role of economic and non-economic factors and the impact of the global financial and sovereign debt crises. *The European Journal of Finance*, 1–33.

Cao, X., & Ward, M. D. (2014). Do democracies attract portfolio investment? Transnational portfolio investments modeled as dynamic network. *International Interactions, 40*(2), 216–245.

Capponi, A., Dooley, J. M., Oet, M. V., & Ong, S. J. (2017). Capital and resolution policies: The US interbank market. *Journal of Financial Stability, 30*, 229–239.

Chiu, W. Y., Tzeng, G. H., & Li, H. L. (2013). A new hybrid MCDM model combining DANP with VIKOR to improve e-store business. *Knowledge-Based Systems, 37*, 48–61.

Claessens, S., & Horen, N. (2014). Foreign banks: Trends and impact. *Journal of Money, Credit and Banking, 46*(s1), 295–326.

Demirgüç-Kunt, A., Kane, E., & Laeven, L. (2015). Deposit insurance around the world: A comprehensive analysis and database. *Journal of financial stability, 20*, 155–183.

Dimitrios, A., Helen, L., & Mike, T. (2016). Determinants of non-performing loans: Evidence from Euro-area countries. *Finance research letters, 18*, 116–119.

Drummond, H. (2003). Did Nick Leeson have an accomplice? The role of information technology in the collapse of Barings Bank. *Journal of Information Technology, 18*(2), 93–101.

Düll, R., König, F., & Ohls, J. (2017). On the exposure of insurance companies to sovereign risk —Portfolio investments and market forces. *Journal of Financial Stability, 31*, 93–106.

Ghosh, A. (2015). Banking-industry specific and regional economic determinants of non-performing loans: Evidence from US states. *Journal of Financial Stability, 20*, 93–104.

Gozgor, G. (2014). Determinants of domestic credit levels in emerging markets: The role of external factors. *Emerging Markets Review, 18*, 1–18.

Grintzalis, I., Lodge, D., & Manu, A. S. (2017). *The implications of global and domestic credit cycles for emerging market economies: measures of finance-adjusted output gaps* (No. 2034). ECB Working Paper.

Herrera-Restrepo, O., Triantis, K., Seaver, W. L., Paradi, J. C., & Zhu, H. (2016). Bank branch operational performance: A robust multivariate and clustering approach. *Expert Systems with Applications, 50*, 107–119.

Honohan, P. (2008). Cross-country variation in household access to financial services. *Journal of Banking & Finance, 32*(11), 2493–2500.

Hsu, C. C., & Liou, J. J. (2013). An outsourcing provider decision model for the airline industry. *Journal of Air Transport Management, 28*, 40–46.

Hsu, C. C., Liou, J. J., & Chuang, Y. C. (2013). Integrating DANP and modified grey relation theory for the selection of an outsourcing provider. *Expert Systems With Applications, 40*(6), 2297–2304.

Hsu, C. H., Wang, F. K., & Tzeng, G. H. (2012). The best vendor selection for conducting the recycled material based on a hybrid MCDM model combining DANP with VIKOR. *Resources, Conservation and Recycling, 66*, 95–111.

Hu, S. K., Lu, M. T., & Tzeng, G. H. (2014). Exploring smart phone improvements based on a hybrid MCDM model. *Expert Systems with Applications, 41*(9), 4401–4413.

Hugonnier, J., & Morellec, E. (2017). Bank capital, liquid reserves, and insolvency risk. *Journal of Financial Economics, 125*(2), 266–285.

Hwang, C. L. & Yoon, K. (1981). "Multiple Attribute Decision Making: Methods and Application", Springer Publications, Berlin.

Jegede, C. A. (2014). Effects of automated teller machine on the performance of Nigerian banks. *American Journal of Applied Mathematics and Statistics, 2*(1), 40–46.

Joseph, M., Allbright, D., Stone, G., Sekhon, Y., & Tinson, J. (2015). Customer Perceptions of Bank Service Delivery Technologies in the United States and England. In *Marketing, Technology and Customer Commitment in the New Economy* (pp. 44–44). Springer, Cham.

Joseph, R., & Fernandez, M. (2016). Growth of Stock Market in the UAE through Merger: A Comparative Study of GCC Stock Markets. *Accounting and Finance Research, 5*(3), 190.

Kocaarslan, B., Sari, R., Gormus, A., & Soytas, U. (2017). Dynamic correlations between BRIC and US stock markets: The asymmetric impact of volatility expectations in oil, gold and financial markets. *Journal of Commodity Markets, 7*, 41–56.

Konheim, A. G. (2016). Automated teller machines: their history and authentication protocols. *Journal of Cryptographic Engineering, 6*(1), 1–29.

Lane, P. R., & McQuade, P. (2014). Domestic credit growth and international capital flows. *The Scandinavian Journal of Economics, 116*(1), 218–252.

LaPlante, A. E., & Paradi, J. C. (2015). Evaluation of bank branch growth potential using data envelopment analysis. *Omega, 52*, 33–41.

Liu, H. C., You, J. X., Zhen, L., & Fan, X. J. (2014). A novel hybrid multiple criteria decision making model for material selection with target-based criteria.*Materials & Design, 60*, 380–390.

Narteh, B. (2015). Perceived service quality and satisfaction of self-service technology: The case of automated teller machines. *International Journal of Quality & Reliability Management, 32* (4), 361–380.

Oh, S., & Park, J. (2015). *Does Bank Branch Competition Alleviate Household Credit Constraints? Evidence from Korean Household Data* (No. 1501).

Paradi, J. C., Sherman, H. D., & Tam, F. K. (2018). Bank Branch Operational Studies Using DEA. In *Data Envelopment Analysis in the Financial Services Industry* (pp. 145–158). Springer, Cham

Polodoo, V., Seetanah, B., Sannassee, R. V., Seetah, K., & Padachi, K. (2015). An econometric analysis regarding the path of non performing loans-a panel data analysis from Mauritian banks and implications for the banking industry. *The Journal of Developing Areas, 49*(1), 53–64.

Prasad, U. D., & Madhavi, S. (2012). Prediction of churn behavior of bank customers using data mining tools. *Business Intelligence Journal, 5*(1), 96–101.

Rajha, K. S. (2016). Determinants of Non-Performing Loans: Evidence from the Jordanian Banking Sector. *Journal of Finance, 4*(1), 125–136.

Samarina, A., & Bezemer, D. (2016). Do capital flows change domestic credit allocation?. *Journal of International Money and Finance, 62*, 98–121.

Sridharan, S., Pramod, T. C., & Sunitha, N. R. (2014, November). Architecting an integrated framework for utility payment services using automated teller machines. In *Science Engineering and Management Research (ICSEMR), 2014 International Conference on* (pp. 1–6). IEEE.

Thierry, B., Jun, Z., Eric, D. D., Yannick, G. Z. S., & Landry, K. Y. S. (2016). Causality Relationship between Bank Credit and Economic Growth: Evidence from a Time Series Analysis on a Vector Error Correction Model in Cameroon. *Procedia-Social and Behavioral Sciences, 235*, 664–671.

Tobe, S. (2017). Domestic Credit Growth, International Capital Inflows, and Risk Perception in Global Markets. *Economics Bulletin, 37*(2), 631–636.

Wu, D., & Olson, D. L. (2010). Enterprise risk management: coping with model risk in a large bank. *Journal of the Operational Research Society, 61*(2), 179–190.

Yang, Y. P. O., Shieh, H. M., Leu, J. D., & Tzeng, G. H. (2008). A novel hybrid MCDM model combined with DEMATEL and ANP with applications. *International journal of operations research, 5*(3), 160–168.

Yüksel, S. (2017). Determinants of the Credit Risk in Developing Countries After Economic Crisis: A Case of Turkish Banking Sector. In *Global Financial Crisis and Its Ramifications on Capital Markets* (pp. 401–415). Springer, Cham.

Due Diligence for Bank M&A's: Case from Turkey

Veclal Gündüz[(✉)]

University of Mediterranean Kaprasia, Nicosia, Cyprus
veclal.gulay@akun.edu.tr

1 Introduction

In this study the main target is to give detailed steps for due diligence in banking sector experienced after the crisis in Turkey in 2000 and 2001. Before giving details, the merger and acquisition must be analyzed briefly, what was done and what is the gap for literature. The unique part for this research will be the guide for future bank M&As with examples from the latest bank M&As in Turkey.

Unfortunately for the banking sector there are some lists and details given by the auditing companies, but the due diligence details are not given. Due diligence details for each department in the banks is the unique part for this study. Before giving the details for due diligence, we must check out the information given for merger and acquisitions for the companies. It must be parallel for the banking sector also.

Three broadly defined schools of thought exist that offer insights into merger and acquisition activity. For the sake of reporting convenience, we refer to them as the capital market school, the strategy school, and the organizational behavior school. Recently also a number of scholars have combined strategic and organizational considerations, adopting what we call a process school on acquisitions. Although all of these schools pursue questions related to mergers and acquisitions, each line of research is anchored in a different central questions, and each approaches its question from a particular perspective, with different sets of assumptions, and with a different set of methodologies.

The central question asked by financial economists on whose research the capital markets view is based, is, "Do mergers and acquisitions create value and if so for whom?" Their broad conclusion after studying stock prices of acquiring and target firms during periods surrounding the merger announcement is that, in general, the shareholders of the acquired firm benefit but those from the acquiring firm do not. Overall they conclude that acquisitions create value, and hence, that an active market for corporate control should be encouraged.

Strategy researchers look at two issues of interest to individual firms. Some empirical researchers examine what types of acquisitions are more likely to be successful for an acquiring firm. This group often focuses on the extent to which an acquisition is related to the firm's existing businesses. Other strategy researchers are interested in providing firms with logical advice on how to search for and evaluate acquisitions so as to have a proper "strategic fit".

Organizational behavior scholars in turn are concerned with the broad questions of what effect acquisitions have on individuals and organizations. Their studies generally

N. Ozatac and K. K. Gökmenoglu (eds.), *Emerging Trends in Banking and Finance*, Springer Proceedings in Business and Economics,
https://doi.org/10.1007/978-3-030-01784-2_14

focus on determining the impact of acquisitions on the individuals in each firm and on the problems relating to a lack of "organizational fit" or "cultural fit".

Finally, some researchers are combining strategic and organizational considerations to address how the acquisition process affects the attainment of strategic objectives.

2 Literature Review

Angwin (1995) found that national cultural differences do play an important role in affecting acquirer's perceptions of target companies and suggest that this may have important consequences for the negotiation of deals and the subsequent management of the postacquisition phase. For the merger and acquisitions many studies just analyzed the before and after the merger and acquisition period according to the types of the measures under qualitative and quantitative methods.

Grundy (1996) explored a number of process and tools for managing acquisitions for both strategic and financial value.

Some of the measures are classified under type of the measures as financial domain, that are market performance and accounting performance, and non-financial domain such as operational performance and overall performance by Meglio and Risberg (2011). They also analyzed the factors shaping the M&A process and found out that it is not possible to talk about M&A performance as if it was a universal construction.

Editorial of Scandinavian Journal of Management (2012) point out M&As have been common corporate practice for 120 years, in contrast, the academic study of M&As has a history of less than 60 years. The study reviewed published top-tier M&A research and analyzed from both thematical and methodological lenses.

2.1 Hypothesis in Bank M&A's

M&As is the need of business enterprises for achieving the economies of scale, growth, diversification, synergy, financial planning, globalization of economy, and monopolistic approach also creates interest amongst companies for M&As in order to increase the market power (Khan 2011). Specific hypotheses examined related to the objective of maximizing shareholder wealth. The examples from Turkey are classified in this study according to these hypotheses. The explanations of them are as follows:

The information hypothesis contends that the bidders have private information about the targets that permits them to identify undervalued firms. In banking, for example, correspondent banks may have private information about correspondent banks.

The market power hypothesis claims that the acquiring firm (by gaining monopoly power through horizontal mergers) can raise product prices after buying up competitors. A pragmatic motivation may be that banks want to strengthen their competitive position on their home markets through consolidation (Vennet 1996). When a bank enters to a new market, the costs of market analysis, expenditure investments, new employee, marketing and advertising expenses.

Mergers are considered to be an important means to achieve operational synergies (Vennet 1996). The synergy hypothesis focuses on cost reductions or synergies related to economies of scale or scope lower distribution or marketing costs or elimination of redundant assets. Acquisition-based cost cutting has been a major driver of bank mergers in the 1990s. M&A of banks can generate more value of their total worth. This increase will be after the M&A result and the decrease of the costs.

The tax hypothesis claims that reduced tax liabilities drive mergers. Although taxes are potential a cost of doing business, the tax hypothesis is viewed as a financial synergy rather than a cost-reducing synergy.

The managerial efficiency theory explains takeovers as an answer to the failure of internal monitoring mechanism (Vennet 1996). It is hypothesized that banks with a significantly lower performance than an efficient use of their assets and input factors might produce have a higher probability of being acquired than well-managed banks. The inefficient-management hypothesis contends that firms with inept managers are potential takeover targets because the existing managers are not maximizing the value of the firm.

The earnings-diversification hypothesis argues that the acquiring firm wants to diversify earnings in an attempt to generate higher levels of cash flow for the same level of total risk. This approach substitutes reductions in business risk (earnings fluctuations) for greater financial risk (leverage). By diversification the risk is decreased and by this way the market value of the banks' shares increase. After M&A the banks can increase the product and services with a wide range of geographic area, which will decrease the risk and increase the market value of both banks' shares.

2.2 Success of M&As

Clark (1991) summarized the success of M&As under six foundations. They are the pricing structure, timing, related acquisition emphasis, a tough-minded postacquisition agenda, financial progress indicators and back-up actions, a supportive asset and divestment program.

Wen et al. (2005) summarized the reasons for failed mergers as:

- Poor strategic fit
- Cultural and social differences
- **Incomplete and inadequate due diligence**
- Poorly managed integration
- Paying too much
- Overly optimistic.

3 The M&A's in Turkey Banking Sector

In Turkey, M&As in banking sector can be divided into two reasons. First one is done under the restructuring mechanisms for the failed bank after the crisis by the government intervention. The second one is related with the market share hypothesis, which will increase the competitive strength and financial performance with higher profit and returns.

3.1 Bank M&A's 2001–2011 Period in Turkey

The main bank M&A's in Turkey between 2001 and 2011 are listed by Sarıgül and Kurşunel (2012) as follows:

Emlak Kredi Bankası - Ziraat Bankası: Emlak Kredi Bankası, which completely lost its equity, was liquidated in 2001 by combining with the Ziraat Bankası. It has been assessed under the synergy that can be achieved due to the internal savings through synergy hypothesis in this merger.

Mergered banks under TMSF: During 2001–2002 BDDK; merged Sümerbank, Egebank, Yaşarbank, Yurtbank, Bank Kapital, Ulusal Bank under name of Sümerbank and Bayındırbank, İnterbank, Esbank, Etibank, İktisat Bankası, Kentbank, EGS Bank, Toprakbank under Birleşik Fon Bankası (Bayındırbank). Local, mandatory, and horizontal mergers were designed under the same Board of Directors Committee and reconstructed for financial and operational activities. Mergers were done for the internal savings that supported by synergy hypothesis.

Körfezbank - Osmanlı Bankası - Garanti Bankası: Doğuş group banks, Körfezbank and Osmanlı Bankası were taken over by Garanti Bankası in 2001; corporate banking and post banking of Körfezbank, management of deposits and commercial banking of Osmanlı Bankası and retail banking and SME banking of Garanti combined together and became second private bank in Turkey. This merger can be classified under the diversification, market share and synergy hypothesis.

Tekfen Yatırım ve Finansman Bankası - Bank Ekspres: Tekfen Holding bought Bank Ekspres in 2001, that had commercial banking licence from TMSF and increased the number of its product and services, also improved its financial statements. This local, optional and vertical merger is an example for the diversification, market share and synergy hypothesis.

Demirbank - HSBC: Demirbank had been transferred to TMSF in 2001, when it had wide locations of branches and alternative banking channels and was sold to HSBC which was the second largest finance group in the world. After this sale, HSBC could find possibilities for corporate banking in Turkey. Cross-border and optional take over was related with diversification, market share and synergy hypothesis.

Sümerbank - Oyak Bank: Sümerbank, which was under TMSF, was sold to Oyak Group in 2002. Oyak Bank could find opportunity to widen its branches with its several members and its largest automotive manufacturer company in the country after the takeover. Local, horizontal, optional takeover represented diversification, market share and synergy hypothesis.

Milli Aydın Bankası (Tarişbank) - Denizbank: Tarişbank was sold to Denizbank by TMSF in 2002. Tarişbank had given credits to agricultural sector in Aegean region, by taking over all of the credits with its bankers Denizbank built the agricultural services and products by that way. Local, horizontal, optional takeover is an example for market share and synergy hypothesis.

Koçbank - UniCredito Italiano: UniCredito Italiano bought Koçbank's 50% shares and established a strategic partnership in 2002. Optional, cross-border merger is classified under diversification and market share hypothesis.

Pamukbank - Halkbank: Pamukbank was under TMSF and transferred to Halkbank in 2004 after the insufficient merger offers. With its alternative service channels, educated bankers, retail banking services, MIS Halkbank became fourth bank in Turkey after took over Pamukbank. Local, mandatory, horizontal and take over indicates this merger is under diversification, market share and synergy hypothesis.

Türk Ekonomi Bankası - BNP Paribas: 42% of TEB's shares were sold to BNP Paribas, the largest bank in Euro region in 2004. TEB could widen internationally and especially retail banking, foreign trade facilities increased that supported synergy hypothesis.

Dışbank - Fortis Bank: Dışbank was sold to Fortis in 2005. Fortis was one of the largest 20 financial intermediary in Europe at that date. Optional, cross-border, take over is under the market share and synergy hypothesis.

Koçbank - Yapı Kredi Bankası: Koçbank was transferred to Yapı Kredi in 2006. Koç Group announced its willingness about being a leader in banking sector with the merger that was done for synergy. Local, optional, horizontal and full merger was under market share and synergy hypothesis.

Garanti Bankası - General Electronics CF: GE bought some shares of Garanti Bankası, one of the Doğuş Group's banks in 2007. GE has changed its strategy for shrinkage in finance sector by selling its shares in the market, increased the market value of its shares from 2 billion 470 million TL to 5.85 billion TL. Optional, cross-border merger was for market share hypothesis.

Finansbank - National Bank of Greece: Finansbank sold its shares to National Bank of Greece (NBG) in 2006. Regional, optional, horizontal took over was one of the synergy and market share hypothesis.

Denizbank - Dexia PB: 75% of Denizbank shares were sold to Dexia, one of the largest 15 banks in Europe, in 2006. Retail banking and a new market were the advantages for synergy.

Şekerbank - Bank Turan Alem Securities JSC: Şekerbank sold its 34% paid-in-capital to Bank Turanalem, the biggest bank in middle Asia, in 2006. By this merger Şekerbank increased its facilities both internally and internationally. Bank Turan Alem merged cross-border and entered in western market. Optional, cross-border, horizontal merger was an example for diversification and market share hypothesis.

Akbank - Citigroup: Akbank sold its 20% shares to Citigroup with 3,1 billion US Dollar, the biggest sale in banking sector in Turkey, in 2006. Optional, cross-border, merger was an example for market share hypothesis.

Oyakbank - ING: ING was listed in the first ten biggest in the ranking of Fortune Global and bought Oyakbank in 2007. After this merger, ING Group has advantages for retail banking with Oyakbank's portfolio and wide number of branches. Optional, cross-border took over had diversification, market share and synergy hypothesis.

Türk Ekonomi Bankası (TEB) - Fortis Bank: Fortis Group was sold to BNP Paribas after it had financial difficulties. BNP Paribas merged its two banks under the name TEB in 2011. Both banks' services and products in corporate, commercial and retail banking were same, but according to the internal saving it was classified as synergy hypothesis.

3.2   2017 Figures for M&A's in Turkey

According to the Ernest and Young (2018) report on Merger and Acquisitions in Turkey for 2017, the total number of M&As in Turkey was 251. This number was mentioned as 298 according to Deloitte. The expectation for 2018 is 10 billion USD in total.

In 2016, the financial services sector ranked third in terms of transaction volume with 25 transactions generating a total transaction volume of US$525 million. In 2017, the sector again ranked third in terms of transaction volume (US$998 million) and ninth in terms of number of transactions (10). The largest transaction in the sector was the acquisition of a 9.95% stake in Garanti Bank by Banco Bilbao Vizcaya Argentaria (BBVA) for US$917 million (M&A Report Turkey 2018).

E&Y also made the survey to determine the evaluations and expectations of prominent members of the Turkish business community with respect to M&A activity in 2017. The sample target group of the study is comprised upper management and shareholders of prominent public and private sector institutions in various sectors in Turkey. Survey results showed that in 2017, 66% of transactions took, from start to finish, less than twelve months to close, 23% between twelve and eighteen months and 11% more than eighteen months. Like 2016, most of the transactions were completed within one year in 2017.

3.3   Problems in M&A for 2017

47% of the participants rated the difficulty in agreeing on price as the main problem arising during negotiations, in line with previous years. This was followed by strategic compliance and legislation/permits with 15%. Corporate culture with 8% was also cited as problematic.

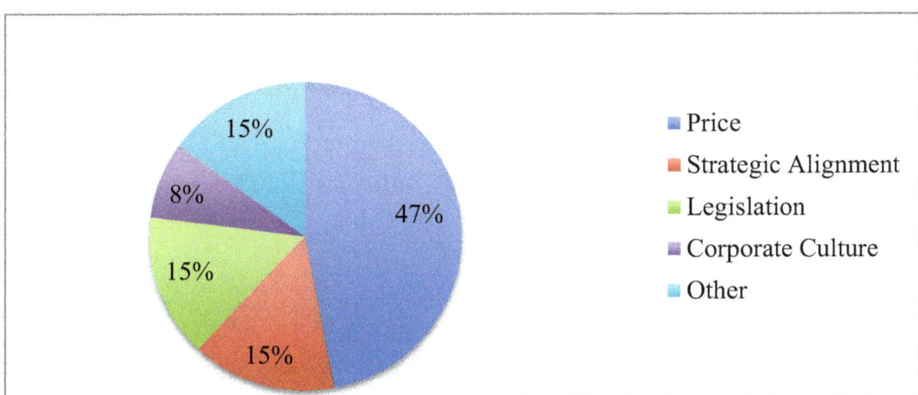

4 Due Diligence

Springer (2013) describes due diligence as a high level of care, a dedication to accuracy, a striving for excellence, and a step past plain old diligence.

Harvey and Lusch (1995) examined the nature and scope of due diligence. The due diligence auditing process is given under three basic issues as (1) what technique/procedure can be used to collect both tangible/intangible data in each of the seven fields[1]; (2) what the appropriate sequence of audits is to increase the value of the collection of data to answer questions in the seven fields; and (3) composition of the due diligence team.

Due Diligence is intended to be an objective & independent examination of the acquisition target. Prime role of due diligence is to understand the risk associated with the purchase. Using due diligence findings to assist in price negotiations.

In simple terms, the purpose of due diligence is to identify the risks in the target bank, and, if appropriate, adjust for those risks in the pricing (Gerrish 2014).

Due diligence practitioners aspire to produce a perfect synopsis of the target company's condition, the reality is one of time and cost constraints.

Tissen and Sneidere (2014) develop a due diligence matrix for main users of financial analysis based on the data of Statistical Bureau of Latvia.

4.1 M&A Value with Due Diligence

How can management and the owners of a bank decide if a proposed merger is good for the organization? The answer involves measuring both the costs and benefits of a proposed merger. Academics and practitioners have generally devoted great attention to the roles time and speed play in creating value from acquisition (Meglio and Risberg 2009). Because the acquiring and acquired banks may have different reasons for pursuing a merger, this is not an easy cost-benefit calculation. Even so, the most important goal of any merger should be to increase the market value of the surviving firm so that its stockholders receive higher returns on the funds they have invested in the bank.

The different kinds of the strategic values by acquisition are listed as follows by Grundy (1992);

- Protective Value
- Enhancing Value
- Synergistic Value
- Future Opportunity Value.

The benefit of a bank merger can be stated as the difference between the total present value of the merged banks and the sum of their present values if they do not merge. This definition of benefit emphasizes the economic value of the bank merger

---

[1] Seven fields are: macro-environment audit, legal/environment audit, marketing audit, production audit, management audit, information/system audit, financial audit (5 year historical).

with the value-estimation process being similar to a capital-budgeting problem in financial management.

Once a company decides to engage in a merger or acquisition, a business valuation can protect it from paying more than the target is worth or help to gain more profits or benefits (Wen et al. 2005).

The following items are the principal factors usually reviewed by the acquiring bank organization in order to make a deal:

- Age and history of the bank
- Background of management
- Comparative management styles of the merging organizations
- Types of services offered
- Recent history of changes in deposits, loans, and market shares
- Principal customers served
- Geographic fit
- International control procedures
- Personnel situation
- Compatibility of accounting and management information systems
- Condition/depreciation schedule for offices and other physical assets
- Adequacy of capital, earnings per share, and ownership dilution before and following the proposed merger
- Growth of expenses
- Before-tax and after-tax income and rate of return.

4.2   Bank Due Diligence Check List

The Independent Bankers Association of Texas listed check list for bank M&As in 2017. The list is as follows:

(1) General Information
(2) Corporate Records
(3) Accountant, Internal Audit
(4) Bank Premises and Equipment
(5) Capital
(6) Compliance
(7) Data Processing
(8) Deposit Accounts and Borrowings
(9) Documents/Material Contracts
(10) Environmental/Real Property
(11) Financial-General Ledger
(12) Human Resources
(13) Insurance
(14) Investments
(15) Legal
(16) Loan Information and Reports

(17) Securities
(18) Shareholder/Insider Agreements
(19) Taxes
(20) Other.

4.3 Analysis of the Departments in a Bank

The fields can be categorized according to the type of the bank. The acquirer bank can organize some groups and analyze department's organization chart, working style, valuation and figure out the total worth of the bank. In simple terms, the purpose of due diligence is to identify the risks in the target bank, and, if appropriate, adjust for those risks in the pricing (Gerrish 2014).

In general the financial analysis of the balance sheet details, the valuation of the sources and the uses of the bank finalize the calculation of the worth of analyzed bank and the decision makers of the acquirer bank decide to buy or not to buy the seller bank.

Gerrish (2014) summarized the due diligence categories as follows:

(a) *Corporate records and financial information*

This includes the target's governing documents, stockholders' list, board and committee meeting minutes, stockholders' meeting minutes, and financial statements and regulatory reports for the past few years.

(b) *Loan and investment portfolio*

Loan policies and procedures, allowance methodology, detailed lending reports, loan portfolio summary, list of OREO, list of restructured and impaired loans, list of nonaccrual and delinquent loans, investment policy, securities portfolio report, and list of classified securities.

(c) *Deposits and other funding sources*

Funding and liquidity Policies, summary of deposit accounts, detailed breakdown of deposits by banking office, and breakdown of non-deposit liabilities.

(d) *Interest rate risk management*

Asset/liability management and interest rate risk policies, interest rate sensitivity analysis report, and interest rate shock analysis report.

(e) *Fixed assets*

Summary of the bank's offices and locations, including ATM documentation; deed and lease documentation; title and insurance documentation; environmental reports; maintenance contracts; and depreciation information.

(f) *Legal and supervisory matters*

Summary of any pending or threatened litigation against the bank; Community Reinvestment Act documentation; summary of completed and pending business transaction; Certificate of Authority and any documentation related to the bank's authority to conduct operations; Reports of Examination; and regulatory enforcement actions (current and terminated).

(g) *Human resources*

Summary of compensation and benefits, including deferred compensation plans, life insurance, incentive stock option plans, and employee stock ownership plans; material employment contracts and severance packages; and employee salary schedule.

(h) *Material agreements*

Shareholder agreements, tax allocation agreements, and dividend.

(i) *Taxes and insurance*

Recent federal and state tax returns and audits, outside tax opinions, summary of tax loss carry forwards, summary of all insurance programs and policies, and workers' compensation policies.

(j) *Data processing/operations/technology*

Summary of hardware and software systems, services providers, including services contracts, core processor contracts, outsourcing agreements, and licensing agreements.

4.4   Due Diligence Example from Turkey

In this section the information of the acquired bank is given that held after the crisis in 2000 and 2001. Analysis groups can be classified parallel to the departments as, Treasury, Commercial Banking, Cash Management, Law, Investments, Individual Banking (Credits, Call Center, Online Banking, Credit Cards, POS, Insurance, Deposits, Funds), Operation, International Relations, Construction, Human Resources and MIS.

4.4.1   Valuation of the Investments

The general problem for the due diligence is the correct valuation and deal price between the buyer and the seller. The investment portfolio and its portion under the income statement of the bank are important. The bond portfolio, repurchase amount, maturity, diversification, average interest, FX difference, treasury loans, stock portfolio and the other details are analyzed under this section. By this way the bank's portfolio, especially maturities and the interest rates are valued in the secondary market and the ability for selling is measured.

At the date of M&A the portfolio must be controlled and physically counted. The analyst also has to check out if the account records are correct or not with the physical count.

4.4.2   Commercial Banking

The credit portfolio is generally examined and the auditor tries to figure out what is its worth. The marketing and the credit departments are compared if the rules and the organization are similar with the buyer and the seller. The similarity makes M&A easy for the investor bank. The credit lines are merged and the credit risk of the portfolio can be easily determined.

The organization chart is divided under the head office and the branches. The branches are observed into two sections as commercial and individual banking.

Credit procedures of the banks also affect the credit policy of an investment bank after M&A. So the details about the credit portfolio must be analyzed carefully. The limitations of a branch manager, credit portfolio and the guarantees must be reported. The separation for cash and non-cash credits, their region and sectors must be included under the reports in detail.

The products of the bank are cash management products, such as utility payment, salary payment that are reported monthly.

The efficiency analysis is important for commercial marketing. The budgeting amounts, controls, the reporting system and their similarity with the investor bank are also important for M&A.

For commercial marketing, the performance of a branch is measured by the analysis of the profitability. The branch facilities are important for the buyer. The budgeting figures, the auditing periods, the matching of the other reports with MIS will be reported. MIS reports are also audited with the accordance of the buyer bank.

The customer profile of commercial credit, the credit types with their maturities, the credit lines of the other banks are all analyzed in details.

The guarantees of the credit portfolio are one of the most important details. The NPL's are closed by the liquidation of the collaterals. The credit risk is calculated by the risk rating of all of the credits. The risk depth must be measured also for the credit portfolio.

The concentration of the credit portfolio can change the ability of hedging the credit risk according to the companies. The deterioration of the financial statement of the big companies will increase the amount of NPL's of the bank.

The credit risk must be separated by currencies as TL and FX loans. The FX risk will be measured by the diversification.

The credit lines of the seller bank's subsidiaries can also change the credit risk of the bank. The limitations and the regulations must be analyzed according to the law.

The worth of the portfolio, NPL's must be considered. If a credit is reused without any payment, it must be transferred under the NPL's. If the total amount of the NPL's is high the buyer bank can decide not to buy the seller bank. The liquidation of the NPL's must be analyzed and reported which will affect the valuation of the portfolio.

4.4.3   Retail Banking

The timing for the retail banking is analyzed and compared with the buyer bank. The seller bank's market share and the market value, swot analysis by its strength, weakness, opportunities and threads are figured out.

The questions for the report and analysis departments, the working groups and their responsibilities, reporting group are all well-organized.

After auditing the retail banking department, the followings must be in the report:

- Retail credits, credit cards details (ATM, POS)
- NPL's details,

- Alternative banking channels,
- Marketing of retail banking product and services,
- Swot analysis,
- Valuation of market value.

The buyer bank tries to figure out the market value of the seller bank by swot analysis, questioners, volume of the retail banking product and services (number of customers of call center) the credit risk and collaterals.

Retail credits details must be analyzed like corporate credit portfolio, diversification as currencies, TL or FX credits, type of the credits, cost of credits, collaterals, etc.

The market share of seller bank's retail banking, deposits, credits, bank accounts, credit cards, debit cards, ATM, POS are reported in details.

The follow up of the repayment of credits with existing MIS is controlled and compared with the buyer bank's system.

For the credit card report the types of the cards like visa or master, or any other types if there will be any, the seller bank's income, cost or commissions from the cards are all calculated.

Organization chart like the other departments, branch limitations, the retail banking details are compared with the buyer bank's organizations.

The existing POS and ATM's numbers are also physically counted, and controlled with the account records. Investment accounts, utility payments, salary payments, mortgages, social security payments, standing orders, marketing are the other services and products.

The call center is analyzed according to the number of calls, transaction, customer number, existing and future projects, percentages of calls, and other details. The costs for each detail are important for reporting.

4.4.4   Accounting in General

The organization chart of Accounting and budgeting department, regulations, managerial reports are analyzed. All of the budgeting reports like retail banking, corporate banking, treasury department, branches, responsibilities, periods of the reports, other reports that are given to TCMB and BDDK, consolidation of the reports, MIS support, subsidiaries are the details.

The sources and the uses of the bank, journal records, general journals, financial statements, following of the assets, all of the costs, payments, utility payments, other payments are all reported under accounting department.

4.4.5   Non-current Assets

All of the fixed assets' title deeds must be controlled, expertise reports, the purchase date, market value, square meter, address details are all reported.

The rental branches, their costs, the period of rent, the beginning and the ending dates, rent payment, the owner, rent amount, address are all analyzed.

After M&A the seller bank's concept must be changed as the buyer's bank concept. The cost for change is calculated, the costs from seller bank is reported for ATM, air conditioners, Q-matic, fixed asset, automobiles, insurance policies.

4.4.6   Subsidiaries

The subsidiary details are important, because after the merger all of them can be transferred to the buyer bank records. The establishment dates, paid-in-capital, shareholder structure, sector, market share, financial statements of the subsidiaries; the participation, income and cost of the subsidiaries for seller bank are analyzed.

4.4.7   Law Department

The organization chart is the first part that must be reported. The comparison of seller and buyer bank is done. The cases against or in favor of the seller bank are reported. Details of the cases like dates, amounts, sides, rights, problems of the bank are all examined.

The paid-in capital, unpaid taxes, fees and funds, obligations, legal status of the subsidiaries, share of the stocks, shareholders, syndication credits, agreements, intellectual rights, asset details are reported.

4.4.8   MIS

The existing information system of the seller bank is compared with the buyer bank's system. Infrastructure compliance, the system support, purchasing if there will be needed are important details in MIS department.

While examining the information technology department, the system working style, central or other, headquarters or branch database, application development software, the structure of customer and account numbers, the quality of services offered in a bank, the average monthly transactions and transaction count for measuring compute density and quality, other external systems used for automatic payments are the details that are used to provide detailed information about SWIFT and EFT systems.

After the merger of the two banks, they will combine the systematic structure and will invest in information technology, if necessary. These investments should be considered in the short and long term. The market share in the sector can be increased by the quality of the services offered. Therefore, the systematic infrastructure of the seller bank and capital expenditures that will be made for the desired level plays a role to affect the determination of the bank's bid price of seller bank.

The system used as outsource supporting affects the costs. The organizational structure of the information systems department, as in other departments, authorities, information elements and shifts are important details. Besides access privileges to access the system, the system of care, to be contacted in case of emergency personnel information on the structure of the bank will be purchased until it is examined.

Computer hardware structures, such as operating systems, database platforms and features (number of processors, data storage unit size, version, licenses), the use of the system rates, bank hosts and contingency plans are some of the other topics discussed. The backup of all system that was received on a regular system backup procedures, backup plans, in a place other than a copy of the information processing building the backup cartridge hosts will be investigated in detail.

4.4.9   Human Resources

Human resource report is perhaps one of the most important observations in the bank M&A's. Because the report can give information about the available human resources structure opportunities after the merger. Staff Disciplinary regulations and the regulations, the number of staff at headquarters and branches, title structure, gender distribution of staff, the average age, seniority, training analysis are analyzed.

The costs of the quality of human resources need to be identified. For example, the low level in terms of education, age and thus seniority year high, correspondingly greater indemnity load, the number of employees per branch and per person vested employee costs the industry average will be taken of the cost of buying a bank which is above and long results can be obtained in the future. The seniority to determine the costs, termination benefits and vacation liability is determined by providing Headquarters and attempted distribution of branches and total personnel costs.

The indemnity for staff at the bank the sum of unused annual paid leave money with cargo, personnel age, education, retirement and so on. The distribution of angles, the structure of personnel, distribution, feature-supplying and/or term contracts involving criminal terms, payments/rights package, scope, vested employee costs, overtime costs, social security issues (trade unions, collective bargaining, etc.). As questions with topics directed banks to be purchased. The purpose of the questions are asked, the bank thought the purchase of short, medium and long-term material and/or human resources of the legal requirements of "processed", "investment grade" to evaluate whether the character.

All the factors mentioned above have an effect on the value of the bank that will be taken over. But this is the point where the most direct effect is the sum of money by allowing compensation burden in terms of human resources. The total load, with the most pessimistic scenario, in case of dismissal of the entire staff of the bank will be faced to express monetary burden. The cost of the bulge staff and personnel costs are also other material factors that affect bid value.

After examination of the human resources formed working groups to clarify the division of labor to be done in terms of compulsory legal process will occur on merger/notifications determined, the bank's staff in terms of organization and joining was performed. After the merger has been some layoffs, some of the remaining staff of the duties, responsibilities, jurisdiction and titles are revised. United case, the database engine has been created to be used, studies have been done for all the banks in terms of the standardization of HR.

Due to the organization's growth, some business functions and/or on the basis of dividing the powers and responsibilities are shared. HR, the increased number of employees and expanding service network provided standardization in all applications due to the wage system was established.

4.4.10   Operations

Some of the questions posed to the bank will be taken over on the Department of Operations is as follows:

- General Manager operations organization,
- Branch operating organization,
- Central OPS unit
- Foreign exchange authorization in the branch,
- Been out source jobs

- Rapid transfer system,
- Letters of commitment, issued bills of exchange, date and amount castings,
- Insurance agency, the
- Regulatory tracking,
- ATM number, location, model, amount of stock,
- Call center,
- Corporate payments,
- Salary payment agreements, conditions,
- Information on Reporting,
- Follow-up of Commitments,
- Guarantee letters/letters of guarantee terms,
- Letters discount/redemption are checks and dumps.

Operation section is made detailed studies about the systems used in connection with. S.W.I.F.T. next to the ATM management, TELEX-TEST KEY system used in EFT and payment institutions (software/hardware testing and backup systems), message statistics (outgoing/incoming) and collected information about the archive.

5 Conclusion and Future Dimensions

The success of M&As is correlated with the detailed analysis for banks. The culture, relations with customers, services, products, targets and many things must be given as a report to the acquirer. The performance of the banks were analyzed as preacquisition and postacquisition with some financial ratios or correlated with some of the financial indicators. In the literature the gap is for the due diligence, the questions that will be asked and reported preacquisition.

Each merger is simply a financial transaction that results in one or more banks being absorbed by another banking institution. The acquired bank (usually the smaller of the two) gives up its charter and adopts a new name (usually the name of the acquiring organization). The assets and liabilities of the acquired bank are added to those of the acquiring bank. A merger normally occurs after the managements of the acquiring and acquired organizations have struck a deal. The proposed transaction must then be ratified by the board of directors of each organization and possibly by a vote of each firm's common stockholders.

There are some differences between audit and financial due diligence. It is summarized below:

Area	Audit	Financial due diligence
Who	• Independent accountants/auditors	• Accountants, typically those experienced in M&A
Objective	• Provide professional opinion on whether the financial statements fairly reflect financial	• Quality of earnings assessment; • Historical working capital needs; • Sales and operating expense trends;

(*continued*)

(continued)

Area	Audit	Financial due diligence
	performance and position in accordance with GAAP.[1]	• Assessment of assumptions in management's forecast; • Assessment of key accounting personnel and accounting information systems; • Identification of deal issues specific to the transaction
Scope	• Dictated by Generally Accepted Auditing Standards ("GAAS"); • Involves detailed verification testing • Typically covers results as of fiscal year end	• Variable; dictated by scope of work determined by the buyer; • Focused on deal issues; • Limited detailed verification testing, although may include a proof of cash • Typically covers the last two fiscal years and the trailing twelve months period
Deliverable	• Audit opinion	• Typically a formal written report, but may be a brief summary of key deal points or a verbal communication
Stakeholders	• Wide range of stakeholders, including investors, banks, suppliers and customers	• Buyers, lenders and secondary investors
Cost	• Largely fixed with scope dictated by GAAS;	• Variable depending on negotiated scope of procedures;
Timing	• Dependent on stakeholder requirements	• Can range from a one day desk review to several weeks of on-site due diligence;

[1] Generally Accepted Accounting Principles

Source https://www.mlrpc.com/articles/understanding-the-differences-between-an-audit-and-financial-due-diligence/

In this study M&As in general, is summarized and the importance of the due diligence is mentioned. The department analyses are given according to the experiences after the crises in Turkey as of 2000 and 2001, and carried as a due diligence for some of the proposed banks as acquired. Mostly common M&As in Turkey is given with the adjustment of M&As hypothesis.

For future research in this area could be the study of comparison of pre and post merger performances with financial figures for bank M&As in Turkey.

References

Angwin, M. (1995). Competitiveness and the future of work. The Future of Work. Leichhardt, Pluto Press.

CLARK Peter J. (1991). Beyond The Deal, Optimizing Merger and Acquisition Value, New York, p 35.

Ernest and Young. (January 2018). Merger and Acquisitions in Turkey 2017. Turkey: EY.
Gerrish, J. (2014). Due diligence—checking out a bank. Banking Exchange. Retrieved from the Banking Exchange website: http://m.bankingexchange.com
GRUNDY A.N. (1992). Corporate Strategy and Financial Decisions, Kogan Page.
GRUNDY Tony (1996). Strategy, Acquisitions and Value, European Management Journal, Vol. 14, No. 2, pp 181–188.
HARVEY Michael G., LUSCH Robert F. (1995). Expanding The Nature and Scope of Due Diligence, Journal of Business Venturing 10, pp 5–21.
KHAN Azeem Ahmad (2011). Merger and Acquisitions (M&As) in the Indian Banking Sector in Post Liberalization Regime, International Journal of Contemporary Business Studies, Vol: 2, No: 11, pp 31–45.
Meglio, O., & Risberg, A. (2009). Mergers and Acquisitions: Time for a Rejuvenation of the Field?.
Meglio, O., & Risberg, A. (2011). The (mis) measurement of M&A performance—A systematic narrative literature review. Scandinavian journal of management, 27(4), 418–433.
RASHID Abdul, NAEEM Nazia (2017). Effects of Mergers on Corporate Performance: An Empirical Evaluation Using OLS and the Empirical Bayesian Methods, Borsa İstanbul Review, 17-1, pp 10–24.
SARIGÜL Haşmet, KURŞUNEL Fahri (2012). Bankacılık Sektöründe Birleşme ve Satın Alma Nedenleri: 2001 – 2011 Türkiye Örnekleri, https://www.researchgate.net/publication/248393000.
Scandinavian Journal of Management (2012).
SPRINGER L. B., (2013). Due Diligence, Journal of The Association of Nurses in Aids Care, Vol. 24, No. 6, pp 469–470.
TISSEN Maria, SNEIDERE Ruta (2014). Due Diligence Matrix for Main User Groups of Financial Analysis, 19th International Scientific Conference; Economics and Management 2014, ICEM 2014, 23–25.
VENNET Rudi Vander (1996). The Effect of Mergers and Acquisitions on the Efficiency and Profitability of EC Credit Institutions, Journal of Banking & Finance 20, pp 1531–1558.
Wen, W., Wang, W. K., & Wang, T. H. (2005). A hybrid knowledge-based decision support system for enterprise mergers and acquisitions. Expert Systems with Applications, 28(3), 569–582.

International Insurance Industry and Systemic Risk

Necla Tunay[1]([✉]), K. Batu Tunay[2], and Nesrin Özataç[3]

[1] Marmara University, Göztepe, Istanbul, Turkey
necla.tunay@marmara.edu.tr
[2] Yildiz Technical University, Maslak, Istanbul, Turkey
btunay@yildiz.edu.tr
[3] Department of Banking and Finance, Eastern Mediterranean University,
Famagusta, North Cyprus, Turkey
nesrin.ozatac@emu.edu.tr

1 Introduction

After the 2008 global crises there has been an increase in the systemic risk. The main reason for the rise in the systemic risk is the role of financial intermediaries. These are the mortgage institutions, commercial banks and investment banks. Moreover, the related studies proved that US finance companies have more effect among others. As well as in USA, Europe and in rest of the World, the large sized insurance companies are themselves systemic risk source and the interactions among have important dynamics. It is widely known that in developed economies, insurance companies have strong bounds among each other.

However, there has been a huge pressure on them during the globalization process. The banking sector as well as the insurance sector indicated a growth in the modern financial system. Global competitiveness caused the bank assurance both nationally and internationally. These developments made the huge insurance companies systemically risky. Recently, the "too big to fail" approach is used for such companies. On the other hand, the other small-sized insurance companies are also part of the systemic risk.

Although the systemic risk of the companies is an important topic, there is a paucity of the related research. The lack of the data is another reason for the limitation of the research in this area. However, there has been a small rise in the number of the studies done on global life and non-life insurance sector's systemic risk level in regard to banking sector.

2 Literature Review

When there is a growth in the insurance companies and their role, the systemic risk rise in regard to it. Deepening in the National insurance sector process global financial pressure was immense. In such process, the insurance companies rise with a systemic

N. Ozatac and K. K. Gökmenoglu (eds.), *Emerging Trends in Banking and Finance*, Springer Proceedings in Business and Economics,
https://doi.org/10.1007/978-3-030-01784-2_15

risk source and the small sized national companies exposed to such risk. There is a plenty number of theoretical and applied studies done in the area of finance especially on the banking sector however, less on the insurance sector. Billio et al. (2012), Bernal et al. (2014), Bierth et al. (2015), Mühlnickel and Weiß (2015), Kanno (2016), Bongini et al. (2017), Chang et al. (2017) are the recent studies done on insurance sector. Among these, Kanno (2016) is the only one that is not based on empirical analysis.

Billio et al. (2012) and Bernal et al. (2014) analysed the systemic risk level of the insurance companies and commercial banks. Billio et al. (2012) analyse insurance companies and hedge funds, banks, brokers and dealers' connectedness and principal components and applied Granger causality tests. The findings indicated that financial intermediaries are linked significantly. It can also be seen that systemic risk level of the insurance sector was rising. The global financial crises increased the effect. The biggest role of the spread of the systemic risk belongs to commercial banks.

Bernal et al. (2014) analysed the significance of the systemic risk of the banking and insurance sector within the financial sector. In order to test the systemic risk measurement using the first level value-at-risk, Kolmogorov-Smirnov test is used basing on bootstrap. The findings indicate that during the period of 2004–2012 where there was a financial distress in the Euro area the systemic risk is of high importance. The role of the banking sector compared to insurance is sector was higher whereas in the USA the insurance sector had a bigger role. The reason is the economic and the financial structural differences in the countries.

Bierth et al. (2015), Mühlnickel and Weiß (2015), Kanno (2016), Bongini et al. (2017) concentrated on the factors that increase the systemic risk on international insurance sector. Bierth et al. (2015) investigated 253 international life and non-life insurance sector's risk exposure and the factors. The findings indicate that international insurance sector's systemic risk level is low. The only period is the crises period where the role of the insurance sector is at peak level on financial sector's vulnerability. The leverage ratio of the insurance companies' is also found to be important factor.

Mühlnickel and Weiß (2015) analysed the 394 acquisition of the insurance sector and the role of the insurance sector's density on systemic risk. The results indicate the concentration on the insurance sector and between the insurance sector and banking sector has a moderate systemic risk positively and significantly. Moreover, the size of the firm, non-financial activities and diversification has an important effect on the systemic risk level. According to the researchers the concentration of the insurance sector is a negative factor causing financial instability. Kanno (2016) analysed non-life insurance companies systemic risk level and global reinsurance sector.

Bongini et al. (2017) investigated the systemic risk level of the insurance sector and the effect on biggest 44 insurance companies. The distance to default and the stock prices are analysed. The regulations and deregulations especially the capital adequacy are analysed. The case studies indicated that the regulations and inventors are ineffective on insurance sector's risk level. The inventors on the insurance sector stocks believe that the moral hazard is an important factor on the insurance sector.

The above studies analysed the case for multicounty data. There are studies done specifically on one country. Chang et al. (2017) investigated Taiwan's systemic risk and the added value of the companies to the risk analysing the marginal expected shortfall, systemic risk index and conditional value-at-risk/CoVaR measures for the years between 2005 and 2015. The basic factors for the systemic risk as well as the non-core activities are found to be the main effects in regard to this.

Bierth et al. (2015), Mühlnickel and WeiB (2015), Bongini et al. (2017) investigated the international insurance sector. The findings indicate the firm size, leverage and non-core activities are the basic effects. However, Chang et al. (2017), the share of the insurance system within the finance sector is important as the firm size. For this reason, the similar result can be seen in the studies done by Billio et al. (2012) and Bernal et al. (2014).

It can be noted that both in national and international insurance sectors have similar patterns in case of systemic risk. Regarding the size of the insurance companies are tending to concentration, high financial leverage and the bounds among insurance companies cause a rise in the systemic risk.

3   Econometric Analysis and the Findings

3.1   Methodology

In the study to measure the systemic risk conditional capital shortfall and conditional value-at-risk/CoVaR are used. The measures are followed from the studies from Bernal et al. (2014), Bierth et al. (2015), Chang et al. (2017). The causality is analysed by using these systemic risk measures of life and non-life insurance and commercial banks. Billio et al. (2012) applied causality test on panel causality. North America, Europe and Advances Asia countries are used and observations are made with panel data set. The geographical spread of systemic risk is aimed to be investigated. The causality between variables is not only for life and non-life insurance companies but also for commercial banks. The relation is given with an equation stated below:

$$y_{it} = \left(\Delta LI_{it}, \Delta NLI_{it}, \Delta BNK_{it}\right)' \tag{1}$$

Equation (1) ΔLI_{it} represents the life insurance companies, ΔNLI_{it} non-life insurance companies and ΔBNK_{it} represents bank's alternative systemic risk. i data is the geographical area and t represents time.

In the analysis Dumitrescu-Hurlin tests (Dumitrescu and Hurlin 2012) are used. Although Granger (1969) is developed to use the causality time series, it can also be used for cross-section and time dimensions. Holtz-Eakin et al. (1988), Hurlin and Venet (2001), Hurlin (2004, 2005) developed the panel Granger test, and unlike Granger test can test non-causality. Panel Granger test provides some advantages. Such as Dynamics and aggregation bias (Lin and Ali 2009).

Linear panel data model can test the causality between two variables given below:

$$y_{it} = \alpha_i + \sum_{k=1}^{K} \gamma^{(k)} y_{it-k} + \sum_{k=1}^{K} \beta^{(k)} x_{it-k} + \varepsilon_{it} \tag{2}$$

α_i i individual effect on cross section, $\gamma^{(k)}$ and $\beta^{(k)}$ coefficients are accepted as constant at t-cross section.

$$y_{it} = \alpha_i + \sum_{k=1}^{K} \gamma_i^{(k)} y_{it-k} + \sum_{k=1}^{K} \beta_i^{(k)} x_{it-k} + \varepsilon_{it} \tag{3}$$

In the equation above $\gamma_i^{(k)}$ and $\beta_i^{(k)}$ coefficients for each i unit or cross-section can be changed. Hurlin (2004), i = 1, …, N units for the standard homogenous panel units for standard homogenous panel Granger test combines average individual Wald statistics.

3.2 Data Set

The data is taken from IMF Global Financial Stability Report: Potent Policies for a Successful Normalization 2016. The weekly frequencies between the periods of 30.12.2005 and 23.10.2015 513 observation number for North America, Europe and Advanced Asia. When Life and non-life insurance companies and conditional capital inadequacy and value at risk are taken into consideration the number of observations is six therefore the total observation number is 9234.

3.3 Findings

In the study, two step econometric analyses are used. At first, the stationary of the variables is tested by panel unit tests. In this regard, ADF-Fisher panel unit root tests were applied as "t" developed by Levin, Lin and Chu (2002), "Im" by Im, Pesaran and Shin (2003) and "W" by Choi (2001). The results of the findings are given in Table 1. It can be observed that conditional capital shortfall for banks and life insurance companies and conditional value at risk for non life insurance companies are not stationary at their level. However, the rest of the variables are stationary at their level. Bernal et al. (2014), Bierth et al. (2015), Chang et al. (2017) in their studies accept the first difference of the conditional value at first difference for the systemic risk measure. When the conditional capital shortfall of the non-life insurance sectors measures taken at first level, it is found at stationary and in the second phase of the study the difference of all the variables are used.

In the second stage of the analysis, Dumitrescu-Hurlin panel causality tests were used. The results can be seen Tables 2 and 3. There is bidirectional causality between nonlife insurance companies to commercial banks. There is no causality among others.

The tests on conditional value at risk indicate that between banks and insurance companies and between insurance companies there can be seen causality (Table 3). Between insurance companies there is unidirectional whereas between banks and insurance companies there is bidirectional causality can be seen.

Table 1. Panel unit root tests

	Conditional capital shortfall						CoVaR					
	Banks		Life Insurance Com.		Non-life Insur. Com.		Banks		Life Insurance Com.		Non-life Insur. Com.	
	Statistic	Prob. ***	Statistic	Prob. ***	Statistic	Prob. ***	Statistic	Prob. ***	Statistic	Prob. ***	Statistic	Prob. ***
Panel A—Level												
Levin, Lin & Chu t*	−1.351	0.088	−0.394	0.347	−1.938	0.026	−1.423	0.077	−1.100	0.136	−0.174	0.431
Im, Pesaran and Shin W-stat**	−0.831	0.203	−0.003	0.499	−10.554	0.000	−2.498	0.006	−2.335	0.010	−0.820	0.206
ADF—Fisher Chi-square**	6.929	0.328	5.023	0.541	156.902	0.000	16.937	0.010	15.483	0.017	8.526	0.202
PP—Fisher Chi-square**	51.840	0.000	5.418	0.491	157.438	0.000	20.735	0.002	20.317	0.002	10.170	0.118
Lags	5		0		0		4		4		4	
Panel B—1st Difference												
Levin, Lin & Chu t*	−40.887	0.000	−48.624	0.000	−18.210	0.000	−44.803	0.000	−44.574	0.000	−20.731	0.000
Im, Pesaran and Shin W-stat**	−38.360	0.000	−41.091	0.000	−31.154	0.000	−36.296	0.000	−36.289	0.000	−22.888	0.000
ADF—Fisher Chi-square**	485.238	0.000	510.408	0.000	429.731	0.000	406.106	0.000	406.833	0.000	345.764	0.000
PP—Fisher Chi-square**	350.960	0.000	510.429	0.000	351.948	0.000	375.449	0.000	390.301	0.000	401.912	0.000
Lags	4		0		6		3		3		2	

*H_0: Assumes common unit root process

**H_0: Assumes common unit root process

***Probabilities for Fisher tests are computed using an asymptotic Chi-square distribution. All other tests assume asymptotic normality

Table 2. Dumitrescu-Hurlin panel causality tests: conditional capital shortfall

Null hypothesis	Lags: 1			Lags: 2			Lags: 3			Lags: 4			Lags: 5		
	W-Stat.	Zbar-Stat.	Prob.	W-Stat.	Zbar-Stat.	Prob.	W-Stat.	Zbar-Stat.	Prob.	W-Stat.	Zbar-Stat.	Prob.	W-Stat.	Zbar-Stat.	Prob.
ΔLI $\to$ ΔBNK	0.8071	−0.2394	0.8108	1.4619	−0.4691	0.6390	2.1871	−0.5781	0.5632	3.4910	−0.3184	0.7502	5.6587	0.3458	0.7295
ΔBNK $\to$ ΔLI	1.1745	0.2074	0.8357	2.5664	0.4798	0.6314	2.7905	−0.1552	0.8767	3.8226	−0.1173	0.9066	4.6670	−0.1913	0.8483
ΔNLI $\to$ ΔBNK	0.8507	−0.1864	0.8521	**4.6784**	**2.2944**	**0.0218**	**6.0909**	**2.1576**	**0.0310**	**8.4753**	**2.7034**	**0.0069**	**11.4433**	**3.4792**	**0.0005**
ΔBNK $\to$ ΔNLI	1.3846	0.4630	0.6434	2.0746	0.0572	0.9544	4.0060	0.6966	0.4861	5.9320	1.1615	0.2454	**9.0605**	**2.1885**	**0.0286**
ΔNLI $\to$ ΔLI	0.3944	−0.7414	0.4584	2.0983	0.0776	0.9382	3.4433	0.3022	0.7625	4.9879	0.5892	0.5558	7.1581	1.1580	0.2469
ΔLI $\to$ ΔNLI	2.4354	1.7411	0.0817	2.7424	0.6310	0.5281	2.7825	−0.1608	0.8722	3.2227	−0.4810	0.6305	3.8001	−0.6609	0.5087

Significant test values at 5% and above were shown in bold

Table 3. Dumitrescu-Hurlin panel causality tests: conditional VaR

Null hypothesis	Lags: 1			Lags: 2			Lags: 3			Lags: 4			Lags: 5		
	W-Stat.	Zbar-Stat.	Prob.	W-Stat.	Zbar-Stat.	Prob.	W-Stat.	Zbar-Stat.	Prob.	W-Stat.	Zbar-Stat.	Prob.	W-Stat.	Zbar-Stat.	Prob.
ΔLI → ΔBNK	0.9968	−0.0087	0.9931	**30.9782**	**24.8905**	**0.0000**	**42.3509**	**27.5679**	**0.0000**	**52.5807**	**29.4425**	**0.0000**	**60.9890**	**30.3168**	**0.0000**
ΔBNK → ΔLI	1.7622	0.9223	0.3564	**24.0120**	**18.9053**	**0.0000**	**34.0973**	**21.7840**	**0.0000**	**38.2003**	**20.7244**	**0.0000**	**45.9338**	**22.1618**	**0.0000**
ΔNLI → ΔBNK	**4.9595**	**4.8112**	**0.0000**	**29.8792**	**23.9463**	**0.0000**	**46.2202**	**30.2795**	**0.0000**	**50.2464**	**28.0273**	**0.0000**	**55.3900**	**27.2840**	**0.0000**
ΔBNK → ΔNLI	2.2405	1.5040	0.1326	**23.1376**	**18.1540**	**0.0000**	**34.4102**	**22.0032**	**0.0000**	**37.2253**	**20.1332**	**0.0000**	**40.1690**	**19.0392**	**0.0000**
ΔNLI → ΔLI	**3.3224**	**2.8199**	**0.0048**	**15.8540**	**11.8961**	**0.0000**	**22.5070**	**13.6617**	**0.0000**	**25.1187**	**12.7935**	**0.0000**	**27.1616**	**11.9934**	**0.0000**
ΔLI → ΔNLI	**3.6685**	**3.2409**	**0.0012**	**15.2324**	**11.3621**	**0.0000**	**21.8515**	**13.2024**	**0.0000**	**25.7220**	**13.1593**	**0.0000**	**26.6230**	**11.7016**	**0.0000**

Significant test values at 5% and above were shown in bold

4 Conclusion

In the study, the causality of the systemic risk of life insurance and non-life insurance companies and the commercial banks of North America, Europe and developed Asia countries is analysed. Capital inadequacy and value-at-risk is used for systemic risk. The weekly data set is used for the years 2005–2015. As a method for the analysis, Dumitrescu-Hurlin panel causality test is used. The target is to find out if there is a bi-directional causality of the systemic risk for the life and non-life insurance companies and commercial banks. In the recent literature, the studies that are done on the systemic risk on the banking sector indicate that the banks have dominant influence within the system. The effect of the banking sector can be seen on the insurance sector as well. For this reason, the banking sector is included in the analysis.

The findings indicate that there is significant bidirectional causality between insurance sector and the banking sector when the value at risk is taken as systemic risk. When the conditional capital adequacy is taken as the systemic risk, it can be seen that the causality is uni-directional from life insurance companies to the banking sector. The results prove that the systemic risk in the insurance sector is bi-directional. As the data set is formed from the insurance sector from three different continents, it also shows the potential spread of the systemic risk globally. The findings are similar to the recent studies in the literature. In different regions there is different financial intermediaries' systemic risk have strong bounds indicating the importance of systemic risk in the case of financial stability. The regulatory authorities started to use "too systematic to fail" approach and trying to have precautions for the matter. It should also be noted that the policy makers should also focus on the insurance sector not only on the banking sector for the case.

References

Bernal, Oscar, Gnabo, Jean-Yves, and Guilmin, Gregory. (2014). "Assessing the contribution of banks, insurance and other financial services to systemic risk". Journal of Banking & Finance, 47, 270–287.

Bierth, Christopher, Irresberger, Felix, and WeiB, Gregor N.F. (2015). "Systemic risk of insurers around the globe". Journal of Banking & Finance, 55, 232–245.

Billio, Monica, Getmansky, Mila, Lo, Andrew W., and Pelizzon, Loriana. (2012). "Econometric measures of connectedness and systemic risk in the finance and insurance sectors". Journal of Financial Economics, 104, 535–559.

Bongini, Paola, Nieri, Laura, Pelagatti, Matteo and Piccini, Andrea. (2017). "Curbing systemic risk in the insurance sector: A mission impossible?". The British Accounting Review, 49, 256–273.

Chang, Carolyn W., Li, Xiaodan, Lin, Edward M.H. and Yu, Min-Teh. (2017). "Systemic risk, interconnectedness, and non-core activities in Taiwan insurance industry". International Review of Economics and Finance, 1–12 (forthcoming).

Choi, In. (2001). "Unit Root Tests for Panel Data". Journal of International Money and Finance, 20(2), 249–272.

Dumitrescu, Elena-Ivona, Hurlin, Christophe. (2012). "Testing for Granger non-causality in heterogeneous panels". Economic Modelling, 29(4), 1450–1460.

Granger, C.W.J. (1969). "Investigating Causal Relations by Econometric Models and Cross-spectral Methods". Econometrica, 37(3), 424–438.

Im, Kyung So, Pesaran, M. Hashem, and Shin, Yongcheol. (2003). "Testing for unit roots in heterogeneous panels". Journal of Econometrics, 115(1), 53–74.

Holtz-Eakin, Douglas; Newey, Whitney and Rosen, Harvey S. (1988). "Estimating Vector Autoregressions with Panel Data". Econometrica, 56(6), 1371–1395.

Hurlin, Christophe. (2004). "Testing Granger causality in heterogeneous panel data models with fixed coefficients". Mimeo, University Paris IX.

Hurlin, Christophe. (2005). "Un test simple de l'hypothese de non-causalite dans un modele de panel heterogene". Revue Economique, 56(3), 799–809.

Hurlin, Christophe, and Venet, Baptiste. (2001). "Granger causality tests in panel data models with fixed coefficients". Mimeo, University Paris IX.

Kanno, Masayasu. (2016). "The network structure and systemic risk in the global non-life insurance market, Insurance". Mathematics and Economics, 67, 38–53.

Levin, Andrew, Lin, Chien-Fu, and Chu, C.S. James. (2002). "Unit Root Tests in Panel Data: Asymptotic and Finite-Sample Properties". Journal of Econometrics 108(1), 1–24.

Lin, Eric S. and Ali, Hamid E. (2009). Military spending and inequality: Panel Granger casuality test. MRPA Papers, No. 40159, July.

Mühlnickel, Janina ve WeiB, Gregor N.F. (2015). "Consolidation and systemic risk in the international insurance industry". Journal of Financial Stability, 18, 187–202.

Bounds of Macrofinance and the Quality of Credit Portfolio in Emerging Economies

K. Batu Tunay[1]($\boxtimes$), Necla Tunay[2], and Nesrin Özataç[3]

[1] Yildiz Technical University, Maslak, Istanbul, Turkey
btunay@yildiz.edu.tr
[2] Marmara University, Göztepe, Istanbul, Turkey
necla.tunay@marmara.edu.tr
[3] Department of Banking and Finance, Eastern Mediterranean University,
Famagusta, Northern Cyprus
Nesrin.ozatac@emu.edu.tr

1 Introduction

The principles that the banks apply in portfolio management, portfolio assessment and the quality of the credits as well as the period for providing the credits are the main components. Inevitably, the different types of credits have different risk levels. The components for the credit portfolio is related with the risk level of the credits included. Moreover, the targets for the growth and the reflection of the credit enlargement portfolio strategy has an impact on the components of the portfolio. The general risk is that the credit portfolio measurement is at the risk level when each credit is taken into account. The risk level for each customer and the business is related with the environment they are exposed to; the credit risk market tendency and macroeconomic conditions. As it is well known that bank credit customers' risks can be previsioned and be managed, however, the tendency for the credit risk and the effect of the general economic conditions can be not be foreseen.

The tendency for the credit market and credit pricing decisions have important effects on the credit portfolio components. The market dynamics have an impact on the credit nonperformance as well as on the profit margin. However, the direct and the most important effect is on credit ratios, that is to say on the pricing process. In a competitive credit market, each bank has an access to market ratios. In a less competitive market, especially in an oligopolistic bank market due to the secretive agreements the bank market leader will be placed as the price dealer. A bank should offer an interest rate in regard to the market interest rate.

Macroeconomic conditions and the effect of the economic variables also have huge impact as well as on the credit market conditions thus on bank credits. The economic conditions during the credit offering process are less selective and easy to an extend. Then there can be a decline in the economic activities. The banks naturally tend to provide less credits and be more selective. This is to protect themselves from any risk that can happen to their portfolio.

Within all these Dynamics the banks assess their portfolio according to the weighted average risk of their assets. The size of their portfolio is decided according to

N. Ozatac and K. K. Gökmenoglu (eds.), *Emerging Trends in Banking and Finance*, Springer Proceedings in Business and Economics,
https://doi.org/10.1007/978-3-030-01784-2_16

the conditions in credit market and the macroeconomic development and also the credit products. Generally, the sectors with more growth pace, with less liquidity problems and high profitability ratios have larger part in the loan portfolios. However, during the periods where banks have struggle with their competitors have more agressive strategies. That makes the quality of the loans and the loan portfolios making the overall credit risk to rise.

Along with these identifications and the evaluations, there is a general agreement on credit quality where there are macroeconomic and macrofinancial effects. The starting point is to an extend within an interaction between the credit quality and the macrofinancial variables. For this reason, in recent times a similar study is done with panel VAR (PVAR) methodology by Dumitrescu and Hurlin (2012) causality test.

2 Literature Review

The subject of financial variables along with macro financial interaction has recently been discussed. The progress is inevitably due to the 2008 crises. Along with the Global crises, it is believed that the credits have special cases in the related matter. The 2007 USA mortgage crises as a starting point of the credit crunch, bank credit portfolio and the quality started to be more crucial. The bank credits and the portfolios are influenced by the credit customers, the financial performance of the credit customers, the credit market Dynamics and macroeconomic variables.

Several studies after the crises are analyzed by macrofinancial interactions directly or indirectly (Sun 2010). Some scholars investigate the macrofinancial interactions with the financial stability, the fragility of the financial companies. According to Sun (2010), it is the financial fragility, to Bellego and Ferrara (2012) it is the cyclical Dynamics of the financial variables, to Gerke et al. (2013) financial shocks, to Lama and Rabanal (2014) it is the monetary dynamics. For the Euro Area, the macroeconomic variables as well as the financial variables have effect on economic cycles and make a dynamic structure (Bellego ve Ferrara 2012). It is also clear that for the Euro area to have the monetary union sustainable it is important to have a stable macroeconomy and financial system (Lama ve Rabanal 2014).

Apart from these studies, De Haas et al. (2010), Filip (2015), Böninghausen and Köhler (2015) also investigated and pointed out that credits have important effect on macro-financial interactions. De Haas et al. (2010) in their study for 20 transition countries on 220 banks found that bank governance, bank size and the legal creditor protection are the most important variables. Moreover, the foreign banks have an active role in mortgage loans.

Filip (2015) analyzed macro economic variables and investigated the role of GDP growth, inflation and unemployment rate on non-performing loans. There is a negative relation between NPL and growth, on the other hand positive relation between inflation and unemployment.

The use of growing global operations made it possible to have international diversified credit portfolios. Böninghausen and Köhler (2015) using German bank data investigated why the German banking system is concentrated on certain countries.

The conclusion is that they preferred to have a portfolio of countries that are more developed, institutionally structured and with strong banking regulations.

Tunay (2016a, b) for the study between 2004 and 2014, pointed out that the quality of the bank credits have strong interactions with macro-financial variables. That is to say economic and financial shocks cause the credit quality to go down making the banking system to be fragile. The missing competitive conditions that are valid in the Turkish banking sector made the credit quality of the domestic bank quality well as the foreign banks to diminish.

3   3   Econometric Analysis

3.1   Methodology: Panel VAR Models

In this study, panel vector autoregression/PVAR methodology is used. PVAR models have the same structure as VAR models. It is accepted that all the variables are endogenous and interdependent. The only difference is with the traditional VAR model that is the representation that the cross sectional dimension is included. In addition to traditional VAR models, it makes it possible for unobserved individual heterogeneity (Love and Zicchino 2006; Canova and Ciccarelli 2014).

A first-order panel VAR model can be described as given below (Love and Zicchino 2006):

$$y_{it} = A_{0,i} + A_{1,i} y_{it-1} + f_i + d_{c,t} + u_t \tag{1}$$

the equation numbered (1) y_{it} i (i = 1, …, N) group (or intersection) for t (t = 1, …, T) time is the dependent variable vector. In this equation f_i is used as fixed effects, and the variables at level is described as individual heterogeneity. In order to prevent to have the biased coefficients the mean-differencing procedure was used.

Two different approaches are used for the assumptions. The first one is developed by Love and Zicchino (2006) that is similar to the dynamic panel data model. Love and Zicchino (2006), Arellano and Bover (1995) suggested Helmert approach which is based on forward mean differencing preventing orthogonality.

The second approach is developed by Cagala and Glogowsky (2012, 2014). The assumption period is easier compared to the first one. The PVAR estimations represented by a least square of a dummy variable. In this model each depended variable is estimated with the other variables lags. Love and Zicchino (2006) estimated action and reaction functions by Monte-Carlo simulations where as, Cagala and Glogowsky (2012, 2014) applied bootstrap methodology. For more detailed explanations the studies of Cagala et al. (2017), Glogowsky et al. (2014) can be reviewed.

The causality between variables are going to be investigated by Dumitrescu and Hurlin (2012) tests:

$$y_{it} = \alpha_i + \sum_{k=1}^{K} \gamma_i^{(k)} y_{it-k} + \sum_{k=1}^{K} \beta_i^{(k)} x_{it-k} + \varepsilon_{it} \tag{2}$$

In the equation above $\gamma_i^{(k)}$ and $\beta_i^{(k)}$ coefficients can be changed for each i unit. Hurlin (2004) that is for i = 1, ..., N units combined standard homogenous panel Granger test with average individual Wald statistics. Hurlin (2005) in his study developed his application for unbalanced panel set Dumitrescu and Hurlin (2012), for the heterogenous panel data set developed Granger tests.

In this study, we followed Love and Ariss (2013, 2014) model. However, the model is derived due to different variables that is given below:

$$y_{it} = (crdqual_{it}, crd_{it}, crdgap_{it}, ir_{it}, \inf_{it}, grw_{it}, ca_{it}) \tag{3}$$

$crdqual_{it}$ represents credit quality. In the model non-performing loans/npl_{it} is accepted as the function of the provisions/$prov_{it}$. In the equation crd_{it} is the credit to private sector, $crdgap_{it}$ is the credit to-GDP gap ratio suggested by BIS to measure the systemic risk), ir_{it} is the real average interest rates, inf_{it} is the inflation rate, grw_{it} is the growth rate, ca_{it} is the budget deficit. The countries in the analysis are the ones with high growth rate with structural economic problems with inflation pressure and chronic budget deficit.

The bank credit portfolios and profitability should be structured at maximum level. An efficient credit portfolio, bank liquidity, financial performance and sustainable growth strategically important. Bank credits as they are risky assets, "credit quality" means a performing (Filip 2015). In literature, Love and Ariss (2013, 2014) approach followed by the credit portfolio quality, non-performing loans to total loans. However, in our study a composite variable is used by credit that is provisions for nonperforming loans and total nonperforming loans to total credits with weighted averages:

$$crdqual_{it} = \frac{1}{2} \left(\frac{npl_{it}}{crd_{it}} + \frac{prov_{it}}{npl_{it}} \right) \tag{4}$$

3.2 Data Set

The data set is taken from Morgan Stanley and Capital Group International/MSCI for the 23 emerging countries that are indexed. The common characteristics for these countries is due to high growth rate and relatively low investment opportunities. Despite high inflation, chronic budget deficit and foreign capital investment need such countries had acceptable performance during 2008 crises (Table 6).

The number of observation is 3312 for 23 countries for the years between 1998 and 2015. The definition of the variables and the data source are presented in Table 1 and the descriptive statistics in Table 2.

Table 1. Varible definitions and sources

Variables	Definition	Data source
Npl	Bank nonperforming loans to gross loans	World Bank Global Financial Development Database, 2017
Pnpl	Provisions to nonperforming loans	World Bank Global Financial Development Database, 2017
Crd	Private credit by deposit money banks to GDP (%)	World Bank Global Financial Development Database, 2017
crdgap	Credit-to-GDP gap	World Bank Global Financial Development Database, 2017
İr	Real interest rate	World Bank Global Financial Development Database, 2017
İnf	Inflation, average consumer prices	IMF, World Economic Outlook Database, October 2017
Grw	Gross domestic product, constant prices (percent change)	IMF, World Economic Outlook Database, October 2017
Ca	Current account balance	IMF, World Economic Outlook Database, October 2017

Table 2. Descriptive statistics

	crdqual	crd	crdgap	ri	grw	inf	ca
Mean	4.238	5.086	0.000	5.889	4.303	6.165	0.905
Median	3.849	4.239	−0.109	4.015	4.386	4.204	−0.534
Maximum	1.419	1.659	2.614	7.762	2.617	8.574	3.319
Minimum	0.000	0.000	−1.741	−2.460	−1.313	−4.876	−2.107
Std. Dev.	2.412	3.241	4.880	1.020	3.944	8.856	6.757
Skewness	0.000	1.036	0.000	2.746	0.000	5.737	1.452
Kurtosis	3.978	3.339	7.562	1.522	7.703	4.395	6.971
Jarque-Bera	669.306	760.539	403.166	309.548	381.904	312.030	417.433
Probability	0.000	0.000	0.000	0.000	0.000	0.000	0.000

3.3   Empirical Findings

At the first level, the stationarity of the variables is tested by Levin, Lin and Chu (2002) as "t", Im, Pesaran and Shin (2003) as "W" and finally by Choi (2001) "ADF-Fisher" panel unit root tests. The results are presented in Table 3. It can be seen that all the variables are stationary at their level.

In the second phase of the analysis, panel VAR estimation is applied and action and reaction functions are measured. Table 4 provides the Panel VAR analysis. In regard to this PVAR(4) model coefficient to Cagala and Glogowsky' (2012) approach with fixed effects estimator. The action reaction functions are estimated and given in Graphics 1 and Graphics 2.

Table 3. Panel unit-root tests

	crdqual		crd		crdgap		ir	
	Test	p Value***	Test	p Value***	Test	p Value***	Test	p Value***
Levin, Lin & Chu t*	−3.531	0.000	−1.205	0.000	−6.724	0.000	−10.572	0.000
Im, Pesaran and Shin W-stat **	−2.497	0.006	−8.144	0.000	−7.961	0.000	−10.156	0.000
ADF—Fisher Chi-square**	7.127	0.010	1.385	0.000	14.736	0.000	17.474	0.000
PP—Fisher Chi-square**	7.798	0.002	1.506	0.000	9.150	0.000	25.970	0.000
Lag	2		3		3		2	
	grw		inf		ca			
	Test	p Value***	Test	p Value***	Test	p Value***		
Levin, Lin & Chu t*	−18.933	0.000	−11.653	0.000	−35.035	0.000		
Im, Pesaran and Shin W-stat **	−12.553	0.000	−96.361	0.000	−34.910	0.000		
ADF—Fisher Chi-square**	43.751	0.000	21.111	0.000	82.703	0.001		
PP—Fisher Chi-square**	67.554	0.000	31.776	0.000	64.143	0.040		
Lag	3		2		3			

* Null: Unit root (assumes common unit root process)

** Null: Unit root (assumes individual unit root process)

*** Probabilities for Fisher tests are computed using an asymptotic Chi-square distribution. All other tests assume asymptotic normality

Table 4. Lag length tests

Lag	Log.Likelihood	L.L.R.	F.P.E.	A.I.C.	S.I.C.	H-Q I.C.
1	*−8078.25	–	1.4E+10	41.6074	41.4431	41.5768
2	−6571.68	3013.13	2.89E+08	36.2863	35.9564	36.2225
3	−5602.94	*1937.47	7.15E+07	33.3735	32.8534	33.2688
4	−2024.53	7156.82	*1.246910	*13.8356	*13.0948	*13.6801

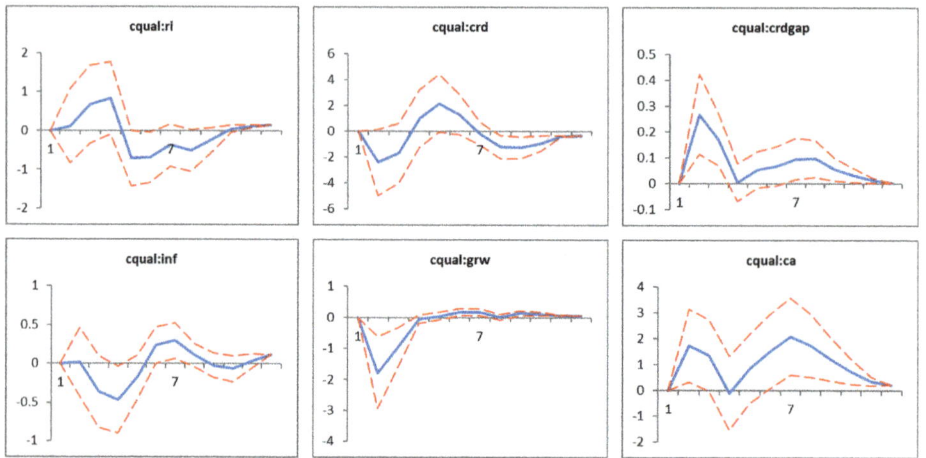

Graph 1. Credit quality response to macro financial shocks

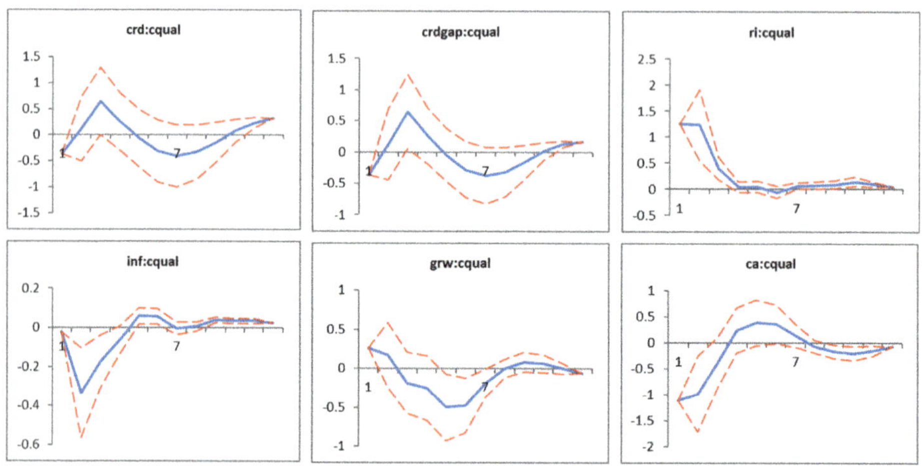

Graph 2. Macro financial variables responses to credit quality shock

Action-reaction functions on credit shocks and systemic risk that is reflected as credit-to GDP gap indicates that the effect on the credit quality is not long-run. The growth and the budget deficit cause a low quality on the credit quality in the long run. When the credit quality shocks are analyzed apart from the growth the long run effect will be appear. When there is a procyclical variables macro financial interactions will be strong.

When the results are analyzed (Table 4). It can be seen that credit quality except growth has bidirectional causality. On the other hand, it can be seen that credit quality and growth have unidirectional sustainable causality (Table 5).

The results of the study indicate that the credit quality is related with the credit-to-GDP gap and besides real interest the macroeconomic variables such as growth, inflation and current deficit are of high importance. During the economic growth, it is observed that credit volume and systemic risk in the banking sector where it causes a contraction in credit-to-GDP gap with a decline in the interest rates and an increase in the credit quality.

In such a period, the sustainability of the current deficit gap (assuming it will not be balanced) as well as the chronical inflationist pressure will go up. However, if the economy will start to shrink all the macrofinancial variables will be influenced negatively causing the credit quality to decline. As the credits indicate a high cyclicality, the credit quality inevitably indicate a similar tendency. Hence, as it is proposed in Basel III counter-cyclical capital buffer applications can be considered as of high effectiveness level.

Table 5. Demitrescu-Hurlin tests

	Lag 1			Lag 2			Lag 3		
	W Test	Z Test	p Value	W Test	Z Test	p Value	W Test	Z Test	p Value
cqual → crd	2.3894	3.1172	0.0018	3.8844	2.2537	0.0242	5.8111	1.7730	0.0762
crd → cqual	7.3256	15.7013	0.0000	7.8360	8.4381	0.0000	11.1723	7.0212	0.0000
cqual → crdgap	2.2751	2.8258	0.0047	3.1801	1.1514	0.2496	5.3668	1.3380	0.1809
crdgap → cqual	2.4798	3.3475	0.0008	7.1788	7.4097	0.0000	8.2509	4.1614	0.0000
cqual → ri	0.6913	−1.2120	0.2255	−3.3011	−3.8258	0.0001	−4.4499	−3.9158	0.0001
ri → cqual	−2.4521	−2.9742	0.0029	−3.8921	−2.2656	0.0366	−5.0198	−0.9983	0.4438
cqual → inf	4.0087	7.2455	0.0000	5.3318	4.5190	0.0000	6.6130	2.5580	0.0105
inf → cqual	1.7213	1.4139	0.1574	4.6561	3.4614	0.0005	7.3499	3.2794	0.0010
cqual → grw	1.1204	−0.1179	0.9061	2.5368	0.1445	0.8851	2.9556	−1.0224	0.3066
grw → cqual	2.0954	2.3676	0.0179	4.4478	3.1355	0.0017	5.7997	1.7618	0.0781
cqual → ca	1.8574	1.7609	0.0783	4.9615	3.9394	0.0001	6.0454	2.0023	0.0453
ca → cqual	1.9940	2.1091	0.0349	2.4684	0.0374	0.9701	3.0298	−0.9498	0.3422

Note → Casuality directions

4 Results

In this study, the interactions between the credit quality and macro financial links are investigated for 23 raising economies where there are some structural economic problems. In the analysis panel VAR models and also Dumitrescu-Hurlin panel causality tests are applied. The results indicate that credit quality, credit volume, credit-to-GDP gap, real interest rate, inflation rate and current account deficit are all interacted. The relation between credit quality and the growth has a one way relation. The credit amount, credit budget, growth and current account deficit are sensitive in case of shocks. The countries that are investigated have chronic current account deficit and the growth period have the same causality with a larger effect in regard to external sources. For this reason, current account deficit and growth based shock cause deep effect on such economies. Likewise the credit volume and credit deficit, the banking system variables show high cyclicality and growth Dynamics.

The results indicate that in rising economies bank credits and the bank quality are sensitive to the economic tendency volume however such sensitivity have higher effect on such economies rather than on developed economies. Chronic structural economic problems and external funding dependency make such economies to have negative results with the shocks and make them become more fragile. For this reason, financial shocks and economic contraction cause macro financial variables to change rapidly. In such a period, the fall in the credit quality and the nonperforming loans can be experienced. Today, macroeconomic and financial variables have strong interdependency on shocks trying to eliminate the structural problems especially if they can manage to have a strategy based on saving with slower growth rate.

Annex

See Table 6.

Table 6. Countries in samples

Brazil	Mexico
Chile	Pakistan
China	Peru
Colombia	Philippines
Czech Republic	Poland
Egypt, Arab Rep.	Qatar
Greece	Russian Federation
Hungary	South Africa
India	Thailand
Indonesia	Turkey
Korea, Rep.	United Arab Emirates
Malaysia	

References

Arellano, Manuel ve Bover, Olympia. (1995). "Another Look at the Instrumental Variable Estimation of Error-components Models", Journal of Econometrics, 68, 29–51.

Bellego, C. ve Ferrara, L. (2012). "Macro-financial Linkages and Business Cycles: A Factor Augmented Probit Approach", Economic Modelling, 29(5): 1793–1797.

Böninghausen, B. ve Köhler, M. (2015). "Diversification and Determinants of International Credit Portfolios: Evidence from German Banks", International Review of Economics and Finance, 39: 57–75.

Canova, Fabio, Ciccarelli, Matteo. (2014). "Panel Vector Autoregressive Models: A survey", Advances in Econometrics, 32, 205–246.

Cagala, Tobias ve Glogowsky, Ulrich. (2012). "Panel Vector Autoregressions for Stata (xtvar)", October, Friedrich-Alexander University of Erlangen-Nuremberg.

Cagala, Tobias ve Glogowsky, Ulrich. (2014). "XTVAR: Stata Module to Compute Panel Vector Autoregression", Statistical Software Components S457944, Boston College Department of Economics, Revised 02 April 2015.

Cagala, Tobias, Glogowsky, Ulrich, Grimm, Veronika ve Rincke, Johannes. (2017). "Public Goods Provision with Rent-Extracting Administrators", CESifo Working Paper Series 6801, CESifo Group Munich.

Choi, In. (2001). "Unit Root Tests for Panel Data", Journal of International Money and Finance, 20(2), 249–272.

De Haas, R., Ferreira, D. ve Taci, A. (2010). "What Determines the Composition of Banks' Loan Portfolios? Evidence from Transition Countries", Journal of Banking and Finance, 34: 388–398.

Dumitrescu, Elena-Ivona, Hurlin, Christophe. (2012). "Testing for Granger non-causality in heterogeneous panels". Economic Modelling, 29(4), 1450–1460.

Filip, B.F. (2015). "The Quality of Bank Loans within the Framework of Globalization", Procedia – Economics and Finance, 20: 208–217.

Gerke, R., Jonsson, M., Kliem, M., Kolasa, M., Lafourcade, P., Locarno, A., Makarski, K. ve McAdam, P. (2013). "Assessing Macro-financial Linkages: A Model Comparison Exercise", Economic Modelling, 31: 253–264.

Glogowsky, Ulrich, Cagala, Tobias, Rincke, Johannes ve Grimm, Veronika. (2014). "Cooperation and Trustworthiness in Repeated Interaction," Annual Conference 2014 (Hamburg): Evidence-based Economic Policy 100437, Verein für Socialpolitik/German Economic Association.

Hurlin, Christophe. (2004). "Testing Granger causality in heterogeneous panel data models with fixed coefficients". Mimeo, University Paris IX.

Hurlin, Christophe. (2005). "Un test simple de l'hypothese de non-causalite dans un modele de panel heterogene". Revue Economique, 56(3), 799–809.

Im, Kyung So, Pesaran, M. Hashem, and Shin, Yongcheol. (2003). "Testing for unit roots in heterogeneous panels". Journal of Econometrics, 115(1), 53–74.

Lama, R. ve Rabanal, P. (2014). "Deciding to Enter a Monetary Union: The Role of Trade and Financial Linkages", European Economic Review, 72: 138–165.

Levin, Andrew, Lin, Chien-Fu, and Chu, C. S. James. (2002). "Unit Root Tests in Panel Data: Asymptotic and Finite-Sample Properties", Journal of Econometrics 108(1), 1–24.

Love, I. ve Ariss, R. T. (2013). "Macro-financial Linkages in Egypt: A Panel Analysis of Economic Shocks and Loan Portfolio Quality", IMF Working Paper, No: WP/12/271.

Love, I. ve Ariss, R. T. (2014). "Macro-financial Linkages in Egypt: A Panel Analysis of Economic Shocks and Loan Portfolio Quality", Journal of International Financial Markets, Institutions and Money, 28: 158–181.

Love, Inessa ve Zicchino, Lea. (2006). "Financial Development and Dynamic Investment Behavior: Evidence from Panel VAR", The Quarterly Review of Economics and Finance, 46, 190–210.

Sun, T. (2010). "Identifying Vulnerabilities in Systemically Important Financial Institutions in a Macro-Financial Linkages Framework", Journal of Economic Asymmetries, 7(2): 77–103.

Tunay, K. Batu. (2016a). "The Determinants of Loan Portfolio Quality and the Role of Macro-Financial Linkages", Finans Politik & Ekonomik Yorumlar, 53(616), 49–60 (in Turkish).

Tunay, K. Batu. (2016b). "Macro-Financial Linkages and Its Effects to Loan Portfolio Quality", Journal of Management and Economics Research, 14(4), 25–44 (in Turkish).

Profitability Determinants of Islamic and Conventional Banks During the Global Financial Crises: The Case of Emerging Markets

Alimshan Faizulayev[✉] and Eralp Bektas

Department of Banking and Finance, Eastern Mediterranean University, Famagusta, North Cyprus, Turkey
{alimshan.faizulayev, eralp.bektas}@emu.edu.tr

1 Introduction

Nowadays the banks play a significant role in our society, and it is not even possible to imagine the life without banks, in other words the banks have become a blood vein of our economy. In order to stimulate the economy of any specific country the government does this via banking system by using "Monetary Tools". Moreover, all of the finance and business transactions that we are being involved in are done through the banks. The first establishment of conventional bank was with no interest, and then it was added and has become the main source of earnings of banking system.

In addition to, many alternatives viewed in contrast to Conventional Banking System but only one is reflected as an optimum option in the horizon that may replace Conventional Banking System (CB System) which is Islamic Banking System (IB System). Alongside of Traditional Banks, Islamic Banks have started playing a vital role in contribution to economy of a country since 1970s. One of the significant differences between Conventional Banking and Islamic Banking is that in IB the interest rate is prohibited. Furthermore, the interest rate is the main source of income that conventional banks are receiving, whereas in Islamic Banks "profit/loss sharing" and buying/selling methodologies are being used. It shows that incomes generated in both banks are different.

Moreover, many studies have been conducted to measure profitability of Islamic Banks, Akhtar et al. (2011), they measured the factors that influence the profitability of Islamic Banks of Pakistan. The main focus of this study is to evaluate and measure the financial performance of the Islamic banking firms operating cross countries. In other words, it is very significant to learn which variable exerts more influence on profitability in Islamic Banks, and so all concentration will be directed to that specific variable. Furthermore, they are many existing studies where profitability determinants differences have been measured between Islamic and Conventional Banks. In contrast to one of the studies of Samad and Hassan (1999), our paper deviates in terms of main earnings indicator such as Spread. This indicator has not been used in the article of Bashir (2001). To evaluate performance of the banks empirically, different financial ratios are going to be employed as well. Likewise, in this work the economic factor and

© Springer Nature Switzerland AG 2018
N. Ozatac and K. K. Gökmenoglu (eds.), *Emerging Trends in Banking and Finance*, Springer Proceedings in Business and Economics,
https://doi.org/10.1007/978-3-030-01784-2_17

the efficiency of banks will be adopted, unlike the study of Alkassim (2005) and Akhtar et al. (2011). In accordance with this aim of this study several banks randomly have been selected across the countries and whose performances were measured to find out the relationship between profitability determinants and variables. The measurement of performance will be based on CAMEL framework. In this study, regression analysis will be applied to see the influence of explanatory variable on determinants of profitability. First of all, OLS has been employed which is based on country cross bank level data: General Model Regression and Specific Model Regression Analysis. General Model Regression Analysis of All Banks includes all banks across the countries. However, Specific Model Regression Analysis all banks are separated into Islamic and Conventional Banking. As result it can be said that profitability indicators of all banks are positively related to capital adequacy of the banks, except ROE. So the probability of defaults is low because the banks have sufficient amount of capital that keeps out the banks of any difficulties in payments that banks may face. However we found that economic growth does not exert any influence on determinants of profitability because they are statistically insignificant, but only Net Interest Margin is inversely related to GDP growth over period 2006–2012. As a separate comparison of Islamic and Conventional Banks showed differences in profitability measures with relation of, management, asset quality and capital adequacy, but scales of banks do not exert any impact on profitability of banks. However, the impact of SPREAD on both IB and CB tells different story; that is to say, interest rate spread does not exert an influence on both of profitability indicators.

2 Literature Review

2.1 Islamic Banks

The comparative analysis of Islamic and Conventional Banks in terms of profitability determinants which is based on CAMEL approach is very vital. All banks are playing a significant role in contribution to the growth of the economy. And many studies are done to improve the profitability indicators and bank characteristics. Recent paper works have employed different characteristic, structures, macroeconomic variables of bank level data across countries. Those papers which are outlined in this chapter done by Bashir (2001), Samad and Hassan (1999), Ariss (2010), Alkassim (2005), Hassan and Bashir (2003), Chukwuogor (2008), Liu and Tripe (2003), Kosmidou et al. (2004) and Spathis (2002).

Hassan and Bashir (2003) have continued to conduct regression analysis of Bashir (2001) study, in order to improve the estimation by adding some dependent and independent variables such as: macroeconomic variables, profitability indicator and financial structure. The added dependent variable as a profitability indicator is Net Non Interest Margin. First of all, they both preceded empirical analysis on relationship of bank characteristics with performance measure of Islamic Banks. As a result, they found that profitability indicators is positively related to capital ratio and it is consistent with previous study of Bashir (2001) and it has inverse association with loan ratios.

The empirical results disclosed that high of capital ratio or equity over assets directs to higher profit margin. Furthermore, they had found that NNIM (net non interest margin) positively related to OVERHEADS, that tells us the more banks are earning the more the salaries and wage will be distributed. The tax structure of government is the same empirically important impact on profitability indicators as in previous study of Bashir (2001). However the reserve requirement ratio does not have a strong impact on financial performance measure of Islamic banks. On one hand, the favorable macroeconomic environment is said to have positive impacts on profit margins, GDP growth increases which lead to an increase in performance measure of Islamic Banks. However, the GDP per capita and Inflation are not statistically significant, in other words they don't have much effect on performance measure of Islamic Banks. Finally, the size of banking system has negative impact on determinants of profitability, except of NNIM.

According to study of Alkassim (2005) who aimed to identify profitability of determinants of Islamic Banks and Conventional Banks. The profitability indicators ROE, ROA, and NIM of two different types of banks are compared. As independent variable he used: logarithmic of total assets, equity to assets, deposit to assets, total loans to assets and etc. He used cross country bank level data for Gulf Cooperation Council GCC countries to conduct Ordinary Least Square. He found the results which are consistent with Hassan and Bashir (2003) for Islamic Banks, and he also found in his analysis relationships between banks' characteristics and profitability indicators for Conventional Banks. The result of variables showed their reflection towards profitability indicators differently. The logarithmic total assets TA have negative relationship with performance measure in Conventional Banking System, but positive in Islamic Banking System. The capital ratio or equity ratio has got negative association with performance measure of Conventional Banks and positive connection with Islamic Banks' profitability indicators. He also found that lending improves the profitability of both Islamic and Conventional Banks, in other words total loans are positively related to determinant of profitability of both banks. In addition to, he had found that deposit ratio has inverse relationship with profit margins for Islamic banks which is consistent with previous studies of Bashir (2001), Hassan and Bashir (2003). However, deposits are positively related with profitability determinants for Conventional Banks. OVERHEADS of both Islamic and Conventional Banks are positively related to determinant of profitability.

Spathis (2002) study, he aimed to investigate the difference between profitability and efficiency of small and large Conventional Banks in Greek. In other words, he just classified the conventional banks into small ones and large ones, based on their scale or total assets. In order to investigate profitability and efficiency of Greek banks, Spathis (2002) has used a multicriteria methodology, that is to say he applied M.H.DIS and UTADIS to identify that affect the ratios of Greek banks. The evidence points out those large banks are more efficient than small ones. In his study, he found that small banks described by high capital yield ROE, high interest yield MARG, high financial leverage TA/TE, and high capital adequacy TE/TA. Large banks are distinguished by asset yield, and low capital and interest rate yield. M.H.DIS and UTADIS support the results of regression analysis.

Samad and Hassan (1999) assessed the differences of performance measures of Bank Islam Malaysia Berhad BIMB and eight Conventional banks in terms of profitability, liquidity, risk and solvency. They come up with output of empirical results stating that BIMB relatively is more liquid and less risky compared to the group of eight Conventional banks. In addition, Islamic banks showed significant progress on ROA and ROE during 1984–1997. However Samad and Hassan (1999) found that comparison of BIMB with group of 8 banks showed that difference in performance measures are statistically insignificant. They also found that the risk in BIMB increased and it is statistically significant.

Kosmidou et al. (2004) evaluated performance and efficiency of commercial and cooperative bank in Greece and Europe for the period 2003–2004. He has taken 16 cooperative banks and 14 commercial banks. And banks are divided into two group large banks and small ones in terms of total asset. Evaluation based on CAMEL framework by employing financial accounting ratios such as equity to assets, EBT/TA, EBT/TE, Loans to assets, and etc. He used multi criteria method to evaluate performances of commercial and cooperative banks. In comparison to cooperative banks, commercial banks are likely to increase their accounts, more competitive, and increasing market share in general.

Liu and Tripe (2003) studied the relationship between capital level and return on equity of banks in New Zeeland and Australia for the period 1996–2002. He took 9 Australian banks and 6 New Zeeland banks. GDP and interest rate was considered in empirical analysis as well. He categorized Australian banks into large and small banks, but New Zeeland banks were estimated separately. Ganger causality test used to see whether there is relationship between the capital ratio and return on equity. As a result he found moderate positive relationship between capital level and ROE in both countries. There is economic environmental positive effect on profitability, and in New Zeeland interest rate has same effect on profitability, but it is unclear whether it has causative relationship with profitability.

3 Methodology

We use the standard model used by Hassan and Bashir (2003) and Spathis (2002) to test the determinants of profitability of Islamic bank and conventional bank. However, in this study, we use three dependent variables, as proxy for financial performance, i.e., return on equity (ROE), return on assets (ROA) and net interest margin (NIM), but Net Income Margin (NIM) for IB. Each dependent variable is separately specified as follows:

$$ROE = \alpha 1 + \beta 1(CR) + \beta 2(TETA) + \beta 3(PLLTL) + \beta 4(LD) + \beta 5(LTA) + \beta 6(LIQD) + \beta 7(GGDP) + \beta 8(SPREAD) + \varepsilon$$
$$ROA = \alpha 2 + \beta 1(CR) + \beta 2(TETA) + \beta 3(PLLTL) + \beta 4(LD) + \beta 5(LTA) + \beta 6(LIQD) + \beta 7(GGDP) + \beta 8(SPREAD) + \varepsilon$$
$$NIM = \alpha 3 + \beta 1(CR) + \beta 2(TETA) + \beta 3(PLLTL) + \beta 4(LD) + \beta 5(LTA) + \beta 6(LIQD) + \beta 7(GGDP) + \beta 8(SPREAD) + \varepsilon$$

where CR represents the Cost to Revenue, CR represents the Cost to Revenue, TETA represents Total Equity to Total Asset, PLLTL represents Provision of Loan Losses over Total Loans; LD represents Loans to Deposits, LTA represent the logarithmic of Total Assets, LIQD represents Liquid Assets to Deposits, GGDP represents Gross Domestic Product Growth, SPREAD represents Interest rate Spread or difference between Lending rate and Deposit rate, and E represents error term.

The balanced panel data has been used to conduct the empirical analysis on determinants of profitability of Islamic and Traditional Banks that comes from financial statements in emerging markets. The cross-country bank-level data has been gathered from Bankscope, Bankersalmanac, World Bank databases and Central Bank of Turkey for the selected countries over period of 2006–2012. This period specifically has been selected to cover fully global financial crises period. The number of countries and banks both Islamic and Conventional are 5 and 36 respectively. The size of both Islamic and Traditional banks is approximately same, and number of Islamic Banks are 18. Countries are: Turkey, Egypt, Malaysia, Pakistan and UAE.

In order to test the data whether data is stationary or not, panel root test have been employed to each variable. According to methodologies developed by Levin, Lin and Chu (LLC) the data reject the null hypothesis, that is to say the unit root does not exist in our whole model or the data is stationary. Likewise, if data was not stationary then Level Equation and ECM by using ARDL method, Bound Test and Ganger Causality test would be applied, in order to find out whether there is or not long run relationship between the variables as it was applied in contrast Katircioglu (2009). Furthermore, the presence of multicollinearity in our regression model is tested. According to correlation between independent variables are very low in both regression model, Whole and Pure Models Regression, and R square are very low which proves the absence of multi-collinearity, correlation table is represented in Chap. 4 and it has been corrected for heteroskedasticity.

Accounting ratios are classified as dependent and explanatory variables. Dependent variables are Return On Equity, Return On Asset; Net Interest Margin expressed as percentages. Explanatory or independent variables are Total Equity over Total Assets, Liquid Assets over Deposits, Provision Loan Losses to Total Loans, Cost to Revenue, Loans over Deposits, Gross Domestic Product growth as % percentages, logarithmic of Total Assets and Interest rate Spread. The main focus of this study will be on SPREAD that stands for interest rate spread, and it is expected that SPREAD will have positive association with profitability determinants in conventional banking system. These variables are used correspondingly with selected five countries which are Turkey, Malaysia, Pakistan, United Arab Emirates and Egypt. Moreover, while measuring, evaluating and comparing the financial performances of Islamic and Conventional Banks, all important financial and operational factors will be taken into account by using CAMEL approach in this comparative study. CAMEL is rating system which measure financial performance of financial institutions and banks that gives information about financial validity.

In this comparative study ordinary regression equation is employed to measure and evaluate the difference in financial performance of the Islamic and Conventional Banks, and next step is taken to compare those results between two different types of banks. We conduct regression analysis by using Eviews software program to estimate our equation. In accordance with Hausman test which is done in panel data regression analysis as well, the "Cross Section Random Effects" model has been used because our sample data does not represent whole population. Additionally, and due to small number of groups which is 36 and time is only 4 years we have used cross section random effects model. Furthermore, three dependent variables used in this ordinary least squares: ROE, ROA and NIM. Other variables are considered as independent ones and demonstrated bellow in the models.

4   Empirical Analysis and Results

4.1   Correlation Analysis

The Correlation analysis points out the relationship of variables among themselves. The correlation is demonstrated in (Table 1). The variables are classified into three groups: All banks, Conventional banks and Islamic Banks. Correlation Analysis is applied to predict how independent variables that are based on CAMEL approach will be correlated with profitability indicators or dependent variables. Another purpose of correlation is to test for multicollinearity problem, in other words whether independent variables are highly correlated with each other or not.

Let us see first part or group. The efficiency of the all banks is inversely correlated to ROE and ROA, except NIM. However the positive correlation between CR and NIM is very low. In other words, the earnings quality of the banks reacts negatively to any change of profitability determinants. The scale of banks is negatively correlated with profitability determinants of banks and it is consistent with Alkassim (2005). Furthermore, the asset quality is inversely related to ROE, ROA and NIM, but coefficient correlation of ROE is low. The Economic growth is positively related to profitability measures and it is consistent with findings of Bashir (2001), Hassan and Bashir (2003). However, NIM is the opposite. The capital adequacy is positively associated with ROA and NIM, except the ROE. Previous findings of Alkassim (2005) which is different. Liquidity indicator has inverse correlation with profitability indicators and which is inconsistent with previous findings.

On other hand, we have run correlation analysis separately for each type of bank namely Islamic and Conventional ones. The efficiency of both types of banks is cost to revenue correlated to profitability indicators, but NIM. Capital adequacy ratio of Islamic and Conventional Banks are only negatively associated with ROE, however towards other both determinants of profitability for only CB, TE_TA is positively related. Alkassim (2005) found same output of his correlation analysis. In both banks the liquidity is inversely correlated to profitability measures. The asset quality ratio is negatively correlated with ROE in CB, but in IB it is positively associated with ROE. And it is the same with the size of banks, that is to say the scale of banks are positively

Table 1. Correlation analysis

All banks

	ROA (%)	ROE (%)	NIM (%)	TETA (%)	PLLTL (%)	LD (%)	CR (%)	LIQD (%)	GDPG (%)	LTA (%)	SPREAD (%)
ROA	100	77	−13	−20	−43	15	−74	11	16	−12	−31
ROE	77	100	−5	−35	−27	−2	−64	2	16	1	−22
NIM	−13	−5	100	26	−9	7	26	−27	−21	25	20
TETA	−20	−35	26	100	5	25	32	11	−12	−7	19
PLLTL	−43	−27	−9	5	100	−5	44	7	7	−5	28
LD	15	−2	7	25	−5	100	−25	−5	2	17	−12
CR	−74	−64	26	32	44	−25	100	−4	−11	7	41
LIQD	11	2	−27	11	7	−5	−4	100	13	−38	−46
GDPG	16	16	−21	−12	7	2	−11	13	100	−2	10
LTA	−12	1	25	−7	−5	17	7	−38	−2	100	25
SPREAD	−31	−22	20	19	28	−12	41	−46	10	25	100

Conventional banks

	ROA (%)	ROE (%)	NIM (%)	TETA (%)	PLLTL (%)	LD (%)	CR (%)	LIQD (%)	GDPG (%)	LTA (%)	SPREAD (%)
ROA	100	85	−16	−35	−55	16	−75	17	19	−22	−45
ROE	85	100	−18	−51	−41	−1	−71	20	21	−16	−33
NIM	−16	−18	100	36	12	20	24	−39	−21	21	36
TETA	−35	−51	36	100	34	51	42	−8	−9	21	10
PLLTL	−55	−41	12	34	100	−8	58	−7	5	7	52
LD	16	−1	20	51	−8	100	−30	−5	6	33	−26
CR	−75	−71	24	42	58	−30	100	−11	−13	7	48
LIQD	17	20	−39	−8	−7	−5	−11	100	20	−40	−61
GDPG	19	21	−21	−9	5	6	−13	20	100	−2	7
LTA	−22	−16	21	21	7	33	7	−40	−2	100	26
SPREAD	−45	−33	36	10	52	−26	48	−61	7	26	100

Islamic banks

	ROA (%)	ROE (%)	NIM (%)	TETA (%)	PLLTL (%)	LD (%)	CR (%)	LIQD (%)	GDPG (%)	LTA (%)	SPREAD (%)
ROA	100	74	−12	−19	−9	8	−72	−14	16	13	0
ROE	74	10	−3	−32	4	−2	−52	−17	10	23	−11

(continued)

Table 1. (*continued*)

All banks

	ROA (%)	ROE (%)	NIM (%)	TETA (%)	PLLTL (%)	LD (%)	CR (%)	LIQD (%)	GDPG (%)	LTA (%)	SPREAD (%)
NIM	−12	−3	100	27	−19	−11	43	16	−22	33	2
TETA	−19	−32	27	100	−15	13	37	34	−14	−22	26
PLLTL	−9	4	−19	−1	100	−1	8	16	12	−26	−2
LD	8	−2	−11	13	−1	100	−9	−12	−4	−16	20
CR	−72	−52	43	37	8	−9	100	8	−8	6	31
LIQD	−14	−17	16	34	16	−12	8	100	4	−48	−22
GDPG	16	1	−22	−14	12	−4	−8	4	100	−3	13
LTA	13	23	33	−22	−26	−16	6	−48	−3	100	24
SPREAD	0	−11	2	26	−2	20	31	−22	13	24	100

related to ROE for IB, but opposite for CB. And it is consistent with previous findings. The profitability measures of Islamic banks are positively correlated to loan to deposit ratio LD that is loans which are being funded through deposits, whereas in Conventional Banks are inversely related.

4.2 Regression Analysis

In this chapter we will talk about the output of regression analysis which is applied on financial ratios of both Islamic and Conventional banks, in order to explain how any changes in independent or explanatory variables may affect the determinants of profitability or the dependent variables of these banks which are Return On Equity, Return On Asset and Net Interest Margin/Net Income Margin. We have estimated nine regression analyses which are categorized into two main models: General and Specific Regression Models. Moreover, General Model consists of regression analyses of all banks, in other words firstly all banks have been taken into consideration namely Islamic Banks and Conventional Banks to regress dependent variables or profitability determinants. Then, regression analysis is applied on both Conventional and Islamic Banks separately and the results are compared.

4.3 General Model Regression Analysis of All Banks

Firstly, according to classification all banks show the effect of bank characteristics, macroeconomic variable and dummies of banks on financial performance of all banks over period 2006–2012. General Model of Regression Analysis is shown below in (Table 2). There are three dependent variables in our model ROE, ROA, and NIM. In the first regression estimation model, only ROA has positive significant association with capital adequacy ratio TETA, that is to say the more capital in the banks will lead to more profits. There is negative relationship between ROA and NIM with asset quality ratio "provision of loan losses over total loans", so the lower the ratio the better the banks are in terms of profitability. As PLLTL ratio increases it means the written off loans goes up and that lost amount will be excluded from net income in the statement of profit and loss account, that's why net income to total assets ratio goes down. The bigger the PLLTL in the banks the more problems bank will have. Furthermore, there is inverse association between ROE and management quality ratio total loans over total deposits, simply to say, the reduction in the ratio is due to increase in Total Deposits which will lead to increase in interest expenses in Income Statement that will reduce Net Income as result, it will decrease the ROE. In general the banking sector they could not finance their accepted deposits in efficient way; in other word they were not able to find creditworthy borrowers. ROE and ROA have statistically significant negative relationship with cost to revenue ratio, as efficiency of banks increases the ROE and ROA increases. Alkassim (2005) has come up with same results where he estimated all banks of gulf countries. On other hand, determinants of profitability of all banks are not affected by the size LTA logarithmic total assets due to statistical insignificance over period 2006–2012, except NIM. There is positive effect exerted on NIM by size of banks which indicates that as banks decide to expand their businesses by opining new branches, it will make the banks to generate more profits by lending to potential borrowers. As we know that large banks are serving large customers such big enterprises. Likewise, Liquid assets to deposits ratio exerts no effect on the profitability determinants ROE, ROA and NIM all banks at all for the period 2006–2011 because they are statistically insignificant. GDP growth does not have any influence on determinants of profitability of ROE and NIM. This is due to limitation on data. However, ROA has been positively affected by GDPG and statistically significant. So the profitability of bans is affected by economic growth of a specific country. The Dummy of banks that coded Islamic bank as 1 and Conventional Banks as 0. According to results there is positive relation with NIM and ROE which are statistically significant. In other words, the coefficient is close to 1 that states there is difference in profitability determinants between Islamic Banks and Conventional Banks. NIM is referred for Islamic Banks as net income margin such as, fees from foreign exchanges, from profit loss and share PLS from financing activities, service charges and etc. almost whole the profits of Islamic banks are coming from NIM. The whole models of ROE, ROA and NIM are reliable and best fitted due to F-test probability values which are statistically significant. R's squared are all very low less than 50%, that depicts the variation in profitability can be explained by variation in financial ratios by less than 50%.

Table 2. All banks

	ROA		ROE		NIM	
IND. variables	Coefficient	Prob. value	Coefficient	Prob. value	Coefficient	Prob. value
C	4.248934	0.0069*	15.49868	0.0183**	−0.487892	0.7138
TETA	0.01079	0.0383**	−0.070909	0.1789	0.020136	0.1842
PLLTL	−0.046495	0.0613***	−0.035556	0.7782	−0.027865	0.0771***
LD	0.001236	0.5975	−0.008981	0.0006*	−0.000253	0.9034
CR	−0.035014	0.0000*	−0.22631	0.0000*	0.011324	0.1736
LIQD	−0.001345	0.8578	0.049866	0.4105	−0.002921	0.5197
DUM	−0.458399	0.2255	2.568093	0.0693***	0.909031	0.0272**
GDPG	0.061139	0.0639***	0.345227	0.3442	−0.062832	0.2027
LTA	−0.135989	0.1609	0.159208	0.7240	0.291203	0.0047*
SPREAD	0.026629	0.7756	0.780333	0.5499	0.00039	0.9979
	R-squared	0.499529	R-squared	0.384558	R-squared	0.210391
	F-statistic	10.97928	F-statistic	6.873319	F-statistic	2.842123
	P-VALUE	0.000000	P-VALUE	0.000000	P-VALUE	0.005204
	D.-Watson	1.745841	D.-Watson	1.506459	D.-Watson	1.668997

4.4 Specific Model Regression Analysis of Islamic and Conventional Banks

As we go through the results of regression analysis of Islamic Banks and Conventional Banks separately by comparing the relationship between profitability determinants and explanatory variables. According to empirical results of regression analysis on conventional banks, assuming nothing changes in the independent variables, the ROA and ROE will increase by 6.49 and 18.40 units respectively, and they are statistically significant. But in Islamic Bank, if nothing changes the ROE will increase by 25.85 units and NIM will go down by 3.5 units. Capital adequacy in Conventional Banking affects the return on assets positively and it is statistically significant. As total asset increases, the both ROA and Capital Adequacy fall down. However there is inverse relationship between ROE and Capital Adequacy, which is statistically significant. This is due to decision to keep more capital inside the bank, as banks increase total equity which will reduce ROE, but the ratio of capital adequacy will increase. In contrast to Conventional banking system, in Islamic banking system ROA and ROE positively associated with Capital adequacy. There is negative relationship between all profitability determinants and asset quality ratio "provision of loan losses over total loans" in both banking system, so the lower the ratio the better the banks are in terms of profitability. As PLLTL ratio increases it means the written off loans goes up and that lost amount will be excluded from net income in the statement of profit and loss account, that's why net income to total assets ratio goes down. The bigger the PLLTL in the banks the more problems bank will have. In addition to, management quality ratio has negative effect on ROE only and it is statistically significant in Conventional Banking system. The inverse association between ROE and management quality ratio total loans over total deposits, simply to say, the reduction in the ratio is due to increase in Total Deposits which will lead to increase in interest expenses in Income Statement that will reduce Net Income as result, it will increase the ROE. But in Islamic Banking, NIM has got negative significant relationship. According to the result of both Islamic and Conventional Banking systems, ROE and ROA have statistically significant negative relationship with cost to revenue ratio, as efficiency of banks increases the ROE and ROA increases, except NIM. Likewise, as expenses are increasing, the profits are going down. In Conventional Banking GDPG is affecting negatively NIM, it is statistically significant which is not consistent with one of the outstanding articles of Bashir (2001) and Hassan and Bashir (2003). The reason is that as the whole economy grows, people receive high paid salary and the need for loan falls, as the demanded loans go down, the bank's interest charges will go down so that profitability determinants is expected to fall down. However in Islamic Banking, ROE is positively related with GDPG and it is statistically significant. As economy grows that Islamic banks start to generate more revenue, as a result the net income will increase that will lead to an increase in ROE. To sum up, three models of Islamic Banking are best fitted due to significance of "F" coefficients, whereas in Conventional one, only 2 models are best fitted, ROA and ROE (Tables 3 and 4).

Table 3. Conventional banks

IND. variables	ROA		ROE		NIM	
	Coefficient	Prob. value	Coefficient	Prob. value	Coefficient	Prob. value
C	6.49177	0.00140*	18.40609	0.00060*	1.37874	0.53690
TETA	0.00645	0.86430	−0.24841	0.00660*	0.07228	0.02370**
PLLTL	−0.05168	0.08490***	−0.01934	0.89820	−0.04058	0.02170**
LD	−0.00007	0.98350	−0.01822	0.00560*	0.00464	0.32630
CR	−0.03570	0.00000*	−0.21469	0.00000*	0.00564	0.36490
LIQD	−0.00324	0.73410	0.05536	0.31680	−0.00333	0.43360
GDPG	0.12498	0.13900	0.43637	0.27170	−0.11805	0.02240**
LTA	−0.30858	0.07080***	0.11221	0.82470	−0.07794	0.69630
SPREAD	−0.09362	0.66070	0.52315	0.49010	0.27708	0.39390
	R-squared	0.61293	R-squared	0.57886	R-squared	0.18711
	F-statistic	9.69882	F-statistic	8.41900	F-statistic	1.38110
	P-VALUE	0.00000	P-VALUE	0.00000	P-VALUE	0.22887
	D.-Watson	1.45757	D.-Watson	1.36613	D.-Watson	1.97013

Table 4. Islamic banks

IND. variables	ROA		ROE		NIM	
	Coefficient	Prob. value	Coefficient	Prob. value	Coefficient	Prob. value
C	0.7053	0.4011	25.851	0.003	−3.54064	0.00290
TETA	0.0356	0.0087	0.140	0.034	−0.01446	0.52770
PLLTL	−0.0380	0.0139	−0.043	0.814	0.00984	0.55260
LD	−0.0002	0.9389	−0.005	0.783	−0.00293	0.04490
CR	−0.0224	0.0014	−0.230	0.000	0.00853	0.30880
LIQD	−0.0001	0.9840	−0.013	0.807	−0.00436	0.52610
GDPG	0.0223	0.2861	0.397	0.066	−0.03252	0.41670
LTA	0.0205	0.6949	−0.592	0338	0.76306	0.00000
SPREAD	0.1524	0.1394	0.472	0.400	0.01447	0.92050
	R-squared	0.92632	R-squared	0.9333	R-squared	0.89817
	F-statistic	22.35045	F-statistic	24.8738	F-statistic	14.70002
	P-VALUE	0.00000	P-VALUE	0.0000	P-VALUE	0.00000
	D.-Watson	1.73830	D.-Watson	1.9100	D.-Watson	2.51800

5   Conclusion

Alongside with traditional banks, Islamic banks have started involving with their principles and rules that exclude interest rate and speculative transactions. And the purpose of this study is not to say that Islamic banks are better off than traditional banks from our empirical results of regression analysis. There are the differences in financial performances between Conventional Banks and Islamic banks which are found in overall picture of all banks in terms of NIM by using DUM. Then we estimated Islamic banks and Conventional Banks separately to touch those differences in detail. Firstly all banks are examined to find differences and similarities in terms of profitability and then both Islamic and Conventional Banks are evaluated separately.

For instance, as it is shown in our empirical results as the cost increases the profitability decreases for all banks, in other words the efficiency is positively related with profitability indicators, except NIM which is positively related to cost to revenue and they are all statistically significant. This relationship is unexplainable and this may be because of limitation on data. GGDP is inversely related with profitability indicator NIM and statistically significant for the period 2006–2012, that is to say during this period there was recession which affected financial organizations' profitability negatively. Finally, the difference found between Islamic Banks and Conventional banks in terms of profitability determinant NIM, in other words DUM variable is positively related and statistically significant with NIM. NIM is main source of income for Islamic banks.

First of all, let us consider the capital adequacy, TETA has inverse relationship with profitability indicators such as ROE for Conventional banks and statistically insignificant, unlike Islamic banks. No difference found between Islamic banks and conventional ones in terms of profitability determinant ROA which is negaively related to provision of loan losses to total loans PLLTL and statistically significant for IB, unlike CB. Generally as PLLTL increases the more problem the bank may face. No difference found in relationship of profitability determinants and Cost to Revenue ratio. The size of banks is affecting negatively the ROA in conventional banking system, and it is statistically significant. As total assets increase the ratio of ROA falls. However, the LTA has positive significant effect on NIM in Islamic Banks. So well capitalized Islamic banks will earn more profits. The growth of economy has got negative impact on NIM of Conventional Banks, whereas in Islamic banks GDPG has positive significant relationship with ROE. The empirical results showed that dependent variable or all profitability determinants are affected by all independent variables in some ways were the different, but in some ways were same.

In further research, by increasing number of banks, macroeconomic variables and countries we will have more accurate evaluation the profitability measure of two different types of Banks. In this research accessibility of data was limited and that's why there might be unreasonable relationship between variables as well. For example, Cost to Revenue is positively related and statistically significant with Net Interest Margin. We need full access to databases such as Bankscope and Bankersalmanaca so that we will be able to do comprehensive empirical evaluation of profitability determinants.

References

Akhtar, M. F., Ali, K., & Sadaqat, S. (2011). Factors influencing the profitability of Islamic banks of Pakistan. International Research Journal of Finance and Economics, 66(66), 1–8.

Alkassim, F. A. (2005). The profitability of Islamic and conventional banking in the GCC countries: A comparative study. Journal of Review of Islamic Economics, 13(1), 5–30.

Ariss, R. T. (2010). Competitive conditions in Islamic and conventional banking: A global perspective. Review of Financial Economics, 19(3), 101–108.

Bashir, A. H. M. (2001). Assessing the performance of Islamic banks: Some evidence from the Middle East. Topics in Middle Eastern and North African Economies, 3.

Chukwuogor, C. (2008). An econometric analysis of African stock market: Annual returns analysis, day-of-the-week effect and volatility of returns. International Research Journal of Finance and Economics, 14, 369–378.

Hassan, M. K., & Bashir, A. H. M. (2003). Determinants of Islamic banking profitability. In 10th ERF annual conference, Morocco (Vol. 7).

Katircioglu, S. T. (2009). Revisiting the tourism-led-growth hypothesis for Turkey using the bounds test and Johansen approach for cointegration. Tourism Management, 30(1), 17–20.

Kosmidou, K., Pasiouras, F., Doumpos, M., & Zopounidis, C. (2004). Foreign versus domestic banks' performance in the UK: a multicriteria approach. Computational Management Science, 1(3-4), 329–343.

Liu, B., & Tripe, D. (2003). New Zealand bank mergers and efficiency gains. Journal of Asia-Pacific Business, 4(4), 61–81.

Samad, A., & Hassan, M. K. (1999). The performance of Malaysian Islamic bank during 1984–1997: An exploratory study. International journal of Islamic financial services, 1(3), 1–14.

Spathis, C. T. (2002). Detecting false financial statements using published data: some evidence from Greece. Managerial Auditing Journal, 17(4), 179–191.